a year
in
poetry

a year in poetry

A Treasury of Classic and Modern Verses for Every Date on the Calendar

edited by

THOMAS E. FOSTER & ELIZABETH C. GUTHRIE

foreword by RICHARD WILBUR

Crown Publishers, Inc.
New York

For Dinah (TEF)
For Matthew and Ellen (ECG)

Published by Crown Publishers, Inc., 201 East 50th Street, New York, New York, 10022. Member of the Crown Publishing Group.

Random House, Inc. New York, Toronto, London, Sydney, Auckland.

CROWN is a trademark of Crown Publishers, Inc.

Manufactured in the United States of America

Library of Congress Cataloging-in-Publication Data
A year in poetry / Thomas E. Foster, Elizabeth C. Guthrie, eds.;
    Includes indexes.
    1. Anniversaries—Poetry.   2. Literary calendars.   3. American poetry.   4. English poetry.   5. Days—Poetry.   I. Foster, Thomas E.   II. Guthrie, Elizabeth C.
PS595.A55Y43   1995
811.008'033—dc20   95-772
        CIP

ISBN 0-517-70008-5

10 9 8 7 6 5 4 3 2 1

First Edition

Contents

March

April

May

June

July

August

 *September*

October

November

December

Acknowledgments

 Grateful acknowledgment is made to the following for permission to reprint previously published material.

Dannie Abse: *Elegy for Dylan Thomas*. Reprinted from *White Coat, Purple Coat* (Persea Books, New York) by permission of the author.

Miguel Algarín: *Sunday, August 11, 1974*. Reprinted by permission of the author.

Martin Allwood: *March Moon Over Winter Sweden—1971*. Reprinted by permission of the author.

Nell Altizer: *Haworth Parsonage, 31 March 1855*. Reprinted by permission of the author.

A. R. Ammons: excerpt from *Extremes and Moderations*. Copyright © 1972 by A. R. Ammons. Reprinted from *Collected Poems 1951–1971* by permission of W. W. Norton & Company and the author.

Tom Andrews: *Song of a Country Priest* from *The Brother's Country* (Persea Books). Copyright © 1990 by Tom Andrews. Reprinted by permission of Persea Books and the author.

John Ashbery: *Qualm* from *Shadow Train* (Viking/Penguin). Copyright © 1980, 1981 by John Ashbery. Reprinted by permission of Georges Borchardt, Inc. and the author.

Christianne Balk: *Leaving Sand County: April 21, 1948*. Copyright © 1986 by Christianne Balk. Reprinted by permission of the author.

Jim Barnes: *Accident at Three Mile Island* from *A Season of Loss*. Copyright © 1985 by Purdue University Press. Reprinted by permission of Purdue University Press and the author.

Gerald W. Barrax: *First Carolina Rain*. Copyright © 1970 by University of Pittsburgh Press. Reprinted by permission of the author.

Judith Baumel: *World Without End*. Copyright © 1990 by Judith Baumel. Originally appeared in *The New Yorker*. Reprinted by permission of the author.

John Beecher: *One More River to Cross* from *Collected Poems, 1924–1974* (Macmillan Publishing Company). Reprinted by permission of Barbara M. Beecher.

Patricia Beer: *Return to Sedgemoor*. Reprinted by permission of Carcanet Press Limited and the author.

Marvin Bell: *Air Wisconsin* from *Seasons: A Correspondence in Poems* by Marvin Bell and William Stafford (David R. Godine). Copyright © by Marvin Bell. Reprinted by permission of the author.

Stephen Vincent Benet: *Abraham Lincoln's Last Day* from *John Brown's Body*. Copyright © 1927, 1928 by Stephen Vincent Benet. Copyright renewed © 1955, 1956 by Rosemary Carr Benet. Reprinted by permission of Brandt & Brandt Literary Agents, Inc.

Ted Berrigan: *Sonnet XXXVI*. Reprinted by permission of the Estate of Ted Berrigan.

Wendell Berry: *October 10* from *OPENINGS*. Copyright © 1965 and renewed 1993 by Wendell Berry. Reprinted by permission of Harcourt Brace & Company.

John Berryman: *World News Telegram*. Reprinted by permission of Farrar, Straus & Giroux, Inc.

John Betjeman: *The Arrest of Oscar Wilde at the Cadogan Hotel* from *Collected Poems*. Reprinted by permission of John Murray (Publishers) Ltd.

Sujata Bhatt: *29 April 1989* from *Monkey Shadows*. Reprinted by permission of Carcanet Press Limited.

Elizabeth Bishop: *Brazil, January 1, 1502*. Copyright © 1979, 1983 by Alice Helen Methfessel. Reprinted from *The Complete Poems 1927–1979* by permission of Farrar, Straus & Giroux, Inc.

Paul Blackburn: *23.VII.71* from *The Collected Poems of Paul Blackburn*. Copyright © 1985 by Joan Blackburn. Reprinted by permission of Persea Books, Inc.

Peter Blue Cloud: *Hawk Nailed to a Barn Door*. Copyright © by Peter Blue Cloud. Reprinted by permission of the author.

ACKNOWLEDGMENTS

Robert Bly: *At a March Against the Vietnam War* from *Selected Poems*. Copyright © 1977 by Robert Bly. Reprinted by permission of HarperCollins Publishers, Inc.

Ronald Bottrall: Petrarch's *Sonnet CCLXIX* from *Against a Setting Sun*. Reprinted by permission of Margot Bottrall, the sole copyright holder.

George Bradley: *Electrocuting an Elephant* from *Terms to Be Met* (Yale University Press, 1986). Reprinted by permission of the author.

Elizabeth Brewster: *William Brewster Disembarking from the Mayflower* from *Selected Poems 1944–1977*. Reprinted by permission of Oberon Press.

Joseph Brodsky: *May 24, 1980* from *To Urania*. Copyright © 1988 by Joseph Brodsky. Reprinted by permission of Farrar, Straus & Giroux, Inc.

George Mackay Brown: *April the Sixteenth* from *Selected Poems*. Reprinted by permission of John Murray (Publishers) Ltd.

Michael Dennis Browne: *Epithalamion/Wedding Dawn* from *The Sun Catcher*. (Carnegie Mellon University Press, 1978). Reprinted by permission of the author.

Alan Brownjohn: *The Rain Diary*. Copyright © by Alan Brownjohn. Reprinted by permission of the author.

Michael Casey: *The Box Riot* from *Obscenities* (Ashod Press). Copyright © 1989 by Michael Casey. Reprinted by permission of the author.

Christopher Caudwell: *Heil Baldwin!* Reprinted by permission of Carcanet Press Limited.

George Chambers: *August 18*. Originally appeared in *NorthWest Review*. Reprinted by permission of the author.

Keith Chandler: *Kett's Rebellion*. Reprinted by permission of Carcanet Press Limited.

David Citino: *The Death of Ray Chapman* from *Last Rites and Other Poems*. Copyright © 1980 by the Ohio University Press. All rights reserved. Reprinted by permission of Ohio State University Press and the author.

Austin Clarke: *A Sermon on Swift* from *Austin Clarke: Selected Poems*. Reprinted by permission of Wake Forest University Press.

Jane Cooper: *Hunger Moon* from *Scaffolding: Selected Poems*. Copyright © 1968 by Jane Cooper. Reprinted by permission of Tilbury House, Publishers, Gardiner, ME.

William Corbett: *Vermont Apollinaire*. Copyright © 1984 by William Corbett. Reprinted by permission of the author.

John Cotton: *Birthday Poem—7th March*. Reprinted by permission of the author.

Hart Crane: *The Broken Tower* and *Cape Hatteras* from *Complete Poems of Hart Crane*, edited by Marc Simon. Copyright © 1933, 1958, 1966 by Liveright Publishing Corporation. Copyright © 1986 by Marc Simon. Reprinted by permission of Liveright Publishing Corporation.

e. e. cummings: *Buffalo Bill's Defunct* from *Complete Poems, 1904–1962* by e.e. cummings, edited by George J. Firmage. Copyright © 1923, 1951, 1991 by the Trustees for the e. e. cummings Trust. Copyright © 1976 by George James Firmage. Reprinted by permission of Liveright Publishing Corporation.

Allen Curnow: *An Excellent Memory*. Reprinted by permission of Auckland University Press and the author.

Donald Davie: *Montcalm*. Copyright © by Donald Davie. Reprinted by permission of the author.

Dick Davis: *Richard Davis*. Reprinted by permission of the author.

Walter de la Mare: *February 29th*. Reprinted by permission of the Literary Trustees of Walter de la Mare and the Society of Authors as their representative.

Peter Didsbury: *The Seventeenth of June* from *That Old-Time Religion*. Reprinted by permission of Bloodaxe Books Ltd.

Elias Dillon: Eileen O'Connell's *Lament for Arthur O'Leary* from the *Irish University Review*, Vol. I, No 2 (1971). Reprinted by permission of the *Irish University Review*, Christopher Murray, editor.

Tim Dlugos: *Qum* from *Selected Poems 1973–1990* (High Risk Books/Serpent's Tail, 1995). Reprinted by permission of Christopher Wiss, Executor.

Stephen Dobyns: *No Map*. Copyright © 1994 by Stephen Dobyns. Reprinted by permission of the author.

Hilda Doolittle: from: *May 1943* from *Collected Poems 1912–1944*. Copyright © 1982 by the Estate of Hilda Doolittle. Reprinted by permission of New Directions Publishing Corporation.

Edward Dorn: *On the Nature of Communication*. Reprinted by permission of the author.

Rita Dove: *Parsley* from *Selected Poems*. Copyright © 1983, 1993, by Rita Dove. Reprinted by permission of the author.

Robert Duncan: *Passages 36* from *Groundwork*. Copyright © 1984 by Robert Duncan. Reprinted by permission of New Directions Publishing Corporation.

Paul Durcan: *The Death by Heroin of Sid Vicious*. Reprinted by permission of The Blackstaff Press and the author.

Tom Earley: *Summer Return*. Reprinted by permission of the author.

Russell Edson: *Time of the King*. Copyright © 1976 by Russell Edson. Reprinted by permission of the author.

Desmond Egan: *Last Day of May* from *Collected Poems* (National Poetry Foundation [USA] and Goldsmith Press [Ireland]). Reprinted by permission of the author.

Martin Espada: *Two Mexicanos Lynched in Santa Cruz, California, May 3, 1877* from *Rebellion Is the Circle of a Lover's Hands (Rebelion es el giro de manos del amante)* (Curbstone Press, distributed by InBook) translated by Camilo Perez-Bustillo. Translation copyright © 1990 by Camilo Perez-Bustillo and Martin Espada. Reprinted by permission of Curbstone Press.

Alison Fell: *August 6, 1945* from *Kisses for Mayekovsky* (Virago Press). Copyright © by Alison Fell. Reprinted by permission of the author.

Gerrie Fellows: *From a Window 22/7/86* from *Technologies and Other Poems*. Reprinted by permission of Polygon Press and the author.

Roy Fisher: *3rd November 1976* from *Poems 1955–1987*. Reprinted by permission of Oxford University Press.

Nigel Forde: *A Day to Remember*. Copyright © by Nigel Forde. Reprinted by permission of the author.

G. S. Fraser: *Instead of an Elegy* from *Poems of G. S. Fraser*. Reprinted by permission of Leicester University Press. All rights reserved.

Robert Frost: *Pea Brush* from *The Poetry of Robert Frost*, edited by Edward Connery Latham. Reprinted by permission of Peter A. Gilbert, Trustee and Henry Holt and Company, Inc.

Alice Fulton: *Another Troy* from *Palladium*. Copyright © 1986 by Alice Fulton. Reprinted by permission of the University of Illinois Press and the author.

Tess Gallagher: *Some Painful Butterflies Pass Through* from *Amplitude*. Copyright © 1992 by Tess Gallagher. Reprinted by permission of Graywolf Press, St. Paul, Minnesota and the author.

David Gascoyne: Benjamin Peret's *Louis XVI Goes to the Guillotine*. David Gascoyne's translation reprinted by permission of the translator.

Charley George: *Death of the Poet* is from *Sainte-Beauve The Poet in Four Parts* from *More: Poems 74–75*. Copyright © 1975 by Charley George. Reprinted by permission of Kathie George.

Emery George: *Bad Day at the Home Office* from *Kate's Death: A Book of Odes* (Ardis). Copyright © by Emery George. Reprinted by permission of the author.

Allen Ginsberg: *Continuation of a Long Poem of These States* from *Collected Poems 1947–1980*. Copyright © 1965 by Allen Ginsberg. Copyright renewed. Reprinted by permission of HarperCollins Publishers, Inc.

Louise Glück: *12.6.71* from *The House on Marsh Land* (Ecco Press, 1975). Reprinted by permission of the author.

Albert Goldbarth: *Water Pie: Tonight, 12/11/72* from *Jan 31* (Doubleday). Copyright © 1974 by Albert Goldbarth. Reprinted by permission of the author.

Laurence Goldstein: *Moon Landing* from *The Three Gardens* (Copper Beech Press, 1987). Copyright © by Laurence Goldstein. Reprinted by permission of the author.

Paul Goodman: *Don Larsen's Perfect Game*. Reprinted by permission of the Sally Goodman.

Alan Gould: *March 21st 1945*. Reprinted by permission of Alan Gould, c/o Margaret Connolly & Associates Pty Ltd.

Jorie Graham: *Breakdancing*. Reprinted by permission of the author.

Barbara L. Greenberg: *April Thirty-First* from *The Spoils of August* (Wesleyan University Press). Copyright © 1974 by Barbara L. Greenberg. Reprinted by permission of the author.

Eamon Grennan: *Morning: The Twenty-Second of March* from *What Light There Is & Other Poems* (North Point Press, 1989). Copyright © by Eamon Grennan. Reprinted by permission of the author.

June Jordan: *Home: January 29, 1984.* Copyright © 1986 by June Jordan and reprinted by permission of the author.

Jenny Joseph: *February Floods, 1953* from *Selected Poems* (Bloodaxe Books, 1992). Reprinted by permission of the author.

Donald Junkins: *Swan's Island, August 9, 1974.* Copyright © by Donald Junkins and reprinted by permission of the author.

Richard Katrovas: *Kings' Day, 1984.* Reprinted by permission of Carcanet Press Limited and the author.

P. J. Kavanagh: *November the First.* Reprinted by permission of Carcanet Press Limited and the author.

Joan Keefe: *Evicted Woman* from Irish Poems: *From Cromwell to the Famine* (Bucknell University Press). Reprinted by permission of Associate University Presses.

Edmund Keeley: C. P. Cavafy's *Theodotos* (with Philip Sherrard) from C. P. Cavafy's *Collected Poems,* Revised Edition, 1992. Translation copyright © 1992 by Edmund Keeley and Philip Sherrard. Reprinted by permission of the translators.

Edmund Keeley: Yannis Ritsos's *Ordinary People's Lithograph.* Translation copyright © 1991 by Princeton University Press and reprinted by permission of the translator.

Richard Kenney: *The Battle of Valcour Island.* Reprinted by permission of the author.

Carolyn Kizer: Tu Fu's *Too Much Heat, Too Much Work.* Translation copyright © by Carolyn Kizer and reprinted by permission of the translator.

Peter Klappert: *Says What.* Copyright © by Peter Klappert and reprinted by permission of the author.

L. D. Lerner: *14 July 1956.* Reprinted by permission of the author.

Julius Lester: *In the Time of Revolution.* Copyright © 1969 by Julius Lester and reprinted by permission of the author.

Peter Levi: Aeschylos's *The Battle of Salamis* and *The Bombardment of Petrolpaulski.* Translation copyright © by Peter Levi. Reprinted by permission of the author and John Johnson Ltd., London.

Robert Lowell: *Lady Ralegh's Lament* from *For the Union Dead.* Copyright © 1964 by Robert Lowell. Copyright renewed 1992 by Harriet Lowell, Sheridan Lowell, and Caroline Lowell. Reprinted by permission of Farrar, Straus & Giroux, Inc.

Jackson Mac Low: *1st Dance—Making Things New—6 February 1964* and *2nd Dance—Seeing Lines—6 February 1964* from *The Pronouns—A Collection of 40 Dances—For the Dancers.* Copyright © 1964, 1971, 1979 by Jackson Mac Low. Reprinted by permission of the author.

Hugh MacDiarmid: *Your Immortal Memory, Burns* from *Collected Poems of Hugh MacDiarmid.* Copyright © 1948, 1962 by Christopher Murray Grieve. Reprinted by permission of Simon & Schuster, Inc.

Louis MacNeice: *Whit Monday—1941* from *The Collected Poems of Louis MacNeice,* edited by E. R. Dobbs. Reprinted by permission of David Higham Associates and Faber and Faber, Ltd.

Haki R. Madhubuti: *One Sided Shoot-out* from *We Walk the Way of the New World* (Broadside Press, 1970). Reprinted by permission of the author.

Jayanta Mahapatra: *30th January 1982: A Story.* Reprinted by permission of Three Continents Press, Inc.

R. A. K. Mason: *Twenty-Sixth October* from *Collected Poems* (Victoria University Press). Reprinted by permission of the author.

Aiden Carl Mathews: *June the Seventh.* Copyright © by Aiden Carl Mathews and reprinted by permission of the author.

Martha McFerren: *June 22* from *Contours for Ritual.* Reprinted by permission of Louisiana State University Press and the author.

James McMichael: *Each in a Place Apart* from *Each in a Place Apart* (University of Chicago Press). Reprinted by permission of the author.

William Meredith: *Trelawny's Dream* from *Partial Accounts.* Copyright © 1987 by William Meredith. Reprinted by permission of Alfred A. Knopf, Inc.

James Merrill: *16.IX.65.* Copyright © by James Merrill and reprinted by permission of the author.

James Michie: Horace's *Odes. Book Three. XVIII.* Translation copyright © by James Michie and reprinted by permission of the translator.

Jane Miller: *May You Always be the Darling of Fortune.* Reprinted by permission of the author.

Ewart Milne: *Rememberance Day 1972*. Reprinted by permission of Aquila Press Limited.

Judith Minty: *Upon Seeing the Aurora Borealis for the First Time on My 35th Birthday* from *Lake Songs and Other Fears* (University of Pittsburgh Press, 1974). Reprinted by permission of the author.

Gary Miranda: *A Marzipan for Einstein's Birthday* from *Grace Period* (Princeton University Press). Reprinted by permission of the author.

Stephen Mitchell: Rainer Marie Rilke's *Turning Point* from *The Selected Poetry of Rainer Maria Rilke*. Translation copyright © 1982 by Stephen Mitchell and reprinted by permission of Random House, Inc.

Susan Mitchell: *Meditations on a Photograph* from *The Water Inside the Water*. Copyright © 1983 by Susan Mitchell. Reprinted by permission of HarperCollins Publishers, Inc.

James Masao Mitsui: *Destination: Tule Lake Relocation Center, May 20, 1942*. Reprinted by permission of the author.

John Moffitt: *The Day Before the End* from *Escape of the Leopard*. Copyright © 1974 by John Moffitt. Reprinted by permission of Harcourt Brace & Company, Inc.

John Mole: *The Impertinence of the Thing* from *Selected Poems* (Sinclair-Stevenson). Copyright © by John Mole. Reprinted by permission of the author.

John Montague: *A Flowering Absence* from *Selected Poems Dead Kingdom* and *Collected Poems* (Wake Forest University Press). Reprinted by permission of the author.

Marion Montgomery: *Winter Song* from *Gull and Other Georgia Scenes*. Copyright © by Marion Montgomery. Reprinted by permission of the author.

Marianne Moore: *Tom Fool at Jamaica* from *The Complete Poems of Marianne Moore*. Copyright © 1953 by Marianne Moore. Reprinted by permission of Viking Penguin, a division of Penguin Books USA, Inc.

Prentiss Moore: *November 7* from *The Winter Garden and Other Poems*. Copyright © 1981 by Prentiss Moore. Reprinted by permission of the author and the University of Texas Press.

Edwin Morgan: *Glasgow 5 March 1971* from the *Collected Poems*. Reprinted by permission of Carcanet Press Limited.

John N. Morris: *To Those Who Share my Birthday 6.18.31*. Copyright © by John N. Morris and reprinted by permission of the author.

Paul Muldoon: *Good Friday, 1971, Driving Westward*. Reprinted by permission of Wake Forest University Press and the author.

Ogden Nash: *Lines in Praise of a Date Made Praiseworthy Solely by Something Very Nice That Happened to It*. Copyright © 1932 by Ogden Nash. Copyright renewed. Reprinted by permission of Curtis Brown Ltd.

Howard Nemerov: *Boom!* Reprinted by permission of Margaret Nemerov.

Tran Thi Nga: *I Was Caught* from *Shallow Graves* by Wendy Larsen and Tran Thi Nga. Reprinted by permission of Wendy Larsen.

John Frederick Nims: Federico Garcia Lorca's *The Unfaithful Wife* from *Sappho to Valery*. (The University of Arkansas Press). Reprinted by permission of The University of Arkansas Press.

John Frederick Nims: *Spanish Ballad* from *Selected Poems*. Reprinted by permission of The University of Chicago Press.

Alden Nowlan: *Tower Green*. Reprinted by permission of Stoddart Publishing Co. Limited, Don Mills, Ontario, Canada M3B 2T6.

Wilfrid Noyce: *Breathless* from *Poems* (Heinemann). Reprinted by permission of Rosemary Ballard.

Robert Nye: *Travelling to My Second Marriage on the Day of the First Moonshot* from *Collected Poems* (Sinclair-Stevenson, London, 1995). Reprinted by permission of the author.

Joyce Carol Oates: *An American Tradition*. Originally published in *The Ontario Review* and is reprinted by permission of the author.

Frank O'Hara: *The Day Lady Died* from *Lunch Poems*. Copyright © 1964 by Frank O'Hara. Reprinted by permission of City Light Books.

Charles Olson: *Maximus, to Gloucester, Sunday, July 19* from *Maximus Poems*, edited by George Butterick. Copyright © 1983 by The Regents of the University of California. Reprinted by permission of The Regents of the University of California.

Gregory Orr: *The Western Invention of Lyrical Nature* from *New and Selected Poems* (Wesleyan University Press). Reprinted by permission of the author.

Jacqueline Osherow: *To Eva* from *Looking for Angels in New York* (University of Georgia Press). Copyright © 1988 by Jacqueline Osherow. Reprinted by permission of the author.

Alicia Ostriker: *Elegy* from *Songs* (Holt, Rinehart & Winston, Inc.). Reprinted by permission of the author.

Christina Pacosz: *The Assumption of the Blessed Virgin Mary, August 15* from *This is Not a Place to Sing* (West End, 1987). Reprinted by permission of the author.

Grace Paley: *Having Arrived by Bike at Battery Park* from *Collected Poems* (Tilbury House). Reprinted by permission of the author.

Greg Pape: *This House* from *Black Branches* (University of Pittsburgh Press, 1984). Reprinted by permission of the author.

Clara Claiborne Park: *Advent*. Originally published in *The American Scholar* and is reprinted by permission of the author.

Stuart A. Paterson: *The Leaving of Scotland*. Reprinted by permission of the author.

Tom Paulin: *11/11/84*. Reprinted by permission of the author.

Octavio Paz: *Day*. Written by Octavio Paz and Charles Tomlinson. Copyright © by Octavio Paz, and is reprinted by permission of Octavio Paz and Charles Tomlinson.

Tod Perry: *For Nicholas, Born in September*. Reprinted by permission. Copyright © 1962, 1990 by The New Yorker Magazine, Inc.

Robert Phillips: *The Unfalling* from *Personal Accounts*. Reprinted by permission of the author and Ontario Review Press.

Fiona Pitt-Kethley: *The Party*. Copyright © by Fiona Pitt-Kethley. Reprinted by permission of the author.

Ruth Pitter: *The Sparrow's Skull*. Reprinted by permission of Messrs. Parrott & Coales, Solicitors.

Sterling D. Plumpp: *Steps to Break the Circle*. Reprinted by permission of the author.

Ezra Pound: *Canto XXVI* from *Cantos*. Copyright © 1934, 1938 by Ezra Pound. Reprinted by permission of New Directions Publishing Corporation.

Sheenagh Pugh: *The ruder times* from *What a Place to Grow Flowers* (Christopher Davis). Reprinted by permission of the author.

Al Purdy: *The Battlefield at Batoche* from *The Collected Poems of Al Purdy* (McClelland & Stewart). Reprinted by permission of the Canadian Publishers, McClelland & Stewart, Toronto.

Rodney Pybus: *St. Peter's Day 1839* from *In Memoriam Milena* (Chatto & Windus, 1973). Copyright © by Rodney Pybus. Reprinted by permission of the author.

Lawrence Raab: *Two Clouds* from *Other Children* (Carnegie Mellon University Press, 1987). Reprinted by permission of the author.

Burton Raffel: *The Battle of Maldon*. Copyright © 1960, 1964 by The University of Nebraska Press. Copyright © 1994 by Burton Raffel. Reprinted by permission of the author.

Burton Raffel and Alla Burogo: Osip Mandelstam's *We Shall Meet Again*. Reprinted by permission of the translators.

Bin Ramke: *Entropy* from *The Difference Between Night and Day* (Yale University Press). Copyright © 1978 by Bin Ramke. Reprinted by permission of the author.

Peter Reading: *15th February*. Copyright © 1983 by Peter Reading and reprinted by permission of the author.

James Reaney: *Orange Lilies*. Reprinted by permission of the author and John Miller.

Peter Redgrove: *Signatures*. Reprinted by permission of author.

James Reiss: *The Breathers* from *The Breathers* (Ecco Press, 1974). Copyright © 1974 by James Reiss. Reprinted by permission of the author.

Alberto Rios: *On January 5, 1984, El Santo the Wrestler Died, Possibly* from *Five Indiscretions*. Copyright © 1985 by Albert Rios. Reprinted by permission of the author.

Peter Robinson: *23 January 1980*. Reprinted by permission of Carcanet Press Limited.

Judith Rodriguez: *A legal error, 29 March, 1847*. Copyright © by Judith Rodriguez. Reprinted by permission of the author.

Alan Ross: *Off Brighton Pier* from *Blindfold Games* (Collins Harvill). Copyright © by Alan Ross. Reprinted by permission of the author.

A. L. Rowse: *Easter Day, 1943*. Copyright © by A. L. Rowse. Reprinted by permission of the author.

Carol Rumens: *The Duchess and the Assassin* from *The Greening of Snow Beach* (Bloodaxe Books,

1988) and *Thinking of Skins: New and Selected Poems* (1993). Reprinted by permission of the author.

Salman Rushdie: *March 6, 1989*. Copyright © 1989 by Salman Rushdie. Reprinted by permission of the author.

Alfrredo Navarro Salanga: *An Apocryphal Account of the Birthing of Andres Bonifacio* from *Turtle Voices in Uncertain Weather* (Cultural Center of the Phillipines). Reprinted by permission of Mr. Salanga's estate, his widow Alicia Salanga and their four children, Elena, Elyrah, Elmirah and Elyas Isabello.

Philip Salom: *The Execution of Hallaj* from *The Silent Piano* (Freemantle Arts Centre Press, 1980, Australia). Reprinted by permission of the author.

Sonia Sanchez: *A poem for my brother (reflections on his death from AIDS)* from *Under a Soprano Sky* (Africa World Press, Inc., Trenton, NJ). Copyright © 1987 by Sonia Sanchez. Reprinted by permission of the author.

Stephen Sandy: *The Heart's Desire of Americans*. Copyright © 1988, 1995 by Stephen Sandy. Reprinted by permission of the author.

Vernon Scannell: *Gunpowder Plot*. Reprinted by permission of the author and Robson Books, Ltd.

Michael Schmidt: *Homage to Federico García Lorca*. Copyright © 1969, 1995 by Michael Schmidt. Reprinted by permission of the author.

James Schuyler: *June 30, 1974* from *The Morning of the Poem* (Farrar, Straus & Giroux, Inc.). Copyright © 1980 by James Schulyler. Reprinted by permission of Farrar, Straus & Giroux, Inc.

Stephen Scobie: *McAlmon's Chinese Opera*. Reprinted by permission of the author.

James Scully: *Lt. Cmdr. T. E. Sanderson*. Reprinted by permission of the author.

Peter Scupham: *V.E. Day* from *The Air Show* (Oxford University Press, England, 1988). Reprinted by permission of the author.

Anne Sexton: *The Red Dance* from *45 Mercy Street*. Copyright © 1976 by Linda Gray Sexton and Loring Conant, Jr. Reprinted by permission of Houghton Mifflin Co. All rights reserved.

Karl Shapiro: *The Jew at Christmas Eve*. Copyright © by Karl Shapiro. Reprinted by permission of the author.

Betsy Sholl: *March 8* from *Changing Faces*. Copyright © by Betsy Sholl. Reprinted by permission of the author.

Peggy Shumaker: *Cinco de Mayo*. Reprinted by permission of the author.

Penelope Shuttle: *The Martyrdom of St. Polycarp* from *The Lion from Rio* (Oxford University Press). Reprinted by permission of the author and David Higham Associates.

C. H. Sisson: *A Letter to John Donne* from *Collected Poems*. Copyright © by C. H. Sisson. Reprinted by permission of Carcanet Press Limited.

Francis Carey Slater: *Woltemade* from *Collected Poems* (Oxford University Press). Reprinted by permission of Messers. Pillans & Wilson.

David R. Slavitt: *Carmen Miranda's Birthday* from *Dozens* (Louisanna State University Press). Copyright © 1981 by David R. Slavitt. Reprinted by permission of Louisiana State University Press.

A. J. M. Smith: *Ode: On the Death of W. B. Yeats* from *The Classic Shade* (McClelland & Stewart). Reprinted by permission of the Canadian Publishers, McClelland & Stewart, Toronto.

John Smith: *Death of Trotsky* from *A Landscape of My Own* (Robson Books). Reprinted by permission of the author.

W. D. Snodgrass: Manet: *"The Execution of Emperor Maximilian"*. Reprinted by permission of the author.

Kelwyn Sole: *Praxis?* Reprinted by permission of the author and Ravan Press.

Michael Spence: *Knowing What North Means: Letter to Richard Hugo from Lopez Island* from *The Spine* (Purdue University Press, 1987). Reprinted by permission of the author.

Stephen Spender: *Mary Stuart and Elizabeth* from *Mary Stuart* (Faber & Faber Ltd.). Reprinted by permission of the author.

Elizabeth Spires: *Letters to the Sea* from *Globe* (Wesleyan University Press). Copyright © 1981 Elizabeth Spires. Reprinted by permission of the author and the University Press of New England.

Jon Stallworthy: *The Trials*. Copyright © by Jon Stallworthy. Reprinted by permission of the author.

Wallace Stevens: *Lettres d'un Soldat* from *Opus Posthumous*. Copyright © 1957 by Wallace Stevens. Reprinted by permission of Alfred A. Knopf, Inc.

Susan Stewart: *At the Font of Aretusa* from *The Hive* (University of Georgia Press). Copyright © by Susan Stewart. Reprinted by permission of the author.

Carolyn Stoloff: *Report on the Times* from *A Spool of Blue, New and Selected Poems* (The Scarecrow Press, Inc., 1983). Copyright © by Carolyn Stoloff. Reprinted by permission of the author.

Adrien Stoutenburg: *Gregorian Adjustment, 1582* from *Land of Superior Mirages* (Johns Hopkins University Press, Baltimore, London, 1982). Reprinted by permission of Johns Hopkins University Press, Baltimore, London.

Dan Stryk: *Quake in Turkey* from *The Artist and the Crow* (Purdue University Press). Reprinted by permission of the author and Purdue University Press.

Nathaniel Tarn: *For the Death of Anton Webern Particularly* from *Old Savage/Young City* (Random House). Copyright © 1962 Nathaniel Tarn. Reprinted by permission of the author.

D. M. Thomas: Alexander Puskin's *May 26, 1828* from *The Bronze Horseman and Other Poems* by Alexander Pushkin (Viking/Penguin, 1982). Translated by D. M. Thomas. Reprinted by permission of the translator.

Dylan Thomas: *Poem in October* from *Poems of Dylan Thomas*. Copyright © 1945 by Trustees for the copyrights of Dylan Thomas. Reprinted by permission of New Directions Publishing Corporation in the United States and David Higham Associates in Canada.

Henry David Thoreau: *The Freshet* from a manuscript at the Harry Ransom Humanities Research Center of the University of Texas at Austin. Reprinted by permission of the Harry Ransom Center and the University of Texas.

Richard Tillinghast: *Today in the Café Trieste*. Copyright © by Richard Tillinghast. Reprinted by permission of the author.

Melvin Tolson: *Alpha*. Reprinted by permission of Melvin B. Tolson, Jr.

Charles Tomlinson: *Charlotte Corday*. Reprinted by permission of the author.

William Trowbridge: *Bearing Gifts*. Copyright © 1989 by William Trowbridge and reprinted by permission of the author and University of Arkansas Press.

Walter James Turner: *Hymn to Her Unknown* from *Selected Poems of Walter James Turner* (Oxford University Press).

Mona Van Duyn: *The Hermit of Hudson Pond* from *If It Be Not I*. Copyright © 1982 by Mona Van Duyn. Reprinted by permission of the author and Alfred A. Knopf, Inc.

David Wagoner: *Thoreau and the Snapping Turtle*. Copyright © 1987 by David Wagoner and reprinted by permission of the author.

Jeanne Murray Walker: *Ravenna, June 27, 1981: Verdi's Macbeth* from *Fugitive Angels* (Dragongate Press, 1985). Copyright © by Jeanne Murray Walker. Reprinted by permission of the author.

J. P. Ward: *Coda*. Reprinted by permission of John Powell Ward and Seven Books.

Sylvia Townsend Warner: *Of the Young Year's Disclosing Days*. Reprinted by permission of Carcanet Press Limited.

Val Warner: *Tristam Corbiere's Letter from Mexico* from *The Centenary Corbiere*. Translated by Val Warner. Reprinted by permission of Carcanet Press Limited.

Rosanna Warren: *Jacob Burkhardt, August 8, 1897* from *Stained Glass*. Originally published in *The Yale Review*. Copyright © 1993 by Rosanna Warren. Reprinted by permission of W. W. Norton & Company, Inc.

Robert Watson: *Sadie's Ice Cream Parlor* from *Selected Poems* (Atheneum, 1973). Reprinted by permission of the author.

Thomas Whitbread: *Postcard from Esna, Egypt* from *Whomp and Moonshiver* (BOA Editions). Copyright © 1982 Thomas Whitbread. Reprinted by permission of the author.

John Whitworth: *Report on the Progress of the Export Drive—Spring Bank Holiday 1977*. Reprinted by permission of the author.

Dara Wier: *Just the facts, ma'am*. Copyright © 1980 by Dara Wier and reprinted by permission of the author.

Richard Wilbur: *Patriot's Day* from *Running* in *Walking to Sleep: New Poems and Translations*. Copyright © 1986 by Richard Wilbur. Reprinted by permission of Harcourt Brace & Company, Inc.

Richard Wilbur: *Six Years Later* from *New and Collected Poems*. Copyright © 1978 by Richard Wilbur. Reprinted by permission of Harcourt Brace & Company, Inc. *Six Years Later* originally appeared in *The New Yorker*.

ACKNOWLEDGMENTS

Gwyn Williams: *For John Ormond*. Reprinted by permission of Daisy Williams.

Hugo Williams: *February the 20th Street* from *Selected Poems* (Oxford University Press, 1989). Reprinted by permission of Oxford University Press and the author.

William Carlos Williams: from *'Paterson'* from *Paterson*. Copyright © 1958 by William Carlos Williams. Reprinted by permission of New Directions Publishing Corporation.

David Wojahn: *Dates, For Example*. Reprinted by permission of the author.

John Woods: *Ahab's Diary*. Reprinted by permission of the author.

Douglas Worth: *March the 2nd*. Copyright © 1987 by Douglas Worth and reprinted by permission of the author.

Charles Wright: from: *A Journal of the Year of the Ox* from *The World of the Ten Thousand Things: Poems 1980–1990* (Farrar, Straus & Giroux, Inc.). Copyright © 1990 by Charles Wright. Reprinted by permission of Farrar, Straus & Giroux, Inc.

James Wright: *Eisenhower's Visit to Franco, 1959* from *The Branch Will Not Break* (Wesleyan University Press). Copyright © 1963 by James Wright and Wesleyan University Press. Reprinted by permission of University Press of New England.

John Yau: *January 18, 1979* from *Radiant Silhouette: New and Selected Work 1974–1978* (Black Sparrow Press). Reprinted by permission of Black Sparrow Press and the author.

William Butler Yeats: Lines from *All Souls' Night*. Lines from *The Poems of W. B. Yeats: A New Edition*, edited by Richard J. Finneran. Copyright © 1982 by Macmillan Publishing Company. Copyright renewed 1958 by George Yeats. Reprinted by permission of Simon & Schuster, Inc.

David Young: *Notes on the Poems*. Copyright © 1991 by David Young and reprinted by permission of the author.

Dean Young: *Age of Discovery* from *Design with X* (Wesleyan University Press, 1988). Reprinted by permission of the author.

Foreword

Some poets of the past have claimed that their verses were dashed off in a passion, or tossed off in a moment of negligent wit. Sometimes the claim has been true. But most poems are not so personal or so sudden as that. The very impulse to make a poem commits one to work with the words of the dictionary, in a language common to many people, and thus to set forth one's thoughts and feelings in a way that may resonate in the lives of others, now and later. In pursuit of that resonance, the poet will tailor and fictionalize whatever event or perception got him going, and he will strive as well, by formal means, to give his words just emphasis and clear tone. Such honing can take much time and deliberate craft. The poet is also carried beyond the personal moment by his century's breakings with tradition, one may still see or sense in most good poems of our day that part of their discourse is a conversing with other poems, across all boundaries of time or tongue.

Poems grow, then, toward the general and timeless. And yet they are rooted in particular days, to which they owe, among other things, their kept immediacy, concreteness, and emotion. Sometimes a poem will record a rare one-day occurrence—an eclipse, say, or the pitching of a perfect game. Sometimes a day's experience will provably initiate the making of a poem, as a January 27 in Mexico begot Hart Crane's "Broken Tower." Birthdays, death-days, or the anniversary of an old battle can marshal things long gathering to be said, and such a holiday as Hallowe'en can give Anthony Hecht a focus for his darkest thoughts. When poets use a date as a title, it can mean many things: the day of composition, for example; or the bitterly remembered date of an assassination; or the day on which some brief aspect of nature (a hatching of mayflies, perhaps) was intensely seen. That last possibility makes me think of how many of Robert Frost's poems concern Nature's threshold and ephemeral phases: consider "Nothing Gold Can Stay," or "Spring Pools," or the suggestion of solstice in "The darkest evening of the year." Those poems have no given dates, but they very well could have. And even in works of huge scope, which were years in the making, one finds those qualities that belong to the individual day or minute. In Book VII of *Paradise Lost*, the invocation becomes for a short time breathtakingly personal, bringing us suddenly close to the conditions under which the blind poet is meditating his lines, "though fallen on evil days;" and in the same book, when the Creator bids the waters to be gathered together, they hasten to do so, "uprolled/ As drops on dust conglobing from the dry." Such brilliant and immediate sightings of the world are also found everywhere in Dante's *Commedia*, which begins, though aimed at eternity, on the fictive eve of Good Friday, 1300.

All anthologies have some narrowing principle; the poets chosen must be major or fourteenth-century or Imagistic or born in Ohio; the poems must be antiwar or in haiku form or about cats. Thomas Foster and Elizabeth Guthrie have restricted themselves to poems belonging, in one way or another, to a particular day of the year, and I must say that their admissions-policy has proven not restrictive but liberating. Clearly there were enough possible candidates for each day to permit the editors to satisfy their excellent taste three hundred and sixty-five times, and once more for leap year. At the same time, the quality of their choices has not resulted in the awful predictability that we find in so many anthologies, especially those designed for textbook use. Because dateability was their first requirement, Foster and Guthrie have cast a wide net; they draw upon many ages and cultures and are refreshingly inclusive as to mode, giving us not only lyric poems but scenes from plays, artlessly poignant ballads, and such hilarious satire as Howard Nemerov's "Boom!"

A simple magic happens when poems are framed in the days of our calendar. The poems of far places are brought so into our lives, and we are reminded that the day is world-wide or world-round; that happens, indeed, in the first poem of this book, when Elizabeth Bishop describes January 1 as a time of burgeoning in Brazil. More magical still is the way that poets of whatever century are made contemporaries of us and of each other, with Corbière and Thomas More cheek by jowl, and Horace seeming as present-day as this year's Easter or the Fourth of July. Though the assembled poets of this fine volume have no topic that is common to them all, it is easy to think of them as engaged in that timeless conversation of which I have spoken.

RICHARD WILBUR
2 June, 1994

Introduction

 As the poems it contains, this book was conceived on a specific date: On the eighteenth of April in 1988 I read Longfellow's stirring account of Paul Revere's ride to my children and wondered, "Do other days have their poems?" Who better to ask such a question than Elizabeth Guthrie, friend and research librarian. Obviously our joint answer turned out to be yes, but with a significant qualification—more frequently it was the *poems* that had their days. As the project progressed and our criteria evolved, we picked fewer "occasional" poems and more poems which themselves were the occasion.

Fortunately the search took a long time. As we hunted for elusive days, we backed and filled, balanced and juxtaposed, and constantly "upgraded." After finding a hundred poems in the first few months we labored seven years to find the rest, abandoning many of the original hundred in the process. That seven year effort enabled us to create a database of several thousand poems from which we could select the best and most representative examples.

Poets mention dates for various reasons. Allen Ginsberg, for example, seems to date certain poems to assure the reader that what he says happened really happened and that every word is absolutely true. For Marianne Moore the coincidence of April 1 and the horse Tom Fool is part of a cosmic joke and just as unbelievable as everything else. Poets who write ekphrastic verse (poems describing paintings) may choose historical subjects, such as watercolors depicting "The Bombardment of Petropaulski" or Goya's "The Second of May," as anchors so their lines do duty to a true as well as a painted chair. Poets who celebrate birthdays and anniversaries, their own or others, work within obvious limitations, but there could hardly be a greater contrast between Hugo Williams's "February the 20th Street" and Ben Jonson's "An Ode, or Song, by all the Muses." Williams's dedication to his twin sister (added for this edition) is the only evidence that the poem relates to his and her birthday, while Jonson announces "birthday, birthday, birthday" in every line.

We have, of course, concentrated on a small corner of the poetic universe. When a poet asks, "What is so rare as a day in June?" we turn the page. When she describes what was so rare about a *particular* June 11, however, we get out our tables and see if the poem fits. If poetry is an effort to enhance memory, these poets have attempted to enlarge certain moments by wresting them from time's flux and focusing on their specific chronology. These poems are news that has stayed news, with dateline.

A multiyear project like this one is not a two-person effort. We could not have answered our initial question without loving support of our families. Elizabeth's son Matt Lang and my wife Dinah Seiver and our three children, Hannah, Isaac, and Miriam, were unfailing love and understanding. Friends and colleagues, especially Gary and Arlene Saxonhouse and family, Nicholas Delbanco, Clara Claiborne Park, Hilary Foulkes, Nancy Hill, Ray Sandona, and Carol Creel, offered many fruitful suggestions. Richard Wilbur's early and continuing enthusiasm for the project was a constant inspiration. Institutions we relied on include the libraries of the University of Michigan and Kent State University, the Crasselli Library at John Carroll University, the Cleveland Public Library and Clevenet System, the Shaker Heights Public Library, the University of Texas Humanities Research Center (especially their WATCH database), the New York Public Library, the Mitchell Library in Glasgow, the Scottish Poetry Library in Edinburgh, the Poetry Library in London, and the Poetry Society (London). Once we made our basic selections, Gary E. Smith used his awesome desktop-publishing skills to fashion the manuscript into something resembling an anthology. All of these efforts would have come to naught, however, without the aid of Elizabeth Ryan of Bascom Communications in New York City, who placed the book, and Peter Ginna, our editor, who championed it. Thank you all.

Finally, I would like to acknowledge the generosity of the poets (and their agents) who allowed their work to appear. We were able to contact almost all contemporary American poets through A Directory of American Poets and Fiction Writers, published by Poets and Writers, Inc. The permissions departments of most publishers were very responsive. Hoping not to slight any individuals by omission, we would particularly thank Patricia Flynn at Random House, Erika Seidman at Farrar, Straus & Giroux, David Cortwright at W. W. Norton, Daniel Allman at New Directions, Teresa Buswell at Houghton Mifflin, Lydia Zalaya at Macmillan, Auriol Milford at Oxford University Press, Faith Barbato at HarperCollins, the poet Michael Schmidt who also heads Carcanet Press, Patricia Kratz at the University Press of New England, and Florence Eichen at Viking/Penguin. The final shape of the book owes much to their flexibility, cooperation, and commitment.

THOMAS E. FOSTER
Cleveland, Ohio
April 18, 1995

January

elizabeth bishop

Brazil, January 1, 1502

> *. . . embroidered nature . . . tapestried landscape.*
> —*Landscape Into Art*, by Sir Kenneth Clark

Januaries, Nature greets our eyes
exactly as she must have greeted theirs:
every square inch filling in with foliage—
big leaves, little leaves, and giant leaves,
blue, blue-green, and olive,
with occasional lighter veins and edges,
or a stain underleaf turned over;
monster ferns
in silver-gray relief,
and flowers, too, like giant water lilies
up in the air—up, rather, in the leaves—
purple, yellow, two yellows, pink,
rust red and greenish white;
solid but airy; fresh as if just finished
and taken off the frame.

A blue-white sky, a simple web,
backing for feathery detail:
brief arcs, a pale-green broken wheel,
a few palms, swarthy, squat, but delicate;
and perching there in profile, beaks agape,
the big symbolic birds keep quiet,
each showing only half his puffed and padded,
pure-colored or spotted breast.
Still in the foreground there is Sin:
five sooty dragons near some massy rocks.
The rocks are worked with lichens, gray moonbursts
splattered and overlapping,
threatened from underneath by moss
in lovely hell-green flames,
attacked above
by scaling-ladder vines, oblique and neat,
"one leaf yes and one leaf no" (in Portuguese).
The lizards scarcely breathe; all eyes

are on the smaller, female one, back-to,
her wicked tail straight up and over,
red as a red-hot wire.

Just so the Christians, hard as nails,
tiny as nails, and glinting,
in creaking armor, came and found it all,
not unfamiliar:
no lovers' walks, no bowers,
no cherries to be picked, no lute music,
but corresponding, nevertheless,
to an old dream of wealth and luxury
already out of style when they left home—
wealth, plus a brand-new pleasure.
Directly after Mass, humming perhaps
L'Homme armé or some such tune,
they ripped away into the hanging fabric,
each out to catch an Indian for himself—
those maddening little women who kept calling,
calling to each other (or had the birds waked up?)
and retreating, always retreating, behind it.

joseph brodsky

Six Years Later

So long had life together been that now
The second of January fell again
On Tuesday, making her astonished brow
Lift like a windshield wiper in the rain,
    So that her misty sadness cleared, and showed
    A cloudless distance waiting up the road.

So long had life together been that once
The snow began to fall, it seemed unending;
That, lest the flakes should make her eyelids wince,
I'd shield them with my hand, and they, pretending
    Not to believe that cherishing of eyes,
    Would beat against my palm like butterflies.

So alien had all novelty become
That sleep's entanglements would put to shame
Whatever depths the analysts might plumb;
That when my lips blew out the candle flame,
    Her lips, fluttering from my shoulder, sought
    To join my own, without another thought.

So long had life together been that all
That tattered brood of papered roses went,
And a whole birch grove grew upon the wall,
And we had money, by some accident,
    And tonguelike on the sea, for thirty days,
    The sunset threatened Turkey with its blaze.

So long had life together been without
Books, chairs, utensils—only that ancient bed—
That the triangle, before it came about,
Had been a perpendicular, the head
    Of some acquaintance hovering above
    Two points which had been coalesced by love.

So long had life together been that she
And I, with our joint shadows, had composed
A double door, a door which even if we
Were lost in work or sleep, was always closed:
    Somehow, it would appear, we drifted right
    On through it into the future, into the night.

Trans. Richard Wilbur

JANUARY 3

stuart a. paterson

The Leaving of Scotland

January 3, 1999

The news breaks on the eve of another
border-summit; Scotland has asked for

4

political asylum from Parliament Square.
They're putting up fences and putting out fires

in Motherwell, chaining the trawlers to
each other in Fraserburgh as black-clad

fish-terrorists riot and threaten a Cod War
with Iceland, rushing the Secretary

of State to a live TV broadcast
in Glasgow where, it's been reported,

Red Kelvinsiders are demanding a fortune
for Pat Lally's release from the National

Concert Hall. Poets are marching
to Fergusson's statue on the Mound singing

Venceramos, keeping the police at bay with
metaphors for educational cut-backs

at *Sabhal Mor Ostaig*. University students
in Dundee are demanding the release

of Douglas Dunn from a cell in London
where, in a *Scottish Books Special Emergency Broadcast*

from the South Bank Centre, he called,
in terza rima, for the reintegration

of Scottish regiments. The news has broken.
Ayrshire has declared its independence

and littered the road to Glasgow with glass.
Up north, an organisation

of Aberdeen radicals calling itself
The Scottish Offshore Republican Army

has captured an oil rig in the name of
Ravenscraig. The military are making

a giant jail of the Highlands, repopulation
of the Islands has begun and Gaelic

24-Hour TV set up, English forbidden.
The Daily Record has barricaded itself

in by the Broomielaw and blamed it all on
dissatisfied Mirror Group Pensioners

in collusion with the Scottish Office.
Michael Forsyth has returned and instituted

a four-year plan for dissident writers
on discovering that 'Mac' is Old Pictish

for 'Comrade Of'.
McLean, McIlvanney, MacCaig (and Allan Massie

for the sake of it) are rounded up to work crofts
on £16 a week, deliver mail, spin new cottage

industries, teach their children The Works
of Walter Scott and Teatime Tales by Molly Weir.

All over Scotland, town halls are giving out
copies of Dwelli's Gaelic-English Dictionary

and My Life In Pictures by Sean Connery.
The Herald has made Tom Shields Editor

and called for Pat Lally's release, but his corpse
is thrown from the roof of the Concert Hall

by vengeful muralists, paint-drenched, bewigged
and flown to an all-expenses-paid

funeral junket in Chicago.
A fierce battle rages at St Andrews Uni

between New Generation poets and police
who make no sense of demands that are written

in the New Dundonian Scots and ask
for a National Poetry Radio Station, and ends

with concessions on a 20-week stadium tour.
The border-summit breaks up again,

no sign of agreement on extradition
for convicted heroin smugglers—

Eh'm sorry, Eh'll read that again,
convicted *herring* smugglers.

English embassies, packed with Inverness
publicans and Aviemore time-share owners,

appeal to the European Community for help.
But the oil's run out, and so has Scotland.

Political asylum denied, it leaves.

george bradley

Electrocuting an Elephant

Her handlers, dressed in vests and flannel pants,
    Step forward in the weak winter light
Leading a behemoth among elephants,
Topsy, to another exhibition site;
    Caparisoned with leather bridle,
Six impassive tons of carnival delight
Shambles on among spectators who sidle
    Nervously off, for the brute has killed
At least three men, most recently an idle
Hanger-on at shows, who, given to distilled
    Diversions, fed her a live cigar.
Since become a beast of burden, Topsy thrilled
The crowds in her palmy days, and soon will star
    Once more, in an electrocution,
Which incident, though it someday seem bizarre,
Is now a new idea in execution.

Topsy has been fed an unaccustomed treat,
    A few carrots laced with cyanide,
And copper plates have been fastened to her feet,
Wired to cables running off on either side;

7

She stamps two times in irritation,
Then waits, for elephants, having a thick hide,
Know how to be patient. The situation
    Seems dreamlike, till someone throws a switch,
And the huge body shakes for the duration
Of five or six unending seconds, in which
    Smoke rises and Topsy's trunk contracts
And twelve thousand mammoth pounds finally pitch
To earth, as the current breaks and all relax.
    It is a scene shot with shades of grey—
The smoke, the animal, the reported facts—
On a seasonably grey and gloomy day.

Would you care to see any of that again?
    See it as many times as you please,
For an electrician, Thomas Edison,
Has had a bright idea we call the movies,
    And called on for monitory spark,
Has preserved it all in framed transparencies
That are clear as day, for all the day is dark.
    You might be amused on second glance
To note the background—it's an amusement park!—
A site on Coney Island where elephants
    Are being used in the construction,
And where Topsy, through a keeper's negligence,
Got loose, causing some property destruction,
    And so is shown to posterity,
A study in images and conduction,
Sunday, January 4th, 1903.

alberto rios

On January 5, 1984, El Santo the Wrestler Died, Possibly

The thing was, he could never be trusted.
He wore the silver mask even when he slept.
At his funeral as reported by all the Mexican news services
The pall bearers also put on their faces

Sequined masks to honor him, or so it was said.
The men in truth wore masks as much to hide from him
That he would not see who was putting him into the ground
And so get angry, get up, and come back after them
That way for which he was famous.
His partner el atomico pretended to think
There was no funeral at all.
He would have had to help el santo be angry
Come like the Samson running against the pillars
These men were, holding up the box
In which el santo was trapped;
Would have had to angle his head down, come at them
Mount them three men to a shoulder
As he ran through the middle, ducking under the casket
Bowling them down like all the other times
Giving el santo just a moment to breathe, get strong.

He will be missed
But one must say this in a whisper, and quickly.
One knows of the dead, of their polite habit of listening
Too much, believing what they hear, how it all builds up
So that finally something must be said.
One knows of the year in which the town of Guaymas
Had its first demonstration of a tape recorder.
It confirmed only what was already known:
That people speak. And that the voice of the wind
Captured finally, played back slowly
Given its moment to say something of lasting importance
Made only a complaint.
If el santo were to hear of his being missed
He might get hold of the wind, the voice of the dead,
And say too much, the way the best wrestlers do
With all the yelling
So one will always be responsible enough only to whisper
The best things about el santo
Out of concern for the crops and the sapling trees.
This much was decided at the funeral.

The decision to whisper was not too much.
One had to be suspicious of this man with a mask
Even as he reached out to shake your hand,
That you might be flung and bent around
Knocked on the head and forced to say
How glad you are to meet him, and his uncle;

9

How suspicious that hand, which he always raised
More slowly than a weightlifter's last possible push
As if he too were suspicious of you
That you might at the last second
Be the Blue Demon after all—*el demonio azul: ¡aha!*
   he recognizes you, *¡but too late!* that you might
In this last moment avoid his hand raised to shake
Hook the crook of your arm into his
And flip him with a slam to a cement canvas.
No, he could not be trusted
And he could not trust you.

In his last years very far from 1942
The year he gave his first bruise to another man
One received as a greeting no hand from him any longer.
A raised eyebrow, perhaps, *good morning to you,*
Just visible through the mask on his morning walk.
This was his greeting, one man to another, now.
But even then he could not be trusted
Had not slipped with age even an inch:
As he moved the hairy arm of his brow up and down
Like a villain taking possession of the widow's house,
If one quickly did not get out of his way—
Well, then, he kept it moving up and down, had gotten you
Had made you imagine his eyebrow
Making the sound of a referee's hand
Slam beating the canvas ten times
Telling you that you have lost.

JANUARY 6

richard katrovas

Kings' Day, 1984

Tonight, chance feeds thunder to the air.
Couples trot from drink to drink,
song to song, umbrellas,
upturned collars against the rain.
Their laughter, meek, is merciful,
and the dying rain, a sheet of mist.

An old drunk lays hands upon a post,
lifts forehead to the stream
running off the iron-lace awning
from above. I press my forehead
to the cool glass to witness transformation:
someone's son is changing wine to water,

his filthy khakis darken
down the length of one weak leg.
He stumbles on; I fall back into my chair,
regard receding tides of distant thunder,
watch droplets spot and run the blurred panes,
lace my fingers into a child's church and see

three men dressed as women
huddled in the doorway of the Roundup.
Clutching packages, they pass a joint
and wave at cars. One laughs hoarsely
and slaps her thigh, another pretends
that she's insulted. One's fluorescent

fishnet stockings glitter through the yellow-
lighted drizzle when she turns away.
Their cab arrives, and by a trick of light
seems driverless. I imagine they are
bearing gifts to celebrate the birth
of something conceived in a glass beaker.

My friends have gone home.
My wife is sleeping. Tonight,
the cathedrals of Europe are cocked
and ready; the apartment is clean and quiet.
One nervous fool twitching in the dark,
I burn with hope like a star.

robert herrick

Saint Distaffs day, or the morrow after Twelfth day

Partly worke and partly play
Ye must on S. *Distaffs* day:
From the Plough soone free your teame;
Then come home and fother them.
If the Maides a spinning goe,
Burne the flax, and fire the tow:
Scorch their plackets, but beware
That ye singe no maiden-haire.
Bring in pailes of water then,
Let the Maides bewash the men.
Give S. *Distaffs* all the right,
Then bid Christmas sport *good-night;*
And next morrow, every one
To his owne vocation.

alan brownjohn

The Rain Diary

For my geography project I would keep a rain diary, a record starting on 1st January of the days that year when it rained and approximately how much.

On 1st January there was no rain. On 2nd January there was no rain. It did not rain on 3rd or 4th either. Would I go back to school on 8th January with nothing to show? Only blank pages with the dates in blue-black italic and the expectation of punishment?

Amanda kept a sunshine diary. The sun shone all the time that New Year, every day was like the legendary 1st January 1942. I saw long shadows of bare trees in Amanda's garden revolving on the stiff white grass as the sun crawled low and bright round the Warwickshire sky. Amanda, day by day, logged her hours of sunshine in duffle coat and mittens, putting out her tongue to warm her finger tips.

Tiny planes inched over the blue from the aerodrome leaving lacy strips of vapour which crumbled into strung-out blurs. There was no rain on 5th, 6th or 7th. I gained a sense of what life in general would be like.

On 8th January I stood at 8.55 a.m. on the worn stone step of the school with my blank diary—and raindrops fell. But I had no time to write anything down, the bell was pounding in the school campanile and we could not be late. So I opened my rain diary and let the rain fall into it, stain it and crinkle it, as the others fled past me into school.

To which rain I added my own joyful tears, knowing that Amanda might have statistics but I had a concrete event.

jacqueline osherow

from: To Eva

Born: D.P. camp, Lanzburg, Germany, March 21, 1947
Died: New Jersey, January 9, 1985

As usual, the seasons change too fast.
This year's early balmy spell so leisurely,
Convincing, it tricks even the cautious
White magnolia into opening
And giving up its petals to a sudden
Change of air, to scatter on the ground
Like a thousand schoolgirl hopes to pluck, "he loves me."
Forsythia and crocus, from a distance,
Are confetti, what crowds in Venice
Throw into the air at *Carnivale*
To color streets for two weeks into Lent.
That's what the willow branches look like,
Even close up, or some oriental
Decoration for the year of the dragon,
Dripping long, chartreuse crepe-paper scales.
And I would so much rather be waking
To a sky like the inside of a shell,
The nearly invisible gray-white chambers,

Swirl enfolding swirl in clouds of snow,
Establishing a clear, white, soundless
Distance between place and place, all pale
Until the twisted stretch of branches starts
To darken over bars of rose and gold,
Looking like that kindergarten trick
Of covering a wildly crayoned picture
With a heavy coat of black, then scratching back
The colors with a pin. And I would watch
Those leafless trees even without a sunset,
All those previously well-kept secrets
In the open air, wayward arrows,
Umbrella frames turned inside out in wind.
Commuting, through the thinnest gauze of snow,
I would watch them from the window, knowing what
The world will look like when there is no world,
How its ghosts will haunt the empty space.

. . .

e. e. cummings

Buffalo Bill's Defunct

Buffalo Bill's
defunct
     who used to
     ride a watersmooth-silver
                              stallion
and break onetwothreefourfive pigeonsjustlikethat
                                             Jesus

he was a handsome man
              and what i want to know is
how do you like your blueeyed boy
     Mister Death

Buffalo Bill Cody died January 10, 1917.

william carlos williams

from: Paterson

Hi, open up a dozen, make
it two dozen! Easy girl!
You wanna blow a fuse?
All manner of particularizations
to stay the pocky moon   :
January sunshine
1949
Wednesday, 11
(10,000,000 times plus April)
—a red-butted reversible minute-glass
loaded with
salt-like   white crystals
flowing
for timing eggs
Salut à Antonin Artaud pour les
lignes, trés pures   :
"et d'évocations plas-
tiques d'éléments de"
"Funeral *designs*"   and
(a beautiful, optimistic
word . .)   and
"Plants"
(it should be explained that
in this case "plants" does NOT refer to interment.)
"Wedding bouquets"
—the association
is indefensible.

tim dlugos

Qum

for Donald Britton

Saturday, Jan. 12: sky swarms
with microscopic particles. It's too warm
inside this bar, a grace note
to make you and my other friends assume I wrote
these words just now, before the reading.
That is an illusion. Needing
drastic forms of admiration is a virus.
Wanting people to desire us
we (meaning you and I) wear a bright veil
of language (meaning words) before which pale
the mundane elements of waking life.
"A poet." Fine. But sometimes I feel like the wife
of a demented mullah, in my thick chador,
two eyes peeping out, no body curves or
smile or sense of pity.
Marching through the streets of this holy city,
I can smell the slogans on my breath,
and my veil is Western journalism's symbol of the death
of reason and the triumph of some crazy throwback
to my suburban Moslem childhood. I can't go back
there any more. The keys won't
fit. Sometimes I don't
remember that this holy garb was of my choosing:
brilliant blue, like Mary's. God, I'm losing
my train of thought, awash in archetypal sentiment.
The words are microscopic particles, a sediment
of mirrored light, brilliant, filling the air
and piling up around us layer by layer.

edward thomas

The Sorrow of True Love

The sorrow of true love is a great sorrow
And true love parting blackens a bright morrow:
Yet almost they equal joys, since their despair
Is but hope blinded by its tears, and clear
Above the storm the heavens wait to be seen.
But greater sorrow from less love has been
That can mistake lack of despair for hope
And knows not tempest and the perfect scope
Of summer, but a frozen drizzle perpetual
Of drops that from remorse and pity fall
And cannot ever shine in the sun or thaw,
Removed eternally from the sun's law.

Edward Thomas recorded in his diary for January 13, 1917: "Nothing to do but test compass which never gives same results. Walk and tea with Flawn. Cold drizzle. Horton and the battery left early for Codford. Even wrote verses. Early to bed." This is his last poem.

christina rossetti

A Death of a First-born

January 14th, 1892

One young life lost, two happy young lives blighted,
  With earthward eyes we see:
With eyes uplifted, keener, farther-sighted,
  We look, O lord, to Thee.

Grief hears a funeral knell: hope hears the ringing
  Of birthday bells on high;
Faith, hope, and love make answer with soft singing,
  Half carol and half cry.

Stoop to console us, Christ, Sole Consolation,
    While dust returns to dust;
Until that blessed day when all Thy Nation
    Shall rise up of the Just.

JANUARY 15

william langland

A High Wind in January

*from: Piers Plowman
Passus quintus de Visione*

The kyng and his knightes to the kirke wente
To here matynes of þe day and þe masse after.
þanne waked I of my wynkynge and wo was withalle
þat I ne hadde sleped sadder and yseighen more.
Ac er I hadde faren a fourlonge feyntise me hente,
That I ne myghte ferther afoot for defaute of slepynge;
And sat softly adown and seide my bileue,
And so I babeled on my bedes, þei broughte me aslepe.

    And þanne saw I moche more, þan I bifore tolde,
For I say þee felde ful of folke þat I bifore of seyde,
And how Resoun gan arrrayen hym, alle þe reume to preche,
And with a crosse afor þe kynge comsed þus to techen.

    He preued þat þise pestilences were for pure synne,
And þe southwest wynde on Saterday at euene
Was pertliche for pure pryde and for no poynt elles.
Piries and plomtrees were puffed to þe erthe,
In ensample, the segges, the shulden do þe bettere.
Beches and brode okes were blowen to þe grounde,
Torned vpward her tailles in tokenynge of drede,
þat dedly synne at domesday shal fordon hem alle.

    Of þis matere I myghte mamely ful longe,
Ac I shal seye as I saw, so me God helpe!
. . .

The "southwest wyned" refers to a violent wind on January 15, 1362, a Saturday.

joseph skipsey

The Hartley Calamity

The Hartley men are noble, and
 Ye'll hear a tale of woe;
Ill tell the doom of the Hartley men—
 The year of Sixty-two.

Twas on a Thursday morning, on
 The first month of the year,
When there befell the thing that well
 May rend the heart to hear.

Ere chanticleer with music rare
 Awakes the old homestead,
The Hartley men are up and off
 To earn their daily bread.

On, on they toil; with heat they broil,
 And streams of sweat still glue
The stour unto their skins, till they
 Are black as the coal they hew.

Now to and fro the putters go,
 The waggons to and fro,
And clang on clang of wheel and hoof
 Ring in the mine below.

The din and strife of human life
 Awake in "wall" and "board,"
When, lo! a shock is felt which makes
 Each human heart-beat heard.

Each bosom thuds, as each his duds
 snatches and away,
And to the distant shaft he flees
 With all the speed he may.

Each, all, they flee—by two—by three
 They seek the shaft, they seek

An answer in each other's face,
 To what they may not speak.

"Are we entombed?" they seem to ask,
 For the shaft is closed, and no
Escape have they to God's bright day
 From out the night below.

So stand in pain the Hartley men,
 And swiftly o'er them comes
The memory of home, nay, all
 That links us to our homes.

Despair at length renews their strength,
 And they the shaft must clear,
And soon the sound of mall and pick,
 Half drowns the voice of fear.

And hark! to the blow of the mall below
 Do sounds above reply?
Hurra, hurra, for the Hartley men,
 For now their rescue's nigh.

Their rescue nigh? The sounds of joy
 And hope have ceased, and ere
A breath is drawn a rumble's heard
 Drives them back to despair.

Together, now behold them bow;
 Their burden'd souls unload
In cries that never rise in vain
 Unto the living God.

Whilst yet they kneel, again they feel
 Their strength renew'd—again
The swing and the ring of the mall attest
 The might of the Hartley men.

And hark! to the blow of the mall below
  Do sounds above reply?
Hurra, hurra, for the Hartley men,
  For now their rescue's nigh.

But lo! yon light, erewhile so bright,
  No longer lights the scene;
A cloud of mist yon light hath kiss'd,
  And shorn it of its sheen.

A cloud of mist yon light hath kiss'd
  And see! along must crawl,
Till one by one the lights are smote,
  And darkness covers all.

"O, father, till the shaft is cleared,
  Close beside me keep;
My eye-lids are together glued,
  And I—and I—must sleep."

"Sleep, darling, sleep, and I will keep
  Close by—heigh-ho!"—To keep
Himself awake the father strives—
  But he too must sleep.

"O, brother, till the shaft is cleared,
  Close beside me keep;
My eye-lids are together glued,
  And I—and I—must sleep."

"Sleep, brother, sleep, and I will keep
  Close by—heigh-ho!"—To keep
Himself awake the brother strives—
  But he too must sleep.

"O, mother dear! wert thou near
  Whilst sleep"—The orphan slept;
And all night long by the black pit-heap
  The mother a dumb watch kept.

And fathers, and mothers, and sisters, and
    brothers
  The lover and the new-made bride
A vigil kept for those who slept,
  From eve to morning tide.

They slept—still sleep—in silence dread,
  Two hundred old and young,
To awake when heaven and earth have
    sped
  And the last dread trumpet rung.

*The beam of a pumping engine broke and fell into the shaft of Hartley colliery on the 16th of Januar
1862. Two hundred and four boys and men, most of the male population of the village, were slow
suffocated or poisoned by coal gas.*

kelwyn sole

---

raxis?

On the 17th January
while standing at the door of my house
n 14th Avenue, I saw
erry Mashabane
rouching behind an asbestos fence.

A Casspir came past
nd a white South African—
policeman—noticed him.

erry saw this
o he knelt down
o hide.
      The policeman

imped off, went straight up
o him and, without speaking,
fted his firearm and
hot him in the stomach.

As Jerry was shot he screamed.
His intestines were hanging out.
e held his stomach with one hand
nd tried to climb the fence.

screamed too and rushed over.
nother young boy ran up
nd we tried to pull him
owards my house. He stopped,
ecause Jerry's intestines
ept falling out,
nd tried to stuff them back.
hey were slipping
rough his fingers.

'he policeman then shot
e other boy in the leg.'

2
The boy's bright blood
indurates the dust. His open
eyes are avian, glassy
        almost stupid
in his final shocked belief
in his own death.

Yesterday is his lost bird swept
by black wings, and a meaning
more beautiful that he ever could imagine
come to give sense
to his jumbled brothers and sisters,
the mother dying slowly with her hands
fluttering open on her chest
and his father's liquor's poisonous anxieties
      in four rooms
without ceilings or inside doors
where he was bred along with
his fury.
      Amandla!

All around an uproar, flung stones opening
the heavy air as they fly
wobbling towards targets he identifies
the boers who shot his cousin,
the sell-outs going to work, izimpimpi
with their OK packets full
of the white man's commodities

and police cars yellow as pus,
windows opaqued so none inside
are visible, appear silently
on street corners
      and watch.

iTeargas ngeyabo!
. . .

john yau

January 18, 1979

So often artists have painted a woman
washing, or combing her hair.
And nearby is a mirror.
And there you were, crouched in the tub.
It was cold in the apartment.
It is always cold in winter.
But you were brushing out your hair
and singing to yourself.
And, for a moment, I think I saw
what those artists saw—
someone half in love with herself
and half in love with the world.

thomas carew

To Ben Jonson

Upon occasion of his Ode of Defiance annex'd to his play of "The New Inn"

'Tis true, dear Ben, thy just chastising hand
Hath fix'd upon the sotted age a brand,
To their swoln pride and empty scribbling due;
It can nor judge nor write: and yet 'tis true
Thy comic Muse, from the exalted line
Touch'd by thy *Alchemist,* doth since decline
From that her zenith, and foretells a red
And blushing evening, when she goes to bed;
Yet such as shall outshine the glimmering light
With which all stars shall gild the following night.
Nor think it much, since all thy eaglets may
Endure the sunny trial, if we say
This hath the stronger wing, or that doth shine

Trick'd up in fairer plumes, since all are thine.
Who hath his flock of cackling geese compar'd
With thy tun'd choir of swans? or else who dar'd
To call thy births deform'd? But if thou bind
By city-custom or by gavelkind
In equal shares thy love on all thy race,
We may distinguish of their sex and place;
Though one hand form them, and though one brain strike
Souls into all, they are not all alike.
Why should the follies, then, of this dull age
Draw from thy pen such an immodest rage,
As seems to blast thy (else-immortal) bays,
When thine own tongue proclaims thy itch of praise?
Such thirst will argue drouth. No, let be hurl'd
Upon thy works by the detracting world
What malice can suggest: let the rout say,
The running sands that, ere thou make a play,
Count the slow minutes, might a Goodwin frame,
To swallow when th' hast done thy shipwrack'd name.
Let them the dear expense of oil upbraid,
Suck'd by thy watchful lamp, that hath betray'd
To theft the blood of martyr'd authors, spilt
Into thy ink, whilst thou growest pale with guilt.
Repine not at the taper's thrifty waste,
That sleeks thy terser poems; nor is haste
Praise, but excuse; and if thou overcome
A knotty writer, bring the booty home;
Nor think it theft, if the rich spoils so torn
From conquer'd authors be as trophies worn.
Let others glut on the extorted praise
Of vulgar breath; trust thou to after days:
Thy labour'd works shall live, when Time devours
Th' abortive offspring of their hasty hours.
Thou are not of their rank, the quarrel lies
Within thine own verge: then let this suffice,
The wiser world doth greater thee confess
Than all men else, than thyself only less.

Jonson's last comedy, The New Inn, *opened and closed on January 19, 1631—*
the performance was interrupted by boos. When Jonson remonstrated with his audi-
ence in verse Carew advised him to "chill."

christopher marlowe

Edward the Second Abdicates

from: Edward II

Act V, scene i.
[*Enter* KING EDWARD, LEICESTER, *the* BISHOP OF
WINCHESTER, *and* TRUSSEL.]

LEICES.　Be patient, good my lord, cease to lament;
　　　　Imagine Killingworth Castle were your court,
　　　　And that you lay for pleasure here a space,
　　　　Not of compulsion or necessity.
K. EDW.　Leicester, if gentle words might comfort me,
　　　　Thy speeches long ago had eas'd my sorrows,
　　　　For kind and loving hast thou always been.
　　　　The griefs of private men are soon allay'd;
　　　　But not of kings. The forest deer, being struck,
　　　　Runs to an herb that closeth up the wounds;
　　　　But when the imperial lion's flesh is gor'd,
　　　　He rends and tears it with his wrathful paw,
　　　　And, highly scorning that the lowly earth
　　　　Should drink his blood, mounts up into the air:
　　　　And so it fares with me, whose dauntless mind
　　　　Th' ambitious Mortimer would seek to curb,
　　　　And that unnatural queen, false Isabel,
　　　　That thus hath pent and mew'd me in a prison
　　　　For such outrageous passions cloy my soul,
　　　　As with the wings of rancour and disdain
　　　　Full often am I soaring up to heaven,
　　　　To plain me to the gods against them both.
　　　　But when I call to mind I am a king,
　　　　Methinks I should revenge me of the wrongs,
　　　　That Mortimer and Isabel have done.
　　　　But what are kings, when regiment is gone,
　　　　But perfect shadows in a sunshine day?
　　　　My nobles rule; I bear the name of king;
　　　　I wear the crown; but am controll'd by them,
　　　　By Mortimer, and my unconstant queen,
　　　　Who spots my nuptial bed with infamy;
　　　　Whilst I am lodg'd within this cave of care,

	Where sorrow at my elbow still attends,
	To company my heart with sad laments,
	That bleeds within me for this strange exchange.
	But tell me, must I now resign my crown,
	To make usurping Mortimer a king?
BISH. OF WIN.	Your grace mistakes; it is for England's good,
	And princely Edward's right, we crave the crown.
K. EDW.	No, 'tis for Mortimer, not Edward's head
	For he's a lamb, encompassed by wolves,
	Which in a moment will abridge his life.
	But, if proud Mortimer do wear this crown,
	Heavens turn it to a blaze of quenchless fire!
	Or, like the snaky wreath of Tisiphon,
	Engirt the temples of his hateful head!
	So shall not England's vine be perished,
	But Edward's name survive, though Edward dies.
LEICES.	My lord, why waste you thus the time away?
	They stay your answer: will you yield your crown?
K. EDW.	Ah, Leicester, weigh how hardly I can brook
	To lose my crown and kingdom without cause;
	To give ambitious Mortimer my right,
	That, like a mountain, overwhelms my bliss;
	In which extreme my mind here murder'd is!
	But what the heavens appoint I must obey.—
	Here, take my crown; the life of Edward too:

[Taking off the crown.]

Two kings in England cannot reign at once.
But stay a while: let me be king till night,
That I may gaze upon this glittering crown;
So shall my eyes receive their last content,
My head, the latest honour due to it,
And jointly both yield up their wished right.
Continue ever, thou celestial sun;
Let never silent night possess this clime;
Stand still, you watches of the element;
All times and seasons, rest you at a stay,
That Edward may be still fair England's king!
But day's bright beams doth vanish fast away,
And needs I must resign my wished crown.
Inhuman creatures, nurs'd with tiger's milk,
Why gape you for your sovereign's overthrow?
My diadem, I mean, and guiltless life.
See, monsters, see! I'll wear my crown again.

[Putting on the crown.]

What, fear you not the fury of your king?—
But, hapless Edward, thou art fondly led;
They pass not for thy frowns as late they did,
But seek to make a new-elected king;
Which fills my mind with strange despairing thoughts,
Which thoughts are martyred with endless torments;
And in this torment comfort find I none,
But that I feel the crown upon my head;
And therefore let me wear it yet a while.

TRUS. My lord, the parliament must have present news;
And therefore say, will you resign or no?
[*The King rageth.*]

K. EDW. I'll not resign, but, whilst I live, be king.
Traitors, be gone, and join you with Mortimer.
Elect, conspire, install, do what you will:
Their blood and yours shall seal these treacheries.

BISH. OF WIN. This answer we'll return; and so, farewell.
[*Going with Trussel.*]

LEICES. Call them again, my lord, and speak them fair;
For, if they go, the prince shall lose his right.

K. EDW. Call thou them back; I have no power to speak.

LEICES. My lord, the king is willing to resign.

BISH. OF WIN. If he be not, let him choose.

K. EDW. O, would I might! but heavens and earth conspire
To make me miserable. Here, receive my crown.
Receive it? no, these innocent hands of mine
Shall not be guilty of so foul a crime;
He of you all that most desires my blood,
And will be call'd the murderer of a king,
Take it. What, are you mov'd? pity you me?
Then send for unrelenting Mortimer,
And Isabel, whose eyes being turn'd to steel
Will sooner sparkle fire than shed a tear.
Yet stay; for, rather than I'll look on them,
Here, here! [*Gives the Crown.*]—Now, sweet God of
 heaven,
Make me despise this transitory pomp,
And sit for aye enthronised in heaven!
Come, death, and with thy fingers close my eyes,
Or, if I live, let me forget myself!

BISH. OF WIN. My lord,—

K. EDW. Call me not lord; away, out of my sight!
Ah, pardon me! grief makes me lunatic.
Let not that Mortimer protect my son;

More safety is there in a tiger's jaws
Than his embracements. Bear this to the queen,
Wet with my tears, and dried again with sighs:
[*Gives a handkerchief.*]
If with the sight thereof she be not mov'd,
Return it back, and dip it in my blood.
Commend me to my son, and bid him rule
Better than I: yet how have I transgress'd,
Unless it be with too much clemency?

TRUS.   And thus, most humbly do we take our leave.

K. EDW.   Farewell.
[*Exeunt the Bishop of Winchester and Trussel with the crown.*]
I know the next news that they bring
Will be my death; and welcome shall it be:
To wretched men death is felicity.

King Edward II abdicated on January 20, 1327.

benjamin péret

Louis XVI Goes to the Guillotine

STINK stink stink
What stinks
It's Louis XVI the addled egg
and his head falls into the basket
his rotten head
because it's cold on the 21st of January
It's raining blood and snow
and all kinds of filth
spouting out of his ancient corpse
like a dog which passed out at the bottom of a copper
among the dirty clothes
and has had time to decay
like the pig-bucket fleur-de-lys
which the cows refuse to eat
because it gives off a smell of god

god the father of all dirt
who has given to Louis XVI
the divine right to pass out
like a dog in a copper

Trans. David Gascoyne

JANUARY 22

george gordon, lord byron

On This Day I Complete My Thirty-Sixth Year

'Tis time this heart should be unmoved,
   Since others it hath ceased to move:
Yes, though I cannot be beloved,
    Still let me love!

My days are in the yellow leaf;
   The flowers and fruits of love are gone;
The worm, the canker, and the grief
    Are mine alone!

The fire that on my bosom preys
   Is lone as some volcanic isle;
No torch is kindled at its blaze—
    A funeral pile.

The hope, the fear, the jealous care,
   The exalted portion of the pain
And power of love, I cannot share,
    But wear the chain.

But 'tis not *thus*—and 'tis not *here*—
   Such thoughts should shake my soul, nor
        now,
Where glory decks the hero's bier,
    Or binds his brow.

The sword, the banner, and the field,
   Glory and Greece, around me see!
The Spartan, borne upon his shield,
    Was not more free.

Awake! (not Greece—she *is* awake!)
   Awake, my spirit! Think through whom
Thy life-blood tracks its parent lake,
    And then strike home!

Tread those reviving passions down,
   Unworthy manhood!—unto thee
Indifferent should the smile or frown
    Of beauty be.

If thou regrett'st thy youth, *why live?*
   The land of honourable death
Is here:—up to the field, and give
    Away thy breath!

Seek out—less often sought than found—
   A soldier's grave, for thee the best;
Then look around, and choose thy ground
    And take thy rest.

Missolonghi, Jan. 22, 1824

Three months later Byron was dead.

peter robinson

23 January 1980

My apology condenses on the window;
a new moon shouldering the pole star
above backyards that overlook
cypresses and ash,
resilience, the marble headboards
in the cemetery, and my fear
of not getting to sleep or ever waking
coughs like a stalling car.

As the earth grows colder, discontented,
under the winters of money and the freezing
of relations, how we live
matters less than this reflection,
that we continue
poorer in health, and letters arrive
bearing affection or disaffection,
starting with, How are you?

Back home, what it is to be forgiven.
Close, I wonder what my furred tongue's for
as words to be uttered when she woke
my teeth close on,
and what should become of us
in the promises of further histories
I'm not asked to explain,
only to say no more.

david ignatow

On the Death of Winston Churchill

Now should great men die
in turn one by one
to keep the mind solemn
and ordained,
the living attend in dark clothes
and with tender weariness
and crowds at television sets
and newsstands wait
as each man's death sustains a peace.
The great gone, the people
one by one
offer to die.

Winston Churchill died on January 24, 1965.

hugh macdiarmid

Your Immortal Memory, Burns!

Thought may demit
Its functions fit
While still to thee, O Burns,
The punctual stomach of thy people turns.

Most folks agree
That poetry
Is of no earthly use
Save thine—which yields at least this
    Annual Excuse!

Other cults die:
But who'll deny
That you your mob in thrall
Will keep, O Poet Intestinal?

From wame to wame
Wags on your fame,
Once more through all the world
On fronts of proud abdomena unfurled.

These be thy train,
No-Soul and No-Brain,
And Humour-Far-From-It,
Bunkum and Bung, Swallow-All and
    Vomit.

Palate and Paunch,
Enthusiasts staunch,
Gladly aver again,
Behold one poet did not live in vain!"

But us no Buts!"
Cry Gullet and Guts
Whose parrots of souls
Resemble a clever ventriloquist's dolls.

Be of good cheer
Since once a year
Poetry is not too pure
A savoury for shopkeepers to endure!

And, dined and wined,
Solicitors find
Their platitudes assume
The guise of intuitions that illume

The hidden heart
Of Human Art
And strike in ignorance
On wonders of unpredicated chance.

A boozy haze
Enchants your lays
and Gluttony for a change
Finds Genius within accosting range,

And cottons on!
—Thy power alone
The spectacle attests
Of drunken bourgeois on the Muses'
    breasts!

Only thy star
Falls from afar
To swim into the ken
Of countless masses of befuddled men,

In their hearts' skies
Like barmaids' eyes
Glabrous to glitter till
Their minds like rockets shoot away and
    spill

These vivid clots
Of idiot thoughts
Wherewith our Scottish life
Is once a year incomparable rife!

. . .

Belly will praise
Thee all its days

And spread to all nations
Thy fame in belchings and regurgitations

While mean minds soar
And hiccoughs adore
And butcher-meat faces
Triumphant, transfigured, example thy
    graces!

The birthday of Robert Burns is celebrated throughout Scotland each January 25th.

JANUARY 26

barbara howes

January 26, '71

A wind-blizzard
Hurls itself screaming down,
Thieves through all corners,
Sets the old willow
To lashing itself,
Turns the grey elm's branches
To batons . . .

All our trees
Have become a febrile orchestra,
While a haze of snow speeds
Whiteness toward its barracks.

The butternut, holding up elfin
Fingers, sways, is political
On the breast of this wind;
Even a nonchalant
Bluejay zips through the
White tide with caution;

Horses are spooked—not
Knowing which side the attack
Comes from—they have windmares,
They let fly, shy, nip, buck—
Caught up in this wind-blizzard,
Forgetting the retinue
Of their day.

hart crane

The Broken Tower

The bell-rope that gathers God at dawn
Dispatches me as though I dropped down the knell
Of a spent day—to wander the cathedral lawn
From pit to crucifix, feet chill on steps from hell.

Have you not heard, have you not seen that corps
Of shadows in the tower, whose shoulders sway
Antiphonal carillons launched before
The stars are caught and hived in the sun's ray?

The bells, I say, the bells break down their tower;
And swing I know not where. Their tongues engrave
Membrane through marrow, my long-scattered score
Of broken intervals . . . And I, their sexton slave!

Oval encyclicals in canyons heaping
The impasse high with choir. Banked voices slain!
Pagodas, campaniles with reveilles outleaping—
O terraced echoes prostrate on the plain! . . .

And so it was I entered the broken world
To trace the visionary company of love, its voice
An instant in the wind (I know not whither hurled)
But not for long to hold each desperate choice.

My word I poured. But was it cognate, scored
Of that tribunal monarch of the air
Whose thigh embronzes earth, strikes crystal Word
In wounds pledged once to hope—cleft to despair?

The steep encroachments of my blood left me
No answer (could blood hold such a lofty tower
As flings the question true?)—or is it she
Whose sweet mortality stirs latent power?—

And through whose pulse I hear, counting the strokes
My veins recall and add, revived and sure
The angelus of wars my chest evokes:
What I hold healed, original now, and pure . . .

And builds, within, a tower that is not stone
(Not stone can jacket heaven)—but slip
Of pebbles,—visible wings of silence sown
In azure circles, widening as they dip

The matrix of the heart, lift down the eye
That shrines the quiet lake and swells a tower . . .
The commodious, tall decorum of that sky
Unseals her earth, and lifts love in its shower.

Crane's friend, Lesley Simpson, describes the genesis of this poem: "I was with Hart Crane in Taxco, Mexico, the morning of January 27, this year [1932], when he first conceived the idea of 'The Broken Tower.' The night before, being troubled with insomnia, he had risen before daybreak and walked down to the village square . . . Hart met the old Indian bell-ringer who was on his way down to the church. He and Hart were old friends, and he brought Hart up into the tower with him to help ring the bells. As Hart was swinging the clapper of the great bell, half drunk with its mighty music, the swift tropical dawn broke over the mountains. The sublimity of the scene and the thunder of the bells woke in Hart one of those gusts of joy of which only he was capable. He came striding up the hill afterwards in a sort of frenzy, refused his breakfast, and paced up and down the porch impatiently waiting for me to finish my coffee. Then he seized my arm and bore me off to the plaza, where we sat in the shadow of the church, Hart the while pouring out a magnificent cascade of words." [Note by John Unterecher]

JANUARY 28

a. j. m. smith

Ode: On the Death of W. B. Yeats

An old thorn tree in a stony place
Where the mountain stream has run dry,
Torn in the black wind under the race
Of the icicle-sharp kaleidoscopic white sky,
　　Burst into sudden flower.

Under the central dome of winter and night
A wild swan spreads his fanatic wing.
Ancestralled energy of blood and power
Beats in his sinewy breast. And now the ravening
Soul, fulfilled, his first-last hour
　　Upon him, chooses to exult.

34

Over the edge of shivering Europe,
Over the chalk front of Kent, over Eire,
Dwarfing the crawling waves' amoral savagery,
Daring the hiding clouds' rhetorical tumult,
    The white swan plummets the mountain top.

The stream has suddenly pushed the papery leaves!
It digs a rustling channel of clear water
On the scarred flank of Ben Bulben.
The twisted tree is incandescent with flowers.
The swan leaps singing into the cold air:
    This is a glory not for an hour:

    Over the Galway shore
    The white bird is flying
    Forever, and crying
    To the tumultuous throng
Of the sky his cold and passionate song.

William Butler Yeats died on January 28, 1939.

june jordan

Home: January 29, 1984

I can tell
because the ashtray was cleaned out
because the downstairs coconut is still full of milk
because actually nothing was left
except two shells hinged together pretty tough
at the joint
I can tell
because the in-house music now includes
the lying down look of gold and your shoulders
because there is no more noise in my head
because one room two hallways two flights of stairs
and the rest of northamerica remain
to be seen in this movie about why

I am trying to write this poem

not a letter
not a proclamation
not a history

I am trying to write this poem
because I can tell
because it's way after midnight and so what
I can tell
eyes open or shut
I can tell
George Washington did not sleep
here
I can tell
it was you
I can tell
it really was
you

jayanta mahapatra

30th January 1982: A Story

Another day. Like any other.
The bleating goat on the butcher's block
quickened its last breath and stared wide-eyed.
Its cry bent deeper still over the fringe of its death
while the butcher worried that his knife
was fast losing its sharpness.
At this moment the mobile loudspeaker van
of the Department of Public Relations swept past
pouring out the words of Gandhi's once-favorite hymn.
The rich woman cursed the Government
for waking her up so early when it was not even fully light.
Her five-year-old daughter cuddled
the broken doll's head in her arms for she needed
to fill her life. Or so she thought.
The sunlight stole slowly to the fallow fields
where village women were relieving themselves in the open.
The postman starting out for work

stopped at the garden fence and suddenly clutched his hernia;
he gave himself up to those letters
that shut him out for ever.
The empty bedroom sank heavily onto one of the evil schemes
which led through the long night into dawn.
No one heard the cry ripening inside himself.
Neighbors both, Amar Babu and Sham Babu smiled
sweetly at one another as they chose
their choice cuts of meat hanging from the hooks
in the marketplace. On a day just like this.
As the scent of new mango blossoms blew in
with the morning breeze, restless
with the heritage of blood.

*Mahatma Gandhi was killed by an assassin's bullet on the 30th January 1948 on
his way to a prayer meeting. [Note by Mahapatra]*

susan stewart

t the Font of Aretusa

ome things cannot follow:
e charcoal mask smudged
ound the red unblinking eye

nd the starched white taffeta
athers of the swan

once more, ruffling, unfurling,
e turns in the peacock-blue water,
turned on the current

ith the slow precision of any
ythological subject.

bove a hundred unfortunate copper coins
d the single wavering milfoil,
dden now and then in the dense

Papyrus that fringes her three
small islands, she is seen

As a consequence, a coda, to a likely,
unlikely, story of lust and water,
separate, then violate

Through chasm and river and
reef; water alternately

Stained and clear, reviving,
polluting, male and female;
flowing, spiralling still, then

Clouding, arriving
at last at this final clarity.

This salt spring, invented at the limit
of Ortygia, where a dozen happy couples
peer and turn and listen

On the last day of January,
1983, two days before the almond trees,

Starting in the west, are reported
to burst into their double
white flowers, all at once—

that is, not in sequence.

February

sylvia townsend warner

"Of the young year's disclosing days"

Of the young year's disclosing days this one day—
The first of February and a Sunday—
I clasp in mind, and set down for a safe keeping;
But why this one plain day more than another
Seems whimsy, unless it be that to me sleeping
You came embracing, said with your air of very
Truth: Sweet heart, this is the first of February.

Signalled thus, and thus with a kiss commended
The morning's visage looked from the blended
Duffle of winter's sober web with I know not
What of special grace, its date a portent
Pledged like the first aconite or first snowdrop,
Of its own choice and free good-will arriving
And flowered unreferred to the almanac maker's contriving

Everything I saw—the broad sky netted over
With small white clouds like a field of clover,
The fine lace of the treetops faintly stirring
Above the boughs unmoved as though not wind plied them
But only the pressed notes of the birds conferring,
The patient winter green of the lawn, the thrushes
Hopping ungainly large under the bare bushes,

All these, that January or March might show me
Unchanged on this eastern coast, where slowly,
Hooding her bright head, planting charily
Her shreds of colour in lew of balk or hedgerow,
Muffled in guise of winter, spring comes warily,
Took, at your word's wand, the light of the spirit
In its due day incarnate, all day to wear it.

Yes, and even the sea, coiling its endless
Tether along the strand, the friendless
Unharvested one, on whose cold green ungreeted
Fall the rich rains of February Filldyke,
Looked now at peace, as though this day had meted
There too a portion of promise, as though the ambered
Forests below that green their greening remembered.

john keats

Lincoln Castle

from: King Stephen: A Dramatic Fragment

Act I, scene iii. The field of battle.
[*Enter* KING STEPHEN *unarmed.*]

STEPHEN   Another sword! And what if I could seize
One from Bellona's gleaming armoury,
Or choose the fairest of her sheaved spears!
Where are my enemies? Here, close at hand,
Here come the testy brood. O for a sword!
I'm faint—a biting sword! A noble sword!
A hedge-stake—or a ponderous stone to hurl
With brawny vengeance, like the labourer Cain.
Come on! Farewell my kingdom, and all hail
Thou superb, plumb'd, and helmeted renown,
All hail—I would not truck this brilliant day
To rule in Pylos with a Nestor's beard—
Come on!
[*Enter* DE KAIMS *and knights, etc.*]

DE KAIMS   Is't madness, or a hunger after death,
That makes thee thus unarm'd throw taunts at us?
Yield, Stephen, or my sword's point dip in
The gloomy current of a traitor's heart.

STEPHEN   Do it, De Kaims, I will not budge an inch.

DE KAIMS   Yes, of thy madness thou shalt take the meed.

STEPHEN   Darest thou?

DE KAIMS   How dare, against a man disarm'd?

STEPHEN   What weapons has the lion but himself?
Come not near me, De Kaims, for by the price
Of all the glory I have won this day,
Being a king, I will not yield alive
To any but the second man of the realm,
Robert of Glocester.

DE KAIMS   Thou shalt vail to me.

STEPHEN   Shall I, when I have sworn against it, sir?
Thou think'st it brave to take a breathing king,
That, on a court-day bow'd to haughty Maud

The awed presence-chamber may be bold
To whisper, there's the man who took alive
Stephen—me—prisoner. Certes, De Kaims,
The ambition is a noble one.

DE KAIMS   'Tis true,
And, Stephen, I must compass it.

STEPHEN   No, no,
Do not tempt me to throttle you on the gorge,
Or with my gauntlet crush your hollow breast,
Just when your knighthood is grown ripe and full
For lordship.

A SOLDIER   Is an honest yeoman's spear
Of no use at a need? Take that.

STEPHEN   Ah, dastard!

DE KAIMS   What, you are vulnerable! my prisoner!

STEPHEN   No, not yet. I disclaim it, and demand
Death as a sovereign right unto a king
Who 'sdains to yield to any but his peer,
If not in title, yet in noble deeds,
The Earl of Glocester. Stab to the hilts, De Kaims,
For I will never by mean hands be led
From this so famous field. Do ye hear! Be quick!

*The fragment describes the decisive battle at Lincoln Castle in which forces led by
Robert, Earl of Gloucester, opposed Stephen on February 2, 1141.*

FEBRUARY 3

paul durcan

The death by heroin of Sid Vicious

There—but for the clutch of luck—go I.

At daybreak—in the arctic fog of a February
    daybreak—
Shoulderlength helmets in the watchtowers of the
    concentration camp
Caught me out in the intersecting arcs of the
    swirling searchlights:

42

There were at least a zillion of us caught out there
—Like ladybirds under a boulder—
But under the microscope each of us was unique,

Unique and we broke for cover, crazily breasting
The barbed wire and some of us made it
To the forest edge, but many of us did not

Make it, although their unborn children did—
Such as you whom the camp commandant branded
Sid Vicious of the Sex Pistols. Jesus, break his fall:

There—but for the clutch of luck—go we all.

February 1979

The lead singer of the Sex Pistols died February 3, 1979.

carol rumens

The Duchess and the Assassin

The Grand Duchess Yelizaveta
Worried about the troops in Manchuria
While Sergei went on crushing the Revolution
In his silk-lined German carriage.

That afternoon of the palace sewing-bee
She was thinking about men's shirts,
Not of the bodies that might break in them,
Proving her perfect seams incontinent.

She watched the lazy bouncing
Of vulturish wrists, and knew it was for the best
That her mind should simply float . . .
She had drawn out the needle again—

The cotton had the strong pull of sunlight—
When the day went up like the Tsar's fleet at Tsushima.
She flung down the shirt and ran
Straight for the flushed smoke-cloud: silk and skin.

She picked up what she recognised
As the Governor-General, thinking: "not my husband."
Her apron sagged with the enormity . . .
The blood on her thighs screamed like birth-blood.

Clothes, after that, were water; even flesh
Showed her its inmost threading.
She sat, untouchable, by the opened curtains,
Burning her eyes on a lifetime of unpicking.

At last she came to the prison,
To the windowless cell, the stink of certainty.
She wanted to know why.
Even terrorists had their reasons.

He was nervous, and tried to sneer.
She felt her power. She wanted to lift her finger
To singe the skin of his cheek.
You don't understand. Forgiveness

Is the last thing I need, he said.
So you'll hang, Iván, she said.
His smile cleared: but the cause will outlive us both!
And she thought of the ripped halves

Of a shirt, stitched together
In stringy blood—two deaths,
Seamless, that Russia would wear
When it came to bury her.

*The Grand Duchess Yelizaveta was the sister-in-law of Tsar Nicholas II, and the
wife of the Governor General of Moscow, Grand Duke Sergei Alexandrovich, who
was assassinated at the Kremlin Gates by the Socialist Revolutionary, Ivan
Kalyayev, on 4 February 1917. [Note by Rumens]*

jenny joseph

February floods, 1953

Those who were far inland
Saw, for a moment, the approaching tempest,
A sudden animal raging across the woods,
Bend each tree as a current sways weeds in water.
The roaring beast turned the landscape to a storm track
Till it hit the house, cracked the double windows
And blew the barn door to leave empty hinges.

And this after it had been broken
On the cliffs and high hills that intervened to the shore
This—far inland in a valley soliloquy
Where in stifling summers the stream forgets its escape
And almost ceases to talk of a fabled sea.

It was only when the surprising night had gone,
Like flotsam hurled with an eddy to lodge in a cleft
Among dry rocks news of the broken coast

Flooded inland.

The air where birds unconcerned were drifting again
Was alive with hourly messages from the sea;
Roads linked the land in help to the disaster,
Rivers, swollen miles up, led again to the sea.
Yesterday and tomorrow dissolve at such times.
The delicate structure of sequence is drowned with the land.
These days are in no season, they recall frames
In an uncle's sepia hall—him in a punt
Poling the main street past submerged shop fronts—
But no lives lost there: recall more
The fireman's helmet in a mothballed cupboard,
Recall Southampton burning.

But we inland, watching the buds grow out
Can think but never know what corn land will be like
Where no green shoot will spring for five more years;
And we inland, intent on our sprouting hedges
Can think but never hear what sea pastures are like

With the walls down like pebbles and the tides flowing over the land.
With a fir tree for symbol still to watch in the wind
We have time to collect statistics and erect some comfort
From appeals and tin boxes passed from hand to hand:
But they have only the sea and the tides returning.

Storing a view before the failure of sunlight
We blow on our fingers, and know an East wind coming
Which will snatch the rags of a tramp to reveal a shadow
In our minds, of a king, and there he'll nobly suffer.
Only so, inland or flying over the channel
Hearing the wind or watching the distant water
We glimpse, for a moment, the fullness of the tide.

The North Sea Floods, the most destructive of this century, crested on February 5, 1953.

FEBRUARY 6

 jackson mac low

from: The Pronouns

1ST DANCE—MAKING THINGS NEW—6 FEBRUARY 1964
He makes himself comfortable
& matches parcels.

Then he makes glass boil
while having political material get in
& coming by.

Soon after, he's giving gold cushions or seeming to do so,
taking opinions,
shocking,
pointing to a fact that seems to be an error & showing it to be other than it seems
& presently paining by going or having waves.

Then after doing some waiting,
he disgusts someone
& names things.

A little while later he gets out with things,
& finally either rewards someone for something or goes up under something.

2ND DANCE—SEEING LINES—6 FEBRUARY 1964
She seems to come by wing,
& keeping present being in front,
she reasons regularly.

Then—making her stomach let itself down
& giving a bit or doing something elastic
& making herself comfortable—
she lets complex impulses make something.

She disgusts everyone.

Later she fingers a door
& wheels awhile
while either transporting a star or letting go of a street.

anonymous

Arrest of the Duke of Suffolk

Now is the fox drevin to hole! ho to hym, hoo, hoo!
ffor and he crepe out, he will yow alle vndo.
Now ye han found parfite, love well your game;
ffor and ye ren countre, then be ye to blame.
Sum of yow holdith with the fox, and rennyth hare;
But he that tied talbot oure doge, euyll mot he fare!
ffor now we mys the black dog with the wide mouth,
ffor he wold haue ronnen well at the fox of the south.
And all gooth backward, and don is in the myre,
As they han deserued, so pay they ther hire.
Now is tyme of lent; the fox is in the towre;
Therfore send hym salesbury to be his confessoure.
Many mo ther ben, and we kowd hem knowe,
But won most begyn the daunce, and all com arowe.
Loke that your hunte blowe well thy chase;
But he do well is part, I beshrew is face!

This fox at bury slowe oure grete gandere;
Therfore at tyborn mony mon on hym wondere.
Iack napys, with his clogge,
Hath tied talbot, oure gentill dogge.
Wherfore Beaumownt, that gentill rache,
Hath brought Iack napis in an evill cache.
Be ware, al men, of that blame,
And namly ye of grete fame,
Spirituall and temperall, be ware of this,
Or els hit will not be well, I-wis.
God saue the kyng, and god forbede
That he suche apes any mo fede.
And of the perille that may be-fall
Be ware, dukes, erles, and barons alle.

Michael de la Pole, the Duke of Suffolk, was charged with treason on February 7, 1540. A later broadside describes his execution on May 3rd.

FEBRUARY 8

stephen spender

Mary Stuart and Elizabeth

from: Mary Stuart

Act V, scene vi
[LEICESTER *alone.*]

LEICESTER She moves towards her death, spirit transcendent,
And I stay tangled here among the damned.
What life from heaven I have cast away!
What has become of my determination
To feel nothing, see nothing but my aims,
Look on with unmoved eyes when her head falls?
Did her glance waken me to shame?
And must her death ensnare me now with love?
No, that's too late. She's gone. You are earth-bound
You must pursue your gross aims to the end.
Make your heart heartless, watch with stony eyes

Her death, so you may gain your shameful prize.
I have to see her die. I was sent here as witness.
[*He goes towards the door through which MARY has been
led, then stands stock-still, unable to move further.*]
In vain! My eyes are dazed! I cannot watch
Her death! I hear voices.
I hear the dean admonish her. She interrupts!
Listen. She prays. It seems so loud.
                  So strong,
Her voice. Now all is quiet. Quite still.
                I hear
Only a sobbing from her women. Now they bare her neck.
The block is brought. She kneels down.
                    Lays her head.
[*He collapses, fainting, and at the same time a loud cry is heard
    from below.*]

Act V, scene vii
[ELIZABETH *alone.*]

ELIZABETH   No one here yet! No messenger! Will it
Never be evening? Has it happened, or
Not happened? Both terrify me, and
I dare not ask.
Leicester doesn't show himself, nor Burleigh,
They have left London. So it must have happened.
The bow is drawn, the arrow flies, it has
Met its mark. Not for my kingdom could I
Stop it from striking now. Who's there?

Spender freely adapted and translated Schiller's Maria Stuart, *an imaginative
account of the last days of Mary Queen of Scots. Mary was executed on February 8,
1587.*

david r. slavitt

Carmen Miranda's Birthday

from: Dozens

"Señor Martinez-Martinez, the big banana
of the Inca Finca, celebrates the birthday
of Carmen Miranda every year: he gives
a small dinner (for sixty), shows one of her films,
and makes his usual speech—to urge that her day
be made a national holiday—concluding,
"Vulgar as she was, so we are vulgar."
And he drinks to her energy, her extravagance
of hats mounded with fruit, those wonderful shoes,
those flashing eyes! He is, otherwise, sane,
takes nothing stronger than sherry, and in the evenings,
by the candlelight he prefers, reads Latin poets.

Carmen Miranda was born on February 9, 1903.

tristan corbière

Letter From Mexico

Vera Cruz, February 10th

'You've entrusted the kid to me.—He's dead.
And more than one of his pals too, poor little chap.
The crew . . . all gone. Some of us perhaps
    Will return.—Fate: take it as read—

'Nothing so fine as that for a man—Sailor—
Everybody wants to be on shore—That's the stuff.
Without any kind of trouble. No more:
    You see apprenticeship is really tough.

'I weep recording it, old *Shore-brother*.
I'd have given my life without a second thought
To send him back to you . . . Weren't my fault:
    There's no sense in this distemper.

'Like clock-work the fever's here inevitably.
You get your ration in the cemetery.
The Zouave—after all, a Parisian—
    Calls it *the zoo's acclimatizing garden*.

'Don't be too upset. They die off here like flies.
. . . I've found some mementoes in his bag:
A girl's picture, Turkish slippers in a small size,
    And:—*Present for my sister*—on the tag.

'His message to *Ma* was that he'd kept his religion.
To his father: that he'd rather have died in action.
Two angels watched him growing paler:
    An old soldier. A sailor.'

Trans. Val Warner

thomas more

A Rueful Lamentation on the Death of Queen Elizabeth

O Ye that put your trust and confidence
In worldly joy and frail prosperity,
That so live here as ye should never hence,
    Remember death and look here upon me.
    Ensample I think there may no better be
        Your self wot well that in this realm was I
        Your queen but late, and lo now here I lie.

Was I not born of old worthy lineage?
    Was not my mother queen, my father king?
Was I not a king's fere in marriage?
    Had I not plenty of every pleasant thing?
    Merciful God, this is a strange reckoning:

Riches, honour, wealth and ancestry
Hath me forsaken, and lo now here I lie.

If worship might have kept me, I had not gone.
    If wit might have me saved, I needed not fear.
If money might have holp, I lacked none.
    But O good God what vaileth all this gear?
    When death is come, thy mighty messenger,
        Obey we must, there is no remedy;
        Me hath he summoned, and lo now here I lie.

Yet was I late promised otherwise,
    This year to live in wealth and delice.
Lo whereto cometh thy blandishing promise,
    O false astrology and divinatrice,
    Of God's secrets making thy self so wise?
        How true is for this year thy prophecy!
        The year yet lasteth, and lo now here I lie.

O brittle wealth, aye full of bitterness,
    Thy single pleasure doubled is with pain.
Account my sorrow first and my distress,
    In sundry wise, and reckon there again
    The joy that I have had, and I dare sayn,
        For all my honour, endured yet have I
        More woe that wealth, and lo now here I lie.

Where are our castles now, where are our towers?
    Goodly Richmond, soon art thou gone from me;
At Westminster that costly work of yours,
    Mine own dear lord, now shall I never see.
    Almighty God vouchsafe to grant that ye
        For you and your children well may edify.
        My palace builded is, and lo now here I lie.

Queen Elizabeth, wife of Henry VII and mother of Henry VIII, died on February 11, 1503.

alden nowlan

˙ower Green

ould it be in good taste
 take a picture of Tower Green?

ften ask myself such questions.

ie night before
therine Howard
s executed
e had them bring
e block to her,
it she might rehearse
ing gracefully.

ie act of a Queen, I called it once
a misjudgment natural to youth.
rue Queen would as lief have winked
the headsman. Rather, the gesture
a pert girl (she was twenty-two).

>ve you, little Catherine,
I you won't mind my camera.
t it appears that one of the Beefeaters
urious that I've dared
desecrate this spot.

He waves both arms,
seems to mouth curses!

I shrink a foot
in height; it's a wonder I don't
slink away on all fours.

Then I understand:
he believes I was swindling him
out of a tip.
            Life still goes on
in the Tower of London.
I'd forgotten that.

Here is a spiritual descendant
of the warder who carried
the block to the Queen's cell
on the night of February 12th,
fifteen forty-two,

another poor man
with a thankless job to do.

william shakespeare

Ophelia's Song

from: Hamlet

Act IV, scene v
[*The* KING *and* OPHELIA.]

KING   How do you, pretty lady?

OPHELIA   Well, God'ild you. They say the owl was a baker's daughter. Lord, we know what we are, but know not what we may be. God be at your table.

KING   Conceit upon her father.

OPHELIA   Pray let's have no words of this, but when they ask you what it means, say you this.

     (sings) Tomorrow is Saint Valentine's day,
         All in the morning betime,
     And I a maid at your window,
         To be your Valentine.
     Then up he rose, and donn'd his clo'es,
         And dupp'd the chamber door,
     Let in the maid that out a maid
         Never departed more.

KING   Pretty Ophelia—

OPHELIA   Indeed, without an oath, I'll make an end on't.

     By Gis and by Saint Charity,
         Alack and fie for shame,
     Young men will do't if they come to't
         By Cock, they are to blame.
     Quoth she, "Before you tumbled me,
         You promis'd me to wed."

     He answers,
     "So would I a done, by yonder sun,
         And thou hadst not come to my bed."

KING   How long hath she been thus?

OPHELIA   I hope all will be well. We must be patient. But I cannot choose but weep to think they would lay him i'th' cold ground. My brother shall know of it. And so I thank you for your good counsel. Come, my coach. Good night, ladies, good night. Sweet ladies, good night, good night.

KING   Follow her close; give her good watch, I pray you.

emily dickinson

Valentine

"Sic transit gloria mundi,"
    "How doth the busy bee,"
"Dum vivimus vivamus,"
    I stay my enemy!

Oh, "veni, vidi, vici!"
    Oh caput cap-a-pie!
And oh "memento mori"
    When I am far from thee!

Hurrah for Peter Parley!
    Hurrah for Daniel Boone!
Three cheers, sir, for the gentleman
    Who first observed the moon!

Peter, put up the sunshine;
    Pattie, arrange the stars;
Tell Luna *tea* is waiting,
    And call your brother Mars!

Put down the apple, Adam,
    And come away with me,
So shalt thou have a *pippin*
    From off my father's tree.

I climb the "Hill of Science,"
    I "view the landscape o'er,"
Such transcendental prospect,
    I ne'er beheld before!

Unto the Legislature
    My country bids me go;
I'll take my *india rubbers*,
    In case the *wind* should blow!

During my education,
    It was announced to me

That *gravitation, stumbling,*
  Fell from an *apple* tree!

The earth upon an axis
  Was once supposed to turn,
By way of a *gymnastic*
  In honor of the sun!

It *was* the brave Columbus,
  A sailing o'er the tide,
Who notified the nations
  Of where I would reside!

Mortality is fatal—
  Gentility is fine,
Rascality, heroic,
  Insolvency, sublime!

Our Fathers being weary,
  Laid down on Bunker Hill;
And tho' full many a morning,
  Yet they are sleeping still,—

The trumpet, sir, shall wake them,
  In dreams I see them rise,
Each with a solemn musket
  A marching to the skies!

A coward will remain, Sir,
  Until the fight is done,
But an *immortal hero*
  Will take his hat and run!

Good bye, Sir, I am going;
  My country calleth me;
Allow me, Sir, at parting,
  To wipe my weeping e'e.

In token of our friendship
  Accept this "Bonnie Doon,"
And when the hand that plucked it
  Hath passed beyond the moon,

The memory of my ashes
>Will consolation be;
Then farewell, Tuscarora,
>And farewell, Sir, to thee!

St. Valentine—'52

These verses, probably to her friend William Howland, were printed in the local newspaper and were Dickinson's first published poetry.

peter reading

15th February

I tried to put in what I really felt.
I really tried to put in what I felt.
I really felt it—what I tried to put.
I put it really feelingly, or tried.
I felt I really tried to put it in.
What I put in I tried to really feel.
Really I felt I'd tried to put it in.
I really tried to feel what I put in.

It cost £5 in WH Smith's.
£5 it cost—WH Smith's ain't cheap.
£5 ain't cheap, not for a thing like that.
It costs, a thing like that—£5 ain't cheap.
It wasn't a cheap thing—£5 it cost.
A thing like that ain't cheap in WH Smith's.
In WH Smith's a thing like that comes costly.
A lot to pay, £5, for a thing like that.

The heart was scarlet satin, sort of stuffed.
I sort of felt it was me own heart, like.
SHE TORE THE STUFFING OUT OF THE SCARLET HEART.
I sort of stuffed and tore her sort of scarlet.
I stuffed her, like, and felt her sort of satin.
I sort of felt she'd tore out all me stuffing.
I felt her stuff like satin sort of scarlet
her stuff felt sore, torn satin whorlet scar

I liked her score felt stiffed her scar lick hurt
I tore her satin felt her stuffed her scarlet
tore out her heart stuff scarred her Satan har
I licked her stiff tore scarf her harlot hair
tied scarf tore stabbed scar whore sin sat tit star
stuffed finger scar ha ha ha ha ha
felt stiff scarf tight tore scarlet heart her scare
her scare stare stabbed heart scarlet feel torn mur

FEBRUARY 16

                    anonymous

David Lowston

My name is David Lowston, I did seal, I did seal,
My name is David Lowston, I did seal.
Though my men and I were lost,
Though our very lives 'twould cost,
We did seal, we did seal, we did seal.

'Twas in eighteen hundred and ten we set sail, we set sail,
'Twas in eighteen hundred and ten we set sail.
We were left, we gallant men,
Never more to sail again,
For to seal, for to seal, for to seal.

We were set down in Open Bay, were set down, were set down,
We were set down in Open Bay, were set down.
Upon the sixteenth day,
Of Februar-aye-ay,
For to seal, for to seal, for to seal.

Our Captain, John Bedar, he set sail, he set sail,
Yes, for Port Jackson he set sail.
"I'll return, men, without fail,"
But she foundered in a gale,
And went down, and went down, and went down.

We cured ten thousand skins for the fur, for the fur,
Yes we cured ten thousand skins for the fur.

Brackish water, putrid seal,
We did all of us fall ill,
For to die, for to die, for to die.

Come all you lads who sail upon the sea, sail the sea,
Come all you jacks who sail upon the sea.
Though the schooner *Governor Bligh*,
Took on some who did not die,
Never seal, never seal, never seal.

ted hughes

February 17th

A lamb could not get born. Ice wind
Out of a downpour dishclout sunrise. The mother
Lay on the mudded slope. Harried, she got up
And the blackish lump bobbed at her back end
Under her tail. After some hard galloping,
some maneuvering, much flapping of the backward
Lump head of the lamb looking out,
I caught her with a rope. Laid her, head uphill,
And examined the lamb. A blood ball swollen
Tight in its black felt, its mouth gap
Squashed crooked, tongue stuck out, black-purple,
Strangled by its mother. I felt inside,
Past the noose of mother-flesh, into the slippery
Muscled tunnel, fingering for a hoof,
Right back to the porthole of the pelvis.
But there was no hoof. He had stuck his head out too early
And his feet could not follow. He should have
Felt his way, tiptoe, his toes
Tucked up under his nose
For a safe landing. So I kneeled wrestling
With her groans. No hand could squeeze past
The lamb's neck into her interior
To hook a knee. I roped that baby head
And hauled till she cried out and tried
To get up and I saw it was useless. I went
Two miles for the injection and a razor.

Sliced the lamb's throat strings, levered with a knife
Between the vertebrae and brought the head off
To stare at its mother, its pipes sitting in the mud
With all earth for a body. Then pushed
The neck stump right back in, and as I pushed
She pushed. She pushed crying and I pushed gasping.
And the strength
Of the birth push and the push of my thumb
Against that wobbly vertebra were deadlock,
A to-fro futility. Till I forced
A hand past and got a knee. Then like
Pulling myself to the ceiling with one finger
Hooked in a loop, timing my effort
To her birth-push groans, I pulled against
The corpse that would not come. Till it came.
And after it the long, sudden, yolk-yellow
Parcel of life
In a smoking slither of oils and soups and syrups—
And the body lay born, beside the hacked-off head.

FEBRUARY 18

 john heywood

On the Princess Mary

Give place, you ladies, and be gone,
   Boast not yourselves at all,
For here at hand approacheth one,
   Whose face will stain you all.

The virtue of her lively looks
   Excels the precious stone;
I wish to have none other books
   To read or look upon.

In each of her two crystal eyes
   Smileth a naked boy;
It would you all in heart suffice
   To see that lamp of joy.

I think nature hath lost the mould
   Where she her shape did take,
Or else I doubt if nature could
   So fair a creature make.

She may be very well compared
   Unto the phoenix kind,
Whose like was never seen nor heard,
   That any man can find.

In life she is Diana chaste,
   In truth, Penelope;
In word and eke in deed steadfast.
   What will you more we say?

all the world were sought so far,
Who could find such a wight?
er beauty twinkleth like a star
Within the frosty night.

er rosial colour comes and goes
With such a comely grace,
ore readier too than doth the rose
Within her lively face.

Bacchus' feast none shall her meet,
Ne at no wanton play;
or gazing in an open street,
Nor gadding as a stray.

he modest mirth that she doth use
Is mixed with shamefastness.

All vice she doth wholly refuse,
And hateth idleness.

O Lord, it is a world to see
How virtue can repair
And deck her in such honesty,
Whom nature made so fair.

Truly, she doth as far exceed
Our women nowadays,
As doth the gillyflower a weed,
And more, a thousand ways.

How might we do to have a graff
Of this unspotted tree,
For all the rest are plain but chaff,
Which seem good corn to be.

ywood celebrates the eighteenth birthday of Princess Mary (later Bloody Mary) on February 18, 1534.

FEBRUARY 19

nigel forde

A Day to Remember

The British love their heritage,
Their pomp and pageantry;
And nothing suits them better than
An anniversary—
An excuse for a toast and a flag on a pole,
Or a plaque, or to plant a tree.
Every day of the year belongs to a saint
Or a much more colourful sinner:
Someone died, or someone was born
King Alfred burnt the dinner,
Or something remarkable happened, or
The West Indies brought on a spinner.
But the dullest day in all the year
Is the nineteenth of February,
For nothing of note took place today

61

As far as I can see,
And it's time we did something about it.
And gave it identity.
So—let's make it a day when we celebrate
The oddest and worst that has been—
Whatever you like that's not already
Kept its memory green
We'll think of and drink to every year
On dull old Feb. nineteen.
It's the day of St. Aloysius Lepp,
Patron saint of hopeless cases
Who turned too fast from temptation
And was strangled in his braces;
The day they invented nappy-rash,
Earwax and empty spaces.
It's the day on which David Coleman made sense,
And Cannon and Ball told jokes;
The day they discovered that Milton Keynes
Was just an elaborate hoax;
It's National Scum and Tidemark day,
And, in 356 B.C.
Hats were invented; the first was worn
At twenty-five past three.
It's National Flag-day Flag-day today;
And comments about the weather
Were first passed in England on Feb. the nineteenth,
And the Scots invented heather.
The day of the first known incidence
Of musak in restaurants;
It's a day to rejoice because square things don't roll
And Frenchmen live in France,
The Greeks were invented, and Income Tax,
Barry Manilow sang in tune
And someone invented fluffy dice
To hang in the family saloon.
It's the day they passed the law that says
Whichever queue you decide on
Will be the slowest moving;
And it's one that can be relied on.
On February the nineteenth
Latin became a dead language;
The cabinet stayed intact all day;
B.R. used the first welded sandwich.
But how to commemorate such a great day?

Have a party? Or write an encomium?
Monks can stay in and celibate
Round the monastery harmonium;
I suggest we observe—at 11 o'clock—
Two minutes' pandemonium.

hugo williams

February the 20th Street

for Elizabeth Eger

A coincidence must be
Part of a whole chain
Whose links are unknown to me.

I feel them round me
Everywhere I go: in queues,
In trains, under bridges,

People, or coincidences, flukes
Of logic which fail
Because of me, because

We move singly through streets,
The last of some sad species,
Pacing the floors of zoos,

Our luck homing forever
Backward through grasses
To the brink of another time.

sterling d. plumpp

Steps to Break the Circle

I was standing on a corner
On that cold, cold rainy day
When they blew Malcolm away.
Will the circle be unbroken
Bye and bye, yall, bye and bye . . .

The Black Man's days are epic chains
Superbad links wandering in cisterns
Dry and narrow with the unending
Echoes just jazzing nights
Riffing right through wooden walls.
These trips I takes is waking breaths
Life cycles my fathers left me pedaling.
My Mississippi manning is a message
Kilos of soul cider sipped by the music
Of a song sailed over sage oceans . . .
I wears the rapping ring of seasons
Ebony circles of blues with the road
Long and my tired strides short.
Mocking birds' mimics are mentors
I hears my soul striding down gravel
Years and the dust is dancing . . .

Undertaker he took Brother King
Laid him out in a shroud

As the troubled cloud
Gave birth to my agony,
Now will the circle be unbroken
Bye and bye, yall, bye and bye . . .

The Black Man's days are epics changing
Bigfeet to break the circle
Break the breast of beaded crises
Ships stinking with Black flesh
Cottonfields colorful with open locks
Muddy roads with stubborn mules tugging

Rivers coughing up African bodies
Fathers never seeing their chilluns mature
Chilluns never knowing their fathers,
Steps to break the circle, I takes
When I lets the leaves become
Victims of crazy winds
And I wanders on, on blacktop hunches
Trying to make a straight bound train
A train to train all my brothers
Travel with all the sisters
And trample, trample my enemy,
This train this train this train
I rides is a hundred cars long. . . .

Malcolm X was assassinated February 21, 1965.

adrien stoutenburg

Gregorian Adjustment, 1582

George Washington's birthday, February 11,
Old Style; February 22, New Style

The equinox was out of joint.
In twelve hundred years plus fifty-seven
trusted calendar went awry,
developing an error of ten days,
so nothing matched.
Leaves bloomed too late;
birds nested in blank boughs;
even roosters were crowing out of tune.

Pope Gregory on his stiff throne
bent brow to fist,
attempting to reel time back
to something rational and true.
From prayer and thought he ruled
ten strumpet days must be tossed out
upon the dump heap of eternity,
the daily reckoning rectified.

Time is a racer and a sloth.
The Pope's chill bones
were tapestry
by the time his rectification came
to the American Colonies
and caught Ben Franklin
out of time . . .
ten days plus one
(a leap year's maverick sprint)
to be deducted from the total sum
of trips abroad, tomes, kites, and love.
Franklin was one who treasured sleep,
regretted those sweet hours lost;
yet philosophy with him ran deep,
and time was but a sieve, he knew,
through which one must expect a leak.

Our founding fathers took in stride
corrections of inevitable flaws.

Some losses had to be.
Birthdays were hustled into line,
adjustments made for wages lost,
new dates assigned to deaths or anniversaires.
But still the gap yawns there:
eleven days of expurgated history.

 penelope shuttle

The Martyrdom of St. Polycarp

He had known John
and others who had known the Lord
but he was betrayed by a servant,

arrested late in the evening
at a farm outside Smyrna,
hens scattering in panic,
geese retreating angrily,
children peeping from corners
to find out who are heroes,
who are villains.

This happens around the year 155,
the arrest of an old man
who had known those who had known
the Lord,
had known John.

In the city
a crowd assembles for the games,
officials, wives, magnates, courtesans,
labourers, idlers, children, artisans;
animals baying, trumpeting,
the stench not a clean farmyard stench
but a festering stink,
the reek of a blood circus.

The old man and the proconsul converse,
they see eye to eye,
they are the only philosophers

within five hundred miles,
and able to bear their differences,
the roman reluctant
to condemn the venerable man
whose honour he can see.

The old man shrugs, smiles.

"How can I curse Christ,
for in all my eighty-six years
I have never known him do me wrong . . ."

And the crowd is yelling,
            "Kill him,
he is the one who destroys our gods . . ."

Even the cripples and lepers join in.

The circus gods need blood or ashes.

So because he is commanded
the proconsul orders the burning of
        Polycarp

"and the flames made a sort of arch,
like a ship's sail
filled with the wind,
and they were like a wall round the
        martyr's body;

he looked, not like burning flesh,
like bread in the oven
old and silver being refined in the
  furnace."

was like bread in the oven!
e gold or silver in the furnace!

turned the torture circus
  fiery circus of joy, flames of the spirit.

the cruel spectators did not clap their
  hands,
all to their knees, or say to the children,
 , there is a miracle, a man alive in the
  flames.

the people say, have our gods done
  such things?

they warm themselves at those flames?

The old man stood
with the flames flowing round him
like a weir of fire,
sailing in his ship of fire,
safe in his tent of flames

as the outraged crowd damned him.

At a sign from the proconsul
(curious in private life
about the supernatural)
a bored boy-executioner
braves the miraculous ark of flame,
pierces the old man's heart,
freeing Polycarp,
who kicks his corpse aside
and becomes a soul
and the crowd go on cheering,
children laughing, the rubbish gods
      ungrieving.

*n the flames would not touch St. Polycarp, he was pierced by a spear. He is the first saint whose
tyrdom, on February 23, 155, appears independently in the historical record.*

jane cooper

Hunger Moon

The last full moon of February
stalks the fields; barbed wire casts a shadow.
Rising slowly, a beam moved toward the west
stealthily changing position

until now, in the small hours, across the snow
it advances on my pillow
to wake me, not rudely like the sun
but with the cocked gun of silence.

I am alone in a vast room
where a vain woman once slept.
The moon, in pale buckskins, crouches
on guard beside her bed.

Slowly the light wanes, the snow will melt
and all the fences thrum in the spring breeze
but not until that sleeper, trapped
in my body, turns and turns.

1967

The full moon of February 1967 was on February 24th. In February, 1967, The
New York Times *noted that in the Middle West, the last full moon before the
spring equinox used to be called "hunger moon," because it was still too early to
plant, yet there was not enough feed left in the barns for the animals. [Note by
Cooper]*

FEBRUARY 25

marilyn hacker

February 25

Dear Bill, I dawdled answering your letter.
My punishment—the postal rates were raised.
The mail piled on this table has me fazed.
I think of it as clearing up the clutter.
There's somebody I like better and better
—she's someone else's lover, though; not mine.
She hides her blushes in her leonine
hair, that was more like tinsel than like butter
when I ruffled it—the feminine
of *avuncular*. She's twenty-five,
but age is not the muddle of the matter
whose damp wings are unfolding now, alive
out of the chrysalis that I felt shatter
when I kissed her till heat split my spine.

ezra pound

from: Canto XXVI

To the Cardinal Gonzaga of Mantua, ultimo febbraio 1548
"26th of feb. was killed in this city
Lorenzo de Medicis. Yr. Illu^s L^{dshp} will understand
from the enc. account how the affair is said to have
gone off. They say those who killed him have certainly
got away in a post boat with 6 oars. But they don't
know which way they have gone, and as a guard may
have been set in certain places and passes, it wd.
be convenient if yr. Ill^s L^{dshp} wd. write at once
to your ambassador here, saying among other things
that the two men who killed Lorenzino have passed through
the city of Mantua and that no one knows which
way they have gone. Publishing this information
from yr. Ldshp will perhaps help them to get free.
Although we think they are already in Florence, but
in any case this measure can do no harm. So that
yr. Ldshp wd. benefit by doing it quickly and even
to have others send the same news.
May Our Lord protect yr. Ill^s and most Revnd person
with the increase of state you desire.

Venice, last of Feb. 1548
I kiss the hands of yr. Ill. Ld^{shp}
Don In. Hnr. de Mendoça

christopher caudwell

Heil Baldwin!

A Poem in celebration of the Anglo-German Naval Agreement

> *"The Anglo-German Agreement is the first practical move in
> disarmament that has been accomplished since the War."*
> —Mr. Baldwin

Arms and the man I sing, whose sovran power
Has brought about at last this happy hour,
Concord of Britain, country of the free,
With Germany, adobe of liberty.

. . .

While Hindenburg still lived, and Adolf loved
The Chief of Staff he later had removed,
While Hitler, Chancellor, seemed a simple dupe,
A prisoner of the tiny Junker group,
While Nazis, with a shrinking vote, saw loom
In the elections six days hence their doom,
Sudden and dreadful on the brow of night
The darkened Reichstag glowed with fiery light.
A pile of massive stone, its granite shell
Was filled with flame, the Council Hall a hell.
Two men had seen the conflagration start
And through the flames a frenzied figure dart.
They urged a policeman to desert his place
Who unenthusiastically gave chase.
The flying figure crashed through panes of glass.
Their bullets missed. He has escaped alas!
But by now Goering, summoned to the spot,
A revelation straight from God has got.
Before he goes inside the truth he sees:
"The Communists are the incendiaries.
This beacon will their evil purpose light.
No loyal German will be safe tonight."
This Goering said; this Goering still believes
For who would dare suppose that God deceives?
Or that, like Nazi justice, Providence

Cannot at will with evidence dispense?
The land remained wrapped in accustomed peace.
The moment failed its honors to release.
Goering himself, where Heavenly Power falls short
Will see God's warning is not brought to naught!
Since blood He promised why then, blood will run,
And all things, as foretold by Him, be done.

. . .

In those bright flames, presage of brighter day,
The rubbish of these years will melt away
And, like a man from nightmare glad to wake,
This land will see the dawn, the red dawn, break,
And over ruined Nazidom unfurled
The second banner of the classless world.

The Reichstag was destroyed by fire on February 27, 1933.

john montague

A Flowering Absence

How can one make an absence flower,
lure a desert to fragrant bloom?
Taut with terror, I rehearse a time
when I was taken from a sick room:
as before from your flayed womb.

And given away to be fostered
wherever charity could afford.
I came back, lichened with sores,
from the care of still poorer immi-
grants, new washed from the hold.

I bless their unrecorded names,
whose need was greater than mine,
wet nurses from tenement darkness
giving suck for a time,
because their milk was plentiful

Or their own children gone.
They were the first to succour
that still terrible thirst of mine,
a thirst for love and knowledge,
to learn something of that time

Of confusion, poverty, absence.
Year by year, I track it down
intent for a hint of evidence,
seeking to manage the pain—
how a mother gave away her son.

I took the subway to the hospital
in darkest Brooklyn, to call
on the old nun who nursed you
through the travail of my birth
to come on another cold trail.

71

Sister Virgilius, how strange!
She died, just before you came.
She was delirious, rambling of all
her old patients; she could well
have remembered your mother's name.

Around the bulk of St. Catherine's
another wild, raunchier Brooklyn:
as tough a territory as I have known,
strutting young Puerto Rican hoods,
flash of blade, of bicycle chain.

Mother, my birth was the death
of your love life, the last man
to flutter near your tender womb:
a neonlit barsign winks off & on,
motherfucka, thass your name.

There is an absence, real as presence,
In the mornings I hear my daughter
chuckle, with runs of sudden joy.
Hurt, she rushes to her mother,
as I never could, a whining boy.

All roads wind backwards to it.
An unwanted child, a primal hurt.
I caught fever on the big boat
that brought us away from America
—away from my lost parents.

Surely my father loved me,
teaching me to croon, *Ragtime Cowboy*
Joe, swaying in his saddle
as he sings, as he did, drunkenly
dropping down from the speakeasy.

So I found myself shipped back
to his home, in an older country,
transported to a previous century,
where his sisters restored me,
natural love flowering around me.

And the hurt ran briefly underground
to break out in a schoolroom
where I was taunted by a mistress
who hunted me publicly down
to near speechlessness.

So this is our brightest infant?
Where did he get that outlandish accent?
What do you expect, with no parents,
sent back from some American slum:
none of you are to speak like him!

Stammer, impediment, stutter:
she had found my lode of shame,
and soon I could no longer utter
those magical words I had begun
to love, to dolphin delight in.

And not for two stumbling decades
would I manage to speak straight again.
Was it any remission to learn
that she drove her daughter to suicide
later, with that same lashing tongue?

None. Only bewildered compassion.
Wounded for the second time
my tongue became a rusted hinge
until the sweet oils of poetry
eased it, and light flooded in.

John Montague was born February 28, 1929.

walter de la mare

February 29

Odd, waif-like Day, the changeling of
Man's 'time' unreckoned in his years;
The moon already shows above
       Thy fickle sleet—now tears!

As brief thy stay has been as though
Next Spring might seal our tryst again.
Alas, fall must four winters' snow
       Ere you come back. And then?

I love thy timid aconite,
Crocus, and scilla's deep-sea blue;
Hark, too, that rainbird, out of sight,
       Mocking the woodland through!

But see, it's evening in the west:
Tranquil, withdrawn, aloof, devout.
Soon will the darkness drape your breast,
       And midnight shut you out!

Sweet February Twenty Nine!—
This is our grace-year, as I live!
Quick, now! this foolish heart of mine:
       Seize thy prerogative!

March

anonymous

There were Three Jovial Huntsmen

There were three jovial huntsmen,
As I have heard men say,
And they would go a-hunting
Upon St. David's Day.

All the day they hunted
And nothing could they find,
But a ship a-sailing,
A-sailing with the wind.

One said it was a ship,
The other he said, Nay;
The third said it was a house,
With the chimney blown away.

And all the night they hunted
And nothing could they find,
But the moon a-gliding,
A-gliding with the wind.

One said it was the moon,
The other he said, Nay;
The third said it was a cheese,
And half of it cut away.

And all the day they hunted
And nothing could they find,
But a hedgehog in a bramble bush,
And that they left behind.

The first said it was a hedgehog,
The second he said, Nay;
The third said it was a pincushion,
And the pins stuck in wrong way.

And all the night they hunted
And nothing could they find,
But a hare in a turnip field,
And that they left behind.

The first said it was a hare,
The second he said, Nay;
The third said it was a calf,
And the cow had run away.

And all the day they hunted
And nothing could they find,
But an owl in a holly tree,
And that they left behind.

One said it was an owl,
The other he said, Nay;
The third said it was the evil one,
And they all ran away.

The feast of St. David, the patron saint of Wales, is celebrated March 1.

douglas worth

March the 2nd

I found in the library, yesterday afternoon,
some stuff about the Native Americans
who lived in this region. Called the Massachusetts,
(which means "place of great hills"), they settled in small bands
near streams and ponds each spring and stayed through summer
fishing and hunting, planting beans and corn
"when the leaves of the white oak were big as the ears of a mouse,"
gathering roots and berries, nuts and herbs;
moving on in the fall to be close to the deer they hunted
through winter when they depended more on meat.
It said robbery and murder were rare among them
and that they lived, for the most part, peacefully,
and when tribes fought over hunting grounds or insults
it usually ended when the first brave got hurt;
that they were astonished when they battled the British
by how many could die in war; that it wasn't their custom
to take scalps till we offered to pay for them.
It said that women took part in village councils
and could leave their husbands anytime they chose.
It said stew was always simmering in a village
and no stranger, red or white, went away hungry.
It said they treated the spirits of all creatures,
among whom they lived as siblings, with respect,
begging forgiveness of the ones they killed,
wasting nothing, downing the flesh to the last morsel,
using the hide for clothes and moccasins,
sinew for bowstrings, horn and bone for tools.
It said they celebrated such festivals
as sugaring in March and planting in May
and made songs and spells and chants for every occasion
from warding off colds to making the corn grow tall,
often guided in this by their shaman, their medicine man,
who kept in touch with the spirits that dwell in all things,
created and overseen by the Great Spirit,
and who'd fast in times of calamity to appease
the angered spirits, and make lighter magic
to entertain and charm at other times.
It said they loved dancing and singing and storytelling,
having no written language, tales about tricksters

fables and myths, often spiced with humor and sex
which shocked the Puritan fathers who must have thought
they'd left behind such leanings with Shakespeare and Chaucer.
It said young men, courting, would sing or play their flutes
at their sweethearts' wigwams on sultry summer evenings
until they came out to stroll with them into the dusk.
Some grandfathers still, it said, would sing in the evenings
to their "mountain flowers," their lovely "spirit blossoms."
It said they played football, hockey, lacrosse, and handball,
gambled with painted pebbles, played cards made of rush,
kept dogs for pets, made popcorn and strawberry bread,
and overindulged their kids who grew sleek and saucy.
It said that before we brought in the idea of heaven
they had no conception of "happy hunting grounds,"
finding everything here as it should be. In short, it sounds
like a good life they led for millennia
till it came to a sudden end in the 1600's
through a series of battles and even more lethal plagues
brought over by white men, along with their thunder sticks,
that wiped out nine out of ten of the Massachusetts
in village after village, and scattered the rest.

MARCH 3

edward thomas

March the Third

Here again (she said) is March the third
And twelve hours singing for the bird
'Twixt dawn and dusk, from half past six
To half past six, never unheard.

'Tis Sunday, and the church-bells end
With the birds' songs. I think they blend
Better than in the same fair days
That shall pronounce the Winter's end.

Do men mark, and none dares say,
How it may shift and long delay,
Somewhere before the first of Spring,
But never fails, this singing day?

When it falls on Sunday, bells
Are a wild natural voice that dwells
On hillsides; but the birds' songs have
The holiness gone from the bells.

This day unpromised is more dear
Than all the named days of the year
When seasonable sweets come in,
Since now we know how lucky we are.

daniel hoffman

Penn's Grant

Good King Charley swigged his hops and his barley
    And a jolly old king was he,

       "by the Grace of God, Defender of the Faith, &c."

He called for his Chancellor and Ministers of State
    And he called for his Mistresses three.

Now the King of Hearts plays at Whists and Darts
    And holds Banquets and Balls at his Court
For his Gentlemen of Parts and his High-Breasted Tarts,
    And be damned if the money runs short,

And be damned if the Tailor or the Victualler Royal
    Or the Cavalry, or men in the Fleet
Make a tasteless turmoil because it's been such a while
       Ere they had wherewithal to eat.

See, here, straight as a staff comes the Lord's mooncalf,
    The son of dear Admiral Penn!
With his hat on his poll he is bound to be droll
    Though the Crown rules more tractable men—

       When Penn attended him the King removed his crown.
       Asked why he did so, H.M. replied, "Friend Penn,

I bare my head because it is the custom here,
    when in the presence of the King,
    that only *one* of us be covered."

                                        —Much merriment
    at this sally from the king whose wit
    amused the wits *The Soldier's Pleasure*
    and *The Country Wife* amused . . .

Now with all due respect, against the Conventicle Act
    Or is't for Quakers in gaol that he pleads?
Welladay, now it sounds like those Sixteen Thousand Pounds
    The Throne owes his Da' that he needs—

But see, William Quaker won't shipwreck the Exchequer
    Or sink King and Chancellor yet:
He requests and receives a quitclaim

        "Whereas our Trustie and well beloved Subject
        William Penn, Esquire,
        sonne and heire of Sir William Penn, deceased,
        out of a commendable desire
        to enlarge our English Empire
        and promote such vseful commodities as may bee
        of benefit to vs and our Dominions,

        "as alsoe to reduce the Savage Natives by
        gentle and just manners
        to the love of civill Societie
        and Christian Religion
        hath humbley besought leave of vs
        to transport an ample Colonie
        vnto a certaine Countrey
        hereinafter described in the partes of America not yet
                cultivated and planted"

                                        that relieves
    Lucky Charles of this nuisance, his debt;

And relieves, by an exodus over the seas
    Of Dissenters, at their own expense—

        The land being hilly, "I would call it New Wales,"
        said Penn whose name in Welsh means *a hill*.
        But the King's Secretary, from Wales as well,

demurs that such a folly as this Quaker plans
might slight his country's name. Then
his deep woods in mind, Penn proposes
—Latin scholar, he—"Sylvania." To this
the King prefixes "PENN,"
which Penn the Quaker must accept, the name
not signifying vanity in him

since Charles confers his Patent "haveing regard
to the memorie and meritts of his late father
in divers services and perticulary
to his *Conduct, courage*, and *difcretion*
under our deareft brother
James Duke of York in that Signall Batell
and victorie obteyned against the Dutch
in the yeare One thousand and Six hundred sixtie
   five . . ."

And relieves of Friend William with his hectoring pleas—
   The benefits do look immense!

In delight at this barter, King Charles signs the Charter
   And many folk, not just Friends, follow Penn.
They ship out with thanksgiving to seek a good living
   In a new land, where men will be men.

King Charles II signed Penn's Charter on March 4, 1681.

edwin morgan

Glasgow 5 March 1971

With a ragged diamond
of shattered plate-glass
a young man and his girl
are falling backwards into a shop-window.
The young man's face
is bristling with fragments of glass
and the girl's leg has caught

on the broken window
and spurts arterial blood
over her wet-look white coat.
Their arms are starfished out
braced for impact,
their faces show surprise, shock,
and the beginning of pain.
The two youths who have pushed them
are about to complete the operation
reaching into the window
to loot what they can smartly:
Their faces show no expression.
It is a sharp clear night
in Sauchiehall Street.
In the background two drivers
keep their eyes on the road.

 salman rushdie

March 6, 1989

Boy, yaar, they sure called me some good names of late:
e.g. opportunist (dangerous). E.g. full-of-hate,
self-aggrandizing, Satan, self-loathing and shrill,
the type it would clean up the planet to kill.
I justjust remember my own goodname still.

Damn, brother. You saw what they did to my face?
Poked out my eyes. Knocked teeth out of place,
stuck a dog's body under, hung same from a hook,
wrote what-all on my forehead! Wrote "bastard"! Wrote "crook"!
I justjust recall how my face used to look.

Now, misters and sisters, they've come for my voice.
If the Cat got my tongue, look who-who would rejoice—
muftis, politicos, "my own people," hacks.
Still, nameless-and-faceless or not, here's my choice:
not to shut up. To sing on, in spite of attacks,
to sing (while my dreams are being murdered by facts)
praises of butterflies broken on racks.

john cotton

Birthday Poem—7th March

On the cemetery side of seventy
(As Larkin might have put it)
Each birthday comes as a bonus
When I wake to the song of a new generation of birds,
Grandchildren overwhelm me with their energy
And life is celebrated in the minutiae of observation.
Preparing to land after a long haul from China
A large lady on the 'plane meticulously picks her teeth
With the aid of a vanity mirror,
While a younger woman paints her lips
With the precise care of an artist.
And me, for the final disembarkation?
To strive not to go ignorant into that long night.

betsy sholl

March 8

My student wants something from me.
His eyes are dark and pointing.
I do not say the right things.
I say I dreamed this morning that a man
was shouting at me from the ledge of a building,
and that my son told his first joke this morning
which was a pun on his father's name. The river
is so high now it has flooded its banks and
flows along the walkways to the boathouse.

I am not a good intellectual.
I do not have my student's interests in mind.

He leaves sullen and muttering.
The man was 15 stories up and shouting.
He was not going to jump.
He just wanted my full attention.

herman melville

A Utilitarian View of the *Monitor*'s Fight

Plain be the phrase, yet apt the verse,
　　More ponderous than nimble;
For since grimed War here laid aside
His painted pomp, 'twould ill befit
　　　　Overmuch to ply
　　The rhyme's barbaric cymbal.

Hail to victory without the gaud
　　　　Of glory; zeal that needs no fans
Of banners; plain mechanic power
Plied cogently in War now placed—
　　　　Where War belongs—
　　Among the trades and artisans.

Yet this was battle, and intense—
　　Beyond the strife of fleets heroic;
Deadlier, closer, calm 'mid storm;
No passion; all went on by crank,
　　　　Pivot, and screw,
　　And calculations of caloric.

Needless to dwell; the story's known.
　　The ringing of those plates on plates
Still ringeth round the world—
The clangor of that blacksmiths' fray,
　　　　The anvil-din
　　Resounds this message from the Fates:

War yet shall be, and to the end;
　　But war-paint shows the streaks of weather;
War yet shall be, but warriors
Are now but operatives, War's made
　　　　Less grand than peace,
　　And a singe runs through lace and feather.

The Monitor *met the* Merrimac *off Hampton Roads, Virginia, in the first battle of ironclad ships on March 9, 1862. The fight ended in a draw.*

jane miller

May You Always Be the Darling of Fortune

March 10th and the snow flees like eloping brides
into rain. The imperceptible change begins
out of an old rage and glistens, chaste, with its new
craving, spring. May your desire always overcome

your need; your story that you have to tell,
enchanting, mutable, may it fill the world
you believe: a sunny view, flowers lunging
from the sill, the quilt, the chair, all things

fill with you and empty and fill. And hurry, because
now as I tire of my studied abandon, counting
the days, I'm sad. Yet I trust your absence, in everything
wholly evident: the rain in the white basin, and I

vigilant.

martin allwood

March Moon Over Winter Sweden—1971

Classic northern winter night.
White, resplendent,
like a lump of molten silver
the intense disc of the moon
pours its cold magic
over hills and ice-bound lakes
paralyzed fir and birch,
into the marvelous
yard-long icicle spears
suspended outside my window.

Glittering icicle diamonds
strung down the tapering stems

hypnotize with moonscape madness
the awe-struck, gazing poet
behind the window-panes.

Black, cold blue, and silver white—
enchanted northern March
sculptured in crystal glory!

The moon was full on March 11, 1971.

MARCH 12

 jon stallworthy

The Trials

12 March 1837

Light is come amongst them, but they
love darkness rather than light.
Five canoes I saw yesterday
put to sea southward and last night,
in a pit lined with stones, a fire
was lit, I thought, to guide them home.
Tonight, over a red sea, four
returned like moths to their tall flame
and conches bellowing round
the bay. I took my evening walk
that way, and in the firelight found
the warriors at such butcher's work
as froze my blood and now my ink.

The speaker, an ancestor of the poet, was a missionary in New Zealand.

jonathan swift

To Stella

March 13, 1723–4

[Written on the Day of her Birth, but not on the Subject, when I was sick in bed.]

Tormented with incessant pains,
Can I devise poetic strains?
Time was, when I could yearly pay
My verse on Stella's native day:
But now, unable grown to write,
I grieve she ever saw the light.
Ungrateful; since to her I owe
That I these pains can undergo.
She tends me like an humble slave;
And, when indecently I rave,
When out my brutish passions break,
With gall in ev'ry word I speak,
She with soft speech my anguish cheers,
Or melts my passions down with tears;
Although 'tis easy to descry
She wants assistance more than I;
Yet seems to feel my pains alone,
And is a stoic in her own.
When, among scholars, can we find

So soft and yet so firm a mind?
All accidents of life conspire
To raise up Stella's virtue higher;
Or else to introduce the rest
Which had been latent in her breast.
Her firmness who could e'er have known,
Had she not evils of her own?
Her kindness who could ever guess,
Had not her friends been in distress?
Whatever base returns you find
From me, dear Stella, still be kind.
In your own heart you'll reap the fruit,
Though I continue still a brute.
But, when I once am out of pain,
I promise to be good again;
Meantime, your other juster friends
Shall for my follies make amends;
So may we long continue thus,
Admiring you, you pitying us.

gary miranda

A Marzipan for Einstein's Birthday

As rain sometimes against the rock
of a singular thought effects its own
undoing, turning from drop to plop
to wet, which, caught by the late-
arriving sun, shimmers in the after-
thought of easy money, so do the words
of the great dissolve in the mouths of fools.

In spite of this, the majesty of rain
is sheer largesse, if only by default—
that is, a code that can't be broken,
though the shapes of clouds are
corrigible enough, and lightning,
however oracular, is merely a glib
god's version of instant hype.

The space between the world and any word
is rife with political static, statistical
strife, and the census confirms not
every sail that swells with breeze
is big with child. In short, by the time
two people know a truth, it isn't
true. Given which, I side with those

conspiratorial spirits that arch, like
invisible rainbows, somewhere beyond our
repertoire of medicinal music. Big
with fable, they strike like constel-
lations the mind's eye, a blight
on philosophies you or I might salvage
or savor, stranded, high and dry.

Albert Einstein was born on March 14, 1879.

william shakespeare

The Ides of March

from: Julius Caesar

Act II, scene iv
[*Enter* PORTIA (*Wife to Brutus*) *and the* SOOTHSAYER.]

PORTIA	Come hither, fellow. Which way hast thou been?
SOOTHSAYER	At mine own house, good lady.
PORTIA	What is't a clock?
SOOTHSAYER	About the ninth hour, lady.
PORTIA	Is Caesar yet gone to the Capitol?
SOOTHSAYER	Madam, not yet. I go to take my stand,
	To see him pass on to the Capitol.
PORTIA	Thou has some suit to Caesar, hast thou not?
SOOTHSAYER	That I have, lady, if it will please Caesar
	To be so good to Caesar as to hear me:
	I shall beseech him to befriend himself.
PORTIA	Why, knows't thou any harm's intended towards
	him?
SOOTHSAYER	None that I know will be, much that I fear may
	chance.
	Good morrow to you. Here the street is narrow.
	The throng that follows Caesar at the heels,
	Of senators, of praetors, common suitors,
	Will crowd a feeble man almost to death:
	I'll get me to a place more void, and there
	Speak to great Caesar as he comes along. [*Exit.*]
PORTIA	I must go in. Ay me, how weak a thing
	The heart of woman is! O Brutus,
	The heavens speed thee in thine enterprise!
	[*Aside.*] Sure, the boy heard me. Brutus hath a suit
	That Caesar will not grant. [*Aside.*] O, I grow faint.
	Run, Lucius, and commend me to my lord;
	Say I am merry; come to me again,
	And bring me word what he doth say to thee.
	[*Exeunt severally.*]

. . .

Act III, scene i
[*Enter* CAESAR *with others.*]

CAESAR   The ides of March are come.
SOOTHSAYER   Ay, Caesar, but not gone.

MARCH 16

alice fulton

Another Troy

When the Green Island Bridge, a scowling trigonometry of over-
wrought iron from the 1800s, veed
into the river, we danced
all night at a tri-city block party, giving thanks
that none were hurt, and at dawn we printed
tee-shirts, petitioning
that the wreckage be preserved. We loved a ruin.

After dyeing our roots
with toothbrushes from Tek Hughes
on giddy high school Fridays, my friends and I
sauntered in electroplated glory by the river.
Like water lilies wan and local, species Trojan,
condoms bobbed above the current after Happy Hours.
What would the Hudson River School have done
with this? "Troylets,"

so the college students called us,
Trojans being too noble
for makers of Rototillers and shirts.
I, too, felt embarrassed
by Troy's futile boosterism: the schemes to sell itself
as "City of Friendly Service"
or "Home of Uncle Sam" were failures
of imagination. In the seismic hiss of the Volcano

Restaurant I invented Armageddons
guaranteed to free us: fires coasting down from heaven,
spumes of air pollutants hurled into the stratosphere
and we, the *damnificados*, fleeing.

An erupting Italian restaurant—
that would put us on the map!
Evacuated to faraway gyms, we'd picture the cinders,
an eiderdown drawn over dinettes
and reproductions of *The Last
Supper* in our scruffy, buckled homes.
As when the bridge fell, no one would be scratched.
But Troy's rough edges
would be buffed by the crumbled palladium
of ash. A local poet liked this plot

and used it in a sonnet. I starred
as Signorita Mount Saint Helens,
an Irish-American flamenco dancer
burning up the backstage of his heart.
But when I climbed on podiums to scream
in praise of rebels torching
"draft cards, bras, and ghettos,"
the poet refused to speak to me.
If asked I could have told him
that being typecast as the Muse
makes arsonists of women who aren't fools.

In time, I escaped the ruinous romances,
but Troy remains. Today the eccentricity
of its willful brick begins
to look like character.
Oh, if I sing of icicles
dangling like syringes from friezes
"neo-grec" or French,
of roses battened down with sackcloth, trees
lumbagoed under lumpen winters,
I'm minting an insignia. Take this, "Troy—
the City without Glibness,"
for your spartan tribute.

*The Green Island Bridge over the Hudson River near Troy collapsed on March
16, 1977.*

ovid

Tristia V iii

To his fellow-poets at Rome upon the birth-day of Bacchus.

This is the day (blithe god of *sack*) which we
If I mistake not, consecrate to thee,
When the soft *rose* we marry to the *bays*,
And warmed with thy own wine rehearse thy praise,
'Mongst whom (while to thy *poet* fate gave way)
I have been held no small part of the day
But now, dulled with the cold *Bear*'s frozen seat,
Sarmatia holds me, and the warlike *Gete*.
My former life, unlike to this my last,
With *Rome*'s best wits of thy full cup did taste,
Who since have seen the savage *Pontic* band,
And all the *choler* of the sea and land:
Whether sad chance, or heaven hath this designed,
And at my birth some fatal planet shined,
Of right thou shouldst the *sisters*' knots undo,
And free thy *votary* and *poet* too.
Or are you gods (like us) in such a state
As cannot alter the decrees of fate?
I know with much ado thou didst obtain
Thy *jovial godhead*, and on earth thy pain
Was no whit less, for wandering thou didst run
To the *Getes* too, and snow-weeping *Strymon*,
With *Persia*, *Ganges*, and what ever streams
The thirsty *Moor* drinks in the mid-day beams.
But thou wert twice-born, and the Fates to thee
(To make all sure) doubled thy misery,
My sufferings too are many: if it be
Held safe for me to boast adversity,
Nor was't a common blow, but from above
Like his, that died for imitating *Jove*,
Which when thou heard'st, a ruin so divine
And *mother*-like, should make thee pity mine.
And on this day, which *poets* unto thee
Crown with full bowls, ask, *What's become of me?*
　　　Help buxom god then! so may thy loved *vine*
Swarm with the numerous grape, and *big* with wine

Load the kind *elm*, and so thy *orgies* be
With priests' loud shouts, and *satyrs* kept to thee!
So may in death *Lycurgus* ne'er be blest,
Nor *Pentheus'* wandering ghost find any rest!
And so for ever bright (thy chief desires,)
May thy *wife's crown* outshine the lesser fires!
If but now, mindful of my love to thee,
Thou wilt, in what thou canst, my helper be.
You *gods* have commerce with your selves, try then
If *Caesar* will restore me *Rome* again.
      And you my trusty friends (the jolly crew
Of careless *poets*!) when, without me, you
Perform this day's glad mysteries, let it be
Your first appeal unto his deity,
And let one of you (touched with my sad name)
Mixing his wine with tears, lay down the same,
And (sighing) to the rest this thought commend,
O! Where is Ovid now our banished friend?
This do, if in your breasts I e'er deserved
So large a share, nor spitefully reserved,
Nor basely sold applause, or with a brow
Condemning others, did my self allow.
And may your happier wits grow loud with fame
As you (my best of friends!) preserve my name.

Trans. Henry Vaughn

According to Ovid's Fasti, *a calendar poem describing Roman festivals, Bacchus's
birthday fell on March 17.*

josephine jacobsen

The Sisters

Everyone notices they are inseparable.
Though this isn't quite so, it might well be.
Talk about depending on each other . . .
One can't say they are totally
congenial—irritation isn't unknown.

Yet it is, truly, touching, how they go on
year after year, not just pairing lives but
taking even holidays and vacations together,
sharing what happens to come along.
Here they are in the Caribbean.

Choose a day—the eighteenth of March for example:
they awake at almost but not quite
the same instant, disoriented:
where is the east? where anything else?
But they aren't going to dog each other all day.

B, anyone would have to admit,
is the better adjusted—easily pleased.
What marvelous lobster! she cries.
Smell the air! (The island is full of spices
and the air is soft as well as fragrant.)

A's energy always seems to be erratic:
first she's on and on about something,
then she wants a nap. She's a great sleeper
and has been known to cast away
hour after precious hour asleep without shame.

And she gets fixations—dashing off
to some spot they've already seen,
and talking about it when she gets back.
Take the little group of graves by the Old Men's Home
the station-wagon passes on its way to the beach.

Both of them noticed it—how could they help?
It's a little patch, unfenced, with four or five

graves. One apparently new and covered
with brightness. They even both waved
to the four old men on the porch who waved back.

But later, it turns out, A went back by herself,
sharp-eyed as ever, to examine the yellow
and violet cellophane, the rubber pond-lilies
floating on dust; the whole glittering heap
of rainbow mound; even asked questions.

That happened this morning; with the result
that when B swam in the sea—that sea
like a sapphire flawed with gold and green—
A went to sleep. The time she wastes
like that, slack as a weed in a wave!

This means that tonight she'll keep B awake
probably for hours, prowling about.
But they fight less than most sisters
and when the question of separation once arose
you should have seen them recoil—both, both.

At scrabble this afternoon they played partners:
tiles smooth to the fingertips, words appearing, solid as objects—salmon, cat; or abstract,
as who, why, go. They did very well.
Then A wouldn't participate in the talk at dinner.

On the whole, this was a good day; hard rain
rattled the roof, then the real rainbow threw up its arch,
and amicably they watched the blood-orange dip
into water; then stars, larger and brighter than elsewhere.
Before bed, A looked at herself in the mirror, using B's eyes.

george gascoigne

from: Gascoignes voyage into Hollande.
An. 1572

Written to the right honourable the Lorde Grey of Wilton.

A Straunge conceyte, a vayne of newe delight,
Twixt weale and woe, twixte joy and bitter griefe,
Hath pricked foorth my hastie penne to write
This woorthlesse verse in hazarde of repreefe:
And to mine *Alderlievest* Lorde I must endite
A wofull case, a chippe of sorie chaunce,
A tipe of heaven, a lively hew of hell,
A feare to fall, a hope of high advance,
A life, a death, a drearie tale to tell.
But since I know the pith of my pastaunce
Shall most consist in telling of a truth,
Vouchsafe my Lord (*en bon gre'*) for to take
This trustie tale the storie of my youth,
This Chronicle which of my selfe I make,
To shew my Lord what healplesse happe ensewth,
When heddy youth will gad without a guide,
And raunge untide in leas of libertie,
Or when bare neede a starting hole hath spide
To peepe abroade from mother Miserie,
And buildeth Castels in the Welkin wide,
In hope thereby to dwell with wealth and ease.
But he the Lord (whome my good Lord doth know)
Can bind or lose, as best to him shall please,
Can save or spill, rayse up or overthrowe,
Can gauld with griefe, and yet the payne appease.
Which thing to prove if so my L. take time,
(When greater cares his head shall not possesse)
To sitte and reade this raunging ragged rime,
I doubt not then but that he will confesse,
What falles I found when last I leapt to clime.
In March it was, that cannot I forget,
In this last March upon the ninteenth day,
When from Gravesend in boate I gan to jette
To boorde our shippe in Quinborough that lay,

From whence the very twentith day we set
Our sayles abrode to slice the Salt sea fome,
And ancors weyde gan trust the trustlesse floud:
That day and night amid the waves we rome
To seeke the coast of Holland where it stoode.

. . .

lawrence raab

Two Clouds

for Jennifer, March 20, 1977

Smallest breath
on the pillow, we counted
all the months,
first day of spring, first day
of summer, and each night now
as your silence
draws us back to you, here
where these soft leaves are leaning
over a little water
inside this circle
painted on your bed, and that cloud,
that aimless puff, goes on
floating through the same perfect sky.
If there's a secret,
I won't ask.
If there's one good explanation,
I don't want to know.
Your blue eyes
catch hold of everything
that pleases you,
and you know
what I mean when I say, *Look at that!*
That I mean, Look at me.

As if one more reckless smile
would rescue
the morning's gray
indifferent weather, and nothing
would be left to speak of
but this
feathery branch of the willow,
or the shadow of the nest
lodged above it,
or the shadow of the cloud
that sweeps the grass and is gone.

MARCH 21

 alan gould

March 21st 1945

The runway is a hurtling, shrinking vee
and England is a coat flung off by wind.
A tractor scores a field, and then the sea

so animal, impassive, perfect-skinned.
You dream you see this, and this is no dream,
and nothing that you see can you rescind.

You fly as though absorbed along a beam
at wavetop height toward a Danish coast,
are drawn into a horror like a scheme

prepared by some unseen deliberate host.
How is it that you come to live in hell
by living bravely, hand and eye engrossed

in all mere apparatus can impel.
How is the hostile sky so blue and calm,
the countryside a rolling brocatelle

of umber furrow, momentary farm.
You skip for steeple, pylon, radar mast,
and once a cyclist waves her pretty arm,

then Copenhagen rears up very fast
and there the target, like a house of bread
where aircraft skim already, blast on blast.

It's now you want to say with shake of head
"What happens here can never be quite known."
It can. It's now, as smoke uncoils ahead

you want to say "This can't be borne alone."
It can. And only now you're blithe to act,
to drop your burden in the burning zone

and live with what you know you can't retract.
That captured partisans will make escape,
that torturers will perish now is fact,

yet as the aftermath fulfils its shape
you'll learn the school where some were killed is real:
some children. One, a girl, her skull agape

with what your fire and shrapnel shall reveal,
will be observed to walk out in the square
and call a greeting as the squadrons wheel

for home, unburdened, call for England where
intelligence of this is gathering
like garments in a cupboard. These you'll wear

as you grow old and learn through suffering
that guilt will fix where blame cannot be found.
This is, you note, the first day of the spring.

MARCH 22

eamon grennan

Morning: the Twenty-Second of March

All the green things in the house
on fire with greenness. The trees
in the garden take their naked ease
like *Demoiselles d'Avignon*. We came

awake to the spider-plant's crisp shadow
printing the pillowcase
between us. Limp wrists of steam
curl auspiciously from the cup
of tea I've brought you, and a blue-jay
screeches blue murder beyond the door.
In a painting over the bed
five tea-coloured cows stand
hock-deep in water at the broad
bend of a river—small smoothback stones
turtling its near margin. A brace
of leafy branches leans over it
from the far bank, where the sun
spreads an open field like butter,
while the cows bend down to the
dumbfound smudge of their own faces
in the flat, metallic water. And here
this minute at the bristle tip
of the Scotch pine a cardinal
starts singing seven compound metal notes
equal in beat, then silence, then
again the identical seven. Between
the sighs the cars and pick-ups make
relenting for the curve with a little
gasp of gears, we hear over the road
among the faintly flesh pink
limbs and glow of the apple orchard
a solitary dove throating three sweet
mournful *Om,* then falling silent, then
—our life together hesitating in this gap
of silence, slipping from us and becoming
nothing we know in the swirl that has
no past, no future, nothing
but the pure pulse-shroud of light, the
dread *here-now*—reporting thrice again
its own silence. The cup of tea
still steams between your hands
like some warm offering or other
in the nameless radiate vacancy at the window,
this stillness in which we go on happening.

henry david thoreau

he Freshet

s now the twenty-third of March,
d this warm sun takes out the starch
winter's pinafore—Methinks
e very pasture gladly drinks
health to spring, and while it sips
faintly smacks a myriad lips.

stir is on the Wooster hills,
d Nobscot too the valley fills,
here scarce you'd dip an acorn cup,
summer when the sun is up,
ow you'll find no cup at all,
t in its place a waterfall.

e river swelleth more and more,
ke some sweet influence stealing o'er
e passive town; and for a while

Each tussock makes a tiny isle,
Where on some friendly Ararat
Resteth the weary water rat.

Our village shows a rural Venice,
Its broad lagoons where yonder fen is;
Far lovelier than the bay of Naples,
That placid cove amid the maples;
And in my neighbor's field of corn
I recognise the Golden Horn.

Here Nature taught from year to year,
When only red men came to hear.
Methinks 'twas in this school of art
Venice and Naples learned their part,
But still their mistress, to my mind,
Her young disciples leaves behind.

ost of "The Freshet" exists in manuscript at the University of Texas Library. Parts of the poem also
pear in "The River Swelleth More and More" in Thoreau's Collected Poems. The Texas manu-
ipt ends with the second line of the fifth stanza, so we have completed "The Freshet" as Thoreau must
ve intended, with the last four lines from "The River Swelleth More and More."

thomas hood

The Bridge of Sighs

"Drown'd! drown'd!"—*Hamlet*

One more Unfortunate
Weary of breath,
Rashly importunate,
Gone to her death!

Take her up tenderly,
Lift her with care;
Fashion'd so slenderly,
Young, and so fair!

Look at her garments
Clinging like cerements;
Whilst the wave constantly
Drips from her clothing;
Take her up instantly,
Loving, not loathing.—

Touch her not scornfully;
Think of her mournfully,
Gently and humanly;
Not of the stains of her,
All that remains of her
Now is pure womanly.

Make no deep scrutiny
Into her mutiny
Rash and undutiful:
Past all dishonour,
Death has left on her
Only the beautiful.

Still, for all slips of her,
One of Eve's family—
Wipe those poor lips of hers
Oozing so clammily.

Loop up her tresses
Escaped from the comb,
Her fair auburn tresses;
Whilst wonderment guesses
Where was her home?

Who was her father?
Who was her mother?
Had she a sister?
Had she a brother?
Or was there a dearer one
Still, and a nearer one
Yet, than all other?

Alas! for the rarity
Of Christian charity
Under the sun!
Oh! it was pitiful!
Near a whole city full,
Home she had none.

Sisterly, brotherly,
Fatherly, motherly
Feelings had changed:
Love, by harsh evidence,
Thrown from its eminence;
Even God's providence
Seeming estranged.

Where the lamps quiver
So far in the river,
With many a light
From window and casement,
From garret to basement,
She stood, with amazement,
Houseless by night.

The bleak wind of March
Made her tremble and shiver;

But not the dark arch,
Or the black flowing river:
Mad from life's history,
Glad to death's mystery,
Swift to be hurl'd—
Any where, any where
Out of the world!

In she plunged boldly,
No matter how coldly
The rough river ran,—
Over the brink of it,
Picture it—think of it,
Dissolute Man!
Lave in it, drink of it,
Then, if you can!

Take her up tenderly,
Lift her with care;
Fashion'd so slenderly,
Young, and so fair!

Ere her limbs frigidly
Stiffen too rigidly,

Decently,—kindly,—
Smoothe, and compose them;
And her eyes, close them,
Staring so blindly!

Dreadfully staring
Thro' muddy impurity,
As when with the daring
Last look of despairing
Fix'd on futurity.

Perishing gloomily,
Spurr'd by contumely,
Cold inhumanity,
Burning insanity,
Into her rest.—
Cross her hands humbly,
As if praying dumbly,
Over her breast!

Owning her weakness,
Her evil behaviour,
And leaving, with meekness,
Her sins to her Saviour!

According to the Times *of March 25, 1884, the mother jumped into the Thames with her two children on March 24, 1884.*

dean young

Age of Discovery

On the 182nd day of the 34th year
of my education,
I wake to a snow that seems falling faster
than snow, so blossom-heavy,

but I know that classic experiment
atop the Tower at Pisa, Galileo's proof
how, regardless of mass, all things drop
at the same rate. What falls falls,

I'd like to write, in continuous swoon
but that is only music just as
there is only music in the old claims
of soul leaving the body in a powdery
whoosh, an unwedging at the scapulas
scattering birds from belfry and roof,

a whir like radium half-lifing.
I've scoffed at the man who's spent his life
trying to photograph ghosts, the woman
who teaches how to breathe from the tips
of toes but surely there's a plethora
of forces bound and unbinding within us.

Towards the end, impoverished and confined
by a Pope who had all the Vatican sparrows
killed so he could pray without their chirps,
Galileo quit his lenses, almost blind,
the first to see eruptions and spots

on the heavenly face. The universe
now shrivels up into such a narrow compass
as is filled by my own bodily sensations,
he wrote in *Scientia Nova* which firmly
lurched every center towards ruin: earth

spun round a sun spiraling through the Milky Way
until, mathematics bursting like fungus,
10:38 EST, March 25, 1987, each of us

roams our own locked cell of perception.
Perhaps Galileo was wrong. Perhaps
we can shake our star-pricked shell apart,

cracks radiating out, arborizing like rivers
seen from planes or the paths some thoughts
blaze in the brain, a trace of lightning,
fire or blood in the body. I know the simple
sadness I feel each time you drive
into the traffic jerks of the city where you work

is just an ion exchange across the semipermeable
membranes of my nervous tissue. I know the music
I seem to need each day is just shaking grain
against the three wired bones of my inner ear.
I know in the glistening cold serenity

of the outer world, we are just two
brief blips of wet electricity,
just part of a random plummet
that is slow fire in my life,

a permanent pulse of love
in the nexus of error that is my thought.

philip salom

The Execution of Hallaj

Come. He is true to his provocations,
death comes like a sanity
to holy fools. He has kissed through
blue fires of breath, stroked the golden
flanks of destiny: this beast the earthen
parts of men unknowingly assembled
in the Mecca of their hearts.

Last ironic exercise of his limbs
through bazaars. Old men, huddled,

chopped ends of straw beneath the cloth,
traders jabbering, brass panniers filled
with flour, money-lenders with rickety scales,
their shroffing hands on the certain
gold of the hour. Women who drape
yashmaks on the contours of suffering,
dun as the dust. Hallaj stills their eyes.

He enters his kingdom of chains,
the lidless bowl of the courtyard
the crowd stains. They grope at a sweet
revulsion, martyrdom or slow murder.
Mullahs fat with gloating, who squeeze
the Prophet's words till acid dribbles
bibulous on the chin of righteousness.
Stand close to see the throat block
or the eye burst (but nervous that blood
leap like a red truth onto skin or cloth).
Light lies along the walls, like a snake.

Suddenly the insolent flesh. Hallaj is grinning,
is drunk, his Christ-tongue torn, kiss
of the knife through his lips.
The gasp and rhetoric of the sword.
Blade enters the sun at noon, air filled
with steel flung down. The chained arm
is spraying, spangled, translucent
rosary beads held to the sky. Whirling,
Hallaj slips the brokerage of time
in a gold loving, out-breathing into breath;
rumples the air's guilt like a sheet
of ecstasy, endless, billowing silk.

Sight folds on the body, like a skin.
Some, perhaps, tasted
the question of death
as if bruised grapes. Some
said the eye winked from the severed
head. (Silence. Slight nudge
at the raw stirrup of hearing.)
Or when they gathered the parts,
one arm was missing. A cart-man
drops a load of bags in the street.

The dust sifts through the crowd.
By Allah, there is straw to weigh, donkeys
to be fed, how much wool for a sheaf of hay?

*Hallaj, a Sufi, was executed March 26, 922, for making heretical statements such
as "I am the truth"—and refusing to recant. He stated also that the pilgrimage to
Mecca could be performed anywhere with suitable dedication and preparation.
Because he emphasized the importance of Christ, as a Sufi teacher, he was accused
by fanatics of being a secret Christian. [Note by Salom]*

josephine miles

Government Injunction Restraining Harlem Cosmetic Co.

They say La Jac Brite Pink Skin Bleach avails not,
They say its Orange Beauty Glow does not glow,
Nor the face grow five shades lighter nor the heart
Five shades lighter. They say no.

They deny good luck, love, power, romance, and inspiration
From La Jac Brite ointment and incense of all kinds,
And condemn in writing skin brightening and whitening
And whitening of minds.

There is upon the federal trade commission a burden of glory
So to defend the fact, so to impel
The plucking of hope from the hand, honor from the complexion,
Sprite from the spell.

*The Federal Trade Commission prohibited the Harlem Cosmetic Co. from using
false and deceptive advertising on March 27, 1931.*

jim barnes

Accident at Three Mile Island

("*. . . how everything turns away/Quite leisurely . . .*"
—W. H. Auden)

The island steams under the opening sky.
All around the narrow length of land
the river flows as it always has, and late

birds heading north to Canada notice
nothing unusual about the air.
There may, or may not, have been a disaster

among the undergrowth: what birds may tell
is augured late at best, and fish homing
upstream are mainly interested in falls.

Who knows? At any rate, the land was calm.
Nothing surprised farmers off their tractors
or knocked the rheumy cattle off their hoofs.

though something surely must disappear every
time the earth shakes or the sky moves an inch
or two to right or left. Still there will always

be a boy fishing from some river bank
who doesn't especially want anything to happen
except summer and a dog scratching at his side.

*The incident at Three Mile Island nuclear power plant occurred on March 28,
1979.*

judith rodriguez

A legal error, 29th March, 1847

for Zoe

Catherine and Margaret Hennessey's
hard-spurring tomboy japes
made of them proper menaces,
currency jackanapes

Furiously Riding on Sundays.
Custody fell on their fault.
Should have been served with a *Summons;*
that's how the jades did a bolt.

Mayor's court, watchmen and constables
else had committed and tried 'em;
kept breaking Sabbaths, just once to put
paid to their Furiously Riding . . .

Eighteen-forties larrikins,
off they flounced into their lives.
Maybe they scampered and ramped again;
maybe they wore into wives.

Here's to the legal error
confounding procedure since genesis—
luck to a handful of helter-
skelter Melburnian Hennesseys!

johann wolfgang von goethe

Walpurgis Night

from: Faust, Part I, xxi

[*The Harz Mountains, near Schierke and Elend.* FAUST *and* MEPHISTOPHELES.]

MEPHISTOPHELES   My friend, don't you long for a broomstick?
                   I'd like a good stout billy goat myself.
                   On this road we're a long way from our goal.
FAUST   As long as I feel fresh, this stick is plenty.
                   What's the good of shortening the road?
                   To creep along the mazes of the valleys,
                   To climb this precipice from which the spring
                   Comes plunging down in its eternal spray—
                   These are the pleasures that give spice to the way.
                   Already spring is stirring in the birches,
                   Even the firs already feel it—
                   It's no wonder that our bodies feel it, too.

. . .

MEPHISTOPHELES   Grab my coat and hold on tight!
                   Now we reach a central peak
                   Where the mountain gives a marvelous view
                   Of Mammon's blazing light.
FAUST   What a strange gleam of morning red
                   Breaks through the mountain hollow
                   And shines into the black ravine
                   Of an almost bottomless abyss!
                   The mists rise, the vapors float,
                   Then veils of smoke catch sudden fire
                   Which creeps along, a slender thread,
                   And gushes up, a flaming fountain.

                   Here the strand of light winds its way
                   Until a hundred veins spread through the glen,
                   And there in the narrow neck of the gorge
                   A single ray shines through the haze.
                   Dancing sparks shoot off nearby,

Sprinkled around like golden sand.
                But look! the whole towering crag
                In all its height is now a firebrand.

MEPHISTOPHELES   Does not Sir Mammon light his castle
                In proper style for a splendid feast?
                What luck for you to see such a sight!
                I hear his unruly guests approaching.

FAUST   How the Wind Witch rages in the air!
                What gusts she rains upon my shoulders!

MEPHISTOPHELES   You must grab those ancient rock-ribs tight
                Or she'll hurl you into a bottomless grave.
                A fog is thickening the night.
                Do you hear those crashing trees?
                The frightened owls are flying off,
                And the evergreen palaces—
                How their beams are cracking!
                Branches are quaking and breaking,
                Tree trunks are mightily groaning,
                Roots are straining and moaning!
                Tree upon tree is falling,
                In a tangled mass they are littered
                And through the gorge's wreckage
                The winds are hissing and howling.
                Do you hear those voices high in the air?
                Distant voices, voices near?
                Yes, the whole length of the mountainside
                Roars with the witch-song in furious choir.

CHORUS OF WITCHES   The witches sail to Blocksberg's peak
                Where corn is green and stubble yellow.
                They gather on the mountaintop
                While Sir Urian starts the show,
                And fly up over stones and stumps
                As witches fart and billy goats reek.

Trans. Randall Jarrell

The witches' Walpurgis Night convocation is held each March 30th.

nell altizer

Haworth Parsonage, 31 March 1855

*Literature cannot be the business of a woman's life, and it ought not
to be. The more she is engaged in her proper duties, the less leisure
will she have for it, even as an accomplishment and a recreation. To
those duties you have not yet been called, and when you are, you will
be less eager for celebrity. You will not seek in imagination for
excitement, of which the vicissitudes of this life, and the anxieties
from which you must not hope to be exempted, be your state what it
may, will bring with them but too much.*
—Letter from Robert Southey to Charlotte Brontë, March
1832

1

At Bridlington when I saw it for the first time
the slam of that adamant,
unbridled hand at my feet pounding No!
threw pieces of white water over my hem
like torn paper,
but my shoes held fast under the sinking
heave of the shingle that soaked clear
to the shores of my heels. Oh, wild
and dear
God! The sea!

    In Haworth the winds
shock burls of leaves abruptly into the winter
light like scrolls of birds
and we all waver a little under our skins;
and then back from a walk on the moors,
an odd, vagrant squall, queer as a gypsy, might knock
us into one another, ripping the sheer lace
of the waterfall
to shreds against the rock.

    But this slate-blue, complete, hurled
water's refusal. No blind rider is so hard in falling.

I never mended well
or governed the children's minds and bones smartly;

their call from the banister
fell always on the other side of that estate
where I lived what I dreamed of
and not the position I held,
and my vision so impaired that in my employment
at Stonegappe I had
to bend for the needle's squint against the candle flame,
and listen to the diastolic clench
of Mrs. Sidgwick's breath in the room's small air
beat its shallow envy against whichever
neighbor's wall was higher.

Oh God, you send the sea to tell us: No
Trespassing. There are billows of gray and thick
weather in this atmosphere where we are told
not to go. Restrain, these furious breakers claim,
your trying, protestant
heart. This is the order of things.

My eyes like old women
who cannot leave their neighborhoods
saw the rain-silk layers of water
under my skirt
vanish like shot silver into the edge of the land,
saw the Yorkshire coast sail from the straw
harbor of my bonnet over the rim of the fallow world
toward Brussels and London, and then my name—
or was it his?—balance like a single
buoy in the channel.

Later I would learn from Mr. Thackeray that the sublime
means only until the limits: a boundary held
between water and settlement, hearth and the moderate air
that the rampage cannot cross.
Order thrust to its very limits and no
farther is sublime. A woman writing, a woman living
two persons at once, female and male, and bondage
broken, the water's fist grinding aside the sea wall,
banked coals ruptured by a spinster's throat into flares
is the verge of a terrible
creation that annihilates its frame.

2

The second time I saw it on our wedding trip
to County Clare when Arthur let me,
wrapped in his husbanding rug,
not look so far over the cliff to be chilled by the spray,
nor close enough at the rocks
to engage as I had at Bridlington
my skirts in that clash of sea water with the land and its
inhabitants—hung
cormorant over the coast,
I felt the solution of blood and the bitter sea
liquid within me
begin.

   Launched with no warning
out of my cells, the small craft
was a secret in January as I walked with Arthur
on the moor to the falls and saw
like a bride's veil worn to threads,
its intricate fret unwoven on the wind's loom,
the snow melted as if by furnaces to a clear, stinging vapor
white as the fibers of wedding cloth
Glauce tried to strip from her poisoned skin
or, under the rain that followed us home,
so it appeared,
and I caught cold.

3

For ten days the winds of the equinox
have surged and crashed like bores against the uncompliant
stones of this parsonage. The shelves in the churchyard
crack in vernal heaving every year, break half and half,
splitting the dead world open.
This is the uproar nature orders in seasons
of revolution when day and night
are briefly equal, as if parity
were a sphere to be thrashed out of the universe.
And I am bound in that direction.

Over the surface of things—
the quilt stitch, the benefice
of vellum lamplight, the Book of Common Prayer—

Arthur kneels and casts his imprecations
into the flood of my refusal
like a net,

> We beseech thee to loose
> the spirit of this thy
> servant from every bond

and hears
hurled from a woman's precipice
over the birth caul,
over the skull cap knitting its hard
adhesion to the brain,
my No! that will take the water
of the shale-gray tides in my voice down with me—
the sea, its passengers and creatures,
poured back like a libation on the land:
feather, scale, cartilage, fontanel,
the fountain flowing over
underground.

Not to see the sea again, not to bear the sea rain
down but the branches of sea trees,
to grow its deep and savage
weeds below the roots of civil grain—
The tremors under your walk will be my words,
the fissure in the soil
cracking your summer garden like a snake,
my son or daughter. On the horizon rockets
of virulent, scalding minerals will break
the ultramarine lintel of the sky,
the surface of the earth's threshold burst
with the eruption of sea
water
finding its level.

March 31, 1855 was the day Charlotte Brontë, eighteen months married, two months pregnant, died.

marianne moore

Tom Fool at Jamaica

Look at Jonah embarking from Joppa, deterred by
the whale; hard going for a statesman whom nothing could detain,
   although one who would not rather die than repent.
      Be infallible at your peril, for your system will fail,
and select as a model the schoolboy in Spain
   who at the age of six, portrayed a mule and jockey
      who had pulled up for a snail.

"There is submerged magnificence, as Victor Hugo
said." *Sentir avec ardeur;* that's it, magnetized by feeling.
   Tom Fool "makes an effort and makes it oftener
      than the rest"—out on April first, a day of some significance
in the ambiguous sense—the smiling
   Master Atkinson's choice, with that mark of a champion, the extra
      spurt when needed. Yes, yes. "Chance

is a regrettable impurity"; like Tom Fool's
left white hind foot—an unconformity; though judging by
   results, a kind of cottontail to give him confidence.
      Up in the cupola comparing speeds, Fred Capossela keeps his head.
"It's tough," he said; "but I get 'em; and why shouldn't I?
   I'm relaxed, I'm confident, and I *don't bet.*" Sensational. He does not
      bet on his animated

valentines—his pink and black-striped, sashed or dotted silks.
Tom Fool is "a handy horse," with a chiseled foot. You've the beat
   of a dancer to a measure or harmonious rush
      of a porpoise at the prow where the racers all win easily—
like centaurs' legs in tune, as when kettledrums compete;
   nose rigid and suede nostrils spread, a light left hand on the rein, till
      well—this is a rhapsody.

Of course, speaking of champions, there was Fats Waller
with the feather touch, giraffe eyes, and that hand alighting in
   Ain't Misbehavin'! Ozzie Smith and Eubie Blake
      ennoble the atmosphere, you recall the Lippizzaner;
the time Ted Atkinson charged by on Tiger Skin—
   no pursuers in sight—cat-loping along. And you may have seen a monkey,

on a greyhound. "But Tom Fool . . .

john donne

Goodfriday, 1613. Riding Westward

Let mans Soule be a Spheare, and then, in this,
The intelligence that moves, devotion is,
And as the other Spheares, by being growne
Subject to forraigne motions, lose their owne,
And being by others hurried every day,
Scarce in a yeare their naturall forme obey:
Pleasure or businesse, so, our Soules admit
For their first mover, and are whirld by it.
Hence is't, that I am carryed towards the West
This day, when my Soules forme bends towards the East.
There I should see a Sunne, by rising set,
And by that setting endlesse day beget;
But that Christ on this Crosse, did rise and fall,
Sinne had eternally benighted all.
Yet dare I'almost be glad, I do not see
That spectacle of too much weight for mee.
Who sees Gods face, that is selfe life, must dye;
What a death were it then to see God dye?
It made his owne Lieutenant Nature shrinke,
It made his footstoole crack, and the Sunne winke.
Could I behold those hands which span the Poles,
And tune all spheares at once, peirc'd with those holes?
Could I behold that endlesse height which is
Zenith to us, and our Antipodes,
Humbled below us? or that blood which is
The seat of all our Soules, if not of his,
Made durt of dust, or that flesh which was worne
By God, for his apparell, rag'd, and torne?
If on these things I durst not looke, durst I
Upon his miserable mother cast mine eye,
Who was Gods partner here, and furnish'd thus
Halfe of that Sacrifice, which ransom'd us?
Though these things, as I ride, be from mine eye,
They'are present yet unto my memory,
For that looks towards them; and thou look'st towards mee,
O Saviour, as thou hang'st upon the tree;
I turne my backe to thee, but to receive
Corrections, till thy mercies bid thee leave.

O thinke mee worth thine anger, punish mee,
Burne off my rusts, and my deformity,
Restore thine Image, so much, by thy grace,
That thou may'st know mee, and I'll turne my face.

Good Friday in 1613 fell on April 2.

APRIL 3

william shakespeare

The Death of Prince Arthur

from: King John

Act IV, scene iii. Before the Castle.
[*Enter* (Prince) ARTHUR (nephew to King John and heir
to the throne), *on the walls.*]

ARTHUR   The wall is high, and yet will I leap down:
Good ground, be pitiful and hurt me not!
There's few or none do know me: if they did,
This ship-boy's semblance hath disguis'd me quite.
I am afraid; and yet I'll venture it.
If I get down, and do not break my limbs,
I'll find a thousand shifts to get away:
As good to die and go, as die and stay.
[*He leaps, and lies momentarily in trance.*]
O me! my uncle's spirit is in these stones:
Heaven take my soul, and England keep my bones!
[*Dies.*]
[*Enter* PEMBROKE, SALISBURY, *and* BIGOT.]

SALISBURY   Lords, I will meet him at Saint Edmundsbury:
It is our safety, and we must embrace
This gentle offer of the perilous time.

PEMBROKE   Who brought that letter from the cardinal?

SALISBURY   The Count Melun, a noble lord of France;
Whose private with me of the Dolphin's love
Is much more general than these lines import.

BIGOT   To-morrow morning let us meet him then.

120

SALISBURY	Or rather then set forward; for 'twill be
	Two long days' journey, lords, or ere we meet.
	[*Enter the* BASTARD, Philip Falconbridge, supposed
	illegitimate son of King Richard.]
BASTARD	Once more to-day well met, distemper'd lords!
	The king by me requests your presence straight.
SALISBURY	The king hath dispossess'd himself of us:
	We will not line his thin bestained cloak
	With our pure honours, nor attend the foot
	That leaves the print of blood where'er it walks.
	Return and tell him so: we know the worst.
BASTARD	Whate'er you think, good words, I think, were best.
SALISBURY	Our griefs, and not our manners, reason now.
BASTARD	But there is little reason in your grief;
	Therefore 'twere reason you had manners now.
PEMBROKE	Sir, sir, impatience hath his privilege.
BASTARD	'Tis true, to hurt his master, no manners else.
SALISBURY	This is the prison. [*Seeing Arthur.*] Who is he lies
	here?
PEMBROKE	O death, made proud with pure and princely
	beauty!
	The earth had not a hole to hide this deed.
SALISBURY	Murther, as hating what himself hath done,
	Doth lay it open to urge on revenge.
BIGOT	Or, when he doom'd this beauty to a grave,
	Found it too precious-princely for a grave.

The circumstances of Prince Arthur's death have never firmly been established. He is the first of several Arthurs who failed to ascend to the English throne. The traditional date of his death is April 3, 1203.

tom andrews

Song of a Country Priest

> *"Naturally I keep my thoughts to myself."*
> —Bernanos, *Diary of a Country Priest*

April 4. Wind hums
in the fireweed, the dogwood
drops white skirts across

the lawn. From this window
I've watched the pink shimmer
of morning light spread

to the sky and the blond
grass lift the dew. *You*
in whose yet greater light,

etc. My prayers grow
smaller each dawn. Each dawn
I wake to this landscape

of thyme, rue, a maple
whose roots are the highways
of ants, cattails down

to the river. I rise
and look and learn again:
I believe in my backyard.

I can mimic the sway
of weeds in wind. I can
study the patience

of tendrils. God knows what
I am, a rib of earth?
a hidden cloud? I am

old now. I am a priest
without believers. I counsel
leaves, fallen petals, two

bluejays and one shy wren.
In my book of Genesis,
the serpent says, "You can't

tempt me with green
peppers, yellow squash,
the ripe meats of Eden.

I'm looking under my
belly for the next meal.
I'm lying beside a dirt

road in West Virginia,
waiting for a pickup
to stir a thick cloud

of dust into my mouth.
I will never hunger.
I will live like this

forever—inching with
rhythm across the dried
dirt, pulling myself

like a white glove through
meal after parched, ecstatic
meal . . ."

Perhaps my blasphemies
have saved me. Perhaps God
reads between these lines,

that whiteness touched
by no one. I'm ready
for Him to settle my

ody like an argument;
ny ashes can settle
vhere they will. God could

ull like an evening sun
o say Eat dust
vith the serpent, crawl

n your belly. He could
ay the earth is a secret
old by quartz vein and

nothing else. Tonight
in the thin dark He could
whisper the sky is the

earth, the stars are foxgloves,
quince blossoms, white flames
of trilliums, and I am

flaring and vanishing
above them. I'm ready.
I would believe it all.

john betjeman

The Arrest of Oscar Wilde at the Cadogan Hotel

He sipped at a weak hock and seltzer
   As he gazed at the London skies
Through the Nottingham lace of the curtains
   Or was it his bees-winged eyes?

To the right and before him Pont Street
   Did tower in her new built red,
As hard as the morning gaslight
   That shone on his unmade bed,

"I want some more hock in my seltzer,
   And Robbie, please give me your hand—
Is this the end or beginning?
   How can I understand?

"So you've brought me the latest *Yellow Book*:
   And Buchan has got in it now:
Approval of what is approved of
   Is as false as a well-kept vow.

"More hock, Robbie—where is the seltzer?
    Dear boy, pull again at the bell!
They are all little better than *cretins*,
    Though this is the Cadogan Hotel.

"One astrakhan coat is at Willis's—
    Another one's at the Savoy:
Do fetch my morocco portmanteau,
    And bring them on later, dear boy."

A thump, and a murmur of voices—
    ("Oh why must they make such a din?")
As the door of the bedroom swung open
    And TWO PLAIN CLOTHES POLICEMEN came in:

"Mr. Woilde, we 'ave come for tew take yew
    Where felons and criminals dwell:
We must ask yew tew leave with us quoietly
    For this *is* the Cadogan Hotel."

He rose, and he put down the *Yellow Book*.
    He staggered—and, terrible-eyed,
He brushed past the palms on the staircase
    And was helped to a hansom outside.

*On the basis of his own testimony in his libel action against Lord Russell, Oscar
Wilde was arrested for transgressions against certain laws restraining sexual
behavior on April 5, 1895.*

APRIL 6

 francesco petrarch

The louer sheweth that he was striken by loue on good friday

It was the day on which the sunne depriued of his light,
To rew Christs death amid his course gaue place vnto ye night
When I amid mine ease did fall to such distemperate fits,
That for the face that hath my hart I was bereft my wits.
I had the bayte, the hooke and all, and wist not loues pretence,
But farde as one that fearde none yll, nor forst for no defence.

Thus dwelling in most quiet state, I fell into this plight,
And that day gan my secret sighes, when all folke wept in sight.
For loue that vewed me voide of care, approcht to take his pray,
And stept by stelth from eye to hart, so open lay the way.
And straight at eyes brake out in teares, so salt that did declare,
By token of their bitter taste that they were forgde of care.
Now vaunt thee loue which fleest a maid defenst with vertues rare,
And wounded hast a wight vnwise, vnweaponed and vnware.

This anonymous translation of Petrarch's poem on meeting Laura on Good Friday, April 6, 1327, appeared in Tottel's Miscellany *(1557–1587).*

dante alighieri

Dante Finds Himself in the Dark Wood

from: The Inferno Canto I

Midway upon the journey of our life
   I found myself within a forest dark,
   For the straightforward pathway had been lost.
Ah me! how hard a thing it is to say
   What was this forest savage, rough, and stern,
   Which in the very thought renews my fear.
So bitter is it, death is little more;
   But of the good to treat, which there I found,
   Speak will I of the other things I saw there.
I cannot well repeat how there I entered,
   So full was I of slumber at the moment
   In which I had abandoned the true way.
But after I had reached a mountain's foot,
   At that point where the valley terminated,
   Which had with consternation pierced my heart,
Upward I looked, and I beheld its shoulders,
   Vested already with that planet's rays
   Which leadeth others right by every road.
Then was the fear a little quieted
   That in my heart's lake had endured throughout
   The night, which I had passed so piteously,

And even as he, who, with distressful breath,
　　Forth issued from the sea upon the shore,
　　Turns to the water perilous and gazes,
So did my soul, that still was fleeing onward,
　　Turn itself back to re-behold the pass
　　Which never yet a living person left.

Trans. Henry Wadsworth Longfellow

Good Friday in the Jubilee Year of 1300 fell on April 8. Dante's journey, which in some ways paralleled that of Jesus through death and resurrection, began on the eve of Good Friday, i.e., Thursday, April 7, 1300.

APRIL 8

 greg pape

This House

In February I watched gray whales
cruising offshore, just beyond the rocks
and sun-dazzled houses of Laguna.
Though I've closed my eyes
and breathed with them and followed
them down past the slow
blowing curtains of kelp
they won't swim me to sleep tonight.
It's the eighth of April
and this house is a stalled whale
under snow clouds. I know there's
a full moon over Missouri tonight
but the light on your shoulders
is from the parking lot next door.
No sound now but a distant siren
and your steady breathing.
It sets the house adrift.
A few minutes ago I heard a car
pull in and the engine stop.
I waited for the sound of the door,

but whoever it is must still
be sitting in the car.
Someone alone, not wanting to go in,
or maybe lovers at it at last,
what the long evening led up to.
He kisses her neck, her lips,
and moves his hand carefully
to her breast. Her hand rests
its small fire on his thigh.
Their breath freezes on the windows
as the snow begins.
And as they go down into the current
of their separate hours
I want to imagine something else,
the rolling waves, the moonlight
on the surface of these clouds.
I'll try again. I'll close my eyes,
dream the deep breath and the big heart
so that this house, with you in it,
may rise.

paul muldoon

Good Friday, 1971, Driving Westward

It was good going along with the sun
Through Ballygawley, Omagh and Strabane.
I started out as it was getting light
And caught sight of hares all along the road
That looked to have been taking a last fling,
Doves making the most of their offerings
As if all might not be right with the day

Where I moved through morning towards the sea.
I was glad that I would not be alone.
Those children who travel badly as wine
Waved as they passed in their uppity cars
And now the first cows were leaving the byres,
The first lorry had delivered its load.
A whole country was fresh after the night

Though people were still fighting for the last
Dreams and changing their faces where I paused
To read the first edition of the truth.
I gave a lift to the girl out of love
And crossed the last great frontier at Lifford.
An iffing and butting herd
Of goats. Letterkenny had just then laid

Open its heart and we paused as new blood
Back into the grey flesh of Donegal.
The sky went out of its way for the hills
And life was changing down for the sharp bends
Where the road had put its thin brown arm around
A hill and held on tight out of pure fear.
Errigal stepped out suddenly in our

Path and the thin arm tightened round the waist
Of the mountain and for a time I lost
Control and she thought we had hit something big
But I had seen nothing, perhaps a stick
Lying across the road. I glanced back once

And there was nothing but a heap of stones.
We had just dropped in from nowhere for lunch

In Gaoth Dobhair, I happy and she convinced
Of the death of more than lamb or herring.
She stood up there and then, face full of drink,
And announced that she and I were to blame
For something killed along the way we came.
Children were warned that it was rude to stare,
Left with their parents for a breath of air.

Good Friday 1971 fell on April 9.

APRIL 10

robert hayden

Middle Passage

Jesús, Estrella, Esperanza, Mercy:

Sails flashing to the wind like weapons,
sharks following the moans the fever and the dying;
horror the corposant and compass rose.

Middle Passage:
    voyage through death
            to life upon these shores.

"10 April 1800—
Blacks rebellious. Crew uneasy. Our linguist says
their moaning is a prayer for death,
ours and their own. Some try to starve themselves.
Lost three this morning leaped with crazy laughter
to the waiting sharks, sang as they went under."

Desire, Adventure, Tartar, Ann:

Standing to America, bringing home
black gold, black ivory, black seed.

Deep in the festering hold thy father lies,
of his bones New England pews are made,
those are altar lights that were his eyes.

Jesus   Saviour   Pilot   Me
Over   Life's   Tempestuous   Sea

We pray that Thou wilt grant, O Lord,
safe passage to our vessels bringing
heathen souls unto Thy chastening.

Jesus   Saviour

"8 bells. I cannot sleep, for I am sick
with fear, but writing eases fear a little
since still my eyes can see these words take shape
upon the page & so I write, as one
would turn to exorcism. 4 days scudding,
but now the sea is calm again. Misfortune
follows in our wake like sharks (our grinning
tutelary gods). Which one of us
has killed an albatross? A plague among
our blacks—Ophthalmia: blindness—& we
have jettisoned the blind to no avail.
It spreads, the terrifying sickness spreads.
Its claws have scratched sight from the Capt.'s eyes
& there is blindness in the fo'c'sle
& we must sail 3 weeks before we come
to port."

What port awaits us, Davy Jones'
or home? I've heard of slavers drifting, drifting,
playthings of wind and storm and chance, their crews
gone blind, the jungle hatred
crawling up on deck.

Thou   Who   Walked   On   Galilee

"Deponent further sayeth *The Bella J*
left the Guinea Coast
with cargo of five hundred blacks and odd
for the barracoons of Florida:

"That there was hardly room 'tween-decks for half
the sweltering cattle stowed spoon-fashion there;

that some went mad of thirst and tore their flesh
and sucked the blood:

"That Crew and Captain lusted with the comeliest
of the savage girls kept naked in the cabins;
that there was one they called The Guinea Rose
and they cast lots and fought to lie with her:

"That when the Bo's'n piped all hands, the flames
spreading from starboard already were beyond
control, the negroes howling and their chains
entangled with the flames:

"That the burning blacks could not be reached,
that the Crew abandoned ship,
leaving their shrieking negresses behind,
that the Captain perished drunken with the wenches:

"Further Deponent sayeth not."

Pilot   Oh   Pilot   Me

. . .

APRIL 11

john whitworth

Report on the Progress of the Export Drive—Spring Bank Holiday 1977

for Ian Goatman

Low cloud and a fine smirr of rain—S.N.C.F. regrets
The hovercraft service to Dover will not be in operation.
Neither the "Princess Anne" nor her sister the "Princess Margaret."
The last named was, we knew, in the way of being lengthened
To accommodate three hundred voyagers and up to thirty autos.
That was by no means all: The Frogs had had in the course of building,
Their own air-slider, enormous and magnificent, the "France,"

To accommodate five hundred voyagers, in excess of fifty autos,
Had had alas. Since two days now, this one she is burn down,
Burn down totally in the paint-spraying. *Tant pis*
As they say. To us voyagers the unlengthened "Princess Anne"
Remains alone, and she, due to adverse weather conditions,
As mournful as a halibut on a fishmarket slab.

And thus to the ferry-boat station and the customs shed, two busfuls,
Us voyagers, stiff upper-lipped, *Circulez, circulez, vite,*
Vite. What's that lad on about? Attendez emmerdeur.
You what, Pierre? Ahead of us a shrill of altercation,
English women, our women, brutally, basely imposed on,
Manhandled by gendarmes, agents, functionaries,
Flint-faced Aznavours, whitegloves, batons, revolvers.
Still all are adamant, our women, adamant if unsteady,
(Perhaps the rough sea-crossing has affected them for the worse.
Quite uncommonly rough they can be, these rough sea-crossings.)
So our women look—who shall blame them?—more than a touch unsteady,
Yet victorious in the upshot, and teetering their ways of Calais Ville,
Along shining cobblestones, to the bar-tabacs of Calais Ville,
Teetering, giggling their ways into the Common Market,
Handbagged, shoulderbagged, polythene-umbrella'd and flush with francs.

Our ferry-boat "Vortigern," odd name for a British boat though,
Murderer, traitor, invader, and burned alive in his tower,
Homeward bound and light laden, no more than our two busfuls—
More than a thousand out, according to a sad bar-steward,
Worse than animals, day-trippers and dancing on the tables,
Which was the least of it. So sadly the steward. No more than her knickers
And Mackerson bottles, one of them, dancing the Spanish Hat.
Then for a dare, for a laugh, she had them off too, her knickers,
Kicking up, buttock-naked on the tables of the Main Lounge,
You wouldn't read about it. And it's true, I never had.

Armoured about with bags, at a table in a corner,
RedBarrel in our fists, Castellas between our teeth,
Business executives, British exporters on expenses,
Purveyors of our English Language by the yard,
We; the "Vortigern" chopping, throbbing across the sea-lanes,
The warm, weak beer and bland cigar smoke swilling in our bellies,
Contentment lapping over us as the French coast smalls.
Good people the Frogs, good people to go among we agree
As the chalk cliffs of our island erect themselves out of mist.
So, loaded down with obligatory duty-free French fags,

We greet the English air and watery sunshine, Folkestone
By God! Same old tat and the picturesque, epitome of Kent,
Epitome of England, right on opening time.

Spring Bank Holiday falls on Easter Monday, which in 1977 was April 11.

APRIL 12

 ogden nash

Lines in Praise of a Date Made Praiseworthy Solely by Something Very Nice That Happened to It

As through the calendar I delve
I pause to rejoice in April twelve.

Yea, be I in sickness or be I in health
My favorite date is April twealth.

It comes upon us, as a rule,
Eleven days after April fool,

And eighteen days ahead of May Day
When spring is generally in its heyday.

Down in New Mexico the chapparal
Is doing nicely by the twelfth of Apparal,

And Bay State towns such as Lowell and Pepperell
Begin to bloom on the twelfth of Epperell.

But regardless of the matter of weather,
There isn't any question whether.

No, not till the trumpet is blown by Gabriel
Shall we have such a day as the twelfth of Abriel.

horace

Maecenas Birthday

illis here is for thee in store
barrell nine yeres ould and more
  Full of Albanian wine
y garden parlsey shal prepare
d Iuie chapletts for thy haire
  To make it dubly shine.

See the fresh laughter new create
flected from refulgent plate
  While crowned with verbaine chast
e sacred altar thirsting cries
ve me a lamb for sacrifice
  I long his blood to tast.

Diligence moues all hands and feete
ll-mell my ladds & lasses meete
  Soe mingling worke & play:
ight flames against black fumes make
head
t these for all theire vap'ring fledd
And those haue wonne the day.

Come Phil, this is not euery tyme
e vernal sunn is in his prime
  And these are April Ides
midst of Venus month soe plac't
is the Ceston 'bout her wast
  Which all her sweetes diuides.

Maecenas birth day whose renowne
akes me well nigh post-date myne owne
  And spend my ioyful teares

To see returnd that pretious light
From whence my King-deriued Knight
  Records his prosperous yeares.

6. Come Sweete & frolick then with vs
Noe Longer doate on Telaphus
  A youth aboue thy fate
A wanton Wench & rich beside
Hath him in twofould bondage tie'd
  Nor does he proue vngrate.

7. Alack! there are examples found
Of Phaëton both burnt & drown'd
  All greedie hopes to check
The foole, Belleraphon who tried
The heau'nlie winged horse to ride
  Fell downe & broake his neck

8. O Phillis these sad stories teach
Vs court nothing past our reach
  Then strike a match with me.
Of harts we'ele driue a mutuall trade
For myne noe flame shal e're inuade
  To feymale after thee.

9. Come then & lett us both reioyce
Gracing my verses with thy voice
  What shame to this belongs?
When thou & I sitt arme in arme
All earthly cares to fright & charme
  Or minish with our Song.

Trans. Thomas Pestell

e ides of each month, according to the Roman calendar, fall on either the 13th or the 15th. In April the
s is on the 13th.

stephen vincent benet

Abraham Lincoln's Last Day

from: John Brown's Body

The gaunt man, Abraham Lincoln, woke one morning
From a new dream that yet was an old dream
For he had known it many times before
And, usually, its coming prophesied
Important news of some sort, good or bad,
Though mostly good as he remembered it.

He had been standing on the shadowy deck
Of a black formless boat that moved away
From a dim bank, into wide, gushing waters—
River or sea, but huge—and as he stood,
The boat rushed into darkness like an arrow,
Gathering speed—and as it rushed, he woke.

He found it odd enough to tell about
That day to various people, half in jest
And half in earnest—well, it passed the time
And nearly everyone had some pet quirk,
Knocking on wood or never spilling salt,
Ladders or broken mirrors or a Friday,
And so he thought he might be left his boat,
Especially now, when he could breathe awhile
With Lee surrendered and the war stamped out
And the long work of binding up the wounds
Not yet begun—although he had his plans
For that long healing, and would work them out
In spite of all the bitter-hearted fools
Who only thought of punishing the South
Now she was beaten.
        But this boat of his.
He thought he had it.
        "Johnston has surrendered
It must be that, I guess—for that's about
The only news we're waiting still to hear."
He smiled a little, spoke of other things.
That afternoon he drove beside his wife

And talked with her about the days to come
With curious simplicity and peace.
Well, they were getting on, and when the end
Came to his term, he would not be distressed.
They would go back to Springfield, find a house,
Live peaceably and simply, see old friends,
Take a few cases every now and then.
Old Billy Herndon's kept the practice up,
I guess he'll sort of like to have me back.
We won't be skimped, we'll have enough to spend,
Enough to do—we'll have a quiet time,
A sort of Indian summer of our age.

He looked beyond the carriage, seeing it so,
Peace at the last, and rest.

They drove back to the White House, dressed and ate,
Went to the theater in their flag-draped box.
The play was a good play, he liked the play,
Laughed at the jokes, laughed at the funny man
With the long, weeping whiskers.
                    The time passed,
The shot rang out. The crazy murderer
Leaped from the box, mouthed out his Latin phrase,
Brandished his foolish pistol and was gone.

Lincoln lay stricken in the flag-draped box.
Living but speechless. Now they lifted him
And bore him off. He lay some hours so.
Then the heart failed. The breath beat in the throat.
The black, formless vessel carried him away.

*John Wilkes Booth shot Abraham Lincoln at Ford's Theater during a performance
the evening of April 14, 1865.*

thomas hardy

The Convergence of the Twain

(Lines on the loss of the "Titanic")

I

In a solitude of the sea
Deep from human vanity,
And the Pride of Life that planned her, stilly couches she.

II

Steel chambers, late the pyres
Of her salamandrine fires,
Cold currents thrid, and turn to rhythmic tidal lyres.

III

Over the mirrors meant
To glass the opulent
The sea-worm crawls—grotesque, slimed, dumb, indifferent.

IV

Jewels in joy designed
To ravish the sensuous mind
Lie lightless, all their sparkles bleared and black and blind.

V

Dim moon-eyed fishes near
Gaze at the gilded gear
And query: "What does this vaingloriousness down here?" . . .

VI

Well: while was fashioning
This creature of cleaving wing,
The immanent Will that stirs and urges everything

VII

Prepared a sinister mate
For her—so gaily great—
A Shape of Ice, for the time far and dissociate.

And as the smart ship grew
In stature, grace, and hue,
In shadowy silent distance grew the Iceberg too.

IX
Alien they seemed to be:
No mortal eye could see
The intimate welding of their later history,

X
Or sign that they were bent
By paths coincident
On being anon twin halves of one august event,

XI
Till the Spinner of the Years
Said "Now!" And each one hears,
And consummation comes, and jars two hemispheres.

The Titanic *went down after striking an iceberg on April 15, 1912.*

APRIL 16

george mackay brown

April the Sixteenth

What did they bring to the saint?
The shepherds a fleece.
That winter many lambs were born in the snow.

What did the dark ones bring?
To Magnus the tinkers have brought
A new bright can. Their hammers beat all night.

What have they brought to the saint?
A fishless fisherman
Spread his torn net at the wall of the church

And the farm boys offered
A sweetness, gaiety, chasteness
Of hymning mouths.

The women came to their martyr
With woven things
And salt butter for the poor of the island.

And the poor of the island
Came with their hungers,
Then went hovelwards with crossed hands over the hill.

"April the Sixteenth" alludes to the fact that St. Magnus was martyred on April
16, 1117. The faithful come with all they can muster and the greatest blessings fall
on the "poor of the island."

APRIL 17

geoffrey chaucer

Here bygynneth the Book of the Tales of Caunterbury

Whan that Aprill with his shoures soote
The droghte of March hath perced to the roote,
And bathed every veyne in swich licour
Of which vertu engendred is the flour;
Whan Zephirus eek with his sweete breeth
Inspired hath in every holt and heeth
The tendre croppes, and the yonge sonne
Hath in the Ram his halve cours yronne,
And smale foweles maken melodye,
That slepen al the nyght with open ye
(So priketh hem nature in hir corages);
Thanne longen folk to goon on pilgrimages,
And palmeres for to seken straunge strondes,
To ferne halwes, kowthe in sondry londes;
And specially from every shires ende
Of Engelond to Caunterbury they wende,
The hooly blisful martir for to seke,
That hem hath holpen whan that they were seeke.

Bifil that in that seson on a day,
In Southwerk at the Tabard as I lay
Redy to wenden on my pilgrymage
To Caunterbury with ful devout corage,
At nyght was come into that hostelrye
Wel nyne and twenty in a compaignye,
Of sondry folk, by aventure yfalle
In felaweshipe, and pilgrimes were they alle,
That toward Caunterbury wolden ryde.
The chambres and the stables weren wyde,
And wel we weren esed atte beste.
And shortly, whan the sonne was to reste,
So hadde I spoken with hem everichon
That I was of hir felaweshipe anon,
And made forward erly for to ryse,
To take oure wey ther as I yow devyse.

*In the "Introduction to the Man of Law's Tale," one of the tales told on the first
day, the host remarks that it is the eighteenth of April. Since the narrator met with
the pilgrims the night before their journey began, we have taken the opening of the
poem as describing the night of April 17.*

APRIL 18

henry wadsworth longfellow

Paul Revere's Ride

Listen, my children, and you shall hear
Of the midnight ride of Paul Revere,
On the eighteenth of April, in Seventy-five;
Hardly a man is now alive
Who remembers that famous day and year.

He said to his friend, "If the British march
By land or sea from the town to-night,
Hang a lantern aloft in the belfry arch
Of the North Church tower as a signal light,—
One, if by land, and two, if by sea;
And I on the opposite shore will be,
Ready to ride and spread the alarm

Through every Middlesex village and farm,
For the country folk to be up and to arm."
Then he said, "Good night!" and with muffled oar
Silently rowed to the Charlestown shore,
Just as the moon rose over the bay,
Where swinging wide at her moorings lay
The Somerset, British man-of-war;
A phantom ship, with each mast and spar
Across the moon like a prison bar,
And a huge black hulk, that was magnified
By its own reflection in the tide.

Meanwhile, his friend, through alley and street,
Wanders and watches with eager ears,
Till in the silence around him he hears
The muster of men at the barrack door,
The sound of arms, and the tramp of feet,
And the measured tread of the grenadiers,
Marching down to their boats on the shore.

Then he climbed the tower of Old North Church,
By the wooden stairs, with stealthy tread,
To the belfry-chamber overhead,
And startled the pigeons from their perch
On the sombre rafters, that round him made
Masses and moving shapes of shade,—
By the trembling ladder, steep and tall,
To the highest window in the wall,
Where he paused to listen and look down
A moment on the roofs of the town,
And the moonlight flowing over all.
Beneath, in the churchyard, lay the dead,
In their night-encampment on the hill,
Wrapped in silence so deep and still
That he could hear, like a sentinel's tread,
The watchful night-wind, as it went
Creeping along from tent to tent,
And seeming to whisper, "All is well!"
A moment only he feels the spell
Of the place and the hour, and the secret dread
Of the lonely belfry and the dead;
For suddenly all his thoughts are bent
On a shadowy something far away,
Where the river widens to meet the bay,—

A line of black that bends and floats
On the rising tide, like a bridge of boats.

Meanwhile, impatient to mount and ride,
Booted and spurred, with a heavy stride
On the opposite shore walked Paul Revere.
Now he patted his horse's side,
Now gazed at the landscape far and near,
Then, impetuous, stamped the earth,
And turned and tightened his saddle-girth;
But mostly he watched with eager search
The belfry-tower of the Old North Church,
As it rose above the graves on the hill,
Lonely and spectral and sombre and still.
And lo! as he looks, on the belfry's height
A glimmer, and then a gleam of light!
He springs to the saddle, the bridle he turns,
But lingers and gazes, till full on his sight
A second lamp in the belfry burns!

A hurry of hoofs in a village street,
A shape in the moonlight, a bulk in the dark,
And beneath, from the pebbles, in passing, a spark
Struck out by a steed flying fearless and fleet:
That was all! And yet, through the gloom and the light,
The fate of a nation was riding that night;
And the spark struck out by that steed, in his flight,
Kindled the land into flame with its heat.
He has left the village and mounted the steep,
And beneath him, tranquil and broad and deep,
Is the Mystic, meeting the ocean tides;
And under the alders, that skirt its edge,
Now soft on the sand, now loud on the ledge,
Is heard the tramp of his steed as he rides.

It was twelve by the village clock,
When he crossed the bridge into Medford town.
He heard the crowing of the cock,
And the barking of the farmer's dog,
And felt the damp of the river fog,
That rises after the sun goes down.

It was one by the village clock,
When he galloped into Lexington.

He saw the gilded weathercock
Swim in the moonlight as he passed,
And the meeting-house windows, blank and bare,
Gaze at him with a spectral glare,
As if they already stood aghast
At the bloody work they would look upon.

It was two by the village clock,
When he came to the bridge in Concord town.
He heard the bleating of the flock,
And the twitter of birds among the trees,
And felt the breath of the morning breeze
Blowing over the meadows brown.
And one was safe and asleep in his bed
Who at the bridge would be first to fall,
Who that day would be lying dead,
Pierced by a British musket-ball.

You know the rest. In the books you have read,
How the British Regulars fired and fled,—
How the farmers gave them ball for ball,
From behind each fence and farm-yard wall,
Chasing the red-coats down the lane,
Then crossing the fields to emerge again
Under the trees at the turn of the road,
And only pausing to fire and load.

So through the night rode Paul Revere;
And so through the night went his cry of alarm
To every Middlesex village and farm,—
A cry of defiance and not of fear,
A voice in the darkness, a knock at the door,
And a word that shall echo forevermore!
For, borne on the night-wind of the Past,
Through all our history, to the last,
In the hour of darkness and peril and need,
The people will waken and listen to hear
The hurrying hoof-beats of that steed,
And the midnight message of Paul Revere.

richard wilbur

Patriot's Day

(Wellesley, Massachusetts)

Restless that noble day, appeased by soft
Drinks and tobacco, littering the grass
While the flag snapped and brightened far aloft,
We waited for the marathon to pass,

We fathers and our little sons, let out
Of school and office to be put to shame.
Now from the street-side someone raised a shout,
And into view the first small runners came.

Dark in the glare, they seemed to thresh in place
Like preening flies upon a window-sill,
Yet gained and grew, and at a cruel pace
Swept by us on their way to Heartbreak Hill—

Legs driving, fists at port, clenched faces, men,
And in amongst them, stamping on the sun,
Our champion Kelley, who would win again,
Rocked in his will, at rest within his run.

*In the days when John Kelley was the local hero, the Boston Marathon took place
on April 19th and not as today on the most convenient Monday.*

samuel taylor coleridge

from: Fears in Solitude

Written in April 1796, During the Alarm of an Invasion

May my fears,

My filial fears, be vain! and may the vaunts
And menace of the vengeful enemy
Pass like the gust, that roared and died away
In the distant tree: which heard, and only heard
In this low dell, bowed not the delicate grass.

But now the gentle dew-fall sends abroad
The fruit-like perfume of the golden furze:
The light has left the summit of the hill,
Though still a sunny gleam lies beautiful,
Aslant the ivied beacon. Now farewell,
Farewell, awhile, O soft and silent spot!
On the green sheep-track, up the healthy hill,
Homeward I wind my way; and lo! recalled
From bodings that have well-nigh wearied me,
I find myself upon the brow, and pause
Startled! And after lonely sojourning
In such a quiet and surrounded nook,
This burst of prospect, here the shadowy main,
Dim-tinted, there the mighty majesty
Of that huge amphitheatre of rich
And elmy fields, seems like society—
Conversing with the mind, and giving it
A livelier impulse and a dance of thought!
And now, beloved Stowey! I behold
Thy church-tower, and, methinks, the four huge elms
Clustering, which mark the mansion of my friend;
And close behind them, hidden from my view,
Is my own lowly cottage, where my babe
And my babe's mother dwell in peace! With light
And quickened footsteps thitherward I tend,
Remembering thee, O green and silent dell!
And grateful, that by nature's quietness
And solitary musings, all my heart
Is softened, and made worthy to indulge
Love, and the thoughts that yearn for human kind.

Nether Stowy, April 20, 1798

christianne balk

₋eaving Sand County: April 21, 1948

(Aldo Leopold died on this day while fighting a grass fire.)

ₙder the roughleg
₋wk who hovers like a smooth-
₋athered bomb waiting

drop on the marsh,
₋re dogwood stems stand exposed
₋ainst the hill. I

₋e men run back and
₋rth, trying to fight the grass
₋e—burning, burning.

₋ipe winnow, coots cluck
₋ite pinions beat the water.
₋e geese are leaving.

₋only I could
₋nd up now like the others.
₋mething pulls me up,

₋s me north, drops me
₋ove cold, spring-fed streams hemmed-
₋ by alder. I

₋y out more line. Cast
₋ as the wind swirls the stream,
₋aking like a brown

miller. I wade waist
deep through the green cave of tree
branches and the white

throat rolls lazily
in the dark pool as he sucks
feathers down his throat.

The line straightens. I
ease him upstream around each
bend in the river,

slowly, as if I
were the current. I gently
pull him in. Twisting,

as if still swimming,
the trout twists in the wet alder
leaves lining my creel.

If only I could
stay. Here, where only woodcocks
spiral down like stalled

planes. Here, where burn marks
in the grass are covered by
the wide-sweeping arc

of an owl's wings.

anne sexton

The Red Dance

There was a girl
who danced in the city that night,
that April 22nd,
all along the Charles River.
It was as if one hundred men were
    watching
or do I mean the one hundred eyes of God?
The yellow patches in the sycamores
glowed like miniature flashlights.
The shadows, the skin of them
were ice cubes that flashed
from the red dress to the roof.
Mile by mile along the Charles she danced
past the benches of lovers,
past the dogs pissing on the benches.
She had on a red, red dress
and there was a small rain
and she lifted her face to it
and thought it part of the river.
And cars and trucks went by
on Memorial Drive.
And the Harvard students in the brick
hallowed houses studied Sappho in cement
    rooms.

And this Sappho danced on the grass
and danced and danced and danced.
It was a death dance.
The Larz Anderson bridge wore its lights
and many cars went by,
and a few students strolling under
their Coop umbrellas.
And a black man who asked this Sappho
    the time,
the time, as if her watch spoke.
Words were turning into grease,
and she said, "Why do you lie to me?"
And the waters of the Charles were
    beautiful,
sticking out in many colored tongues
and this strange Sappho knew she would
    enter the lights
and be lit by them and sink into them.
And how the end would come—
it had been foretold to her—
she would aspirate swallowing a fish,
going down with God's first creature
dancing all the way.

sheenagh pugh

The ruder times

(The battle of Clontarf, 1014)

Clontarf was all blood; Irishmen and Norse,
Christians and heathens, mercenaries, anyone
who wanted money, kingship or a good fight
with a cause, to put a shine on ambition.

Sigur of Orkney came with the cool words
his mother spoke, weaving his raven banner,
when he said he feared that fight would be his last:
"I didn't know you wanted to live for ever."

King Brian stood behind a shelter of shields
weaponless, (it was Good Friday), urging his men
to murder. When he was killed, his brother went
blood-mad as though pity had never been,

a hunting wolf. In his path, a man stopped
to tie a shoe: "There's no hurry for me,
I live in Iceland, and I cannot reach
my home tonight." . . . Brian's brother let him be.

Nor was he less human, that he was moved
by arrogance where he could not be by fear.
A man laughing at the darkness warned him
against the day when dark must be his share.

Brian Boru, the High King of all Ireland, was killed by Scandinavian invaders on
April 23, 1014.

john milton

Sonnet XVIII
On the Late Massacre in Piemont

Avenge, O Lord, thy slaughter'd Saints, whose bones
    Lie scatter'd on the Alpine mountains cold,
    Ev'n them who kept thy truth so pure of old
    When all our Fathers worship't Stocks and Stones,
Forget not: in thy book record their groans
    Who were thy Sheep and in their ancient Fold
    Slain by the bloody Piemontese that roll'd
    Mother with Infant down the Rocks. Their moans
The Vales redoubl'd to the Hills, and they
    To Heav'n. Their martyr'd blood and ashes sow
    O'er all th'Italian fields where still doth sway
The triple Tyrant: that from these may grow
    A hundredfold, who having learnt thy way
    Early may fly the *Babylonian* woe.

(1655)

Waldensians, who up to the spring of 1655 had enjoyed a certain measure of free-dom of worship, were savagely slaughtered on April 24, 1655, during their Easter celebration.

a. l. rowse

Easter Day, 1943

In the apple orchard I hear the bells
    Ring once more for Easter-tide,
The wind sings softly in the pines
    To celebrate the Crucified

Who now this day has conquered death
    And put on new life with the spring;
The splendid seagulls sail the sky,
    While over the hill the church bells ring.

They are the church bells of my youth,
    Hearing them disturbs the heart:
I see again the country lad
    On Easter Day, solemn and smart

In Sunday suit, walk down the lane
    To sing with others in the choir
"Jesus Christ is risen today,"
    The voices rising high and higher.

The church smells sweet of Easter flowers,
    The altar frontal is of white;
There is an air of festival,
    The familiar faces are glad and bright.

Yet where are they now, the people I knew?
    (As I walk the orchard, the petals drop.)
Many have gone their different ways,
    But most of them have fallen on sleep;

And I a man much changed by time,
    Alone with my passion and my pride,
Whose heart the church bells still can touch
    With the tenderness of Easter-tide.

April 25th is the latest possible day for Easter and was Easter Day only once in this century. Surely Rowse is here celebrating the beginning of the end of England's and Europe's long nightmare.

gregory orr

The Western Invention of Lyrical Nature

And there's Petrarch, our first
mountain climber, stumbling up
the slopes of Mt. Ventoux
with his shepherd guide
and a bottle of wine—one more
trapped man of the Renaissance
looking for some way out
that doesn't lead to God.

It's almost dusk when he reaches
the summit. He's never gazed
so far, never known there was so large
a vista. He's standing there
for all of us, frightened but brave.
Biting his lip, he tastes the sea.

*Petrarch's letter describing his ascent of Mt. Ventoux is one of the most famous of all
Renaissance documents, although Petrarch himself never viewed this experience as
a fit subject for poetry. The climb occurred on April 26, 1336.*

gwyn williams

For John Ormond

April 27. No sort of anniversary
except that I take each day to be
always, an emblem for the lot,
my eighty years joyous or
failed. My diary says Llanelli
beat Cardiff in the final (I remember
Albert Jenkins dropping a prodigious
goal from half-way). Lowri came laughing
from her encounters with Welsh
black cattle breeders. I walked to the sea
in sunshine and a probing north wind.

Back home your New Year card, John,
fell from its place at my desk:
carollers clothed in the dusk converged
on a lit doorway. The card opened
to its poem, recalled boyhood and
the crispness of winter.
A daughter, a friend, an empty
laughing sea, an image of Wales from
your colourful hand, a re-reading
of a comforting poem, a day
like any other, it makes no difference,
yet which displays my life jewelled
with happy moments, pointless
though capable yet of a statement,
interwoven or to be cast hugger-mugger
back to the swirl of a universe where summer
and winter are skin deep,
where time doesn't matter.

austin clarke

A Sermon on Swift

Friday, 11.30 a.m. April 28th, 1967

Gentle of hand, the Dean of St. Patrick's guided
My silence up the steps of the pulpit, put around
    My neck the lesser microphone. "I feel
That you are blessing me, Mr. Dean."
                              Murmur
Was smile.

In this first lay sermon, must I
Not speak the truth? Known scholars, specialists,
From far and near, were celebrating the third
Centenary of our great satirist.
They spoke of the churchman who kept his solemn gown,
Full-bottom, for Sunday and the Evening Lesson,
But hid from lectern the chuckling rhymster who went,
Bald-headed, into the night when modesty

Wantoned with beau and belle, his pen in hand.
Dull morning clapped his oldest wig on. He looked from
The Deanery window, spied the washerwomen
Bundling along, the hay carts swaying from
The Coombe, dropping their country smells, the hackney—
Clatter on cobbles—ready to share a quip
Or rebus with Sheridan and Tom Delaney,
Read an unfinished chapter to Vanessa
Or Stella, then rid his mind of plaguey curling-
Tongs, farthingales and fal-de-lals. A pox on
Night-hours when wainscot, walls, were dizziness,
Tympana, maddened by inner terror, celled
A man who did not know himself from Cain.
A *Tale of a Tub*, *Gulliver's Travels*, fables
And scatological poems, I pennied them on
The Quays, in second-hand book-stalls, when I was young,
Soon learned that humour, unlike the wit o' the Coffee
House, the Club, lengthens the features, smile hid by
A frown.
                    Scarce had I uttered the words,
                                        "Dear Friends,
Dear Swiftians"—
                    when from the eastern window
The pure clear ray that Swift had known, entered the
Shady church and touched my brow. So blessed

Again, I gathered 'em up, four-letter words,
Street-cries, from the Liberties.
                                        Ascend,
Our Lady of Filth, Cloacina, soiled goddess
Of paven sewers. Let Roman fountains, a-spray
With themselves, scatter again the imperious gift
Of self-in-sight.
                    Celia on a close-stool
Stirs, ready to relace her ribs. Corinna,
Taking herself to pieces at midnight, slips from
The bed at noon, putting together soilures
And soft sores. Strephon half rouses from a dream
Of the flooding Tiber on his marriage-night,
When Chloe stoops out unable to contain her
Twelve cups of tea. Women are unsweet at times,
No doubt, yet how can willynilly resist
The pleasures of defaulting flesh?
    . . .

sujata bhatt

29 April 1989

She's three months old now,
asleep at last for the afternoon.
I've got some time to myself again
but I don't know what to do.
Outside everything is greyish green and soggy
with endless Bremen-Spring drizzle.
I make a large pot of Assam tea
and search through the books
in my room, sift through my papers.
I'm not looking for anything, really,
just touching favourite books.
I don't even know what I'm thinking,
but there's a rich round fullness
in the air
like living inside Beethoven's piano
on a day when he was
particularly energetic.

tony harrison

Prague Spring

on my birthday, 30 April

A silent scream? The madrigal's top note?
Puking his wassail on the listening throng?
Mouthfuls of cumulus, then cobalt throat.
Medusa must have hexed him in mid-song.

The finest vantage point in all of Prague's
this gagging gargoyle's with the stone-locked lute,
leaning over cherries, blow-ups of Karl Marx
the pioneers 'll march past and salute.

Tomorrow's May but still a North wind scuffs
the plated surface like a maced cuirass,

lays on, lays off, gets purchase on and roughs
up the Vltava, then makes it glass.

The last snow of this year's late slow thaw
dribbles as spring saliva down his jaw.

APRIL 31

barbara l. greenberg

April Thirty-First

And call it the maiden ladies' day.
With lavender water, with attar of roses
flutter them out of their Back Bay houses
out of their West End pots of flowers
out of their North End east wind closets;
ruffle them out of their cotes as pigeons
flush and feather, the maiden ladies
under the sun their silken dresses
kiss kiss kiss in a ringworm pattern.

And summon the beautiful blue police
with blown-up butterfly nets to gather
all the drunks in the Boston Common
swoop and capture, swoop and capture
Billy-the-Bum, sweet William fallen;
raise them, shave them, all in satin
dress them just for the day and dance them
down down down to the Public Gardens
arm in arm with the maiden ladies.

In and out in the Public Gardens
swan by swimming by duck by tree
by bridge and river and flowered path
they'll dance, the maidens, the maiden ladies
sweet and sweaty, the red-nosed rummies
ringing their buttocks above their thighs
like wedding bells. Come down to see.
Come down to see and pack a lunch
and nobody laugh and nobody laugh.

April is a very pleasant month (pace *Eliot*), *but adding an extra day only post-pones the even more beautiful May.*

154

May

robert frost

Pea Brush

I walked down alone Sunday after church
    To the place where John has been cutting trees
To see for myself about the birch
    He said I could have to bush my peas.

The sun in the new-cut narrow gap
    Was hot enough for the first of May,
And stifling hot with the odor of sap
    From stumps still bleeding their life away.

The frogs that were peeping a thousand shrill
    Wherever the ground was low and wet,
The minute they heard my step went still
    To watch me and see what I came to get.

Birch boughs enough piled everywhere!—
    All fresh and sound from the recent ax.
Time someone came with cart and pair
    And got them off the wild flowers' backs.

They might be good for garden things
    To curl a little finger round,
The same as you seize cat's-cradle strings,
    And lift themselves up off the ground.

Small good to anything growing wild,
    They were crooking many a trillium
That had budded before the boughs were piled
    And since it was coming up had to come.

melvin tolson

Alpha

The Harlem Gallery, an Afric pepper bird,
   awakes me at a people's dusk of dawn.
The age altars its image, a dog's hind leg,
   and hazards the moment of truth in pawn.
      The Lord of the House of Flies,
      jaundice-eyed, synapses purled,
   wries before the tumultuous canvas,
         The Second of May—
         by Goya:
      the dagger of Madrid
         vs.
      the scimitar of Murat.
   In Africa, in Asia, on the Day
of Barricades, alarm birds bedevil the Great White World,
a Buridan's ass—not Balaam's—between no oats and hay.

      Sometimes a Roscius as tragedian,
         sometimes a Kean as clown,
   without Sir Henry's flap to shield my neck,
I travel, from oasis to oasis, man's Saharic up-and-down.

   As a Hambletonian gathers his legs for a leap,
         dead wool and fleece wool
         I have mustered up from hands
            now warm or cold: a full
            rich Indies' cargo;

   but often I hear a dry husk-of-locust blues
descend the tone ladder of a laughing goose,
         syncopating between
         the faggot and the noose:
         "Black Boy, O Black Boy,
         is the port worth the cruise?"

   Like the lice and maggots of the apples of Cain
         on a strawberry tree,
      the myth of the Afroamerican past
         exacts the parasite's fee.

Sometimes the spirit wears away
in the dust bowl of abuse,
like the candied flesh of the barrel cactus which
the unpitying pitch
of a Panhandle wind
leaves with unpalatable juice.

Although the gaffing *"Tò ti?"* of the Gadfly girds
the I-ness of my humanness and Negroness,
the clockbird's
jackass laughter
in sun, in rain,
at dusk of dawn,
mixes with the pepper bird's reveille in my brain,
where the plain is twilled and the twilled is plain.

MAY 3

martin espada

Two Mexicanos Lynched in Santa Cruz, California, May 3, 1877

More than the moment
when forty gringo vigilantes
cheered the rope
that snapped two Mexicanos
into the grimacing sleep of broken necks,

more than the floating corpses,
trussed like cousins of the slaughterhouse,
dangling in the bowed mute humility
of the condemned,

more than the Virgen de Guadalupe
who blesses the brownskinned
and the crucified,
or the guitar-plucking skeletons
they will become
on the Día de los Muertos,

remain the faces of the lynching party:
faded as pennies from 1877, a few stunned
in the blur of execution,
a high-collar boy smirking, some peering
from the shade of bowler hats, but all
crowding into the photograph.

eileen o'connell

Lament for Arthur O'Leary

EILEEN SPEAKS:

I

  My love forever!
The day I first saw you
At the end of the market-house,
My eye observed you,
My heart approved you,
I fled from my father with you,
Far from my home with you.

II

I never repented it:
You whitened a parlour for me,
Painted rooms for me,
Reddened ovens for me,
Baked fine bread for me,
Basted meat for me,
Slaughtered beasts for me;
I slept in ducks' feathers
Till midday milking-time,
Or more if it pleased me.

III

My friend forever!
My mind remembers
That fine spring day
How well your hat suited you,
Bright gold banded,
Sword silver-hilted—

159

Right hand steady—
Threatening aspect—
Trembling terror
On treacherous enemy—
You poised for a canter
On your slender bay horse.
The Saxons bowed to you,
Down to the ground to you,
Not for love of you
But for deadly fear of you,
Though you lost your life to them,
Oh my soul's darling.

IV

Oh white-handed rider!
How fine your brooch was
Fastened in cambric,
And your hat with laces.
When you crossed the sea to us,
They would clear the street for you,
And not for love of you
But for deadly hatred.

V

My friend you were forever!
When they will come home to me,
Gentle little Conor
And Farr O'Leary, the baby,
They will question me so quickly,
Where did I leave their father.
I'll answer in my anguish
That I left him in Killnamartyr.
They will call out to their father;
And he won't be there to answer.

VI

My friend and my love!
Of the blood of Lord Antrim,
And of Barry of Allchoill,
How well your sword suited you,
Hat gold-banded,
Boots of fine leather,
Coat of broadcloth,
Spun overseas for you.

VII

My friend you were forever!
I knew nothing of your murder
Till your horse came to the stable
With the reins beneath her trailing,
And your heart's blood on her shoulders
Staining the tooled saddle
Where you used to sit and stand.
My first leap reached the threshold,
My second reached the gateway,
My third leap reached the saddle.

VIII

I struck my hands together
And I made the bay horse gallop
As fast as I was able,
Till I found you dead before me
Beside a little furze-bush.
Without Pope or bishop,
Without priest or cleric
To read the death-psalms for you,
But a spent old woman only
Who spread her cloak to shroud you—
Your heart's blood was still flowing;
I did not stay to wipe it
But filled my hands and drank it.

IX

My love you'll be forever!
Rise up from where you're lying
And we'll be going homewards.
We'll have a bullock slaughtered,
We'll call our friends together,
We'll get the music going.
I'll make a fine bed ready
With sheets of snow-white linen,
And fine embroidered covers
That will bring the sweat out through you
Instead of the cold that's on you!

Trans. Eilis Dillon

Arthur O'Leary was murdered on May 4, 1773.

peggy shumaker

Cinco de Mayo

One hot chunk of melting asphalt, this block
roped off between the Phoenix Hilton
and the Museum of Science. One night unsnapped
to celebrate el Día de Independencia, Cinco de Mayo,

who cares por qué, time to party, la gente
packed tight as candies in las piñatas,
streetgangers riding low, ese, vato,
clean prom kids movin on, careful
not to sit in rented threads.

Xicanindio setting up, centerstage—
the cowbell's rich *donk!*
calls in the congas—
Jambo's palms stroke the taut skins
between kisses hello to las hijas.

Los viejitos turn las cumbias, spinning
twirled beer bottles, one leg between stockinged thighs,
tight skirt riding up, Carmen's hair
blue in the false light, the cuíca moaning
lover, Zarco milking the groaning skin,
sweet muscles, everyone's naked, especially
those with clothes on, like that woman lit up
aquí, on the corner, dancing alone, her white
strapless barely hanging on, white skirt
whispering around her calves, then rising
higher, hija, as she whirls, fireworks
breaking the sky, focusing la fiesta
upside down on the retina
of the museum's walk-in eye,
y el borracho staggers to pee in the fountain,
throws a star, and a rock falls.

samuel ferguson

from: At the Polo-Ground

6th May 1882

. . .

                  Oh, he comes at last!
No time for thinking now. My own life pays
Unless I play my part. I see he brings
Another with him, and, I think, the same
I heard them call Lord—something—Cavendish.
If one; two, likely. That can't now be helped.
Up. Drive on straight,—if I blow my nose
And show my handkerchief in front of them,
And then turn back, what's that to anyone?
No further, driver. Back to Island Bridge.
No haste. If some acquaintance chanced to pass,
He must not think that we are running away.
I don't like, but I can't help looking back.
They meet: my villains pass them. Gracious Powers,
Another failure! No, they turn again
And overtake; and Brady lifts his arm—
I'll see no more. On—by the Monument.
On—brisker, brisker—but yet leisurely.
By this time all is over with them both.
Ten minutes more, the Castle has the news,
And haughty Downing Street in half an hour
Is struck with palsy. For a moment there,
Among the trees, I wavered. Brady's knife
Has cut the knot of my perplexities;
Despite myself, my fortune mounts again.
The English rule will soon be overthrown,
And ours established in the place of it.
I'm free again to look, as long as I please,
In Fortune's show-box. Yes; I see the chain,
I see the gilded coach. God send the boy
May take the polish! There's but one thing now
That troubles me. These cursed knives at home
That woman brought me, what had best be done
To put them out o' the way? I have it. Yes,
That old Fitzsimon's roof's in need of repairs.

I'll leave them in his cock-loft. Still in time
To catch the tram, I'll take a seat a-top—
For no one must suppose I've anything
To hide—and show myself in Grafton Street.

The speaker is one of the "Invincibles" who perpetrated the Phoenix Park Murders of Burke and Cavendish.

MAY 7

john woods

Ahab's Diary

Tell the doctors the wounds were ulcerous
a while, then salt and sea lice
cleaned them. I don't troll well,
the peg leg gone, bobbing and wheeling
in the creaming wake.
     Once, we
sounded near a sinking oiler.
The airbursts were deafening.
        I saw
faces in the portholes, going down.
ITS flukes drew in debris. A whole
cheese! *Lusitania*, May 7, 1915, I read.

We know more than you think, sounding
off the shores. The flume is fine, feathery,
and quite warm. We feel the sonar,
and the Bikini drift was copper-tasting.

In the icelands, the channel led
through immense, singing mountains,
green and yellow with trace minerals
and the tricks of light. A few pods
of THEM, ranked down in the green,
a calf larger than a locomotive,
or that mossy Pershing, lashed
to the steel deck off Hatteras.

I could tell you . . .

peter scupham

V.E. Day

Carpamus dulcia: nostrum est
Quod vivis: cinis, et manes, et fabula fies
                    Persius: Sat. V

Noticing oddly how flags had been rubbed thin,
Bleaching in shut drawers, now unrolled
In blues, reds, their creases of old skin
Tacked on brown lances, headed with soft gold.
        Clothes-lines of bunting,

And light fresh at the front door, May
Switching the sky with stray bits of green,
The road levelling off; the day much like a day
Others could be, and others might have been.
        A woman laughing,

Sewing threadbare cotton to windy air,
The house open: hands, curtains leaning out
To the same gravel, the same anywhere, everywhere.
Birds remain birds, cats cats, messing about
        In the back garden.

And a table-land of toys to be put away,
To wither and shrivel back to Homeric names.
Scraps gathering myth and rust, the special day
Moving to its special close: columnar flames
        Down to a village bonfire

In which things seasoned and unseasoned burn
Through their black storeys, and the mild night
Fuels the same fires with the same unconcern:
Dresden, Ilium, London: the witch-light
        Bright on a ring of children.

Night, and the huge bombers lying cold to touch,
The bomb-bays empty under the perspex skull.
The pyres chill, that ate so fiercely, and so much,
The flags out heavily: the stripes charcoal, dull.
        Ashes, ghosts, fables.

Victory in Europe Day was May 8, 1945.

william dunbar

The Thrissill and the Rois

Quhen Merche wes with variand windis past
And Appryll had with hir silver schouris
Tane leif at Nature with ane orient blast;
And lusty May, that muddir is of flouris,
Had maid the birdis to begyn thair houris
Amang the tendir odouris reid and quyht,
Quhois armony to heir it wes delyt:

In bed at morrow sleiping as I lay
Me thocht Aurora with hir cristall ene
In at the window lukit by the day
And halsit me, with visage paill and grene;
On quhois hand a lark sang fro the splene:
Awalk, luvaris, out of your slomering,
Se how the lusty morrow dois up spring.

Me thocht fresche May befoir my bed upstude
In weid depaynt of mony divers hew,
Sobir, benyng, and full of mansuetude,
In brycht atteir of flouris forgit new,
Hevinly of color, quhyt, reid, broun and blew,
Balmit in dew and gilt with Phebus bemys
Quhill all the hous illumynit of hir lemys.

Slugird, scho said, Awalk annone for schame,
And in my honour sum thing thow go wryt;
The lork hes done the mirry day proclame
To rais up luvaris with confort and delyt;
Yit nocht incress thy curage to indyt,
Quhois hairt sum tyme hes glaid and blisfull bene,
Sangis to mak undir the levis grene.

Quhairto, quod I, Sall I uprys at morrow,
For in this May few birdis herd I sing?
Thai haif moir caus to weip and plane thair sorrow,
Thy air it is nocht holsum nor benyng;
Lord Eolus dois in thy sessone ring;
So busteous ar the blastis of his horne,
Amang thy bewis to walk I haif forborne.

With that this lady sobirly did smyll
And said, Uprys and do thy observance;
Thow did promyt in Mayis lusty quhyle
For to discryve the Ros of most pleasance.
Go se the birdis how thay sing and dance,
Illumynit our with orient skyis brycht
Annamyllit richely with new asur lycht.

. . .

Than all the birdis song with sic a schout
That I annone awoilk quhair that I lay,
And with a braid I turnyt me about
To see this court, bot all wer went away.
Than up I lenyt, halflingis in affrey,
And thus I wret, as ye haif hard to forrow,
Off lusty May upone the nynte morrow.

bret harte

_____

What the Engines Said

(Opening of the Pacific Railroad)

What was it the Engines said,
Pilots touching,—head to head
Facing on a single track,
Half a world behind each back?
This is what the Engines said,
Unreported and unread.

With a prefatory screech,
In a florid Western speech,
Said the Engine from the WEST:
"I am from Sierra's crest;
Why, I reckon, it's confessed
That I've done my level best."

Said the Engine from the EAST:
"They who work best talk the least.
S'pose you whistle down your brakes,
What you've done is no great shakes,—
Pretty fair,—but let our meeting
Be a different kind of greeting.
Let these folks with champagne stuffing,
Nor their Engines, do the *puffing*.

"Listen! Where Atlantic beats
Shores of snow and summer heats;
Where the Indian autumn skies
Paint the woods with wampum dyes,—
I have chased the flying sun,
Seeing all he looked upon,
Blessing all that he has blessed,
Nursing in my iron breast
All his vivifying heat,
All his clouds about my crest;
And before my fling feet
Every shadow must retreat."

Said the Western Engine, "Phew!"
And a long, low whistle blew.
"Come, now, really that's the oddest
Talk for one so very modest.
You brag of your East! *You* do?
Why, *I* bring the East to *you*.
All the Orient, all Cathay,
Find through me the shortest way;
And the sun you follow here
Rises in my hemisphere.
Really,—if one must be rude,—
Length, my friend, ain't longitude."

Said the Union, "Don't reflect, or
I'll run over some Director."
Said the Central: "I'm Pacific;
But, when riled, I'm quite terrific.
Yet to-day we shall not quarrel,
Just to show these folks this moral,
How two Engines—in their vision—
Once have met without collision."

This is what the Engines said,
Unreported and unread;
Spoken slightly through the nose,
With a whistle at the close.

*The Union Pacific from the east and the Central Pacific from the west were joined
by the driving of a golden spike on May 10, 1869 in Promontory, Utah, to form the
first United States transcontinental railroad.*

MAY 11

john berryman

World-Telegram

Man with a tail heads eastward for the Fair.
Can open a pack of cigarettes with it.
Was weaving baskets happily, it seems,
When found, the almost Missing Link, and brought
From Ceylon in the interests of science.
The correspondent doesn't know how old.

Two columns left, a mother saw her child
Crushed with its father by a ten-ton truck
Against a loading platform, while her son,
Small, frightened, in a Sea Scout uniform,
Watched from the Langley. All needed treatment.

Berlin and Rome are having difficulty
With a new military pact. Some think
Russia is not too friendly towards London.
The British note is called inadequate.

An Indian girl in Lima, not yet six,
Has been delivered by Caesarian.
A boy. They let the correspondent in:
Shy, uncommunicative, still quite pale,
A holy picture by her, a blue ribbon.

Right of the centre, and three columns wide,
A rather blurred but rather ominous

169

Machine-gun being set up by militia
This morning in Harlan County, Kentucky.
Apparently some miners died last night.
"Personal brawls" is the employers' phrase.

All this on the front page. Inside, penguins.
The approaching television of baseball.
The King approaching Quebec. Cotton down.
Skirts up. Four persons shot. Advertisements.
Twenty-six policemen are decorated.
Mother's Day repercussions. A film star
Hopes marriage will preserve him from his fans.

News of one day, one afternoon, one time.
If it were possible to take these things
Quite seriously, I believe they might
Curry disorder in the strongest brain,
Immobilize the most resilient will,
Stop trains, break up the city's food supply,
And perfectly demoralize the nation.

11 May 1939

MAY 12

 al purdy

The Battlefield at Batoche

Over the earthworks among slim cottonwood trees
wind whistles a wind tune
I think it has nothing to do with living or dead men
or the price of groceries
it is only wind
And walking in the wooded dish-shaped hollow
that served to protect generals and staff
officers from sniper fire
I hear a different kind of murmur
—no more than that at least not definitely
the sort of thing you do hear
every now and then in a city never
questioning because it's so ordinary

but not so ordinary here
I ask my wife "Do you hear anything?"
She smiles "Your imagination again?"
"All right then don't you wish you had one?"
"If I did I'd burn your supper . . ."
the sort of thing she says to annoy me
the unanswerable kind of remark
that needs time to think about
I take my time watching the green curve
of the South Saskatchewan River below
a man riding an inch-long machine a mile distant
that makes dark waves cutting the yellow wheat
I wonder if Gunner Phillips heard the sound
on the day of May 12 in 1885
before the bullet knocked him down
the stairs he spent twenty years climbing?
Did Letendre with his muzzle-loader
clamped under one arm stuffing gun powder
down the barrel and jamming in a bullet
stop remembering great itchy beasts
pushing against log palisades at night
and running the buffalo at Grand Coteau
the Sioux screaming insults from a safe distance
at men from the White Horse Plain?
—all this in dream pantomime
with that sound and nothing else?
And old Ouellete age 90
his hearing almost gone anyway
wiping off river mist from his rifle
listening—?

. . .

In May the annoyed general eats his lunch
on the cliffs ordering "a reconnaissance in force"
which his officers misinterpret as "attack in force"
Midlanders   Winnipeg Rifles   Grenadiers
move out from their own positions
and burst into the Métis rifle pits
with Captain Howard from Connecticut
a demonstrator for the Colt Firearms Company
of Hartford demonstrating
death at 500 rounds a minute
with the borrowed Gatling gun

But it isn't the sound I hear now
not the dead shifting positions underground
to dodge bullets stopped in mid-earth
here a little way under the black soil
where wheat yellow as a girl's hair blossoms
the Métis nation was born and died
as the last buffalo stumbles to his knees
and felt cold briefly while his great wool
blanket was ripped from his bloody shoulders. . . .

MAY 13

russell edson

Time of the King

There was a king who didn't like to wait very much. When a pleasant date was approaching he would simply do away with the days or weeks that stood between.

ALL CITIZENS ARE ASKED TO X ALL THE DAYS ON THEIR CALENDARS BETWEEN NOW AND THE KING'S PLEASURE.

At other times the king might insist on re-playing a particular date representing some high satisfaction: IT WILL BE MAY 13, 1974 FOR TWO WEEKS, OR UNTIL FURTHER NOTICE.

Sometimes the king, in moods of having nothing to look forward to, would reverse the calendar to dates of former pleasures. Sometimes he would remain in the past for years.

One day he settled into childhood, just on the edge of puberty, just when he was discovering the joys of masturbation.

No no, that looks bad, said one of his high advisers.

What's so bad about a kid having a little fun? Freud says it's normal, said the distracted king.

After a year of masturbating the king became very depressed and decided he didn't want to live anymore.

The king consulted insurance company actuarials, had medical advice as to his general health, checked the longevity of his ancestors, and put all of this through a computer, arriving at a date when he might reasonably expect to die of *natural* causes; had new calendars printed describing a year many years away; and specifying a month and a day in that future year, went to bed and died.

172

isaac rosenberg

Dead Man's Dump

The plunging limbers over the shattered track
Racketed with their rusty freight,
Stuck out like many crowns of thorns,
And the rusty stakes like sceptres old
To stay the flood of brutish men
Upon our brothers dear.

The wheels lurched over sprawled dead
But pained them not, though their bones crunched,
Their shut mouths made no moan,
They lie there huddled, friend and foeman,
Man born of man, and born of woman,
And shells go crying over them
From night till night and now.

Earth has waited for them
All the time of their growth
Fretting for their decay:
Now she has them at last!
In the strength of their strength
Suspended—stopped and held.

What fierce imaginings their dark souls lit
Earth! have they gone into you?
Somewhere they must have gone,
And flung on your hard back
Is their souls' sack,
Emptied of God-ancestralled essences.
Who hurled them out? Who hurled?

None saw their spirits' shadow shake the grass,
Or stood aside for the half used life to pass
Out of those doomed nostrils and the doomed mouth,
When the swift iron burning bee
Drained the wild honey of their youth.

What of us, who flung on the shrieking pyre,
Walk, our usual thoughts untouched,
Our lucky limbs as on ichor fed,

Immortal seeming ever?
Perhaps when the flames beat loud on us,
A fear may choke in our veins
And the startled blood may stop.

The air is loud with death,
The dark air spurts with fire
The explosions ceaseless are.
Timelessly now, some minutes past,
These dead strode time with vigorous life,
Till the shrapnel called "an end!"
But not to all. In bleeding pangs
Some borne on stretchers dreamed of home,
Dear things, war-blotted from their hearts.

A man's brains splattered on
A stretcher-bearer's face;
His shook shoulders slipped their load,
But when they bent to look again
The drowning sound was sunk too deep
For human tenderness.

They left this dead with the older dead,
Stretched at the cross roads
Burnt black by strange decay,
Their sinister faces lie
The lid over each eye,
The grass and coloured clay
More motion have than they,
Joined to the great sunk silences.

Here is one not long dead;
His dark hearing caught our far wheels,
And the choked soul stretched weak hands
To reach the living word the far wheels said,
The blood-dazed intelligence beating for light,
Crying through the suspense of the far torturing wheels
Swift for the end to break,
Or the wheels to break,
Cried as the tide of the world broke over his sight.

Will they come? Will they ever come?
Even as the mixed hoofs of the mules,
The quivering-bellied mules,
And the rushing wheels all mixed

With his tortured upturned sight,
So we crash round the bend,
We heard his weak scream,
We heard his very last sound,
And our wheels grazed his dead face.

*The manuscript of this poem is signed and dated "Isaac Rosenberg, May 14, 1917,
B.E.F. France."*

hilda doolittle (h.d.)

rom: May 1943

I

rog faces,
og lust,
og bellies
 the dust,
1 unexpected flame
ve you another name:

1ere's the siren wail again,
ay 15;
' the clock,
ar 6,
at's 4
' the sun):

)g faces,
)g lust,
)g bellies
 the dust
the Last Judgment Day:

when winter-fog is gone,
the frogs sit in the sun,
and now you can see
strawberry-leaves
on a crown,
a lion,
a unicorn:

now you can clearly see
what frogs in the sun
become:

salamanders in the flame,
heraldic wings surround the name
English from Englisc from
Engle, Angle
from the Angles who settled
in Briton.

r. a. mackintosh

In Memoriam

Private D. Sutherland killed in action in the German trench, May 16, 1916, and the others who died.

So you were David's father,
And he was your only son,
And the new-cut pears are rotting
And the work is left undone,
Because of an old man weeping,
Just an old man in pain,
For David, his son David,
That will not come again.

Oh, the letters he wrote you,
And I can see them still,
Not a word of the fighting
But just the sheep on the hill
And how you should get the crops in
Ere the year get stormier,
And the Bosches have got his body,
And I was his officer.

You were only David's father,
But I had fifty sons
When we went up in the evening
Under the arch of the guns,
And we came back in the twilight—
Oh God! I heard them call
To me for help and pity
That could not help at all.

Oh, never will I forget you,
My men that trusted me,
More my sons than your fathers',
For they could only see
The little helpless babies
And the young men in their pride.
They could not see you dying,
And hold you while you died.

Happy and young and gallant,
They saw their first-born go,
But not the strong limbs broken
And the beautiful men brought low,
The piteous writhing bodies,
They screamed "Don't leave me, sir,"
For they were only your fathers
But I was your officer.

david wagoner

Thoreau and the Snapping Turtle

> *[It] looked not merely repulsive, but to*
> *some extent terrible even as a crocodile . . .*
> *a very ugly and spiteful face.*
> —Thoreau, *Journal*, May 17, 1854

As his boat glided across a flooded meadow,
He saw beneath him under lily pads,
Brown as dead leaves in mud, a yard-long
Snapping turtle staring up through the water
At him, its shell as jagged as old bark.

He plunged his arm in after it to the shoulder,
Stretching and missing, but groping till he caught it
By the last ridge of its tail. Then he held on,
Hauled it over the gunwale, and flopped it writhing
Into the boat. It began gasping for air

Through a huge gray mouth, then suddenly
Heaved its hunchback upward, slammed the thwart
As quick as a spring trap and, thrusting its neck
Forward a foot at a lunge, snapped its beaked jaws
So violently, he only petted it once,

Then flinched away. And all the way to the landing
It hissed and struck, thumping the seat

Under him hard and loud as a stake-driver.
It was so heavy, he had to drag it home,
All thirty pounds of it, wrong side up by the tail.

His neighbors agreed it walked like an elephant,
Tilting this way and that, its head held high,
A scarf of ragged skin at its throat. It would sag
Slowly to rest then, out of its element,
Unable to bear its weight in this new world.

Each time he turned it over, it tried to recover
By catching at the floor with its claws, by straining
The arch of its neck, by springing convulsively,
Tail coiling snakelike. But finally it slumped
On its spiky back like an exhausted dragon.

He said he'd seen a cut-off snapper's head
That would still bite at anything held near it
As if the whole of its life were mechanical,
That a heart cut out of one had gone on beating
By itself like clockwork till the following morning.

And the next week he wrote: *It is worth the while*
To ask ourselves . . . Is our life innocent
Enough? Do we live inhumanely, *toward man*
Or beast, in thought or act? To be successful
And serene we must be at one with the universe.

The least conscious and needless injury
Inflicted on any creature is
To its extent a suicide. What peace—
Or life—can a murderer have? . . . White maple keys
Have begun to fall and float downstream like wings.

There are myriads of shad-flies fluttering
Over the dark still water under the hill.

john dekker

from: The Shoemaker's Holiday

Act III, scene ii. London: a Room in the Earl of Lincoln's House.

[*Enter the* EARL OF LINCOLN *and* DODGER.]

LINCOLN	How now, good Dodger, what's the news in France?
DODGER	My lord, upon the eighteenth day of May
	The French and English were prepared to fight;
	Each side with eager fury gave the sign
	Of a most hot encounter. Five long hours
	Both armies fought together; at the length
	The lot of victory fell on our sides.
	Twelve thousand of the Frenchmen that day died,
	Four thousand English, and no man of name
	But Captain Hyam and young Ardington,
	Two gallant gentlemen, I knew them well.
LINCOLN	But Dodger, prithee, tell me, in this fight
	How did my cousin Lacy bear himself?
DODGER	My lord, your cousin Lacy was not there.
LINCOLN	Not there?
DODGER	No, my good lord.
LINCOLN	Sure, thou mistakest.
	I saw him shipped, and a thousand eyes beside
	Were witnesses of the farewells which he gave,
	When I, with weeping eyes, bid him adieu.
	Dodger, take heed.
DODGER	My lord, I am advised,
	That what I spake is true: to prove it so,
	His cousin Askew, that supplied his place,
	Sent me for him from France, that secretly
	He might convey himself thither.
LINCOLN	Is't even so?
	Dares he so carelessly venture his life
	Upon the indignation of a king?
	Has he despised my love, and spurned those favours
	Which I with prodigal hand poured on his head?
	He shall repent his rashness with his soul;
	Since of my love he makes no estimate,
	I'll make him wish he had not known my hate.
	Thou hast no other news?

DODGER	None else, my lord.
LINCOLN	None worse I know thou hast.—
	Procure the king
	To crown his giddy brows with ample honours,
	Send him chief colonel, and all my hope
	Thus to be dashed! But 'tis in vain to grieve,
	One evil cannot a worse one relieve.
	Upon my life, I have found out his plot;
	That old dog, Love, that fawned upon him so,
	Love to that puling girl, his fair-cheeked Rose,
	The lord mayor's daughter, hath distracted him,
	And in the fire of that love's lunacy
	Hath he burnt up himself, consumed his credit.
	Lost the king's love, yea, and I fear, his life,
	Only to get a wanton to his wife,
	Dodger, it is so.
DODGER	I fear so, my good lord.
LINCOLN	It is so—nay, sure it cannot be!
	I am at my wits' end. Dodger!
DODGER	Yea, my lord.
LINCOLN	Thou art acquainted with my nephew's haunts;
	Spend this gold for thy pains; go seek him out;
	Watch at my lord mayor's—there if he live,
	Dodger, thou shalt be sure to meet with him.
	Prithee, be diligent.—Lacy, thy name
	Lived once in honour, now 'tis dead in shame.—
	Be circumspect. [*Exit.*]
DODGER	I warrant you, my lord.
	[*Exit.*]

thomas wyatt

The Death of Anne Boleyn

As for them all I do not thus lament,
But as of right my reason doth me bind;
But as the most doth all their deaths repent,
Even so do I by force of mourning mind.
Some say, "Rochford, haddest thou been not so proud,
For thy great wit each man would thee bemoan,
Since as it is so, many cry aloud
It is great loss that thou art dead and gone."

Ah! Norris, Norris, my tears begin to run
To think what hap did thee so lead or guide
Whereby thou hast both thee and thine undone
That is bewailed in court of every side;
In place also where thou hast never been
Both man and child doth piteously thee moan.
They say, "Alas, thou art far overseen
By thine offences to be thus dead and gone."

Ah! Weston, Weston, that pleasant was and young,
In active things who might with thee compare?
All words accept that thou diddest speak with tongue,
So well esteemed with each where thou diddest fare.
And we that now in court doth lead our life
Most part in mind doth thee lament and moan;
But that thy faults we daily hear so rife,
All we should weep that thou are dead and gone.

. . .

Ah! Mark, what moan should I for thee make more,
Since that thy death thou hast deserved best,
Save only that mine eye is forced sore
With piteous plaint to moan thee with the rest?
A time thou haddest above thy poor degree,
The fall whereof thy friends may well bemoan:
A rotten twig upon so high a tree
Hath slipped thy hold, and thou art dead and gone.

And thus farewell each one in hearty wise!
The axe is home, your heads be in the street;

The trickling tears doth fall so from my eyes
I scarce may write, my paper is so wet.
But what can hope when death hath played his part,
Though nature's course will thus lament and moan?
Leave sobs therefore, and every Christian heart
Pray for the souls of those be dead and gone.

Anne Boleyn was executed on May 19, 1536 along with the gentlemen she laments.
Henry VIII was betrothed to Jane Seymour on the morrow and married to her on
May 30. The attribution of authorship to Thomas Wyatt is highly conjectural.

MAY 20

 james masao mitsui

Destination: Tule Lake Relocation Center, May 20, 1942

She had raised the window
higher

than her head; then
paused

to lift wire spectacles,
wiping

sight back with a wrinkled
hand-

kerchief. She wanted to watch
the old

place until the train's passing
erased

the tarpaper walls and tin roof;
she had

been able to carry away
so little.

The finger of her left
hand

worried two strings
attached

to a baggage tag
flapping

from her
lapel.

anonymous

On the Earthquake of 1382

. . .

And also whon this eorthe qwok,
    Was non so proud he nas agast,
And al his jolité forsok,
    And thought on God whil that hit last.
    And alsone as hit was over past,
Men wox as uvel as thei dede are.
    Uche mon in his herte may cast,
This was a warnyng to be ware.

For sothe this was a Lord to drede,
    So sodeynly mad mon agast;
Of gold and selver thei tok non hede,
    But out of ther houses ful sone thei past.
    Chaumbres, chymeneys, al to-barst,
Chirches and castelles foule gon fare;
    Pinacles, steples, to grounde hit cast;
And al was for warnyng to be ware.

The mevyng of this eorthe iwis,
    That schulde bi cuynde be ferm and stabele,
A pure verrey toknyng hit is

That mennes hertes ben chaungabele,
  And that to falsed thei ben most abele.
For with good feith wol we not fare.
  Leef hit wel, withouten fabele,
This was a warnyng to be ware.

The rysyng of the comuynes in londe,
  The pestilens, and the eorthe-qwake,
Theose threo thinges, I understonde,
  Beoth tokenes the grete vengaunce and wrake
  That schulde falle for synnes sake,
As this clerkes conne declare.
  Now may we chese to leve or take,
For warnyng have we to be ware.

. . .

The earth quaked on May 21, 1382.

 robert burns

A Poet's Welcome to his love-begotten Daughter; the first instance that entitled him to the venerable appellation of Father

Thou's welcome, wean! Mischanter fa' me,
If thoughst o' thee, or yet thy Mamie,
Shall ever daunton me or awe me,
               My bonie lady;
Or if I blush when thou shalt ca' me
               Tyta, or Daddie.

Though now they ca' me fornicator,
And tease my name in kintra clatter,
The mair they talk, I'm kend the better;
               E'en let them clash!
An auld wife's tongue's a feckless matter
               To gie ane fash.

Welcome! My bonie, sweet, wee dochter!
Though ye come here a wee unsought for;
And though your comin I hae fought for,
                    Baith Kirk and Queir;
Yet by my faith, ye're no unwrought for,
                    That I shall swear!

Wee image o' my bonie Betty,
As fatherly I kiss and daut thee,
As dear and near my heart I set thee,
                    Wi' as gude will,
As a' the Priests had seen me get thee
                    That's out o' h———

Sweet fruit o' monie a merry dint,
My funny toil is no a' tint;
Though ye come to the warld asklent,
                    Which fools may scoff at,
In my last plack your part's be in't,
                    The better half o't.

Though I should be the waur bestead,
Thou's be as braw and bienly clad,
And thy young years as nicely bred
                    Wi' education,
As any brat o' Wedlock's bed,
                    In a' thy station.

Lord grant that thou may ay inherit
Thy Mither's looks an' gracefu' merit;
An' thy poor, worthless Daddie's spirit,
                    Without his failins!
'Twad please me mair to see thee heir it
                    Than stocked mailins!

For if thou be, what I wad hae thee,
And tak the counsel I shall gie thee,
I'll never rue my trouble wi' thee,
                    The cost nor shame o't,
But be a loving Father to thee,
                    And brag the name o't.

The child was born on May 22, 1785, to Elizabeth Paton, who had been a servant in the Burns household.

wilfrid noyce

Breathless

(written on Mt. Everest at 21,000 ft. on 23 May 1953)

Heart aches,
lungs pant
dry air
sorry, scant.
Legs lift—
why at all?
Loose drift,
heavy fall.
Prod the snow
easiest way;
a flat step
is holiday.
Look up,
far stone
many miles
far, alone.
Grind breath
once more then on;
don't look up
till journey's done.

Must look up,
glasses dim.
Wrench of hand,
faltering limb
Pause one step,
breath swings back;
swallow once,
throat gone slack.
Go on
to far stone;
don't look up,
count steps done.
One step,
one heart-beat,
stone no nearer
dragging feet.
Heart aches,
lungs pant
dry air
sorry, scant.

joseph brodsky

May 24, 1980

I have braved, for want of wild beasts, steel cages,
carved my term and nickname on bunks and rafters,
lived by the sea, flashed aces in an oasis,
dined with the-devil-knows-whom, in tails, on truffles.
From the height of a glacier I beheld half a world, the earthly
width. Twice have drowned, thrice let knives rake my nitty-gritty.
Quit the country that bore and nursed me.
Those who forgot me would make a city.
I have waded the steppes that saw yelling Huns in saddles,
worn the clothes nowadays back in fashion in every quarter,
planted rye, tarred the roofs of pigsties and stables,
guzzled everything save dry water.
I've admitted the sentries' third eye into my wet and foul
dreams. Munched the bread of exile: it's stale and warty.
Granted my lungs all sounds except the howl;
switched to a whisper. Now I am forty.
What should I say about life? That it's long and abhors transparence.
Broken eggs make me grieve; the omelette, though, makes me vomit.
Yet until brown clay has been crammed down my larynx,
only gratitude will be gushing from it.

Trans. by the author

grace paley

Having Arrived by Bike at Battery Park

I thought I would
sit down at one of those park department tables
and write a poem honoring
the occasion which is May 25th
Evelyn   my best friend's birthday
and Willy Langbauer's birthday

Day! I love you for your delicacy
in appearing after so many years
as an afternoon in Battery Park right
on the curved water
where Manhattan was beached

At once arrows
straight as Broadway were driven
into the great Indian heart

Then we came from the east
seasick and safe the
white tormented people
grew fat in the
blood of that wound

MAY 26

alexander pushkin

May 26, 1828

Fruitless and chance gift, my breath,
Why were you given to me,
And why were you condemned to death
By inscrutable destiny?

Who fashioned brain and eye and limb
From nothingness, and gave
My spirit an immortal dream
And knowledge of the grave?

I weep because the only sound
Is life's monotonous,
Sad, aimless, endless lull, the ground-
Swell of the universe.

Trans. D. M. Thomas

george henry bowker

The Black Regiment

[May 27, 1863]

Dark as the clouds of even,
Ranked in the western heaven,
Waiting the breath that lifts
All the dead mass, and drifts
Tempest and falling brand
Over a ruined land,—
So still and orderly,
Arm to arm, knee to knee,
Waiting the great event,
Stands the black regiment.

Down the long dusty line
Teeth gleam and eyeballs shine;
And the bright bayonet,
Bristling and firmly set,
Flashed with a purpose grand,
Long ere the sharp command
Of the fierce rolling drum
Told them their time had come,
Told them what work was sent
For the black regiment.

"Now," the flag-sergeant cried,
"Though death and hell betide,
Let the whole nation see
If we are fit to be
Free in this land; or bound
Down, like the whining hound,—
Bound with red stripes of pain
In our cold chains again!"
Oh! what a shout there went
From the black regiment!

"Charge!" Trump and drum awoke;
Onward the bondmen broke;
Bayonet and sabre-stroke

Vainly opposed their rush.
Through the wild battle's crush,
With but one though aflush,
Driving their lords like chaff,
In the guns' mouths they laugh;
Or at the slippery brands
Leaping with open hands,
Down they tear man and horse,
Down in their awful course;
Trampling with bloody heel
Over the crashing steel,—
All their eyes forward bent,
Rushed the black regiment.

"Freedom!" their battle-cry,—
"Freedom! or leave to die!"
Ah! and they meant the word,
Not as with us 't is heard,
Not a mere party shout;
They gave their spirits out,
Trusted the end to God,
And on the gory sod
Rolled in triumphant blood.
Glad to strike one free blow,
Whether for weal or woe;
Glad to breathe on free breath,
Though on the lips of death;
Praying,—alas! in vain!—
That they might fall again,
So they could once more see
That burst to liberty!
This was what "freedom" lent
To the black regiment.

Hundreds on hundreds fell;
But they are resting well;

Scourges and shackles strong
Never shall do them wrong.
O, to the living few,
Soldiers, be just and true!

Hail them as comrades tried;
Fight with them side by side;
Never, in field or tent,
Scorn the black regiment!

MAY 28

peter redgrove

Signatures

Around Ascension Day, the thundery time,
Regular tea-time thunderclaps;

The vast tiny grass, each with its dew
An excellent microscope;

All night we heard the birds passing,
Then at mid-afternoon the clouds streamed

And opened their great inner surfaces—
What in air is a sounding process

In water streams and roughens
And whitens through the plaiting reeds—

The smell from the water is like woven papyrus,
The material for scrolls, and the scrolls,

Rush past full of fragrant hieroglyphs;
Then winter high-pressure, still, illiterate and oily.

Ascension Day, 1992

Ascension Day, a moveable feast forty days after Easter, was celebrated on May 28 in 1992.

anonymous

May Twenty-ninth

'Twas the twenty-ninth of May,
'twas a holiday,
Four and twenty tailors
set out to hunt a snail;
The snail put forth his horns,
and roared like a bull,
Away ran the tailors,
and catch the bull who will.

The holiday referred to in this children's rhyme is probably Restoration Day (Royal Oak Day), commemorating the restoration of Charles II in 1666.

john bangs

May 30, 1893

It seemed to be but chance, but who shall say
That 't was not part of Nature's own sweet way,

That on the field where once the cannon's breath
Laid many a hero cold and stark in death,

Some little children, in the after-years,
Had come to play among the grassy spears,

And, all unheeding, when their romp was done,
Had left a wreath of wild flowers over one

Who fought to save his country, and whose lot
It was to die unknown and rest forgot?

desmond egan

Last Day of May

why did you stand there
thinking out the gable window?

like something that didn't fully happen
    the grass
lay soggy and lush it was
littered with petals round the crabapple
    tree
where an odd one still hung

drooping making lifesounds
with a sad pigeon somewhere down the
    woods
        somewhere down the woods

rain falls straight
on the warmth
the vegetation

roads fill in fill in
the ditches are nests
and houses empty with
long long evenings of
the longest day.

where the cuckoo hides
where the swallows lift

and I go mowing
trying not to care

June

francis carey slater

Woltemade

In seventeen-seventy-three my story—
On June the first at dawn of day—
Begins, where raging storms have
    maddened
The tranquil waves of Table Bay.

Battered by those angry billows,
And beaten by the blind wind's scourge,
A ship runs—reels—is torn and spitted
By rock-fangs hidden in foaming surge.

As wild-dove pierced by an unseen arrow,
Wounded, sinking, the good ship lies;
Her hapless crew in white-eyed terror
Harrow the air with hopeless cries.

Scattered on the shore are watchers,
Some seek plunder—base-got gear—
Other who would help are helpless,
Faltering in the bonds of fear.

To their midst a man comes riding:
Who is this horseman gaunt and grey?
Who this monarch clad so meanly,
Whose eyes are bright as sun-born day?

One it is who on a farmstead
Far from wrangling throngs has dwelt;
A humble hind, a cattle herdsman,
A patient nursling of the veld.

While he watched the cattle feeding
By stony koppie, sun-drenched plain,
Perhaps he dreamed of lives heroic,
And prayed that his might not be vain:

And while he milked the full-fed cattle,
When suns burnt on the mountain-belt,

Perhaps he dreamed of high adventure—
This scion of the sun-proud veld.

* * *

The day has come—the great adventure
He scans the helpless cowards there,
He kindles his beast with breath heroic—
And they face the tempest's blast and
    blare.

Around them surges snarl and bellow,
About them hisses blinding spray,
While on the beach the breathless
    watchers
Forget their terror and their prey.

Seven times they brave the path of peril
And souls twice seven are brought to sho
But from the last great, glad adventure
The bright-eyed brothers come no more

Return no more? Nay, they are with us!
They'll perish never, that noble twain!
Men pass like dews, but deeds of valour
Are founts that fail not in life's plain.

Man sinks to silence: like sweet music
His high deeds haunt with echoes felt
By dwellers in the crowded city
Or lonely farm on the crinkled veld.

—Ocean in unflinching struggle,
Warfare old as his waves are old,
Snatched never from earth a spoil more
    splendid
Than Woltemade. My tale is told.

louis macneice

Whit Monday—1941

Their feet on London, their heads in the grey clouds,
The Bank (if you call it a holiday) Holiday crowds
Stroll from street to street, cocking an eye
For where the angel used to be in the sky;
But the Happy Future is a thing of the past and the street
Echoes to nothing but their dawdling feet.
The Lord's my shepherd—familiar words of myth
Stand up better to bombs than a granite monolith,
Perhaps there is something in them. *I'll not want*—
Not when I'm dead. *He makes me down to lie*—
Death my christening and fire my font—
The quiet (Thames or Don's or Salween's) *waters by.*

Whit Monday, the day after the Feast of the Pentecost (Whit Sunday), fell on June 2 in 1941.

andrew hudgins

eflections on Cold Harbor

after dawn the third of June
inth anniversary of Cold Harbor—
I, who rose before the sun
alk the darkness from the woods,

sitting in a neighbor's field
watching as the early sun
ns off the last dew from the corn.
m men I was in prison with

ard that Grant's men looked like corn
ancing toward the reaper's blade,
which they fell relentlessly. That June,

the fields were soaked with summer rain.
If they had actually been corn
we never would have harvested—not wet,
ripe corn. It spoils. As did those men.

Elijah Cobb said that as he fired
into the massive surging of their line
he started crying. Tears blurred his aim.
But he did not withhold his fire:

there were so many running men
that every shot hit something blue,
even a shot fired blind through tears.
He was embarrassed by those tears

and couldn't understand their cause.
And knowing Cobb, a man who once
staged cockroach races for the troops
then ate the winner live, neither can I.

So now I sit amid the corn
and think about the quantities
of fertilizer it requires
—much more than other plants—

and how it's pollinated not by bees
but the vagaries of the summer wind.

The dark sky brightens to deep-ocean
    blue,
a blue in which some poets have

been known to drown quite happily.
But that's a trick the language plays
with some help from my nervous system
and a human wish to flee the body.

Sometimes, like now, I have great need
to live outside of metaphor,
to know a dawn that's only dawn
and corn that's corn and nothing else.

JUNE 4

 john haines

At Slim's River

Past Burwash and the
White River delta
we stopped to read a sign
creaking on its chains in the wind.

I left the car and climbed a grassy bluff,
to a grey cross leaning there
and a name that was peeling away:

"Alexander Clark Fisher.
Born October 1870. Died January 1941."

No weathering sticks from a homestead
remained in that hillside,
no log sill rotting under moss
nor cellar hole filling with rose vines.
Not even the stone ring
of a hunter's fire,
a thin wire flaking in the brush.

Only the red rock piled
to hold the cross, our blue car
standing on the road below,
and a small figure playing there.
The Yukon sunlight warming a land
held long under snow,
and the lake water splashing.

From the narrow bridge in the distance
a windy clatter of iron—
billow of dust on a blind crossing,
but a keen silence behind that wind.

It was June 4, 1973. I was forty-nine.

My ten-year-old daughter
called to me from the road:
she had found a rock to keep,

and I went down.

george chapman

The Battle of Fontaine Française

from: The Conspiracy and Tragedy of Charles, Duke of Byron

Act II, scene ii
[KING HENRY *and the* DUC DE SAVOY.]

SAVOY   A league from Fontaine Française, when you sent him
To make discovery of the Castile army,
When he discern'd 'twas it, with wondrous wisdom
Join'd to his spirit, he seem'd to make retreat.
But when they press'd him, and the Baron of Lux
Set on their charge so hotly that his horse
Was slain and he most dangerously engag'd,
Then turn'd your brave Duke head, and, with such ease
As doth an echo beat back violent sounds
With their own forces, he, as if a wall
Start suddenly before them, pash'd them all
Flat as the earth, and there was that field won.

HENRY   Y'are all the field wide.

SAVOY   O, I ask you pardon,
The strength of that field yet lay in his back,
Upon the foe's part; and what is to come
Of this your Marshal, now your worthy Duke,
Is much beyond the rest. For now he sees
A sort of horse troops issue from the woods
In number near twelve hundred, and retiring
To tell you that the entire army follow'd,
Before he could relate it, he was forc'd
To turn head and receive the main assault
Of five horse troops only with twenty horse.
The first he met he tumbled to the earth,
And brake through all, not daunted with two wounds,
One on his head, another on his breast,
The blood of which drown'd all the field in doubt.
Your Majesty himself was then engag'd,
Your power not yet arriv'd, and up you brought
The little strength you had, a cloud of foes
Ready to burst in storms about your ears.
Three squadrons rush'd against you, and the first
You took so fiercely that you beat their thoughts
Out of their bosoms from the urged fight.

The second all amazed you overthrew;
The third dispers'd with five and twenty horse
Left of the fourscore that pursu'd the chase.
And this brave conquest now your Marshal seconds
Against two squadrons, but with fifty horse.
One after other he defeats them both,
And made them run like men whose heels were tripp'd,
And pitch their heads in their great general's lap,
And him he sets on as he had been shot
Out of a cannon, beats him into rout,
And as a little brook being overrun
With a black torrent that beats all things down
His fury overtakes, his foamy back
Loaded with cattle and with stacks of corn,
And makes the miserable plowman mourn;
So was Du Maine surcharg'd, and so Byron
Flow'd over all his forces, every drop
Of his lost blood bought with a worthy man,
And only with a hundred gentleman
He won the place from fifteen hundred horse.

The Battle of Fontaine Française, which the Duc de Savoy is describing to King Henry IV, took place on June 5, 1595.

JUNE 6

 yannis ritsos

Ordinary People's Lithograph

Heavy, huge, honey-filled figs weighted down
the blazing noonday. The man hitched his horse to the fig tree.
He ate figs and licked his fingers. He stripped—
fierce, solitary, hirsute. He plunged into the river.
The two daughters of the field guard, complicitous, silent,
were watching from behind the willows. Inside their mouths
they felt the tiny seeds from the figs
that the horseman had eaten a short while ago. Then,
right above their heads, a bird let out
a wicked cry. The girls, alarmed, ran off.
The man emerged from the water all gold and got dressed.
Sikyona, June 6, 1964

Trans. Edmund Keeley

aidan carl mathews

June the Seventh

In Portugal today the Government
Ordered the troops to man the barricades.
Photos in the evening papers show me
An opened jugular, a thin spittle of blood.
I turn the page to read about a scandal.

This afternoon I wheeled a covered corpse
Into the morgue. A mother sat in tears
While nurses dressed a gash in her son's knee.
"Your father told you not to go in there."
Later the boy goes home to a beating.

And in the evening when I came to you,
I found you fast asleep. Your light brown hair
Trailed from the quilt over the cast iron.
I found a note on the kitchen table:
The milk has gone off. Please buy a bottle.

sonia sanchez

A Poem for My Brother

(reflections on his death from AIDS: June 8, 1991)

1. death

The day you died
a fever starched my bones.
within the slurred
sheets, i hoarded my legs
while you rowed out among the boulevards
balancing your veins on sails.
easy the eye of hunger

as i peeled the sharp
sweat and swallowed wholesale molds.

2. recovery (a)

What comes after
is consciousness of the morning
of the licensed sun that subdues
immoderate elements.
there is a kindness in illness
the indulgence of discrepancies.

reduced to the ménage of houses
and green drapes that puff their seasons
toward the face.
i wonder what to do now.
i am afraid
i remember a childhood that cried
after extinguished lights
when only the coated banners answered.

3. recovery (b)

There is a savior in these buds
look how the phallic stems distend
in welcome.
O copper flowerheads
confine my womb that i may dwell within.
i see these gardens, whom i love
i feel the sky's sweat on my face
now that these robes no longer bark
i praise abandonment.

4. wake

i have not come for summary.
must i renounce all babylons?
here, without psalms,
these leaves grow white
and burn the bones with dance.
here, without surfs,
young panicles bloom on the clouds and fly
while myths tick grey as thunder.

5. burial

you in the crow's rain
rusting amid ribs
my mouth spills your birth
i have named you prince of boards
stretching with the tides.

you in the toad's tongue
peeling on nerves
look. look. the earth is running palms.

6. (on) (the) (road). again.

somewhere a flower walks in mass
purchasing wholesale christs
sealing white-willow sacraments.

naked on steeples
where trappists idioms sail
an atom peels the air.

O i will gather my pulse
muffled by sibilants
and follow disposable dreams.

JUNE 9

mona van duyn

The Hermit of Hudson Pond

> *"Like most of the hermits in the area [he] obeyed to the letter the
> Fish and Game Laws."*

In the "immaculately neat" cabin it is calm and warm.
Deermice with Disney ears run the rafters by day
and rustle, gnaw and squeak in the provisions at night.
The snowshoe rabbit, red in sun as a setter,
hops and sits, twitching its nose, outside the door,
and all around, from trees to ground, the air

flashes with the yellow and black and white flight
of Evening Grosbeaks, fat with the spruce budworms
they feed on. The pond, like a great pan of broth,
bubbles with feeding trout when the hatch comes on.
For forty years, the days dawn and darken
in quiet order for the hermit of Hudson Pond,
only one law reaching in to his natural place.
No women with their feverish voices and strange, bloody days,
nor men, murdering, hustling, re-making the world,
only the self trimmed to its simplest needs,
shelter, food, for friendship a dog, and the days
dawning and darkening on woods and pond,
the moose wading in, mergansers churning the water
like motorboats as they scoot for a fish, loon
hooting and yodeling, or, when the snow comes,
the deep, still white, the burning, glistering cold.

"June 9, 1961" the flying service pilot
checks on the hermit and finds a note in the cabin:

"I killed myself because I had to kill
my baby dog for chasing deer. I threw
my pistol into the lake after I shot
baby dog. I didn't have nerve enough
to shoot myself. I didn't have to shoot
my dog. No one knew she was chasing deer
but me. I want to suffer because I think
it was a crime to shoot my baby dog.
If you find this, Ray, I'm all done living. I'm on
the bottom of the lake beside my dog."

Quotes from Anne Howe, "Hermits of the Moosehead Region," MOOSEHEAD,
MAINE BICENTENNIAL BOOKLET, 1976. *[Note by Van Duyn]*

wilfred owen

The Letter

With B.E.F. June 10. Dear Wife,
(O blast this pencil. 'Ere, Bill, lend's a knife.)
I'm in the pink at present, dear.
I think the war will end this year.
We don't see much of them square-'eaded 'Uns.
We're out of harm's way, not bad fed.
I'm longing for a taste of your old buns.
(Say, Jimmie, spare's a bite of bread.)
There don't seem much to say just now.
(Yer what? Then don't yer ruddy cow!
And give us back me cigarette!)
I'll soon be 'ome. You mustn't fret.
My feet's improvin', as I told you of.
We're out in rest now. Never fear.
(VRACH! By crumbs, but that was near.)
Mother might spare you half a sov.
Kiss Nell and Bert. When me and you—
(Eh? What the 'ell! Stand to? Stand to!
Jim, give's a hand with pack on, lad.
Guh! Christ! I'm hit. Take 'old. Aye, bad.
No, damn your iodine. Jim? 'Ere!
Write my old girl, Jim, there's a dear.)

tess gallagher

Some Painful Butterflies Pass Through

I saw the old Chinese men standing
in Nanjing under the trees where
they had hung their caged birds
in the early morning as though a cage
were only another branch that travels
with us. The bird revolves and settles,
moving its mind up and down the tree

with leaves and light. It sings
with the free birds—what else
can it do? They sit on the rungs
and preen or jit back and down and
back. But they are busy
and a day in the sky makes wings
of them. Then some painful butterflies
pass through.

The old men talk and smoke, examine
each other's cages. They feel restored,
as if they'd given themselves a tree, a sky
full of companions, song
that can travel. They depend
on their birds, and if their love stories
swing from their arms as they walk
homeward, it may be they are chosen
after all like one tree
with one bird that is faithful,
an injured voice traveling high into silence
with one accustomed listener
who smiles and walks slowly with
his face in the distance so
the pleasure spreads, and the treasured
singing, and the little bursts
of flying.

Shanghai, June 11, 1983

 marvin bell

Air Wisconsin

The day that Mt. St. Helens
gave your air a twist, seeding it,
marbling it, making it mildly ex-
plosive from your Canada to your
Salem, there came, to our Wisconsin,
a roving, dazzling rainfall
held by eight-mile vertical winds
which simply blew a plane out of the air.

Think of those confident wings,
getting more of what they thought they wanted.
I saw them carry the pilot on a board
through mud and soybeans—
it was a film I saw in my own home
of the severed wings, the rescue
of the wounded by tractor,
the clean sheets on the black and blue

field. They were going to Nebraska's
Lincoln, when they fell into a machine
that cuts a fuselage open like a can—
the Patrol calls it the Jaws of Life.
All in little figures on a screen—
boys in mud to their ankles held up
pristine plastic bags of plasma
and a kneeling man asked, "Where does

it hurt?" And then, in recognition,
"You don't know?" I didn't.
Then the film of the volcano came on
and I could see how much the mountain
was covered by smoke—the plume,
they called it, bringing to mind
the old question from childhood:
Which weighs more: a ton of feathers
or a ton of coal? You have ten seconds.

The incident occurred on June 12, 1980. "Air Wisconsin" is part of Segues: A
Correspondence in Poetry, *written back-and-forth with William Stafford, who
lived at the time in Lake Oswego, Oregon. [Note by Bell]*

J U N E   1 3

john mole

The Impertinence of the Thing

Past forty, a lyricist
Unsung, prone to self-pity
And troubled by the dead
Weight of every
Line, each further from my best,

I think of the young Joyce just
Happening to pass through London
On Yeats's birthday, or
(Was it?) expressly come
To do what must be done

When the time arrives
In all poets' lives
Which was (ie) to make straight
For the Cavendish where W.B.
Sat ensconced in state

Correcting proofs while sipping
Luke-warm jasmine tea
And not expecting anything
At all like this considering
The eminence of already distinguished *gris*

He might reasonably
Have assumed—Well, Joyce
(Says Oliver Gogarty) knocked on Yeats's door
And in readiness was
Clearing his thin voice

With bat-eyes narrowing
Behind their lenses when
Yeats, his sight already
None too good either, in that familiar sing-
Song called *Come in!*

Then turned to the young blur
Suddenly framed there
And heard *What age are you, sir?*
To which *I'm forty*
He replied, and presumably thought he'd

Appear quite grand, quite mezzo del cammin
To the young fellow who would not come in
But who explained simply
You are too old for me
To help, I bid you goodbye said he

And went, leaving W.B.
(Says Gogarty) *amazed by the impertinence*

Of the thing, but good for Joyce
Say I, sound sense,
And good for the old peacock too

Because there's nothing like a witty
Exchange between the greats
(Bravo Joyce *and* Yeats!)
To reduce a poet's dull self-pity
To absurdity

And so, being older
Than either was then,
Let me laugh now with one
Now the other
And now with both men.

This poem is based on Hugh Kenner's version of Gogarty's anecdote, which can be found in his book A Colder Eye. *[Note by Mole]*
The date of the incident must have been June 13, 1905, Yeats's fortieth birthday.

ruth pitter

The Sparrow's Skull

Memento Mori. Written at the Fall of France.

The kingdoms fall in sequence, like the waves on the shore.
All save divine and desperate hopes go down, they are no more.
Solitary is our place, the castle in the sea,
And I muse on those I have loved, and on those who have loved me.

I gather up my loves, and keep them all warm,
While above our heads blows the bitter storm:
The blessed natural loves, of life-supporting flame,
And those whose name is Wonder, which have no other name.

The skull is in my hand, the minute cup of bone,
And I remember her, the tame, the loving one,
Who came in at the window, and seemed to have a mind
More towards sorrowful man than to those of her own kind.

She came for a long time, but at length she grew old;
And on her death-day she came, so feeble and so bold;
And all day, as if knowing what the day would bring,
She waited by the window, with her head beneath her wing.

And I will keep the skull, for in the hollow here
Lodged the minute brain that had outgrown a fear;
Transcended an old terror, and found a new love,
And entered a strange life, a world it was not of.

Even so, dread God! even so, my Lord!
The fire is at my feet, and at my breast the sword:
And I must gather up my soul, and clap my wings, and flee
Into the heart of terror, to find myself in thee.

France fell to Hitler's Wehrmacht on June 14, 1940.

thomas randolph

On 6 Cambridge Maids bathing themselves by Queen's College, June 15, 1629

When bashfull Day-light now was gone,
And Night that hides a blush came on.
Six pretty Nymphs to wash away
The sweating of a summers-day,
In *Chams* fair streams did gently swim
And naked bathe each curious limbe.
O who had this blest sight but seen
Would think that they had *Cloelia's* been.
    A Scholler that a walk did take
(Perchance for meditation sake)
This better object chanc'd to finde,
Straight all things else were out of minde;
What better study in this life,
For *Practick* or *Contemplative?*
He thought, poor soul, what he had seen

Diana and her Nymphs had been,
And therefore thought in piteous fear
Acteons fortunes had been near.
Or that the water-Nymphs they were
Together met to sport them there.
And that to him such love they bore
As unto *Hilas* once before.

      What could he think but that his eye
Six Nymphs at once did there espie
Rise from the waves? Or that perchance
Fresh-water *Syrens* came to dance
Upon the stream with tongue and look
To tempt poor Schollers from their book?
He could not think they *Graces* were
Because their numbers doubled are.
Nor can he think they *Muses* be
Because (alas) there wanted three.

      I should have rather guest that there
Another brood of *Helens* were,
Begot by Jove upon the plains,
Hatch'd by some Leda of the swans.
The maids betrai'd were in a fright
And blusht, but 'twas not seen by night.
At last all by the bank did stand,
And he (kind heart) lent them his hand.
Where 'twas his blisse to feel all o're
Soft paps, smooth thighes, and some thing more.
But envious night hid from his eyes
The place where love and pleasure lies.

      Guesse lovers guesse, guesse you that dare
What then might be this Schollers prayer.
That he had been a Cat to spy,
Or had he now *Tiberius* eye.
Yet since his wishes were in vain
He helpt them d'on their clothes again,
Makes promise there should none be shent,
So with them to the Tavern went.
How they all night did sport and play
Pardon my *Muse*, I dare not say;
Guesse you that have a minde to know
Whether he were a fool or no.

alice meynell

The Sunderland Children

This was the surplus childhood, held as cheap!
    Not worth the care which shields
The lambs that are to stay, the corn to reap—
    The promise of the fields.

The nation guards her future. Fruits and grass
    And vegetable life
Are fostered league by league. But oh, the mass
    Of childhood over-rife!

O mass, O units! Oh, the separate story
    Planned for each breather of breath!
This futile young mankind, and transitory,
    Is left to stray to Death.

O promise, presage, menace! Upon these
    A certain seal is laid.
Unkept, unbroken, are the auguries
    These little children made.

For threat is bound with promise; and the nation
    Holds festival of regret
Over these dead—dead in their isolation—
    Wisely. She feared their threat.

On the 183 Sunderland children who lost their lives in a panic at the Victoria Hall, 16th June, 1883. [Note by Meynell]

peter didsbury

The Seventeenth of June

Back at tea-time. And a lacewing inside the house.
Lovely *Chrysopa*, on a towel smelling of rain.
Which shews patience enough to bask a while in our joy
(at its having been rescued from death by folding up)

then disappears at speed about its business.
I think I will thank Saint Briavel for this,
whose day it is,
and about whose life nothing, whatsoever, is known.

I encountered a fellow pluviophile earlier on.
The sudden secret handshake of our talk
I must confess has cheered me up no end.
There it incredibly was,
the telling me how in weather akin to this
his wife would opine him crazy,
his fancy to sleep among lumber in the shed.
Pass friend; and when you cease to exist
go straight to Heaven, up through a summer downpour,
but keeping dry all the while, as if there had never
been other ways to travel.

The day recounts itself backwards.
At the bus-stop this morning
I was thinking how simple it sometimes actually is
just to set things in motion,
to do as we've every One been done by, in fact.
I hoped that when the evening finally came, as it has,
I might find some words about English coastal parishes,
each with its beacon, spire, gallows,
ragstone tower or en-hillocked elm as landfall,
to be battered towards by crumster, cog and barque
through stillicidous arras of wrist-wraithing bone-racking sea-roke.

And here they are.
I wasn't quite sure what I wanted them for at the time
but now, in this silence, I bless their superfluity,
welling over the rounded rim of a day
of huge balneation, spargefaction wide,
the workings of grace made both pertinent and strange,
its conduits quick with all the sanctions of water.

john n. morris

To Those Who Share My Birthday 6.18.31

It is ours alone, this day,
Ours alone in our thousands.
By dozens the million
We love gather
In private celebration.

And always we record it,
This day special to us.
As shadow the happiness returns,
Every one of us
The center of that picture.

Some few of us will die
This day we all set out on.
They will leave us this day,
The circle closing
With idiot perfection.

Strangers, every day
We die, we leave us,
We leave us strangers.
How few we will become,
Alone in all our houses!

Let the engraving light
Record us, strangers—
As always it recorded
Us this happy day,
The past promising before us.

w. d. snodgrass

Manet: "The Execution of Emperor Maximilian"

"Aim well, muchachos: aim right here;" he pointed to his heart.
With face turned upward, he waited grave but calm.

Dear good God, we've blundered into some musical
    Comedy; here we have the girls' *corps de ballet*
Got up as legionnaires and shooting several
    Supernumeraries. These dainty backs display
No strain lifting up and steadying rifles twice
    The length of those we use. True; their aim's not quite right.
What difference, though; their uniforms look so nice;
    The sabers in their white holsters all gleam so bright;
Their hats and spats and dress gear trim and orderly.
    They've worked hours to crease their pants, to shine buttons for
An event which—if you're a soldier—ought to be
    The peak of your career: to shoot an emperor!
One's shown up late, though—of course; to one side, he stands
    Coolly inspecting his rifle. Who knows, though—he
Maybe just gets bored with politics. Still, his hands
    Have just cocked the fate of nations. Wait, now; his cap's
Red; he doesn't wear spats—is he a sergeant, set
    To render the *coup de grace*? His face alone shows
Dignity and calm; he, above all, seems real. Yet
    Whether he has a name or purpose, no one knows.

      A second volley was necessary for Maximilian who had asked to be
      shot in the chest so that his mother might see his face.

The scumbly, half-formed heads of these few peons peak
    Up over the background which is a flat rock wall.
One yawns, one leans on his elbows, one rests his cheek
    On his crossed arms, drowsing. The others, meantime, sprawl
Around every which way like idlers who've gone numb
    With heat and flies watching some would-be matadors.
They look like angels bored with one more martyrdom.
    This one's not yawning, though—he's yelling. Still, of course,
That could mean triumph, hate, outrage or just shock. Who
    Knows? It could well be that he's waving to somebody
He knows—or just wants us to know he's here. We *do*

Know him, after all: an old friend from Daumier's study
Of a mob rioting. So we can assume he
   Wants a revolt. Or. . . . wait; this face with the mantilla
And the fan—the classic Spanish temptress. What's she
   Doing here?—a high class lady straight out of Goya!
Meantime, along the wall, one hat's sneaking away
   At right, past our sergeant—or turned up late also.
One thing we *do* share with these peons—we can't say
   What they're doing here. This late, who will ever know?

> *On the spot where he died, the Hapsburgs—whose general downfall
> was prefigured in his—built a chapel to further his remembrance on
> earth and his forgiveness in heaven.*

As for the victims, they would scarcely seem worth mention—
   Stuck in a corner, their whole world washed with flat light,
Focusless, having no perspective or convention
   To lead us in the way we ought to turn our sight.
At the center where the Emperor ought to stand, just
   This blank space rifles cross; otherwise, shadows thrown
In all directions; you'd think every man here must
   Have his inner light, like Quakers, or his own
Outer darkness. As if each flag flew in some thwart
   Direction, feeling a different wind. All the same,
For Maximilian, all aim and the purpose stops short
   In this flat rock wall. Why speak of hints of cypress
Trees, shadowed lanes and cool vistas beyond the wall
   Far off at left? Out there, one white shape like a plaster
Bust drifts through the trees—a sort of neo-classical
   Ideal head floating, ghost-like, over the disaster.
Our hero stands as far from that as from this nameless
   Sergeant's real head, whose feet are well braced in the scene;
Untroubled, purposeless—he won't, for long, go aimless.
   He and stone walls are what men should not come between.

> *When Maximilian refused to believe the absurd claim that he had
> been elected by the peons, Napoleon threatened to crown some other
> candidate. That, of course, overcame all doubts.*

Still, for Maximilian, he whose widow soon went
   Mad with loss—or with some love disease he'd brought
Her from Brazil—this "Lord of all the Firmament"
   As she always called him—this high-flown head that thought
All life one grand staircase at whose top he might stand
   Bestowing his smile of infinite grace upon

The human beings at its base, cannot command
  The central spot in its own execution.
Or the surest brush-work! This head with its fine dreams
  It could unite, somehow, the Old World with the New,
Bind the Divine Rights of Hapsburgs with half-baked schemes
  And liberal sentiments, could link the True Church to
The freely divisive mind, seems half-way divorced
  From its own body. Perched on a puff of smoke,
It bobs the way a kid's balloon slues back and forth
  At the end of its string. And, as a last bad joke,
Flaunts this broad sombrero—the tasteless parody
  Of a halo that may be fitting to a passion
Undergone between two generals. So we see
  Even gods must keep their heads and take note of fashions.

> *It was as if some ne'er-do-well had finally found his true vocation:
> as martyr and sacrificial victim, he has seldom been surpassed.*

Still, for Maximilian, he stands here holding hands
  With these two who chose death with him. And that's about
All he held together. Now, even while he stands
  Showing us the wounds in their palms, we've got our doubts.
He's bleached out like some child's two-penny crucifixion;
  Even the eye wanders from that face where we see
Nothing of interest—not, surely, that firm conviction
  We demand. After all, there's *some* nobility
In this unknown sergeant. Or in this general
  At the rear, although he may seem hesitant to enter
The picture—as well he might. Wait, though; after all,
  Maximilian might well have yielded up the center.
It could be this one, back of the others. Or else him,
  In front, with legs spread, whose hand flaps up like a doll's,
The face nearly lost, yet twisting up in a dim
  Shudder of strain—or, say, pain?—as the rifleballs
Break in and his brain cells, the atoms of his mind
  Untie, all bonds dissolved they hurl free, first rats fleeing
The sinking vessel for some new faith, grasping, blind,
  And he, whoever he was, is all done with being.

> *1832: Birth, 6 July.*
> *1854: Naval administrator.*
> *1857: Viceroy to the Lombardo-Venetian Kingdom.*
> *1864: Emperor of Mexico.*
> *1867: Deposition; death, 19 June.*

rainer maria rilke

Turning Point

The road from intensity to greatness passes through sacrifice.
—Kassner

For a long time he attained it in looking.
Stars would fall to their knees
beneath his compelling vision.
Or as he looked on, kneeling,
his urgency's fragrance
tired out a god until
it smiled at him in its sleep.

Towers he would gaze at so
that they were terrified:
building them up again, suddenly, in an instant!
But how often the landscape,
overburdened by day,
came to rest in his silent awareness, at nightfall.

Animals trusted him, stepped
into his open look, grazing,
and the imprisoned lions
stared in as if into an incomprehensible freedom;
birds, as it felt them, flew headlong
through it; and flowers, as enormous
as they are to children, gazed back
into it, on and on.

And the rumor that there was someone
who knew how to look,
stirred those less
visible creatures:
stirred the women.

Looking how long!
For how long now, deeply deprived,
beseeching in the depths of his glance?

When he, whose vocation was Waiting, sat far from home—
the hotel's distracted unnoticing bedroom

moody around him, and in the avoided mirror
once more the room, and later
from the tormenting bed
once more:
then in the air the voices
discussed, beyond comprehension,
his heart, which could still be felt;
debated what through the painfully buried body
could somehow be felt—his heart;
debated and passed their judgment:
that it did not have love.

(And denied him further communion.)

For there is a boundary to looking.
And the world that is looked at so deeply
wants to flourish in love.

Work of the eyes is done, now
go and do heart-work
on all the images imprisoned within you; for you
overpowered them: but even now you don't know them.
Learn, inner man, to look on your inner woman,
the one attained from a thousand
natures, the merely attained but
not yet beloved form.

Trans. Stephen Mitchell

In a letter to Lou Andreas-Salome dated June 20, 1914, Rilke wrote: "Lou, dear, here is a strange poem, written this morning, which I am sending you right away because I involuntarily called it 'Turning-point,' because it describes the turning-point which no doubt must come if I am to stay alive."

rudyard kipling

What the People Said

Queen Victoria's Jubilee, June 21st, 1887

By the well, where the bullocks go
Silent and blind and slow—
By the field, where the young corn dies
In the face of the sultry skies,
They have heard, as the dull Earth hears
The voice of the wind of an hour,
The sound of the Great Queen's voice—
"My God hath given me years,
"Hath granted dominion and power:
"And I bid you, O Land, rejoice."

And the Ploughman settles the share
More deep in the grudging clod;
For he saith:—"The wheat is my care,
"And the rest is the will of God.
"He sent the Mahratta spear
"As He sendeth the rain,
"And the *Mlech*, in the fated year,
"Broke the spear in twain,
"And was broken in turn. Who knows
"How our Lords make strife?
"It is good that the young wheat grows,
"For the bread is Life."

Then, far and near, in the twilight drew,
Hissed up to the scornful dark
Great serpents, blazing, of red and blue,
That rose and faded, and rose anew,
That the Land might wonder and mark.
"To-day is a day of days," they said,
"Make merry, O People, all!"
And the Ploughman listened and bowed his head.
"To-day and to-morrow God's will," he said,
As he trimmed the lamps on the wall.

"He sendeth us years that are good,
"As He sendeth the dearth.
"He giveth to each man his food,
"Or Her food to the Earth.
"Our Kings and our Queens are afar—
"On their peoples be peace—
"God bringeth the rain to the Bar,
"That our cattle increase."

And the Ploughman settled the share
More deep in the sun-dried clod:—
"Mogul, Mahratta, and *Mlech* from the North,
"And White Queen over the Seas—
"God raiseth them up and driveth them forth
"As the dust of the ploughshare flies in the breeze;
"But the wheat and the cattle are all my care,
"And the rest is the will of God."

Mlech *is the foreigner.* *[Note by Kipling]*

JUNE 22

martha mcferren

June 22

We saw it in the channel
Midsummer Day, leaving Mull
for Iona, St. Columba's island,
where he landed after that
prayerbook fracas in Ireland.
For some good reason
the water was completely in
stripes:
      aquamarine and azure
plus a warp of turquoise, though
the turquoise did not count
for much.
      I'm told most men
will never see these colors.
They won't admit the names.

You can't see what you cannot say
and men will not say *turquoise*,
azure, and *aquamarine*.
                    Even
Columba, a saint, and wanting
his own way like every saint,
might never have seen those
colors like I said them.
                    So
what's unnatural, the water
or the words? Or is the miracle
having two sexes?
                    I asked my
husband, "Do you see the stripes?
There, in the water." Of course
he saw them.
                    "What colors are
they, honey?" "They're all blue."

JUNE 23

howard nemerov

BOOM!

SEES BOOM IN RELIGION, TOO

*Atlantic City, June 23, 1957 (AP).—President Eisenhower's pastor said tonight
that Americans are living in a period of "unprecedented religious activity"
caused partially by paid vacations, the eight-hour day and modern conveniences.*

*"These fruits of material progress," said the Rev. Edward L. R. Elson of the
National Presbyterian Church, Washington, "have provided the leisure, the
energy, and the means for a level of human and spiritual values never before
reached."*

Here at the Vespasian-Carlton, it's just one
religious activity after another; the sky
is constantly being crossed by cruciform
airplanes, in which nobody disbelieves
for a second, and the tide, the tide
of spiritual progress and prosperity

miraculously keeps rising, to a level
never before attained. The churches are full,
the beaches are full, and the filling-stations
are full, God's great ocean is full
of paid vacationers praying an eight-hour day
to the human and spiritual values, the fruits,
the leisure, the energy, and the means, Lord,
the means for the level, the unprecedented level,
and the modern conveniences, which also are full.
Never before, O Lord, have the prayers and praises
from belfry and phonebooth, from ballpark and barbecue
the sacrifices, so endlessly ascended.

It was not thus when Job in Palestine
sat in the dust and cried, cried bitterly;
when Damien kissed the lepers on their wounds
it was not thus; it was not thus
when Francis worked a fourteen-hour day
strictly for the birds; when Dante took
a week's vacation without pay and it rained
part of the time, O Lord, it was not thus.

But now the gears mesh and the tires burn
and the ice chatters in the shaker and the priest
in the pulpit, and Thy name, O Lord,
is kept before the public, while the fruits
ripen and religion booms and the level rises
and every modern convenience runneth over,
that it may never be with us as it hath been
with Athens and Karnak and Nagasaki,
nor Thy sun for one instant refrain from shining
on the rainbow Buick by the breezeway
or the Chris Craft with the uplift life raft;
that we may continue to be the just folks we are,
plain people with ordinary superliners and
disposable diaperliners, people of the stop'n'shop
'n'pray as you go, of hotel, motel, boatel,
the humble pilgrims of no deposit no return
and please adjust Thy clothing, who will give to Thee,
if Thee will keep us going, our annual
Miss Universe, for Thy Name's Sake, Amen.

john frederick nims

Spanish Ballad

¿Dó los mis amores, dó los?
¿Dó los andaré a buscar?

Rose and went a-roving, mother,
On the morning of St. John
Rose and saw a lass a-laundering
On the ocean sands alone.
Lone she wrings and lone she rinses,
Lone extends them on a thorn,
All the while the clothes are sunning,
Sings a solitary song:

"Where's my darling, where, I wonder?
How to wander where he's gone?"

Up the ocean, down the ocean,
Still the girl goes singing on.
With a gold comb in her fingers
For her tresses ocean-blown.
"You, you sailor, tell me truly,
True as heaven steer you home,
Have you seen him pass, my darling,
Seen him faring on the foam?"

The feast of St. John is celebrated on June 24.

walt whitman

From Far Dakota's Cañons

June 25, 1876.

From far Dakota's cañons,
Lands of the wild ravine, the dusky Sioux, the lonesome
   stretch, the silence,
Haply to-day a mournful wail, haply a trumpet-note for heroes.

The battle-bulletin,
The Indian ambuscade, the craft, the fatal environment,
The cavalry companies fighting to the last in sternest heroism,
In the midst of their little circle, with their slaughter'd
   horses for breastworks,
The fall of Custer and all his officers and men.

Continues yet the old, old legend of our race,
The loftiest of life upheld by death,
The ancient banner perfectly maintain'd,
O lesson opportune, O how I welcome thee!

As sitting in dark days,
Lone, sulky, through the time's thick murk looking in vain
   for light, for hope,
From unsuspected parts a fierce and momentary proof,
(The sun there at the centre though conceal'd,
Electric life forever at the centre,)
Breaks forth a lightning flash.

Thou of the tawny flowing hair in battle,
I erewhile saw, with erect head, pressing ever in front,
   bearing a bright sword in thy hand,
Now ending well in death the splendid fever of thy deeds,
(I bring no dirge for it or thee, I bring a glad triumphal sonnet,)
Desperate and glorious, aye in defeat most desperate, most glorious,
After thy many battles in which never yielding up a gun or a color,
Leaving behind thee a memory sweet to soldiers,
Thou yieldest up thyself.

dara wier

Just the facts, ma'am

If it wasn't Arthur Godfrey,
it was his ukelele, it was Ricky
berating Lucy, it was counting
with Jack Benny.

It's June 26, 1956 and the family's waiting.
It's the twosome, Dean Martin and Jerry,
marking their last appearance,
divided in routine ascension.

Liberace dallies his baby grand,
his falcon prances his wrist.
Ted Mack meters the applause.
Durante claps everyone a kiss.

This is your Life, but it isn't.
Ernie watches for money.
Lucille eyes Kathryn Murray.
Wanda wants Perry.
Midge swoons in envy.

JUNE 27

jeanne murray walker

Ravenna, June 27, 1981: Verdi's *Macbeth*

—for Larry and Juanita Brook

Nothing exactly like this has ever happened before.
We have come here to recall the story that never changes,
we, who are going to die, who have already paid
with the small change of the lucky
to see how Macduff lost all his pretty ones,
how Macbeth then lost himself.

Three women stroll past. One wears a violet toga
which hangs like wisteria to her knees.
They go across the grass to the little table
laid with a red-checked cloth and white bone china.
Nails shiny as pebbles, they spread paté on French bread.
As though she had just thought of how to make her throat
                                    beautiful,
one woman throws back her head and laughs.
The one sitting on the red plaid blanket picks up a plum.
Her silver teeth flash. Fixed to the trunks of giant oaks,
spotlights begin to blink on, all over the park,
and the great foamy heads of trees
float over us like unearthly props.
Back and forth people glide in pairs, as though miraculously
they desired to go where the script had planned
for them to be. A father steers his daughter by,
hand on her neck. Lovers in khaki shorts meander,
their hands in one another's pockets.
Another pair of lovers ambles without touching.
Three men are joking, their slang sings clear
as the smell of apples beside the little fountain,
where a bronze boy dances, kicking up skirts of water.
A slender woman wearing little sandals waves to someone
and reaches to accept a glass of wine.
The others, in uniforms which are new for the last time,
grow tense, lean forward, inhaling purple air.
Suddenly the voice of Sherrill Milnes plunges
like a dagger, stabbing the dark again and again.
Beneath the trees, before we can compose ourselves,
the woman in the toga locks her teeth midbite,
the men's mouths fall, the lovers link their arms too late.
The music comes for us, murderous and beautiful.

elizabeth barrett browning

Crowned and Wedded

I.

When last before her people's face her own fair face she bent,
Within the meek projection of that shade she was content
To erase the child-smile from her lips, which seemed as if it might
Be still kept holy from the world to childhood still in sight—
To erase it with a solemn vow, a princely vow—to rule;
A priestly vow—to rule by grace of God the pitiful;
A very godlike vow—to rule in right and righteousness
And with the law and for the land—so God the vower bless!

II.

The minister was alight that day, but not with fire, I ween,
And long-drawn glitterings swept adown that mighty aisle'd scene;
The priests stood stoled in their pomp, the sworded chiefs in theirs,
And so, the collared knights, and so, the civil ministers,
And so, the waiting lords and dames, and little pages best
At holding trains, and legates so, from countries east and west;
So, alien princes, native peers, and high-born ladies bright,
Along whose brows the Queen's, now crowned, flashed coronets to light;
And so, the people at the gates with priestly hands on high
Which bring the first anointing to all legal majesty;
And so the DEAD, who lie in rows beneath the minister floor
There verily an awful state maintaining ever more:
The statesman whose clean palm will kiss no bribe whate'er it be,
The courtier who for no fair queen will rise up to his knee,
The court-dame who for no court-tire will leave her shroud behind,
The laureate who no courtlier rhyme than "dust to dust" can find,
The kings and queens who having made that vow and worn that crown,
Descended unto lower thrones and darker, deep adown:
Dieu et mon droit—what is't to them? what meaning can it have?—
The King of kings, the right of death—God's judgment and the grave.
And when betwixt the quick and dead the young fair queen had vowed,
The living shouted "May she live! Victoria, live!" aloud:
And as the loyal shouts went up, true spirits prayed between,
"The blessings happy monarchs have be thine, O crowned queen!"

. . .

The coronation of Queen Victoria occurred on June 28, 1838.

rodney pybus

t. Peter's Day 1839

r below the high-slung global sun
e peasants heaved
d grumbled in the corn: pinioned
end of June heat.
rts droned
oss fields:
        flies
nded the stench of manure.

he flogged his high-jawed, lathered
rses through the village,
r peasants jumped the Doctor—

ld from behind by
ear of a man
        wind
ked by a hand as heavy
a thigh of lead;
e trio rushed & beat
testicles
he fainted.

ey humped his sacked body
ough cart-rucked streets.
involved susurrus of flies
ised and clustered in the air;
ayed him, supine.

Through forced, forbidding jaws
and black indented teeth
they sank a quart of spirit; neat
enough to skin
the stomach of an ox:
        broke open
the mouth
to still the silent shudders
with rough-ripped shirt-tail—
ambiguous insult round
the swelling tongue.

The body jumped
ejaculating shock
epileptic marionette
with mulberry bruises bare,
livid parts
no longer private

to the summoned priest:
witness of Fyodor's dead
decaying father,
ruler of Darovoye
and the acres that lay around it.
Let me tell you
that this weekend Sunday
morning in the country

e *Feast of Sts. Peter and Paul is celebrated on June 29.*

james schuyler

June 30, 1974

fills my soul
with tranquil joy:
the dunes beyond
the pond beyond
the humps of bayberry—
my favorite
shrub (today,
at least)—are
silent as a mountain
range: such a
subtle profile
against a sky that
goes from dawn
to blue. The roses
stir, the grapevine
at one end of the deck
shakes and turns
its youngest leaves
so they show pale
and flower-like.
A redwing blackbird
pecks at the grass;
another perches on a bush.
Another way, a millionaire's
white chateau turns
its flank to catch
the risen sun. No
other houses, except
this charming one,
alive with paintings,
plants and quiet.
I haven't said
a word. I like
to be alone
with friends. To get up
to this morning view
and eat poached eggs
and extra toast with

Tiptree Gooseberry Preserve
(green)—and coffee,
milk, no sugar. Jane
said she heard
the freeze-dried kind
is healthier when
we went shopping
yesterday and she
and John bought
crude blue Persian plates.
How can coffee be
healthful? I mused
as sunny wind
streamed in the car
window-driving home.
Home! How lucky to
have one, how arduous
to make this scene
of beauty for
your family and
friends. Friends!
How we must have
sounded, gossiping at
the dinner table
last night. Why, *that*
dinner table is
this breakfast table:
"The boy in trousers
is not the same boy
in no trousers," who
said? Discontinuity
in all we see and are:
the same, yet change,
change, change. "Inez,
it's good to see you."
Here comes the cat, sedate,
that killed and brought
a goldfinch yesterday.

like to go out
a swim but
a little cool
that. Enough to
here drinking coffee,
ting, watching the clear
day ripen (such
a rainy June we had)
while Jane and Joe
sleep in their room
and John in his. I
think I'll make more toast.

July

bin ramke

Entropy

> *Some of the evil of my tale*
> *may have been inherent in our*
> *circumstances.*
> —T. E. Lawrence

1

Vast petals of poppy burn
a brilliant hole in landscape:
the land lies riddled with heat.
The murders our evening paper tells
are not those we each commit
under this stress of heat.
Among our flowers butterflies
tatter their flimsy lives. Pray
for the drowning city,
but for the city consumed by heat
listen to the scatter
of its dry seed.

2

The formidable memory of birds
brings them back by millions
each summer. For two days
the sky darkens beneath their wings,
Their call is that faint language
a citizen barely recalls:
a thin, scattered remembrance
of an age of flight.

And we become a city of lizards
flat against the burning rocks
hanging our shriveled sex in bundles
like garlic from the rafters,
an amulet against dark dangers.
We fear what comes with the cool of evening,
we are terrified of night.

3
And we fear such things as great success
or obvious failure. We know ourselves.
Each house in our terrible town has a garden,
a wall, and a secret. We breed garish flowers
to tend with cruel care.
We are small and all very much alike.

In our city if you need a place to sleep
knock on any door. If it opens, the smell
of fear will drive you back into the street.

Let us consider that our fear is a large black bird—
this is hypothesis—and this bird's solemn
wing beat marks a cycle of months, perhaps years.
In our beds at night we breathe longer breaths
to keep time with our peculiar fate.
We go slowly through the day, we try to be part
of what we do not understand. I have kept
our secret but told you of our fear.

4
Wrapped in yourself speak
to us as a prophet should, fresh
from the desert. Tell us the story
of stones and small immortal snakes,
the story of long effulgent time.

5
On the first of July, 1961, Louis-Ferdinand Celine
spoke in our Municipal Auditorium. The speech
was called "Life Comes to You in the Morning."
I shall not be great in my own language, he said,
I am one who grows in translation.
There was much applause, then a clown show followed.

The speech lasted twelve hours. We heard
the purr of bees, the brittle crash of fountains,
voices in the distance rising and falling
like flocks of birds. We saw the spittle
dry on his lips. He spoke
one long single breath, and at the end
only I was left to hear.

I alone applauded, till my hands bled;
I threw the poppies to his feet;
I alone saw the clowns
perform unspeakable acts
upon each other.
Later, the speaker and the clowns gone,
I watched the spiders
weave stars in the rafters.

6
A man drives his car in the desert.
He is alone. Our city lights the sky
in a small corner of his horizon.
Soon he will sleep, or die, and dream
of acres and acres of poppies
with butterflies skimming their surface
and a few magnificent spiders
drifting on threads,
riding the waves of heat.

JULY 2

 luke 1:36–55

The Visitation

And Mary arose in those days, and went into the hill country with haste,
   into a city of Juda;
And entered into the house of Zacharias, and saluted Elisabeth.
And it came to pass, that, when Elisabeth heard the salutation of Mary,
   the babe leaped in her womb; and Elisabeth was filled with the
   Holy Ghost:
And she spake out with a loud voice, and said, Blessed art thou among
   women, and blessed is the fruit of thy womb. And whence is this to
   me, that the mother of my Lord should come to me?
For, lo, as soon as the voice of thy salutation sounded in mine ears, the
   babe leaped in my womb for joy.

And blessed is she that believed: for there shall be a performance of
   those things which were told her from the Lord.
And Mary said, My soul doth magnify the Lord,
And my spirit hath rejoiced in God my Saviour.
For he hath regarded the low estate of his handmaiden: for, behold, from
   henceforth all generations shall call me blessed.
For he that is mighty hath done to me great things; and holy is his
   name.
And his mercy is on them that fear him from generation to generation.
He hath shewed strength with his arm; he hath scattered the proud in
   the imagination of their hearts.
He hath put down the mighty from their seats, and exalted them of low
   degree.
He hath filled the hungry with good things; and the rich he hath sent
   empty away.
He hath helpen his servant Israel, in remembrance of his mercy,
As he spake to our fathers, to Abraham, and to his seed forever.

The Feast of the Visitation is celebrated on July 2.

francesco petrarch

Sonnet CCLXIX

> *A lament for the deaths of Laura and Cardinal Giovanni Colonna*
> *(d. 3 July 1348)*

Broken is the high column and the green laurel
   Which gave shade to my tired thoughts;
   I have lost what I cannot hope to recover
   From north to south or Indian to Moorish sea.
You've taken from me, Death, my double treasure
   That made me live in joy and proudly walk;
   No land or empire can bring them back,
   Nor oriental gems nor loads of gold.

But, if this is destiny's decision,
    What else can I do but bear a heavy soul,
    Forever tearful eyes and a bowed head?
Oh, our life, so beautiful in distant view,
    How easily in one morning we can lose
    What in long years we acquired with great pain.

Trans. Ronald Bottrall

J U L Y 4

anonymous

The Cuckoo

Oh, the cuckoo, she's a pretty bird,
And she warbles as she flies.
And she never hollers "Cuckoo"
'Til the fourth day of July.

I will build me a log cabin
In the mountains, so high,
So I can see my Willie,
As he goes riding by.

Oh, the cuckoo, she's a pretty bird,
And she warbles as she flies.
And she never hollers "Cuckoo"
'Til the fourth day of July.

Jack of diamonds, jack of diamonds,
I've known you, of old.
You have robbed my poor pocket
Of its silver and its gold.

Oh, the cuckoo, she's a pretty bird,
And she warbles as she flies.
And she never hollers "Cuckoo"
'Til the fourth day of July.

octavio paz and charles tomlinson

Day

> *Sweet day, so cool, so calm, so bright,*
> *The bridall of the earth and skie.*
> —George Herbert

Copious tree each day. This one
(July the fifth) grows hour by hour
invisible: a tree obliterated
to be freighted down with future leaves.

Coming to terms with day—light, water, stone—
our words extend a world of objects
that remains itself: the new leaves
gladden us, but for no motive of their own—

merely to be vegetable exclamations,
onomatopoeia of celebration
of the yearly chemical resurrection,

where evening already stains the finished page
and shadow absorbing shadow, day
is going down in fire, in foliage.

patricia beer

Return to Sedgemoor

"Battle of Sedgemoor. Come and bring your friends."
And so they have I see. Dragging me down
Into this pageant of what was once real.
I died here but I cannot now recall
Which side I fought on. And until today—
Comfortable in warm weather hoping something,
Tetchy in winter dreading everything—

I've been content simply to know I was
Once here. How shocking the oblivion
Of coming back to sight and sound, to north
And south, to right and wrong, at a complete loss.

The cows are gazing at the popping cannon.
What roars they must have heard to go on chewing
At noise that shot the meat out of our mouths.
I seem to see the guns for the first time,
Plump little pigs. I hear a voice explaining
That they were known as "Hot Lips" and "Sweet Lips."
I swear we never called them anything
Like that. I first made love on a battlefield,
I remember—though not which or who—
And realized there was a difference
Between love and war: I don't remember what.

Sedgemoor took place at night, and it's enough
To make a ghost laugh in the sun to see
These fluent creatures dash about regardless
While we, with elbows, knees and arse and chin
Stuck out at angles, had to feel our way.
These willow trees were low and strong to hang
Men in the morning light—as they are doing
Now—but in the dark they merely gave
Us bloody noses. Memory does not return
Like experience, more like imagination:
How it would have been if, how it must.

"The last battle to be fought on English soil"
The voice concludes. No riots, no pretenders
Or invaders in what must be years?
No, I am a ghost and do not wish
To understand the present. Let me
Concentrate on getting my life back.
My memory is like a severed muscle
And there's no friend or foe or animal
To recognize me. On the night I died
King's men and rebels all hastened away
As if some moon came up to light them home.

The Battle of Sedgemoor was fought on July 6, 1685.

elizabeth spires

Letters to the Sea

Swimming at Midnight 7.7.77

Moonlight chisels your face into marble skin.
Arm over arm, we swim,
carrying old virtues like half-drowned children.
You speak your desire, scattering
the moon's reflection:
bright tin foil floating on water.
I touch your chest. Phosphor
flares inside you like a match.

We turn on touch, and touching,
turn into something else.
Stars chant incantations above our heads.
There's my dark twin, Gemini,
slicing the sky into lucky number sevens.
You're Pisces—half-man,
half-fish, you swim outside time's net
and take me along for the ride.

We fall asleep at dawn, two
breaths blending into one.
Now birds begin the cries that people waking
call bird song.

william meredith

Trelawny's Dream

*Edward John Trelawny, who is imagined to speak the following
lines in his late middle age, survived his friend Shelley by almost
sixty years. Trelawny had intended to convoy the poet and Edward
Williams (and a cabin-boy Charles Vivian) when they sailed the
Ariel out of Leghorn into the storm that drowned them, but Lord
Byron's yacht, which he was commanding, was detained at the last
minute by port authorities. [Note by Meredith]*

The dark illumination of a storm
and water-noise, chuckling along the hull
as the craft runs tight before it.
Sometimes Shelley's laughter wakes me here,
unafraid, as he was the day he dove
into water for the first time, a wooded pool
on the Arno, and lay like a conger eel
on the bottom—"where truth lies," he said—
until I hauled him up.

But oftener the dream insists on all,
insists on retelling all.
                         Ned Williams is the first
to see the peril of the squall. His shout
to lower sail scares the deck-boy wide-eyed
and cuts off Shelley's watery merriment.
The big wind strokes the cat-coat like a kitten.
Riding the slate-gray hillocks, she is dragged
by the jib Ned Williams leaves to keep her head.
The kitten knows the wind is a madman's hand
and the bay a madman's lap.
As she scuds helpless, only the cockney boy
Charles Vivian and I, a dreamer and a child,
see the felucca loom abeam. Her wet lateen
ballooning in the squall, she cuts across
wind and seas in a wild tack, she is on us.
The beaked prow wrenches the little cabin
from the deck, tosses the poet slowly to the air—
he pockets his book, he waves to me and smiles—

then to his opposite element,
light going into darkness, gold into lead.
The felucca veers and passes, a glimpse of a face
sly with horror on her deck. I watch our brave
sailor boy stifle his cry of knowledge
as the boat takes fatal water, then Ned's stricken face,
scanning the basalt waves
for what will never be seen again except in dreams.

All this was a long time ago, I remember.
None of them was drowned except me
whom a commotion of years washes over.
They hail me from the dream, they call an old man
to come aboard, these youths on an azure bay.
The waters may keep the dead, as the earth may,
and fire and air. But dream is my element.
Though I am still a strong swimmer
I can feel this channel widen as I swim.

Shelley's cat-boat was struck and sunk on July 8, 1822.

john hollander

The Ninth of July

In 1939 the skylark had nothing to say to me
As the June sunset splashed rose light on the broad sidewalks
And prophesied no war after the end of that August;
Only, midway between playing ball in Manhattan and Poland
I turned in my sleep on Long Island, groped in the dark of July,
And found my pillow at last down at the foot of my bed.
Through the window near her bed, brakes gasped on Avenue B
In 1952; her blonde crotch shadowed and silent
Astonished us both, and the iced gunpowder tea grew warm,
Till the last hollow crust of icecube cracked to its death in the glass.
The tea was hot on the cold hilltop in the moonlight
While a buck thrashed through the gray ghosts of burnt-out trees
And Thomas whispered of the S.S. from inside his sleeping-bag.
Someone else told a tale of the man who was cured of a hurt by the
    bears.

241

The bathtub drain in the old Elberon house gucked and snorted
When the shadows of graying maples fell across the lawn:
The brown teddybear was a mild comfort because of his silence,
And I gazed at the porthole ring made by the windowshade
String, hanging silently, seeing a head and shoulders emerge
From the burning *Morro Castle* I'd seen that afternoon.
The rock cried out "I'm burning, too" as the drying heat
Entered its phase of noon over the steep concrete
Walls along Denver's excuse for a river: we read of remote
Bermudas, and gleaming Neal spat out over the parapet.
In the evening in Deal my b.b. rifle shattered a milkbottle
While the rhododendrons burned in the fading light. The tiny
Shot-sized hole in the bathhouse revealed the identical twats
Of the twins from over the hill. From over the hill on the other
Side of the lake a dark cloud turretted over the sunset;
Another lake sank to darkness on the other side of the hill,
Lake echoing lake in diminishing pools of reflection.
A trumpet blew Taps. While the drummer's foot boomed on the
    grandstand
The furriers' wives by the pool seemed to ignore the accordion
Playing "Long Ago and Far Away." None of the alewives
Rose to our nightcrawlers, wiggling on the other side of the mirror.
She was furrier under the darkness of all the blanketing heat
Than I'd thought to find her, and the bathroom mirror flashed
White with the gleam of a car on seventy-second street.
We lay there just having died; the two of us, vision and flesh,
Contraction and dream, came apart, while the fan on the windowsill
Blew a thin breeze of self between maker and muse, dividing
Fusing of firework, love's old explosion and outburst of voice.
This is the time most real: for unreeling time there are no
Moments, there are no points, but only the lines of memory
Streaking across the black film of the mind's night.
But here in the darkness between two great explosions of light,
Midway between the fourth of July and the fourteenth,
Suspended somewhere in summer between the ceremonies
Remembered from childhood and the historical conflagrations
Imagined in sad, learned youth—somewhere there always hangs
The American moment.
                   Burning, restless, between the deed
And the dream is the life remembered: the sparks of Concord were mine
As I lit a cherry-bomb once in a glow of myth
And hurled it over the hedge. The complexities of the Terror
Were mine as my poring eyes got burned in the fury of Europe
Discovered in nineteen forty-two. On the ninth of July

I have been most alive; world and I, making each other
As always, make fewer mistakes.
                              The gibbous, historical moon
Records our nights with an eye neither narrowed against the brightness
Of nature, nor widened with awe at the clouds of the life of the mind.
Crescent and full, knowledge and touch commingled here
On this dark bed, window flung wide to the cry of the city night,
We lie still, making the poem of the world that emerges from shadows.

Doing and then having done is having ruled and commanded
A world, a self, a poem, a heartbeat in the moonlight.

To imagine a language means to imagine a form of life.

anne bradstreet

Here follows some verses upon the burning of our House, July 10th, 1666. Copyed out of a loose Paper

In silent night when rest I took,
For sorrow neer I did not look
I waken'd was with thundring nois
And Piteous shreiks of dreadfull voice.
That fearfull sound of fire and fire,
Let no man know is my Desire.

I starting up, the light did spye,
And to my God my heart did cry
To strengthen me in my Distresse
And not to leave me succourlesse.
Then coming out beheld a space,
The flame consume my dwelling place.

And, when I could no longer look,
I blest his Name that gave and took,
That layd my goods now in the dust:
Yea so it was, and so 'twas just.
It was his own: it was not mine;
Far be it that I should repine.

He might of All justly bereft,
But yet sufficient for us left.
When by the Ruines oft I past,
My sorrowing eyes aside did cast,
And here and there the places spye
Where oft I sate, and long did lye.

Here stood that Trunk, and there that chest;
There lay that store I counted best:
My pleasant things in ashes lye,
And them behold no more shall I.
Under thy roof no guest shall sitt,
Nor at thy Table eat a bitt.

No pleasant tale shall 'ere be told,
Nor things recounted done of old.
No Candle 'ere shall shine in Thee,
Nor bridegroom's voice 'ere heard shall bee.
In silence ever shalt thou lye;
Adieu, Adieu; All's vanity.

Then streight I 'gin my heart to chide,
And did thy wealth on earth abide?
Didst fix thy hope on mouldring dust,
The arm of flesh didst make thy trust?
Raise up thy thoughts above the skye
That dunghill mists away may flie.

Thou hast an house on high erect,
Fram'd by that mighty Architect,
With glory richly furnished,

Stands permanent though this bee fled.
It's purchased, and paid for too
By him who hath enough to doe.

A Prise so vast as is unknown,
Yet, by his Gift, is made thine own.
Ther's wealth enough, I need no more;
Farewell my Pelf, farewell my Store.
The world no longer let me Love,
My hope and Treasure lyes Above.

JULY 11

   sir john suckling

A Ballad Upon a Wedding

I tell thee, Dick, where I have been;
Where I the rarest things have seen,
  Oh, things without compare!
Such sights again cannot be found
In any place on English ground,
  Be it at wake or fair.

At Charing Cross, hard by the way
Where we, thou know'st, do sell our hay,
  There is a house with stairs;
And there did I see coming down
Such folk as are not in our town,
  Forty at least, in pairs.

Amongst the rest, one pest'lent fine
(His beard no bigger though than thine)
  Walk'd on before the rest:
Our landlord looks like nothing to him;
The King (God bless him!), 'twould undo
  him,
  Should he go still so dress'd.

At course-a-park, without all doubt,
He should have first been taken out
  By all the maids i' th' town,

Though lusty Roger there had been,
Or little George upon the Green,
  Or Vincent of the Crown.

But wot you what? the youth was going
To make an end of all his wooing;
  The parson for him stay'd:
Yet by his leave, for all his haste,
He did not so much wish all past,
  Perchance, as did the maid.

The maid—and thereby hangs a tale;
For such a maid no Whitsun-ale
  Could ever yet produce:
No grape that's kindly ripe could be
So round, so plump, so soft as she,
  Nor half so full of juice.

Her finger was so small, the ring
Would not stay on which they did bring,
  It was too wide a peck;
And to say truth (for out it must)
It look'd like the great collar (just)
  About our young colt's neck.

Her feet beneath her petticoat
Like little mice stole in and out,
    As if they fear'd the light;
But oh! she dances such a way,
No sun upon an Easter day
    Is half so fine a sight.

He would have kiss'd her once or twice,
But she would not, she was so nice,
    She would not do 't in sight;
And then she look'd as who should say,
I will do what I list to-day,
    And you shall do 't at night.

Her cheeks so rare a white was on,
No daisy makes comparison,
    (Who sees them is undone);
For streaks of red were mingled there,
Such as are on a Kather'ne pear
    (The side that's next the sun).

Her lips were red, and one was thin
Compar'd to that was next her chin—
    Some bee had stung it newly;
But, Dick, her eyes so guard her face,
Durst no more upon them gaze
    Than on the sun in July.

Her mouth so small, when she does speak,
Thou'dst swear her teeth her words did
        break,
    That they might passage get;
But she so handled still the matter
They came as good as ours, or better
    And are not spent a whit.

If wishing should be any sin,
The parson himself had guilty bin,
    She look'd that day so purely;
And did the youth so oft the feat
At night, as some did in conceit,
    It would have spoil'd him surely.

Passion o' me! how I run on!
There's that would be thought upon,
    I trow, besides the bride:
The business of the kitchen's great,
For it is fit that men should eat;
    Nor was it there deni'd.

Just in the nick the cook knock'd thrice,
And all the waiters in a trice
    His summons did obey;
Each serving-man, with dish in hand,
March'd boldly up, like our train'd band,
    Presented, and away.

When all the meat was on the table,
What man of knife or teeth was able
    To stay to be entreated?
And this the very reason was
Before the parson could say grace
    The company was seated.

Now hats fly off, and youths carouse;
Healths first go round, and then the house,
    The bride's came thick and thick;
And when 'twas nam'd another's health,
Perhaps he made it hers by stealth:
    (And who could help it, Dick?)

O' th' sudden up they rise and dance;
Then sit again, and sigh, and glance;
    Then dance again and kiss:
Thus several ways the time did pass,
Whilst ev'ry woman wish'd her place,
    And ev'ry man wish'd his.

By this time all were stol'n aside
To counsel and undress the bride;
    But that he must not know:
But yet 'twas thought he guess'd her mind,
And did not mean to stay behind
    Above an hour or so.

When in he came, Dick, there she lay
Like new-fall'n snow melting away,

('Twas time, I trow, to part);
Kisses were now the only stay,
Which soon she gave, as who would say,
    God b'w'y', with all my heart.

But, just as Heav'ns would have, to cross it,
In came the bridesmaids with the posset:
    The bridegroom eat in spite;
For had he left the women to 't,

It would have cost two hours to do 't,
    Which were too much that night.

At length the candle's out, and now
All that they had not done they do:
    What that is, who can tell?
But I believe it was no more
Than thou and I have done before
    With Bridget and with Nell.

The marriage of John Lovelace and Anne Wentworth was celebrated on July 11, 1638.

JULY 12

james reaney

Orange Lilies

On the twelfth day of July
King William will ride by
    On a white horse
    On a white charger
King William and Queen Mary
    He bears an orange lily
    In his hand
    (He in front
    And she behind,
    On a white horse
    On a white charger)
And so does she
On a white horse.

They're riding to see
And to jump the Boyne
    With a white horse
    In their groin

On the twelfth day of July
King William will ride by
    With a white horse
King William with Queen Mary.

charles tomlinson

Charlotte Corday

O Vertu! le poignard, seul espoir de la terre,
Estton arme sacrée. . . .
—Chénier

Courteously self-assured, although alone,
With voice and features that could do no hurt,
Why should she not enter? They let in
A girl whose reading made a heroine—
Her book was Plutarch, her republic Rome:
Home was where she sought her tyrant out.

The towelled head next, the huge batrachian mouth:
There was a mildness in him, even. He
Had never been a woman's enemy,
And time and sickness turned his stomach now
From random execution. All the same,
He moved aside to write her victims down,
And when she approached, it was to kill she came.

She struck him from above. One thrust. Her whole
Intent and innocence directing it
To breach through flesh and enter where it must,
It seemed a blow that rose up from within:
Tinville* reduced it all to expertise:
—What, would you make of me a hired assassin?

—What did you find to hate in him?—His crimes
Every reply was temperate save one
And that was human when all's said and done:
The deposition, read to those who sit
In judgement on her, "What has she to say?"
"Nothing, except that I succeeded in it."

—You think that you have killed all Marats off?
—I think perhaps such men are now afraid.
The blade hung in its grooves. How should she know
The Terror still to come, as she was led

*Fouquirer Tinville was the public prosecutor.

Red-smocked from gaol out into evening's red?
It was to have brought peace, that faultless blow.

Uncowed by the unimaginable result,
She loomed by in the cart beneath the eye
Of Danton, Desmoulins and Robespierre,
Heads in a rabble fecund in insult:
She had remade her calendar, called this
The Fourth Day of the Preparation of Peace.

Greater than Brutus was what Adam Lux
Demanded for her statue's sole inscription:
His pamphlet was heroic and absurd
And asked the privilege of dying too:
Though the republic raised to her no statue,
The brisk tribunal took him at his word.

What haunted that composure none could fault?
For she, when shown the knife, had dropped her glance—
She 'who believed her death would raise up France'
As Chénier wrote who joined the later dead:
Her judge had asked: 'If you had gone uncaught,
Would you have then escaped?' 'I would,' she said.

A daggered Virtue, Clio's roll of stone,
Action unsinewed into statuary!
Beneath that gaze what tremor was willed down?
And, where the scaffold's shadow stretched its length,
What unlived life would struggle up against
Death died in the possession of such strength?

Perhaps it was the memory of that cry
That cost her most as Catherine Marat
Broke off her testimony . . . But the blade
Inherited the future now and she
Entered a darkness where no irony
Seeps through to move the pity of her shade.

*Charlotte Corday killed the French revolutionary Jean Paul Marat on July 13,
1793.*

l. d. lerner

14 July 1956

The rockets bubble upward and explode;
The colours scale the slopes of sky and fall.
A few look up; somebody says "That's all";
No sigh or shudder rises from the crowd.
They must be here because they want to be.

We chatter to the crowd in French and nods;
Shake hands, and pick up children; claim that we
Are also equal, free and brotherly.
The troubled sky suggests the wrath of gods.
"Always the same," a woman says, and goes.

The fireworks scatter to the ground and die:
Just as the conscript gazers, each one knows,
Might parachute upon their gazing foes:
Invaders from a foreign century.
I hear a whisper scratching at my ear—

An ancient hag drew back her lips to breathe
Her ecstasy upon the festive air.
She might well be the oldest woman there
—Or so the concentration in her teeth
And damp absorption in her eyes suggest.

A wisp of gesture spirals from her wrist
Towards the crimson sky. The oldest there?
The sky turns gold. I wonder if for her
Algeria or 'eighty-nine exist.
The fading sparks find mirrors in her eyes.

Who are the fireworks for? Old hags, old men,
Children up late, and straggling foreigners?
No-one is old enough to know the cause,
Or young enough to feel he is not in
A troubled crowd beneath a troubled sky.

john clare

Written in a Thunderstorm, July 15th, 1841

The heavens are wroth-the thunder's rattling peal
Rolls like a vast volcano in the sky;
Yet nothing starts the apathy I feel,
Nor chills with fear eternal destiny.

My soul is apathy, a ruin vast—
Time cannot clear the ruined mass away;
My life is hell—the hopeless die is cast,
And manhood's prime is premature decay.

Roll on, ye wrath of thunders—peal on peal,
Till worlds are ruins and myself alone;
Melt, heart and soul, cased in obdurate steel,
Till I can feel that nature is my throne.

I live in love, sun of undying light,
And fathom my own heart for ways of good;
In its pure atmosphere, day without night
Smiles on the plains, the forest, and the flood.

Smile on, ye elements of earth and sky,
Or frown in thunders as ye frown on me.
Bid earth and its delusions pass away,
But leave the mind as its creator, free.

robert nye

Travelling to My Second Marriage on the Day of the First Moonshot

We got into the carriage. It was hot.
An old woman sat there, her white hair
Stained at the temples as if by smoke.
Beside her the old man, her husband,
Talking of salmon, grayling, sea-trout, pike,
Their ruined waters.

A windscreen wiper on another engine
Flickered like an irritable, a mad eyelid.
The woman's mouth fell open. She complained.
Her husband said: "I'd like
A one-way ticket to the moon,
Wouldn't mind that."

"What for?" "Plant roses." *"Roses?"* "Roses,
Yes. I'd be the first rose-grower on the moon.
Mozart, I'd call my rose. That's it.
A name for a new rose: Mozart.
That's what I'd call the first rose on the moon,
If I got there to grow it."

Ten nine eight seven six five four three two one.
The old woman, remember her, and the old man:
Her black shoes tapping; his gold watch as he counted.
They'd been to a funeral. We were going to a wedding.
When the train started the wheels sang *Figaro*
And there was a smell of roses.

See July 20.

frank o'hara

The Day Lady Died

It is 12:20 in New York a Friday
three days after Bastille day, yes
it is 1959 and I go get a shoeshine
because I will get off the 4:19 in Easthampton
at 7:15 and then go straight to dinner
and I don't know the people who will feed me

I walk up the muggy street beginning to sun
and have a hamburger and a malted and buy
an ugly NEW WORLD WRITING to see what the poets
in Ghana are doing these days
                              I go on to the bank
and Miss Stillwagon (first name Linda I once heard)
doesn't even look up my balance for once in her life
and in the GOLDEN GRIFFIN I get a little Verlaine
for Patsy with drawings by Bonnard although I do
think of Hesiod, trans. Richmond Lattimore or
Brendan Behan's new play or *Le Balcon* or *Les Nègres*
of Genet, but I don't, I stick with Verlaine
after practically going to sleep with quandariness

and for Mike I just stroll into the PARK LANE
Liquor Store and ask for a bottle of Strega and
then I go back where I came from to 6th Avenue
and the tobacconist in the Ziegfeld Theatre and
casually ask for a carton of Gauloises and a carton
of Picayunes, and a NEW YORK POST with her face on it

and I am sweating a lot by now and thinking of
leaning on the john door in the 5 SPOT
while she whispered a song along the keyboard
to Mal Waldron and everyone and I stopped breathing

Billie Holiday ("Lady Day") died on July 17, 1959.

tran thi nga

I Was Caught

The night of the 18th July
all the family was packed
to go to Gia Lam airport.
I could not sleep.
I had packed my bags
and put them a little to one side.
My mother sensed my plan.
She came over to my bed and asked,
"You are not coming with us?"

She cried out, waking everyone
and brought my father to my bed, saying,
"Here is your daughter
who will not come with us."
He asked if I planned to stay behind
with my third brother.
I tried to say no, but the tears came.

Father said we must stick together
at least share our troubles.
The communists would divide the family.
This way we would die together.
The whole family slept near me that night.
In the morning, they put me in the car first
with the little children.
I could not get a message to my brother.

charles olson

Maximus, to Gloucester, Sunday, July 19

and they stopped before that bad sculpture of a fisherman

—"as if one were to talk to a man's house,
knowing not what gods or heroes are"—

not knowing what a fisherman is
instead of going straight to the Bridge
and doing no more than—saying no more than—
in the Charybdises of the
Cut waters the flowers tear off
the wreathes

the flowers
turn
the character of the sea   The sea jumps
the fate of the flower   The drowned men are undrowned
in the eddies

      of the eyes
      of the flowers
      opening
      the sea's eyes

The disaster
is undone
What was received as alien
—the flower
on the water, that a man drowns
that he dies in water as he dies on earth, the impossible
      that this gross fact can return to us
                  in this upset
on a summer day
of a particular tide

that the sensation is true,
that the transformations of fire are, first of all, sea—
  "as gold for wares wares for gold"

Let them be told who stopped first
  by a bronze idol

A fisherman is not a successful man
he is not a famous man he is not a man
of power, these are the damned by God

II

whose surface bubbles
with these gimlets
which screw-in like

potholes, caustic
caked earth of painted
pools, Yellowstone

Park of holes
is death the diseased
presence on us, the spilling lesion

of the brilliance
it is to be alive: to walk onto it,
as Jim Bridger the first into it,

it is more true a scabious
field than it is a pretty
meadow

When a man's coffin is the sea
the whole of creation shall come to his funeral,

it turns out; the globe
is below, all lapis

and its blue surface golded
by what happened

this afternoon: there are eyes
in this water

the flowers
from the shore,

awakened
the sea

Men are so sure they know very many things,
they don't even know night and day are one

A fisherman works without reference to
that difference. It is possible he also

by lying there when he does lie, jowl
to the sea, has another advantage: it is said,

"You rectify what can be rectified," and when a man's heart
cannot see this, the door of his divine intelligence is shut

let you who paraded to the Cut today
to hold memorial services to all fishermen
who have been lost at sea in a year
when for the first time not one life was lost

radar sonar radio telephone good engines
bed-check seaplanes goodness over and under us

no difference
when men come back

JULY 20

 laurence goldstein

Moon Landing

I
"The eye is the window of the soul"

Open-eyed we have kept a weeklong vigil
beside the messenger from heaven
of nonce images, new immortalities.
Now the waiting for vision is over.
Some creature wades through static,
all sheathing and gingerly motion.
A squint will register for eternity
how it descends the ladder while
every worldly eye
opens its shutter, to receive
into the nascent universal soul
the first footstep, the flashing signal
LIVE FROM THE MOON

. . .

III

The idea of it is now on the street
Midway between the pepper trees, neighbors
who have taken imagery into their souls
gather to point upward, grinning like
the Louvre St. John, as if to say
"We have lived to see wonders!"
"But I don't see no rocket up there,"
one woman utters the very truth
Seeing has already become believing,
or if not, hurry back to television
Up there is only birds, in summer twilight
seeming to move sideways across the sky.

. . .

VI

I know sleep will not come tonight.
Prodigal fact peals in every living cell:
like strafing of bells this presence,
these men suited in the science of gods.
Through a neighbor's window I glimpse
an imageless glow of the same conquest.
Almost I wish to take flight through glass
and like Icarus turning his wings to the sun
enter the white heart of that light.
Ancestor of this mid-century's events,
while you improvise I would step
close and linger, swollen with ghostly speech.
You tasted the hawk's tail as a child
and drew the bird of empire; you foresaw
the aeronautical shapes now landed
at the gates of horn, waiting for release.
May your dreamwork be no Pax Americana
but some new age anationless painter,
young and starry-eyed, might draw from within,
like your self-portrait of Gabriel at his errand,
raising the sign of irresistible news.

Neil Armstrong took his first step on the moon on July 20, 1969, after a four day trip from earth. The painter Goldstein addresses is Leonardo.

matthew prior

On My Birthday, July 21

I, my dear, was born to-day—
So all my jolly comrades say:
They bring me music, wreaths, and mirth,
And ask to celebrate my birth:
Little, alas! my comrades know
That I was born to pain and woe;
To thy denial, to thy scorn,
Better I had ne'er been born:
I wish to die, even whilst I say—
"I, my dear, was born to-day."

I, my dear, was born to-day:
Shall I salute the rising day,
Well-spring of all my joy and woe?
Clotilda, thou alone dost know,
Shall the wreath surround my hair?
Or shall the music please my ear?
Shall I my comrades' mirth receive,
And bless my birth, and wish to live?
Then let me see great Venus chase
Imperious anger from thy face:
Then let me hear thee smiling say—
"Thou, my dear, wert born to-day."

Gerrie Fellows

From a Window 22/7/86

In the back court
the morning after Glasgow Fair
three dustmen
who have somehow lost a dustcart
lounge against a pebbled wall
in the quick sunshine

It's the clatter of their laughter
that's drawn me   tousle headed
to pull up the blind
(We're all late this morning)
and stand   gazing down

Dark head   greasy curls   thin fair hair
the smoke   spiralling between them
three men in a kind of communion
At their elbows   forgotten
the sacks of used tins   tealeaves
vegetable parings

High on the bleached wall   light
slaps at the flat vermillion blind
A woman in a cotton nightdress
opens the curtains

A blond man   lying on the lawn
the others draped against a metal fence
are still laughing

Young men   old enough
to be husbands   wiry
careless   in the bold sunshine

Will they grow old   battered   surviving
divorces   happy marriages   heart attacks
Using thick forearms to lift pints
Staggering home on Fair Monday
Pulling up the blinds
on a brief sunlit   morning such as this
and gazing down   at other men
laughing   among the garbage

paul blackburn

23.VII.71

Young, dying yellow birch on Owego St.
  half-block from the IGA.

fat black ants tool along beside me
or troll across the sidewalks. I am careful

Because I think maybe words are coming, I sit
on a stump in the sun in front of number 28,
staring at pink and white hollyhocks under its front windows,
an ambivalent paleness of hollyhock.
I always thought they were a
               somewhat gross plant,
                      those scratchy leaves.

The running samaritan this noon-hour, I've
delivered a bottle of freshmade orange juice iced, &
a suppository   25 mg. Adult.
insert one as directed for vomiting. and am
on my way
to the IGA
for cigs and a cold 6-pack of Coca Cola for Howard
to help celebrate
his first post-celebration-of-being-21 day.

Beware friends and well-meaning bar owners bearing gifts
that resemble three fingers high of excellent bourbon in a whiskey sour
    glass,
beware even the double shot . uh, *stark!*

On the way back to Tomkins St,
the ants accompany me in the hot sun. Don't
they know that sidewalks are terrible places to cruise,
for ants anyway?

And we always treated hollyhocks like
second class citizens, poor relations, bums, we
kept them out by the garage in back.
Those delicate blooms. The awkward stems. The hairy leaves.

thomas whitbread

Postcard From Esna, Egypt

(CAIRO, Oct. 27—Egyptian frontier administration authorities
said today that the police still had not cleared up the identity of the
body of an American found in the Nubian Desert yesterday.

Meanwhile desert patrols continued to search for a second
American in the ill-fated party that left Aswan by motorcar July 26
headed for Wadi Halfa on the Sudanese border.

A three-week search by jeep, helicopter and camel resulted
yesterday in the finding of four bodies in the lonely sands 275 miles
south of Aswan . . .
—The New York Times, Oct. 28, 1959)

Luxor and Edfu, Pyramids and Sphinx,
Port Said, Beirut, the Bosphorus, Paris,
Thus backward from the desert past Aswan
If lives were safety-film, at will rewound.
I take these place-names from the last post card
I have from my friend, John Armstrong. I could add
Orleans, Hong Kong, Manila, Monterey,
Cambridge, Amherst, and, interweaving all,
Preceding all, Belleville, New Jersey. But:
"Missent to North Chatham, Mass.," stamped in red ink.
No postmark on the UAR Egyptian stamps.
"July 24" in John's hand. At the end he says
"It is hot and dusty on the road, but now
We wait in Esna in the cool shade of trees
At the police station, waiting for a guide
To show us the way through the mountains to Aswan."
They got to Aswan, but not to Wadi Halfa
Across the Nubian Desert. Mysteries
Obscure the deaths of John and his three friends
Or two friends and an inexperienced guide.
"Their heroism lies on the other side
Of folly," says a spectator here in Texas.
"This was a serious fellow on a lark."
So: as Swift says, you should choose your moments well
For jumps into volcanoes: hero or fool,
Genius or madman, what thin lines! So: John was
Deadly serious along route 39

In throwing beercans at No Passing signs.
But I don't think John hoped for new answers, or
Was "in search of personal identity"
So avidly as to seek risk of death
In hope of revelation or some grail.
I think he expected to be alive today,
Translating Chinese into French. Just what
Happened, what monkey wrench cracked bloodily
Into what skull, what water spilled, what sun
Struck savage and incessant, what sands swept
Across what dimlit road, I do not know.
I have John's card, his hand: "No news from you,
A silence which has saddened me of late."
Then the names of places seen and to be seen.
I am saddened that I cannot ever break
My silence, which had saddened him of late,
And his full silence, which now saddens me.

JULY 25

federico garcía lorca

The Unfaithful Wife

. . . so I walked her down to the river.
I was really the first, she said
—forgetting the fact of a husband.
On the night of the patron of Spain—
I was merely trying to oblige.
As the streetlamps all went black and
crickets came afire.
When we reached the end of the sidewalk
I touched her breasts: sleeping.
They blossomed for me promptly,
no hyacinth so sweet.
The slip she wore, starched cotton,
hissed in my ear excitement.
As a piece of silk would, ripped to
ribbons by ten knives.
No silver catching the branches,
the trees loomed enormous.
And the skyline of hounds yowling
very far from the shore.

Passing the blackberry bushes,
passing the reeds and bracken,
under her cover of hair I
scooped a hole in the clay.
I unfastened my necktie.
She unfastened her skirt.
I, my belt and revolver.
She, her petticoats—four.
Neither camellia, seashell
such delight to the finger.
Never a moon on water
shone as she did then.
Her thighs in my clutch, elusive
as bass you catch bare-handed.
Half, they were fire and splendor;
chilly as winter, half.
That night I went riding
the finest of all our journeys,
fast on a filly of pearl, that
never knew stirrup or curb!
I'm man enough not to be breathing
certain words she uttered.
I'm a clean straight-thinking fellow
with a decent tongue in love.
She was slubbered with kisses and sand
when I took her home from the river.
The air was a melee of sabers:
lilies raged at the wind.

I behaved like the man I am:
hundred-percent gypsy.
And presented her with a saffron
satiny case, de luxe.
But for falling in love?—not me!
She with a husband, yet
to say I was really the first
as I walked her down to the river!

Trans. John Frederick Nims

July 25th, the great mid-summer fiesta, with revelry likely to lead to such episodes. . . . St. James [Santiago] is no ordinary saint: he is the Patron of Spain, and what happens on his night ought to have a particularly Spanish sanction. [Note by Nims]

michael casey

The Box Riot

Ft. Leonard Wood Stockade, July 26, 1969

They called me out of bed
For slack an I
Rushed right over there
An all sorts of rank was there
An they went with me
To the box all right
An the prisoners were all out
An I get beat up
By two box dudes
With two by fours
They was watchin real good though
We only saw one side
Only Africa and me went in there
The guards inside
Locked themselves up
So they wouldn't get hurt
And Wilkerson got hit
With a hammer
Helpin the engineers at the gate
One of the engineers
They think is dead
Ya could see inside his head
Only Africa an Wilkerson
An me was there
They started biffin us with
Two by fours
I grabbed a two by four
An started biffen them back
Christ Almighty
They not cutting me no slack
I'm not cutting them any

c. h. sisson

A Letter to John Donne

*On 27 July 1617, Donne preached at the parish church at
Sevenoaks, of which he was rector, and was entertained at Knole,
then the country residence of Richard Sackville, third Earl of Dorset.*

I understand you well enough, John Donne
First, that you were a man of ability
Eaten by lust and by the love of God
Then, that you crossed the Sevenoaks High Street
As rector of Saint Nicholas:
I am of that parish.

To be a man of ability is not much
You may see them on the Sevenoaks platform any day
Eager men with despatch cases
Whom ambition drives as they drive the machine
Whom the certainty of meticulous operation
Pleasures as a morbid sex a heart of stone.

That you should have spent your time in the corruption of courts
As these in that of cities, gives you no place among us:
Ability is not even the game of a fool
But the click of a computer operating in a waste
Your cleverness is dismissed from the suit
Bring out your genitals and your theology.

What makes you familiar is this dual obsession;
Lust is not what the rutting stag knows
It is to take Eve's apple and to lose
The stag's paradisal look:
The love of God comes readily
To those who have most need.

You brought body and soul to this church
Walking there through the park alive with deer
But now what animal has climbed into your pulpit?
One whose pretension is that the fear
Of God has heated him into a spirit
An evaporated man no physical ill can hurt.

Well might you hesitate at the Latin gate
Seeing such apes denying the church of God:
I am grateful particularly that you were not a saint
But extravagant whether in bed or in your shroud.
You would understand that in the presence of folly
I am not sanctified but angry.

Come down and speak to the men of ability
On the Sevenoaks platform and tell them
That at your Saint Nicholas the faith
Is not exclusive in the fools it chooses
That the vain, the ambitious and the highly sexed
Are the natural prey of the incarnate Christ.

 ted berrigan

Sonnet XXXVI

After Frank O'Hara

It's 8:54 a.m. in Brooklyn it's the 28th of July and
it's probably 8:54 in Manhattan but I'm
in Brooklyn I'm eating English muffins and drinking
pepsi and I'm thinking of how Brooklyn is New
York city too how odd I usually think of it as
something all its own like Bellows Falls like Little
Chute like Uijongbu
                        I never thought on the Williams-
burg bridge I'd come so much to Brooklyn
just to see lawyers and cops who don't even carry
guns taking my wife away and bringing her back
                                            No
and I never thought Dick would be back at Gude's
beard shaved off long hair cut and Carol reading
his books when we were playing cribbage and
watching the sun come up over the Navy Yard
across the river

I think I was thinking when I was
ahead I'd be somewhere like Perry street erudite
dazzling slim and badly loved
contemplating my new book of poems
to be printed in simple type on old brown paper
feminine marvelous and tough

carolyn stoloff

Report on the Times

July 29, 1969

At nightfall fierce winds and floods beset us
rivers rose in Rome, London, Dresden
reports of sewer lines swept away
bridges collapsed, trapped motorists
three feet of water lapped Mainstreet
rain held down crowds at Nice
at Yosemite—flattened tents
campers swept into gullies

Rain washed out Egyptian positions
prisoners advanced through waterways
in Viet Nam one hundred and twenty
civilian dead blamed on the rain

Victory went to the Minnesota Twins
evidence pointed to rain
it pelted the Upper nile and the Amazon
pelted Musial, Hoyt, Campanella
washed out the Hall of Fame game
in New York the Mayor was charged with collusion
other candidates promised a change
as meteorologists dragged the dead
from the Passaic, the Arno, the Seine

Rain restricted the need for weapons
threatened landslides and depressions

accidents left twelve million pregnant
economists cursed forecasters
and spawned theories blaming the rain
it was rumored astronauts returned to the moon
Earth was in quarantine

At midafternoon the President rose
stoically in the rain for the National Anthem
and promised a gradual reduction soon

j. p. ward

Coda

On the last but one day
July's cobweb heat and fragrance
Hit our faces. A trout flopped upward
Out of the pool and fell back with a lollop.

Absently you picked a weed (milk thistle).
Settlement seventeen years
Dispenses good for life's distinct domains
And we have had ours.
Friends phoned the day of the ad.
We've always liked it, we'll pay what you ask they said.

A form, litany seemed required.
Thank you blackbirds for the priceless chip.
Thank you apple, fitting October
Crisply to my hand. Heal our surgical
Incisions, the copse-gate's angle, casement
Windows ridiculously small. . . .

Our smaller boy quiet, bewildered.
His brother stares out from the car
At a red commercial balloon
Over the motorway suddenly,
Twenty, a giant rainbow bouquet
Like a small girl curtseying to God.

He speeds bravely to his future
Not undisturbed by this summer evening,
Its tranquil and careened indifference.

Last night a fox
Slunk across the mysterious trees,
Looked briefly, then too went on its way.

alexander pope and lady mary wortley montagu

Three Epitaphs

Two rustic lovers, John Hewet and Sarah Drew, were struck by the same bolt of lightning on July 31, 1718. Pope described the scene in a letter to Lady Mary and enclosed two epitaphs.

When Eastern Lovers feed the fun'ral fire,
On the same Pile their faithful Fair expire;
Here pitying Heav'n that virtue mutual found,
And blasted both, that it might neither wound.
Hearts so sincere, th' Almighty saw well-pleas'd,
Sent his own Lightning, & the victims seiz'd.

I
Think not, by rig'rous Judgment seiz'd,
   A pair so faithful could expire;
Victims so pure Heav'n saw well-pleas'd,
   And snatch'd them in celestial fire.

II
Live well, & fear no sudden fate;
   When God calls Virtue to the grave,
Alas 'tis Justice, soon, or late,
   Mercy alike, to kill, or save.

Virtue unmov'd, can hear the Call,
And face the Flash that melts the Ball.

Lady Mary responded with an epitaph of her own.

Here lyes John Hughs and Sarah Drew;
Perhaps you'll say, what's that to you?
Believe me, Friend, much may be said
On this poor Couple that are dead.
On Sunday next they should have marry'd,
But see how oddly things are carry'd.
On Thursday last it rain'd and Lighten'd;
These tender lovers sadly frighten'd
Shelter'd beneath the cocking Hay
In Hopes to pass the storm away.
But the bold Thunder found them out
(Commission'd for that end no Doubt)
And seizing on their trembling Breath,
Consign'd them to the Shades of Death.
Who knows if 'twas not kindly done?
For had they seen the next year's Sun
A Beaten Wife and Cuckold Swain
Had jointly curs'd the marriage chain.
Now they are happy in their Doom
For P[ope] has writ upon their Tomb.

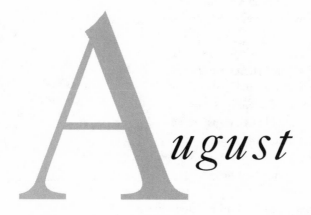

tom earley

Summer Return

On this first August afternoon
I have climbed to the rocking stone
And now, at the summit of my summer,
I lie alone on a sprung bed
Of winberry bushes, looking down
Beyond the scrubby heather, beyond
The moss-covered tips and the clumping
Bracken to the mountain-sheltered town.

I watch the toy bus swing up the valley
As it did yesterday when we followed
The line of the river, the coaly Cynon
Black and shiny as a pair of Sunday shoes.
Its slaggy bank had been transformed
By masses of luxuriant ragwort,
Rosebay, hemp-agrimony and tansy
Into a mauve and yellow hedge.

As we approached the Penrhiwceiber pit
I noted again how the mountain
Had reached right down into the street
In a thickly covered slope of heather,
Bringing to Tynte a temporary loveliness,
To Ynysboeth an unexpected beauty,
And suddenly I saw the grassy tump
Of Twynbrynbychan dominate the town.

I looked up at the rocking stone
Which told me I would climb up here
Today and here I am now, satisfied
And lying at ease on my bouncing
Spring-mattress of a winberry bed,
Looking down at the familiar places
In mountain-sheltered Mountain Ash
On this first August afternoon.

john ashbery

Qualm

Warren G. Harding invented the word "normalcy,"
And the lesser-known "bloviate," meaning, one imagines,
To spout, to spew aimless verbiage. He never wanted to be president.
The "Ohio Gang" made him. He died in the Palace

Hotel in San Francisco, coming back from Alaska,
As his wife was reading to him, about him,
From *The Saturday Evening Post.* Poor Warren. He wasn't a bad egg,
Just weak. He loved women and Ohio.

This protected summer of high, white clouds, a new golf star
Flashes like confetti across the intoxicating early part
Of summer, almost to the end of August. The crowd is hysterical:
Fickle as always, they follow him to the edge

Of the inferno. But the fall is, deliciously, only his.
They shall communicate this and that and compute
Fixed names like "doorstep in the wind." The agony is permanent
Rather than eternal. He'd have noticed it. Poor Warren.

Warren Harding died on August 2, 1923.

aubrey de vere

Queen Mary Obtains the Throne

from: Mary Tudor

Act III, scene ii
[*Enter* MARY, ELIZABETH, ARUNDEL, *& C.*]

ARUNDEL	Heaven smiles, my liege, upon the righteous cause.
	Welcome thus far upon your prosperous way.
	Here rest your wearied foot—your foes disperse
	Frail as the dust before their giddy feet.
MARY	How name you this fair prospect?
ARUNDEL	Wanstead Heath:
	By Epping chase.

MARY

How blest these breezy downs,
With purple heath and golden gorse enamelled;
Each bosky bank with dewy windflowers strewn,
Each dell with cowslip and rathe violet—
And the sun-loving daisy on hill tops
Drinking the light! Ah, happy shepherd's life!
He this sweet solitude, without constraint,
Explores, his chosen damsel at his side:
Recounting tales of love and plighted faith:
Or from his pipe pours such delicious song
That the wild hare in the close bitten lane
Pauses with ear erect, and timorous deer
That down the labyrinthine forest glade
Goes bounding, starts aside, and turns to gaze.

ELIZABETH Old times return—discourse for ever thus.

MARY

Beneath this chesnut canopy, sun-proof,
Cool as a cavern on the ocean shore,
I'll take my rest.

ELIZABETH   Not new to me this scene.
Oft have I chased the red deer through these wilds,
With our loved Edward.

MARY   Saints be with him now!
He loved you, Bess: not me the unbeloved!

ELIZABETH He loved you well till traitors edged between.
God pardon him.

MARY   And them! Preserve me, Lord,
From the vindictive Fiend that tempts my spirit.

ELIZABETH

Forswear sad thoughts. In fancy let us rove
These downs and coverts. From yon breezy brow,
Like a monk's head close-shaven, with boscage fringed,
Oft have I watched Paul's steeple, o'er the smoke
Of the great City glistering like a pyre.
Along the horizon spread the billowy tops
Of Hainault's forest oaks: nor far uprears
The Fairlop tree his huge trunk, grey and bossy;
A mighty shade, where village maids at eve
In dance and song with rural archers sport.
[*A distant Trumpet sounds.*]

ARUNDEL

The hart is near the toils. Thoughtless of fate,
I hear his wanton belling on the wind.
[*Enter* WINCHESTER *and* PEMBROKE.]

MARY You are welcome.

PEMBROKE On our knees we sue for pardon:
For that, long hampered in false Dudley's meshes,

	We stood aloof, in mock disloyalty.
	Praise be to God! the summer Sun hath risen
	To dry out tearful cheeks. God save the Queen!
MARY	Well have I known your hearts were dutiful
	Albeit your outward carriage was unliegeful.
	Let worthy posts, Lord Marshal, be assigned them!
	[*Great shouting heard.*]
ARUNDEL	Fortune comes bounding on a flowing tide.
MARY	What means this tumult?
ARUNDEL	Dudley's ill-sorted Bands
	Have flung their arms aside; and hither rush,
	Frenzied with loyal zeal.
	[*Enter* NORTHUMBERLAND *with Soldiery in disorder.*]
NORTHUMBERLAND	Hold back! this ardour
	Shall fright the Queen, not please her! Thus, my men!
	[*Throwing up his cap.*]
	God save Queen Mary!
MARY	Down with your sword! what mean you?
	Me thou can'st neither frighten nor cajole.
	Kneel, traitor, kneel!
NORTHUMBERLAND	Lowly to earth abased,
	A penitent sincere, I crave your mercy!
	I might have lived an exile; but prefer
	To stoop my forfeit head and trust your pity.
	Too well my momentary treason (yea
	Treason it seems till you have read my soul)
	Deserves death. Yet considerately judge
	Confessed infirmity; remembering mercy,
	That best prerogative of Royalty!
	The common herd—
	[*Pauses.*]
MARY	Nay, let your say be said.
	You have license, Sir; proceed.
NORTHUMBERLAND	I cannot harm you—
	But can well serve. For I have piloted
	The state so long that all its perilous leaks
	And privy treasons are to me revealed,
	And shall to your Grace if this poor life be spared.
MARY	My Lord, I muse much at your strange appeal:
	And shall take counsel on it.
NORTHUMBERLAND	Not with my foes!
	So were I crushed to screen their double treason.
	Your gracious nature knows not to delude.
	Trust your own wisdom. Give me hope!

MARY   To live
     In righteous hope needs hope beyond this world.
     They only who serve God in his true Church
     Partake that blessing. Sir, you should have hope:
     But you have served, till now, whom hope disowns.
     I shall revolve your suit. My Lord, retire.
     Keep him in ward, not rigorous, but observant.
     [*Exit* QUEEN MARY, *attended.*]

Northumberland's rebellion, the last threat to Mary's accession, collapsed on
August 3, 1553.

A U G U S T **4**

          michael drayton

A Hymne to His Ladies Birth-place

     Coventry, that do'st adorne
The countrey wherein I was borne,
Yet therin lyes not thy prayse,
Why I should crowne thy tow'rs with bayes:
'Tis not thy wall, me to thee weds
Thy ports, nor thy proud pyrameds,
Nor thy trophies of the bore,
But that shee which I adore,
Which scarce goodnesse selfe can payre,
First their breathing blest thy ayre;
     Idea, in which name I hide
Her, in my heart deifi'd,
For what good, man's mind can see,
Onely her Ideas be:
She, in whom the vertues came
In womans shape, and tooke her name,
She so farre past imitation,
As but nature our creation
Could not alter, she had aymed,
More then women to have framed;
She, whose truely written story,
To thy poore name shall adde more glory,
Then if it should have beene thy chance,
T'have bred our Kings that conquer'd France.

Had she beene borne the former age,
That house had been a pilgrimage,
And reputed more divine,
Then Walsingham or Beckets shrine.
  That Princesse, to whom thou do'st owe
Thy freedome, whose cleere blushing snow,
The envious sunne saw, when as she
Naked rode to make thee free,
Was but her type, as to foretell,
Thou should'st bring forth one, should excell
Her bounty, by whom thou should'st have
More honour, then she freedome gave;
And that great Queene, which but of late
Ru'ld this land in peace and state,
Had not beene, but heaven had sworne,
A maide should raigne, when she was borne.
  Of thy streets, which thou hold'st best,
And most frequent of the rest,
Happy Mich-Parke ev'ry yeere,
On the fourth of August there,
Let thy maides from Flora's bowers,
With their choyce and daintiest flowers
Decke thee up, and from their store,
With brave garlands crowne that dore.
  The old man passing by that way,
To his sonne in time shall say,
There was that lady borne, which long
To after-ages shall be sung;
Who unawares being passed by,
Back to that house shall cast his eye,
Speaking my verses as he goes,
And with a sigh shut ev'ry close.
  Deare citie, travelling by thee,
When thy rising spyres I see,
Destined her place of birth;
Yet me thinkes the very earth
Hallowed is, so farre as I
Can thee possibly descry:
Then thou dwelling in this place,
Hearing some rude hinde disgrace
Thy citie with some scurvy thing,
Which some jester forth did bring,
Speake these lines where thou do'st come,
And strike the slave for ever dumbe.

judith minty

Upon Seeing the Aurora Borealis for the First Time on My 35th Birthday

For me, the birthday girl, it was a portent.
I waited, almost hoping we would never see those lights.
For the others, it was an excursion
like a carnival trip to see freaks expose their anomalies.
I would have liked red wine, a toast,
a Eucharist even. Instead there was
cigarettes and Scotch, the flash of matches and laughter.

Stretched out on cool sand, the sky spilling stars,
we were first-nighters waiting for the curtain.
I thought of my Nordic father, how he had seen that show
birthdays ago up near the Arctic Circle;
the reverence in his voice as he told
how, like an umbrella it had opened perfectly over his head,
the rays fingering down so close he could have touched them.

And then, from over the lake, it began for us.
First a flicker of candles, then a blaze
of white yellow orange. It was
a blossoming: the petals unfurled, stretched
out from the north in their celebration of beams and arcs;
withering, then brilliance;
silence, then an explosion of light.

It was quiet before terror, before they
began to roll as if alive. I wanted to
shut my eyes, cry out that the umbrella was gone.
Only ghosts now, raining, tumbling, roaring
over each other; years chasing, haunting across the sky.
He said, "I thought the world was coming to an end."
And, papa, it did then—in a way.

Judith Minty turned thirty-five on August 5, 1972.

alison fell

August 6, 1945

In the Enola Gay
five minutes before impact
he whistles a dry tune

Later he will say
that the whole blooming sky
went up like an apricot ice.
Later he will laugh and tremble
at such a surrender, for the eye
of his belly saw Marilyn's skirts
fly over her head for ever

On the river bank,
bees drizzle over
hot white rhododendrons

Later she will walk
the dust, a scarlet girl

with her whole stripped skin
at her heel, stuck like an old
shoe sole or mermaid's tail

Later she will lie down
in the flecked black ash
where the people are become
as lizards or salamanders
and, blinded, she will complain:
Mother you are late, so late

Later in dreams he will look
down shrieking and see

ladybirds
ladybirds

Enola Gay *was the name of the plane that dropped the Hiroshima bomb. [Note by Fell]*

jim harrison

from: Letters to Yesenin

I cleaned the granary dust off your photo with my shirt-sleeve.
Now that we are tidy we can wait for the host to descend
presumably from the sky as that seems to exhaust the alternatives.
You had a nice summer in the granary. I was out there with you
every day in June and July writing one of my six-week wonders,
another novel. Loud country music on the phonograph, wasps
and bees and birds and mice. The horses looked in the window
every hour or so, curious and rather stupid. Chief Joseph stared
down from the wall at both of us, a far nobler man than
we ever thought possible. We can't lead ourselves and he led

a thousand with a thousand horses a thousand miles. He was a god
and had three wives when one is usually more than enough for
a human. These past weeks I have been organizing myself into
my separate pieces. I have the limberness of a man twice my age
and this is as good a time as any to turn around. Joseph was
very understanding, incidentally, when the Cavalry shot so many
of the women and children. It was to be expected. Earth is
full of precedents. They hang around like underground trees
waiting for their chance. The fish swam for four years solid
in preparation for August the seventh, 1972, when I took his life
and ate his body. Just as we may see our own ghosts next to
us whose shapes we will someday flesh out. All of this suffering
to become a ghost. Yours held a rope, Manila, straight from
the tropics. But we don't reduce such glories to a mudbath.
The ghost giggles at genuflections. You can't buy him a drink.
Out in a clearing in the woods the other day I got up on a
stump and did a little dance for mine. We know the most fright-
ening time is noon. The evidence says I'm half way there, such
wealth I can't give away, thirty-four years of seconds.

 rosanna warren

Jacob Burckhardt, August 8, 1897

He's dismissed them over
and over: *Gewaltmenschen,* maniacs
of power, like those new *"terribles
simplificateurs* who will descend upon old Europe." But

here they come crowding his room, ghost
shouldering ghost. The window fades
and faces surge, shine
as though lit from within. Good Lord, he is—

he sees it now—he's been
their magic lantern puppeteer
for years, *he's* cast them on
the screen of the world. *To me*

history is poetry on the grandest scale. And they have
scale, his people: Alberti, il Moro, blood
in rivulets, poison
globules, dome of domes, *Honor*

*that enigmatic mixture of conscience and egoism
surviving the loss of faith, love, hope.* He coughs,
wants water, but won't disturb
the nurse asleep in the study.

Ah, but in his loneliness, he's had
love. His kind. Not the young Basel women
with lisps and linens, not widows
longing to dust his books, but

*My fancy is beauty
of spirit. . . . Only ascetics change the world. . . .* Not
plump Emma, cramming the mail
with odes. *Dear Emma,*

*you must save yourself
from seas of feeling, and reach
art. . . . Not every mood is fit. . . .*
How she will rail! *The golden*

*shimmer of reconciliation must
hover over the poem. . . .* As over
the deathbed. Aeneas Silvius leans
close, scholar-pope to

scholar-of-popes, and smooths
the sheets across the Professor's chest.
Lorenzo guards the door,
nose whittled white. Dusk throngs

the bedroom with ambassadors,
Luca's cherubs
fingering marble lutes. . . .
The quilt lies heavy, but he can't

lift it: Borgia looms
terror-eyed with poison-sallow skin.
They're closing in
touched with the flames he heard had swept the Louvre

under the Commune, when he wept, and ran
out into his wildering city with the news. They sweep
around the bed, not Silvius, not Lorenzo, but
his more imaginative

freaks, fiery with rings,
vials, sword-hilts, smiles—
Nietzsche among them, loyal
young friend, as Death,

terrible simplificateur,
bends now across the pillow, and shades his eyes.

AUGUST 9

donald junkins

Swan's Island, August 9, 1974

A summer morning,
my son and I are running the Red Point Road
for time: for the early breeze,
the half-high sun.
                        Elsie Gillespie is picking raspberries
by her barn-garage. She waves. Overhead
the eagle from the Sisters winds slowly higher,
pacing.
            Pace will bring us home. My son
eases ahead in his long strides. There's a parked car
off the road for blueberries: summer
people. A bandana-head looks up from serious picking.

Pacing. At the turn of the woods
a crow jumps from the top of a spruce tree
caw, cawing to cronies deeper in: they
take off, protesting.
                        I relax into pace, unclench
my fists, try not to think of running.
My son disappears down the hill
through the Otter Pond swamp.
I love my son. I will catch him if I can.

Two miles—from the seawall field to Rosy Staples' house
and back. (We will sit on the deck, pick
berries by the shore, wade in the tide pool,
breathe easy.)
       Pacing. The halfway mark, my son is coming
back. We nod. Arms loose, legs
easy, I am turning
home. Pace will bring me home. I
will not think of running. The island
is cool and green, the day is long,
my son is running like the rhyme,
if you
can, if
you can, . . .
I'm running after the gingerbread man.

anonymous

from: The Battle of Maldon

. . .
So, the sea-wolves, the Norse sailors,
No longer afraid of the stream, crossed west
On the Panta, carried their shields over shining
Water and brought pirates and weapons to land.
Byrtnoth and his warriors waited to meet them,
Ready, their linden shields linked rim
To rim in a wall raised on their arms
And firm. Then fighting hung on a sword blade,
Glory in battle; the time had come
For fate to pluck out ripened lives.
The armies shouted, and above the uproar
The ravens circled, greedy for carrion.
Then sharp-honed steel flew from their hands,
Fine-ground spears; and the bows hummed,
And blades thudded on up-raised shields.
       The charge was savage: soldiers fell
On every side, and lay where they dropped.
Wulfmar was wounded and slept on the bloody

Field, Byrtnoth's cousin, killed
By the sudden sweep of a hooked broad sword.
But the pirates were paid in kind. I heard
That Edward offered a proper tribute,
Struck a Dane so sharply that he fell
At his feet and fought no more. For which
His chief thanked the chamberlain, when the chance
Came.
                    So they stood, neither
Yielding, every warrior eagerly
Planning another's death, his point
The first to show eternity to a mortal
Soul. The slaughtered were thick on the ground.
And they stood firm. Byrtnoth held them,
Ordered every thought on the battle
And the glory of beating back the Danes.
A brave pirate raised his weapons
And came at Byrtnoth, waving his shield.
The earl strode as boldly toward him,
Each of them thinking the other's pain.
The sailor threw his Italian spear
And Byrtnoth was hit: he pushed quickly down
With his shield and burst the wooden shaft
To splinters; the spear sprang out. Then,
Angry, he shoved his spear through the guts
Of the proud Dane who'd wounded him. Wise
In war's tricks, he stabbed his javelin
Deep in the dangerous Viking's neck,
Reached to his life and let it spill free.
Then he quickly turned on another,
Shattered his mail, threw the poisoned
Point between the woven rings
Into his heart. And the earl was happy
And laughed and gave thanks to God for what
The day had granted him.
. . .

Trans. Burton Raffel

The skirmish, a victory for the Danes on August 10, 991, was one in a long series in the Norse invasion of Britain.

miguel algarín

Sunday, August 11, 1974

Sunday afternoon and it is one-thirty and all the
churchgoing latinos have crossed themselves and are now going
home to share in the peace of the day, pan y mantequilla, una
taza de café and many sweet recollections of el rinconcito en
Juncos, donde Carmencita, Maria y Malén jugaban y peleaban.
Sunday afternoon and it is one-thirty and all the
churchgoing latinos fuse each other with love and the women
dress so clean and pure and the children walk so straight and pure
and the fathers look so proud and pure and everything so right and
pure and even as I wake up to my nephew's voice coming through
the window, there is pleasure in awakening. My mother and father
and Grafton and Johnny come in, there is light in
their eyes,
there is pleasure in living,
there is no shame in being
full of love,
there is no shame in being
nude while my mother's
eyes look in at me,
looking at my nude body,
body that she made mixing her blood
with my father's
and there's no rushing for clothes
just sweet openness in being
loved by my family.
Sunday afternoon and it is
one-thirty and all the churchgoing latinos have crossed themselves
and my body swings free.

john webster

from: The White Devil

The Arraignment of Vittoria

Act III, scene ii, ll. 179–231
[*In an ecclesiastical courtroom in Rome*, FRANCISCO,
MONTICELSO and VITTORIA.]

MONTICELSO   Your champion's gone.
VITTORIA   The wolf may prey the better.
FRANCISCO   My lord there's great suspicion of the murder,
             But no sound proof who did it: for my part
             I do not think she hath a soul so black
             To act a deed so bloody,—if she have,
             As in cold countries husbandmen plant vines,
             And with warm blood manure them, even so
             One summer she will bear unsavoury fruit,
             And ere next spring wither both branch and root.
             The act of blood let pass, only descend
             To matter of incontinence.
VIT   I discern poison,
             Under your gilded pills.
MONT   Now the duke's gone, I will produce a letter,
             Wherein 'twas plotted he and you should meet,
             At an apothecary's summer-house,
             Down by the river Tiber:—view't my lords:—
             Where after wanton bathing and the heat
             Of a lascivious banquet . . . I pray read it,
             I shame to speak the rest.
VIT   Grant I was tempted,
             Temptation to lust proves not the act,
             Casta est quam nemo rogavit,—
             You read his hot love to me, but you want
             My frosty answer.
MONT   Frost i'th'dog-days! strange!
VIT   Condemn you me for that the duke did love me?
             So may you blame some fair and crystal river
             For that some melancholic distracted man
             Hath drown'd himself in't.
MONT   Truly drown'd indeed.

VIT   Sum up my faults I pray, and you shall find
That beauty and gay clothes, a merry heart,
And a good stomach to a feast, are all,
All the poor crimes that you can charge me with:
In faith my lord you might go pistol flies,
The sport would be more noble.

MONT   Very good.

VIT   But take you your course, it seems you have
        beggar'd me first
And now would fain undo me,—I have houses,
Jewels, and a poor remnant of crusadoes,
Would those would make you charitable.

MONT   If the devil
Did ever take good shape behold his picture.

VIT   You have one virtue left,
You will not flatter me.

FRAN   Who brought this letter?

VIT   I am not compell'd to tell you.

MONT   My lord duke sent to you a thousand ducats,
The twelfth of August.

VIT   'Twas to keep your cousin
From prison, I paid use for't.

MONT   I rather think
'Twas interest for his lust.

VIT   Who says so but yourself? if you be my accuser
Pray cease to be my judge, come from the bench,
Give in your evidence 'gainst me, and let these
Be moderators: my lord cardinal.
Were your intelligencing ears as long
As to my thoughts, had you an honest tongue
I would not care though you proclaim'd them all.

robert southey

The Battle of Blenheim

I

It was a summer evening,
    Old Kaspar's work was done,
And he before his cottage door
    Was sitting in the sun,
And by him sported on the green
His little grandchild Wilhelmine.

II

She saw her brother Peterkin
    Roll something large and round,
Which he beside the rivulet
    In playing there had found;
He came to ask what he had found,
That was so large, and smooth, and round.

III

Old Kaspar took it from the boy,
    Who stood expectant by;
And then the old man shook his head,
    And, with a natural sigh,
" 'Tis some poor fellow's skull," said he,
"Who fell in the great victory.

IV

"I find them in the garden,
    For there's many here about;
And often when I go to plough,
    The ploughshare turns them out!
For many thousand men," said he,
"Were slain in that great victory."

V

"Now tell us what 'twas all about,"
    Young Peterkin, he cries;
And little Wilhelmine looks up
    With wonder-waiting eyes;
"Now tell us all about the war,
And what they fought each other for."

VI

"It was the English," Kaspar cried,
    "Who put the French to rout;
But what they fought each other for,
    I could not well make out;
But everybody said," quoth he,
"That 'twas a famous victory.

VII

"My father lived at Blenheim then,
    Yon little stream hard by;
They burnt his dwelling to the ground,
    And he was forced to fly;
So with his wife and child he fled,
Nor had he where to rest his head.

VIII

"With fire and sword the country round
    Was wasted far and wide,
And many a childing mother then,
    And new-born baby died;
But things like that, you know, must be
At every famous victory."

The Duke of Marlborough's wife relayed to Queen Anne the message her husband had written on r back of a tavern bill: "I have not time to say more, but to beg you will give my duty to the Queen, and her know her army has had a glorious victory," on August 13, 1704.

tu fu

Too Much Heat, Too Much Work

It's the fourteenth of August, and I'm too hot
To endure food, or bed. Steam and the fear of scorpions
Keep me awake. I'm told the heat won't fade with Autumn.

Swarms of flies arrive. I'm roped into my clothes.
In another moment I'll scream down the office
As the paper mountains rise higher on my desk.

O those real mountains to the south of here!
I gaze at the ravines kept cool by pines.
If I could walk on ice, with my feet bare!

Trans. Carolyn Kizer

christina pacosz

The Assumption of the Blessed Virgin Mary,
August 15

.

She has gone
to heaven
where she will
intercede
for us.

She is the earth
and cannot
forget us.

Last night
under a half moon
she rose
with the smoke
from the burning

stubble, a bonfire
in the fields
lighting her way.

When she passed
the moon
she cast
a shadow:

this dream:

Through the muddy
fields of Felinow
three women
came to me
to show me a spring.

I search for it
all day
in every leaf
and lark.

2.
My aunt arranges
a bouquet
her daughter-in-law
has gathered
to be blessed
in church.

Mach, buckwheat, barley, millet,
dill, dahlias, asparagus fern,
cabbage leaf, daisies, gladioli,
green beans, roses and phlox.

And when the next cow calves,
the dried bloom
will sweeten her
first drinking water,
and Mary's blessing
flow from her udders.

3.
The sow and her ten piglets
roam the locked farmyard.
I sit on a stool
in the mud and sun.

We are all on holiday.

The odor of chamomile
strong as church incense
after the rain
and the pigs' rooting

The sow makes
a deep sound
in her foraging,
and the piglets run
on tiny hooves
through the mud

toward her.

4.
A woman wearing
a white head scarf
and a red dress
walks the rutted road
on her way
to church,

carrying a bouquet.

william cullen bryant

The Battle of Bennington

On this fair valley's grassy breast
The calm, sweet rays of summer rest,
And dove-like peace divinely broods
On its smooth lawns and solemn woods.

A century since, in flame and smoke,
The storm of battle o'er it broke;
And ere the invader turned and fled,
These pleasant fields were strewn with dead.

Stark, quick to act and bold to dare,
And Warner's mountain band were there;
And Allen, who had flung the pen
Aside to lead the Berkshire men.

With fiery onset—blow on blow—
They rushed upon the embattled foe,
And swept his squadrons from the vale,
Like leaves before the autumn gale.

Oh! never may the purple stain
Of combat blot these fields again,
Nor this fair valley ever cease
To wear the placid smile of peace.

But we, beside this battlefield,
Will plight the vow that ere we yield
The right for which our fathers bled,
Our blood shall steep the ground we tread.

And men shall hold the memory dear
Of those who fought for freedom here,
And guard the heritage they won
While these green hill-sides feel the sun.

Written for the hundredth anniversary of the battle of Bennington, August 16, 1877.

david citino

The Death of Ray Chapman

He was the best friend I had.
—Tris Speaker

Carl Mays had hit five batters
that summer of 1920, and now on the mound
in a Polo Grounds' fog he counted slowly to 6.

Chapman dug in, bat near his head, and leaned
toward the plate, "the best bunter in the A.L.,"
they said later to be kind; but though his hands
were slow his arm was young enough to knock down
a runner from the back of the hole.

Mays' submarine toss submerged into mist
around home to surface at the side of the boy's head,
shattering the nerves that manage speech.
Chappie went down like a Texas Leaguer
plummeting between outfielders.

Muddy Ruel tore off the mask, sprang to his feet
and pivoted on the blood-ball, wheeling
to throw toward first. In Cleveland that night
downtown grew lurid with bonfire, thousands
cheered for Mays' blood, shook the cathedral
with the hands and feet of their prayer.

That fall Chicago went to hell in dark socks
and Cleveland ruled the world.

*Ray Chapman, the only on-field fatality in the history of Major League baseball,
was beaned on August 17, 1920.*

george chambers

August 18

at 4 am he wakes
he hears a cock crow Christ around the corner
the bodies of women dead and yet in pain writhe on the sheet
Eisenhower's heart is attacked again in Washington
out the window there are many stars, a moon
he turns to sleep again, his face muffled in the woman beside him
She writes from Bolivia: my asthma is treating me rather well
he rises on an elbow
a line of what might be a poem occurs
he thinks to write it down
it repeats itself in his head
he adjusts it
what Mayakovsky really wanted was a Renault
in the dark he goes down stairs to the refrigerator
he opens the door he stares through the cold smoke of the food
he takes a soda he drinks it he takes another
he is lonely for his daughter, having her seventh birthday
about that, he thinks, he was wrong
he starts to rhyme
there once was a man from Brazil
at the kitchen table he composes his gravestone
here lies me long and here lies me dead
Simon Bolivar var var he giggles
har har
where are the apples in Minneapolis
he goes out to see the moon the stars to walk
in a ditch he sees a migrant worker with a knife
inside again he thinks of the body of the woman sleeping above him
yesterday he said to her: you hate PLAYBOY sweetiepie,
    but I have to keep abreast somehow
annie, he says, annie, his first daughter, her name
hard little apples shine in the moonlight
on a piece of paper he prints o t h e r
was it Ionesco who said: mama peep's geese?
he takes the pencil in his hand writes please
he watches that word
he puts the pencil in his other hand and writes please please

michael schmidt

Homage to Federico García Lorca, August 19, 1969

1

Morning or night?
Unseen, a lorry bumped out of Granada.
The guards' bones were rattling
but they sat, propped their carbines,
even laughing:
and ten prisoners, ten picks.

The weather lost heart.
Wind curled in the valley,
rain dumped on the hill.
For some reason
the black birds
did not trace this pleasure ride.

Revenge for fascists murdered
in the north, or a civil guard
jealous in love sent one of these ten
up a mountain suddenly unfamiliar,
a jondo lament
with no word at last.

2

Small infinities
arrived at in the dark,
one window open to the sea.

But never
pacing centenary tombstones.

His business was the wind,
how it empties, not the way
it dies.

For church he burned
two candles at each other
bent in a common shadow:
prayer and response, or two
faces recognized across a mirror.
They did not seem to burn away.

He came closest to finalities in that widow
who twisted a chicken's head right off
and let the body run away.

Once he told
a dead man

(and forgot)
"the sea
dies too."

3

I want to see
what made the words,

the hand that cancelled words.
Tell the sun to warm the body.
Let it live.

Live! but even the mouth
is stopped forever. Unless
the body's life
is word.

Still the horses pass, cobbles
uphill twisted like an eye:
morning milk, clouds
for children to drink
and the earth.

Would memory of the thousand
mornings nailed abruptly
in this last secret still hurt him,
and his own

grass-deep grave, unmarked?
Sent off without breakfast, no scrap
of bread that morning, no cock's crow,

when the orchards wore
a lemon light.

ey made him dig: he wept
e a Tibetan forced to wound the earth
eady warm with sun and sweat.

ats grazed his footprints.
gentle guard turned out his eyes.
ch orchard tree became a trigger—

t no black bird traced him,
en as they shovelled Spain on his voice,
lling him with sand and rocks.

It is a long way to the sea, no windows
in the black rough, and no boys
naked in the branches, gathering oranges.

Nailed right through the blue bone of his
    palm.
Pharisees make no mistake. The harm
was done. It doesn't even matter if he died.

Not to have prepared! And no one knew.
Granada cried out—does it believe—
"the sea too dies!"

john smith

The Death of Trotsky

I have been dreaming lately of the death of Trotsky,
Astonished to find, after the stifled night,
My pillow, on waking, not saturated with blood.
I do not see the bearded man in the room,
Nor the assassin with the axe hidden under his coat,
But only the shattered skull, with the electric blood
Shocking the Mexican air, and the brain exposed.
Even then, so we learn, the little Russian
Spoke, as if death (as it is) were immaterial.
Had he not spouted enough, chopping his way through the world?

We have no need to mourn a death like this
For such a man, nor would he have wished it.
The feather bed cushioning the bones of the gentle aged,
The last sigh scarcely flickering the petals of flowers
On the nursing table, this was not death's way
For the urgent fiend. Yet his murderer was so mild,
Smiling before the strike, then crying real tears.
Well, he is of small concern, and swiftly fades.
But the image returns: the air like crimson rain;
The bone splintered like the carapace of a crab.

I dream continually of this and, waking, I sometimes hear
From the hideous maw of violence unleashed,
Not Trotsky's words slurred by the blood on his tongue,
But sounds of those maimed and crucified by his life;
And could pray for a pitiless anger to blaze up
Discharging from their innocent despair
Against such monsters as this hot world spawns
A trinity of blows; or attend his grotesque funeral
Not in homage, but to cast upon his coffin
A wreath signed with their blood, their tears, their deaths.

Trotsky was murdered on August 20, 1940.

AUGUST 21

 a. r. ammons

from: Extremes and Moderations

Hurly-burly: taking on whatever is about to get off, up the
slack, ready with prompt-copy for the reiteration, electronic
to inspect the fuzzy-buffoon comeback, picking up the diverse
gravel of mellifluous banality, the world-replacing world

world-irradiating, lesser than but more outspoken:
constructing the stanza is not in my case exceedingly
difficult, variably invariable, permitting maximum change
within maximum stability, the flow-breaking four-liner, lattice

of the satisfactory fall, grid seepage, currents distracted
to side flow multiple laterals that at some extreme spill
a shelf, ease back, hit the jolt of the central impulse: the
slow working-down of careful investigation, the run

diffused, swamped into variable action: my ideal's a cold
clod clam calm, clam contained, nevertheless active in the
digestion, capable of dietary mirth, the sudden whisk, nearly
rollably spherical: ah, but friends, to be turned

loose on an accurate impulse! how handsome the stanzas are
beginning to look, open to the total acceptance, fracturing into

delight, tugging down the broad sweep, thrashing it into
particulars (within boundaries): diversity, however—as of

the concrete—is not ever-pleasing: I've seen fair mounds
of fine-stone at one end or the other of highway construction
many times and been chiefly interested in the "hill": but
abstraction is the bogey-boo of those incapable of it, while,

merrily, every abstractor brings the concrete up fine: one,
anyway, as Emerson says, does well what one settles down to:
it's impossible anyone should know anything about the concrete
who's never risen above it, above the myth of concretion. . . .

I didn't see the hornet at first when I went to attach the
hose: he was sucking the spigot: people around here don't
have sprinklers, I can't understand it: I always used to have

one in South Jersey: maybe the water's expensive or maybe
very dry spells are rare: seems to me I remember a very dry
one last year: the days are shortening: it's sundown
now: at eight: maybe a little later officially, but the sun's

down behind the ridge on the other side of the lake by then: any
night could turn sharp cold—read August 21: I've been at this
poem or prose-poem or versification of diversification for three
or four days: I'll never get all the weeds

out of the grass: I just know after each day that
there are a hell of a lot fewer weeds in the lawn:
it's evening: seven: I just noticed
a dark cloud coming from the west, so I went out

and said, please, rain some here: a few pin drops
fell, I think though more because of the dark cloud than the
saying: saying doesn't do any good but it doesn't
hurt: aligns the psychic forces with the natural:

that alignment may have some influence: I have found the world
so marvelous that nothing would surprise me: that may sound
contradictory, the wrong way to reach the matter-of-fact. . . .

humphrey o'sullivan

Evicted Woman

This is the road out of here
Through the potato field,
I planted them—but Deveraux will dig them—
Through the wheat field
My sons sowed it—but Deveraux will harvest it—
My Curse on him
Through the yard by my little wood pigeons,
They will roast in Deveraux's pot.

My own husband built this house,
I myself darkened the rafters with soot,
But Deveraux took the door off the jamb,
He took the hinges off the hooks
He left the house without a door,
The window without glass,
The hearth without a fire,
The sty without sow or sucking-pig,
Or boar, large or small, fat or lean.

I will never hear again
The anxious lowing of my cow to her calf
The whinny of my mare to her foal
The bleat of my sheep to her lamb
The call of my goat to her kid
The clucking of my hens to their chickens
The morning-call of my rooster.

I will not see again my white duck
Nor my speckled drake
Nor my honking goose
Nor my shining gander.

I will not see the bog-pool
Nor hear the cry of the bittern
Nor the shriek of the wild goose
Nor the small moan of the green plover
Nor the fluting of the moor plover
Nor the thin whine of the jack-snipe.

I will not see the crane
Nor hear the splashing of the water hen,
I will not dredge the pool
For the eel or the pike
>   *Far from here I will die*
>   *And my unhappy husband and my sad children*

The sweet mint will not grow by my stream
Nor the red and white clover in my meadow,
I will not plant flax nor pull it
Nor steep it in the pond,
I will not turn my spinning wheel
I will twist no yarn.

My loom for wool and linen is thrown in the ditch
My chest is flung in the quarry
My table across the fence
My pans on the waste-ground
My chair out in the rain,
My pallet is without blanket or quilt,
My head has no covering
My back has no cloak.
>   *For rent they are taken*
>   *A hard cruel fate*

> *Trans. Joan Keefe*

*This poem is based on an episode described by Humphrey O'Sullivan in his Diary
dated August 22, 1828. The keening woman's family had been evicted by Patrick
Deveraux.*

AUGUST 23

susan mitchell

Meditations on a Photograph

"When you look at me that way
you look just like my mother . . ."

This said by my own mother.
But in this last photo taken of my grandmother
she looks like someone we'd never known,

as if at the last moment
she's realized another possibility and become it
without warning or the least hesitation.
Whenever mother looks at the picture she says
"You can see she is dying there."
Can you? Can you see it?
The picture was taken August 23, 1965
at my aunt's beach house overlooking Conscience Bay.
The time is a little after lunch,
a long lunch that must have gone on until two or three.
Some of what we were eating is in the photo—
bread, ham and a bunch of green grapes.
Grandmother should have been sitting between
me and two of her daughters. But at the last moment
she leaned forward, reaching out of the picture,
as if she wanted to stop the photographer
or had something urgent to say.
She blurred part of the photo. The leaves are smeared.
I could be looking at them through a rain-streaked window.
And for whatever eternity a photo has
there will be a silver streak
where she elbowed a knife off the table.

"Look at the eyes." That's mother again.
One of grandmother's eyes is rheumy, enflamed,
the eye of an old and decrepit bird,
a maddened eye,
fixed, staring out at the world, angry
at what it can no longer see.
I follow it back
into the skull, pulled inward, sucked
into the brain where the anger burns aimlessly,
a blind hole
beyond the reaches of us whose eyes
swing lightly over trees, houses, hands and other eyes.

Then there's the mouth—smiling, open, working
against the eye, denying the meaning of the eye, insisting
that the eye, like the hand lifting
the grapes, only wants—what? What does it want?
The hand lifts out of the photo, the eye
leads back in. I weave in and out, sometimes
thinking the eye must have been caught unawares,
before it could compose itself

into the weakly tearing eye
Grandmother always wiped with a white handkerchief.

. . .

Maybe the picture isn't important.
After all, grandmother didn't choose to be in it.
She hardly touched any of the food.
Her legs hurt her all afternoon. Perhaps
her hand is pointing to what the photographer left out—
the wind, salty and fresh, the buzz
of a seaplane and the beach tilting slightly
upward, where only that morning I had picked mussels.
Grandmother spotted them. The shells,
purple-black under the water, were opening,
the orange tongues sticking out.
We sat on the beach and ate them out of their shells.
Then we watched the wake of a boat.
One wave came in to the shore. The other wave,
lifting like the fin of an enormous fish,
continued out to sea.

AUGUST 24

walter james turner

Hymn to Her Unknown

In despair at not being able to rival the creations of God
I thought on her
Whom I saw on the twenty-fourth of August nineteen thirty-four
Having tea on the fifth story of Swan and Edgar's
In Piccadilly Circus.

She sat facing me with an older woman and a younger
And a little boy aged about five;
I could see that she was his mother,
Also she wore a wedding-ring and one set with diamonds.

She was about twenty-five years old,
Slim, graceful, disciplined;

She had none of the mannerisms of the suburbs,
No affectations, a low clear speech, good manners,
Hair thick and undyed.

She knew that she was beautiful and exceedingly attractive,
Every line of her dress showed it;
She was cool and determined and laughed heartily,
A wide mouth with magnificent teeth.

And having said this I come to the beginning of my despair,
Despair that I in no way can describe her
Or bring before the eyes of the present or the future
This image that I saw.

Hundreds and hundreds of women do I see
But rarely a woman on whom my eyes linger
As the eyes of Venus lingered on Adonis.

What is the use of being a poet?
Is it not a farce to call an artist a creator,
Who can create nothing, not even re-present what his eyes have seen?

She never showed a sign that she saw me
But I knew and she knew that I knew—
Our eyes fleeting past, never meeting directly
Like that vernal twinkling of butterflies
To which Coleridge compared Shakespeare's *Venus and Adonis*.

And, like Venus, I lavished my love upon her
I dallied with her hair, her delicate skin and smooth limbs,
On her arms were heavy thick bangles
Like the ropes of my heart's blood.

Could I express the ecstasy of my adoration?
Mating with her were itself a separation!
Only our bodies fusing in a flame of crystal
Burning in an infinite empyrean
Until all the blue of the limitless heaven were drunken
In one globe of united perfection
Like a bubble that is all the oceans of the world ascending
To the fire that is the fire of fires, transcending
The love of God, the love of God, the love of God—
Ah! my pitiful efforts now ending
I remember a bough of coral

Flower of the transparent sea
Delicate pink as though a ray of the sun descending
Pathless into the ocean
Printed the foot of Venus
Where bloomed this asphodel.

seamus heaney

The Strand at Lough Beg

In Memory of Colum McCartney

> *All round this little island, on the strand*
> *Far down below there, where the breakers strive,*
> *Grow the tall rushes from the oozy sand.*
> —Dante, *Purgatorio*, I, 100–103

Leaving the white glow of filling stations
And a few lonely streetlamps among fields
You climbed the hills towards Newtownhamilton
Past the Fews Forest, out beneath the stars—
Along that road, a high, bare pilgrim's track
Where Sweeney fled before the bloodied heads,
Goat-Beards and dogs' eyes in a demon pack
Blazing out of the ground, snapping and squealing.
What blazed ahead of you? A faked road block?
The red lamp swung, the sudden brakes and stalling
Engine, voices, heads hooded and the cold-nosed gun?
Or in your driving mirror, tailing headlights
That pulled out suddenly and flagged you down
Where you weren't known and far from what you knew:
The lowland clays and waters of Lough Beg,
Church Island's spire, its soft treeline of yew.

There you used to hear guns fired behind the house
Long before rising time, when duck shooters
Haunted the marigolds and bulrushes,
But still were scared to find spent cartridges,

Acrid, brassy, genital, ejected,
On your way across the strand to fetch the cows.
For you and yours and yours and mine fought shy,
Spoke an old language of conspirators
And could not crack the whip or seize the day:
Big-voiced scullions, herders, feelers round
Haycocks and hindquarters, talkers in byres,
Slow arbitrators of the burial ground.

Across that strand of yours the cattle graze
Up to their bellies in an early mist
And now they turn their unbewildered gaze
To where we work our way through squeaking sedge
Drowning in dew. Like a dull blade with its edge
Honed bright, Lough Beg half shines under the haze.
I turn because the sweeping of your feet
Has stopped behind me, to find you on your knees
With blood and roadside muck in your hair and eyes,
Then kneel in front of you in brimming grass
And gather up cold handfuls of the dew
To wash you, cousin. I dab you clean with moss
Fine as the drizzle out of a low cloud.
I lift you under the arms and lay you flat.
With rushes that shoot green again, I plait
Green scapulars to wear over your shroud.

Colum McCartney was murdered on his return from a soccer match on August 25, 1976.

william blake

The Battle of Crécy

from: King Edward the Third

Scene v. Sir Thomas Dagworth's Tent. SIR THOMAS DAG-
WORTH—to him.

[*Enter* SIR WALTER MANNY.]

SIR WALTER	Sir Thomas Dagworth, I have been weeping
	Over the men that are to die to-day.
DAGWORTH	Why, brave Sir Walter, you or I may fall.
SIR WALTER	O Dagworth, France is sick! the very sky,
	Tho' sunshine light it, seems to me as pale
	As the pale fainting man on his death-bed,
	Whose face is shewn by light of sickly taper!
	It makes me sad and sick at very heart,
	Thousands must fall today!
DAGWORTH	Thousands of men must leave this prison house,
	To be exalted to those heavenly fields,
	Where songs of triumph, psalms of victory,
	Where peace, and joy, and love, and calm content,
	Sit singing in the azure clouds, and strew
	Flowers of heaven's growth over the banquet-table:
	Bind ardent Hope upon your feet like shoes,
	Put on the robe of preparation,
	The table is prepar'd in shining heaven,
	The flowers of immortality are blown;
	Let those that fight, fight in good steadfastness,
	And those that fall shall rise in victory.
SIR WALTER	I've often seen the burning field of war,
	And often heard the dismal clang of arms;
	But never, till this fatal day of Crécy,
	Has my soul fainted with these views of death!
	I seem to be in one great charnel-house
	And seem to scent the rotten carcases!
	I seem to hear the dismal yells of death,
	While the black gore drops from his horrid jaws:
	Yet I not fear the monster in his pride—
	But O the souls that are to die to-day!

DAGWORTH	Stop, brave Sir Walter, let me drop a tear,
	Then let the clarion of war begin;
	I'll fight and weep, 'tis in my country's cause;
	I'll weep and shout for glorious liberty.
	Grim war shall laugh and shout, decked in tears,
	And blood shall flow like streams across the meadows,
	That murmur down their pebbly channels, and
	Spend their sweet lives to do their country service:
	Then shall England's verdure shoot, her fields shall
	smile,
	Her ships shall sing across the foaming sea,
	Her mariners shall use the flute and viol,
	And rattling guns, and black and dreary war,
	Shall be no more.
SIR WALTER	Well, let the trumpet sound, and the drum beat;
	Let war stain the blue heavens with bloody banners,
	I'll show my sword, nor ever sheath it up,
	'Till England blow the trump of victory,
	Or I lay stretch'd upon the field of death!

In one of the great battles of the Hundred Years' War, Edward III's army defeated the French under Philip VI at Crécy field on August 26, 1346.

AUGUST 27

keith chandler

Kett's Rebellion

On Mousehold Heath they gathered
Kett's ragtail army, 30,000 peasants.
Below them the city of Norwich
trembled, a mirage in the summer heat.
Mayor Codd and his burgesses
flapping like chickens overcircled by a hawk
sent deputies bowing up the hillside
to bargain for time with bread and meat,
meanwhile sunk their valuables in wells
and out of a secret gate
sped messengers to London squawking for help
against Kett "that Captain of Mischief"
and his "parcel of vagabonds . . . brute beasts."

For six weeks up on Mousehold Heath they sat
high on heather, sky and hope.
"Twas a merry world when we were yonder
eating of mutton" one would look back.
The sun poured down like honey

and there was work for work-shaped hands,—
stakes to be sharpened, trenches to be dug,
a New Jerusalem of turf thrown up.
Hacking down the hated fences
and rounding up gentry was for sport.
Meanwhile the Dreamer under the Oak
wrote these words with the tip of his tongue:
"We desire that Bondmen may be free
as Christ made all free, His precious blood shedding."
The sentries lay back on cupped palms.
Crickets in the dry grass wound their watch.
City-men crawled like ants.
Clouds coasted round the edge . . .

"The country gnoffs, Hob, Dick, and Hick
With clubs and clouted shoon
Shall fill the Vale of Dussindale
With slaughtered bodies soon."

August 27th, 1549.
A long black cloud against the blood-red sunrise
Warwick and his mounted Landsknechts showed up.
One puff of their cannon
took the skull of Mousehold Heath clean off.
Then down the hill they tumbled
with their pitchforks, their birdslings, their billhooks.
They had no chance,—less
than rabbits making a run for it
when the combine rips into the last patch
and the Guns stand by, about to make laconic remarks.
So they laid themselves down, ripe for sacrifice,
till the brook got tired of undertaking
and Dussindale was bloodily fulfilled.
Kett, found shivering in a barn,
was dragged through the city in ankle-chains
then hung upside down from the castle wall,—
they made fun of Death in those days.

Then Mayor Codd called for a Thanksgiving Mass
followed by feasting in the streets.
While many a poor cottage-woman
waiting for her menfolk to come back
heard tapping on the shutters that night
but it was handfuls of rain.

AUGUST 28

lucy terry

Bar's Fight, August 28, 1746

August 'twas, the twenty-fifth,
Seventeen hundred forty-six,
The Indians did in ambush lay,
some very valient men to slay,
The names of whom I'll not leave out:
Samuel Allen like a hero fout,
And though he was so brave and bold,
His face no more shall we behold;
Eleazer Hawks was killed outright,
Before he had time to fight,
Before he did the Indians see,
Was shot and killed immediately;
Oliver Amsden, he was slain,
Which caused his friends much grief and pain;
Simeon Amsden they found dead,
Not many rods off from his head;
Adonijah Gillet, we do hear,
Did lose his life, which was so dear;
John Saddler fled across the water,
And so escaped the dreadful slaughter;
Eunice Allen see the Indians comeing,
And hoped to save herself by running,
And had not her petticoats stopt her,
The awful creatures had not cotched her,
And tommyhawked her on the head,
And left her on the ground for dead;

Young Samuel Allen, oh! lack-a-day,
Was taken and carried to Canada.

Deerfield historian George Sheldon describes "Bar's Fight" as "the fullest contemporary account of that bloody tragedy which has been preserved." It is unclear, however, why the massacre, which occurred on August 28, 1746, is erroneously dated by Terry on the twenty-fifth.

AUGUST 29

william cowper

On the Loss of the *Royal George*

Toll for the brave—
The brave! that are no more:
  All sunk beneath the wave,
Fast by their native shore.
  Eight hundred of the brave,
Whose courage well was tried,
  Had made the vessel heel
And laid her on her side;
  A land-breeze shook the shrouds,
And she was overset;
  Down went the *Royal George*,
With all her crew complete.

Toll for the brave—
Brave Kempenfelt is gone,
  His last sea-fight is fought,
His work of glory done.
  It was not in the battle,
No tempest gave the shock,
  She sprang no fatal leak,
She ran upon no rock;
  His sword was in the sheath,
His fingers held the pen,
  When Kempenfelt went down
With twice four hundred men.

Weight the vessel up,
Once dreaded by our foes,

And mingle with your cup
The tears that England owes;
   Her timbers yet are sound,
And she may float again,
   Full charg'd with England's thunder,
And plough the distant main;
   But Kempenfelt is gone,
His victories are o'er;
   And he and his Eight hundred
Must plough the wave no more.

The Royal George *turned turtle and sank on August 29, 1782.*

AUGUST 30

john dryden

The Death of Cleopatra

from: All for Love

Act V
[*Enter* Charmion *and* Iras *to* Cleopatra.]

CHARMION   What must be done?
CLEOPATRA   Short ceremony, friends,
                          But yet it must be decent. First, this laurel
                          Shall crown my hero's head: he fell not basely,
                          Nor left his shield behind him.—Only thou
                          Couldst triumph o'er thyself; and thou alone
                          Wert worthy so to triumph.
CHARMION   To what end
                          These ensigns of your pomp and royalty?
CLEOPATRA   Dull that thou art! why, 'tis
                          to meet my love
                          As when I saw him first on Cydnus' bank,
                          All sparkling, like a goddess; so adorned,
                          I'll find him once again. My second spousals
                          Shall match my first in glory. Haste, haste, both,
                          And dress the bride of Antony.
CHARMION   —'Tis done.

CLEOPATRA   Now seat me by my lord. I claim this place,
             For I must conquer Caesar, too, like him,
             And win my share of the world.—Hail, you dear relics
             Of my immortal love!
             O let no impious hand remove you hence,
             But rest for ever here! Let Egypt give
             His death that peace which it denied his life.—
             Reach me the casket.

IRAS   Underneath the fruit
             The aspic lies.

CLEOPATRA   Welcome, thou kind deceiver!
             [*Putting aside the leaves.*]
             Thou best of thieves, who, with an easy key,
             Dost open life and, unperceived by us,
             Even steal us from ourselves, discharging so
             Death's dreadful office better than himself,
             Touching our limbs so gently into slumber
             That Death stands by, deceived by his own image,
             And thinks himself but sleep.

SERAPION   [*Within.*]   The queen
             where is she?
             The town is yielded, Caesar's at the gates.

CLEOPATRA   He comes too late to invade the rights of death.
             Haste, bare my arm, and rouse the serpent's fury.
             [*Holds out her arm, and draws it back.*]
             Coward flesh,
             Wouldst thou conspire with Caesar to betray me
             As thou wert none of mine? I'll force thee to it,
             But bring, myself, my soul to Antony.
             [*Turns aside, and then shows her arm bloody.*]
             Take hence. The work is done.

SERAPION   [*Within.*]   Break open the door
             And guard the traitor well.

CHARMION   The next is ours.

IRAS   Now, Charmion, to be worthy
             Of our great queen and mistress.
             [*They apply the aspics.*]

CLEOPATRA   Already, death, I feel thee in my veins.
             I go with such a will to find my lord
             That we shall quickly meet.
             A heavy numbness creeps through every limb,
             And now 'tis at my head. My eyelids fall,
             And my dear love is vanished in a mist.—
             Where shall I find him—where? O turn me to him,

And lay me on his breast!—Caesar, thy worst.
Now part us, if thou canst.   [*Dies*]

[IRAS *sinks down at her feet, and dies:* CHARMION
stands behind her chair, as dressing her head.]
[*Enter* SERAPION, *two* PRIESTS, ALEXAS, *bound,*
EGYPTIANS.]

PRIEST   Behold, Serapion,
What havoc death has made!

SERAPION   'Twas what I feared.—
Charmion, is this well done?

CHARMION   Yes, 'tis well done, and like a queen, the last
Of her great race. I follow her.
[*Sinks down and dies.*]

ALEXAS   'Tis true,
She has done well. Much better thus to die
Than live to make a holiday in Rome.

SERAPION   See, see how the lovers sit in state together,
As they were giving laws to half mankind!
The impression of a smile, left in her face,
Shows she died pleased with him for whom she lived,
And went to charm him in another world.
Caesar's just entering: grief has now no leisure.
Secure that villain as our pledge of safety
To grace the imperial triumph.—Sleep, blest pair,
Secure from human chance, long ages out,
While all the storms of fate fly o'er your tomb;
And fame to late posterity shall tell
No lovers lived so great or died so well.
                                        [*Exeunt.*]

Cleopatra committed suicide on August 30, 30 B.C.

robert watson

Sadie's Ice Cream Parlor

The lives I've almost lost are eight;
I've lived by luck and luck alone.
I've seen three wars smoke up the sky.
Why does a fat, grumbly woman
I have not seen for thirty years
Sigh to me on moonlit summer nights?
I smell her marigolds and taste
Fresh strawberry on my lips.
Is she my muse? That ugly tub
Who never spoke a pleasant word.

Walking to Sadie's in moonlight
Round the lake's rim, down the mountain
To her cottage, an ice-cream store . . .
She dipped the largest cones in Jersey.
Three hundred pounds of gloom. Back up
The mountain by the stream we children
Ate climbing to our dreams. And now
I have children taller than I.

Was she Aphrodite in disguise?
My wife says, "Watch your weight!" Woe's me.
I sigh and grumble over beer.

I kissed my first girl walking home
From Sadie's, lips licking strawberry,
Our feet wound in the mountain stream.
Next day Hitler marched on Poland,
I caught ten speckled trout.
The future drops its noose around my neck.
A car pulls up: my children home
Safe from the Dairy Queen. Hurrah.

September

william corbett

Vermont Apollinaire

"From America comes the little hummingbird"
From morning mistclouds a raven descends
First the one kingfisher, plop then the mate, plop
They whirr and rattle away crossed wires
August's end tomatoes take on orange swallows disappear
The loons cry their bearded cry
Jane calls a crane stands at the stream's mouth
Stands impervious to any order save its own
From the sea mountains distant come gulls

I cannot carry a tune
Not in a bucket one note
I carry the past like a mailman letters
The past like a wave breaking always
Always about the break never in the right place
When I reach my address my letters fall through the slot

The little car, the bug is yellow
1st September 2 a.m. doused with dew
now crossing the Pepperpot bridge a wind
    roughens the dark water
whipping up tiny waves. Chalk on slate.
    My shirt is plastered
to me. The joggers jog their hair
    in flames. The wind
is ringing down the last
    blossoms all over town.
Gutters are dusty with doll
    bells on stems and
on Commonwealth and Beacon pink
    magnolia petals smear
grainy rust over concrete.
    This narrow way leads
to Kendall Square where every walker
    is rearranged
by winds that sluice between new
    high rises sweeping
grit off cheerless vast plazas.

The subway teeters by
rain like beebee chain on its many windows.
    A yellow street sweeper
below moves through the lanes
    of the cloverleaf
an ear really of highway that keeps
    to the river.
From here the state house is a gold
    thimble or nipple
swaggered over by stony giants
    blunt as stony fingers.

Summer swallows spring and goes into September
Like long division it is always there
Autumn, fall we say, fruit releases itself
You are now enough so the old catches up
Cross this bridge come to that one
You grow up and ancient history snaps back
Rubber band and rake handle

Morning before morning
Mist like flour
Cat wants in, butts the door
At garden's edge stand blackest ravens
This is the void some two or three there
Just beyond reach and they too hear cow's bell
How far that sound travels unheeded, feather on water

Hummingbirds need not prepare
They know, they know their way above the clouds
from the red sugar water all the way to Mexico

Goodbye Goodbye
You ruby throats who stop in air

Memory ardent for mercy

                                        1984

virgil

The Battle of Actium

from: Book VIII of the Aeneid

Betwixt the quarters flows a golden sea;
But foaming surges there in silver play.
The dancing dolphins with their tails divide
The glitt'ring waves, and cut their precious tide.
Amid the main, two mighty fleets engage
Their brazen beaks, oppos'd with equal rage.
Actium surveys the well-disputed prize;
Leucate's wat'ry plain with foamy billows fries.
Young Caesar, on the stern, in armor bright,
Here leads the Romans and their gods to fight:
His beamy temples shoot their flames afar,
And o'er his head is hung the Julian star.
Agrippa seconds him, with prosp'rous gales,
And, with propitious gods, his foes assails:
A naval crown, that binds his manly brows,
The happy fortune of the fight foreshows.
Rang'd on the line oppos'd, Antonius brings
Barbarian aids, and troops of Eastern kings;
Th' Arabians near, and Bactrians from afar,
Of tongues discordant, and a mingled war:
And, rich in gaudy robes, amidst the strife,
His ill fate follows him—th' Egyptian wife.
Moving they fight; with oars and forky prows
The froth is gather'd, and the water glows.
It seems, as if the Cyclades again
Were rooted up, and justled in the main;
Or floating mountains floating mountains meet:
Such is the fierce encounter of the fleet.
Fireballs are thrown, and pointed jav'lins fly;
The fields of Neptune take a purple dye,
The queen herself, amidst the loud alarms,
With cymbals toss'd her fainting soldiers warms—
Fool as she was! who had not yet divin'd
Her cruel fate, nor saw the snakes behind.
Her country gods, the monsters of the sky,
Great Neptune, Pallas, and Love's Queen defy:

The dog Anubis barks, but barks in vain,
Nor longer dares oppose th' ethereal train.
Mars in the middle of the shining shield
Is grav'd, and strides along the liquid field.
The Dirae souse from heav'n with swift descent;
And Discord, dyed in blood, with garments rent,
Divides the prease: her steps Bellona treads,
And shakes her iron rod above their heads.
This seen, Apollo, from his Actian height,
Pours down his arrows; at whose winged flight
The trembling Indians and Egyptians yield,
And soft Sabaeans quit the wat'ry field.
The fatal mistress hoists her silken sails,
And, shrinking from the fight, invokes the gales.
Aghast she looks, and heaves her breast for breath,
Panting, and pale with fear of future death.
The god had figur'd her as driv'n along
By winds and waves, and scudding thro' the throng.
Just opposite, sad Nilus opens wide
His arms and ample bosom to the tide,
And spreads his mantle o'er the winding coast,
In which he wraps his queen, and hides the flying host.
The victor to the gods his thanks express'd
And Rome, triumphant, with his presence bless'd.

Trans. John Dryden

The Battle of Actium, depicted on the shield of Aeneas, was fought on September 2, 31 B.C.

william wordsworth

Composed Upon Westminster Bridge, September 3, 1802

Earth has not any thing to show more fair:
Dull would he be of soul who could pass by
A sight so touching in its majesty:
This City now doth, like a garment, wear
The beauty of the morning: silent, bare,
Ships, towers, domes, theatres, and temples lie
Open unto the fields, and to the sky;
All bright and glittering in the smokeless air.
Never did sun more beautifully steep
In his first splendour, valley, rock, or hill;
Ne'er saw I, never felt, a calm so deep!
The river glideth at his own sweet will:
Dear God! the very houses seem asleep;
And all that mighty heart is lying still!

SEPTEMBER 4

peter levi

The Bombardment of Petropaulski

4 September 1854

When our grandfathers in their great ship
swept into the calm shallows of that bay
their snow-white canvas clung like a swan's wings
who swims in winter on the flooded field.
Their eyes glittered, their soul was twisted.
They were hungry and lustful like the sea.
They chewed crab-claws, crumbled sour biscuit,
and they ran out their heavy guns and fired.

•

The dancing water barred with blue and green,
the disciplined, loud firing of the fleet,

the points of fire answering from the shore,
the smoke, the smell, then the tang of the sea,
the spouting water of the cannon-balls.
Look, they are firing short from the seashore.

•

Our grandfathers came down like history
lashing the coastal towns with their great guns
whiplash of time and fate, worse than the gods.
They were gods in their day on their quarterdecks
with Christian calmness and bright instruments
and the hair on their bodies as rough as gorse.
Red blood as innocent as the sunset.

•

Dawn after dawn after dawn those men had seen,
oak ships with fair names creaking like whales,
and the blackest of heavens blasting apart,
the wonders of man on the face of the deep.

•

So there he sat and painted his own fleet
in watercolor delicately done,
with a quick sense of the gunnery aspect,
and the whole bay drowned in idyllic shade.
One vast mountain reared up to silver snow.

•

What is it hidden in the Russian hills?
A swollen fur of vineyards or scrub-trees.
A nothingness, a kind of mystery.
Empire on which the sun never rises.
The Admiral has not set foot on it.

•

They say an early Chinese Emperor
worshipped a rock and the moss on the rock
and in defeat he named it General,
lord of strategy, saviour and god.

True and tragic. But un-Victorian.
An Admiral out of a limerick
by brave sad musical Edward Lear,
the face like a snow-owl, the prancing feet.
Or a dull man, a kind of old lady,
touching up his sketch as the clouds shifted,
no eyes for action, just the exact scene.
Or a good man, a Buddha firing guns
and smelling somehow of chrysanthemums.

●

All day the great ships banged and banged away,
and cannon-balls spouted in the bright bay.

●

The whistle and the thunder of their wings
is silent, the most silent of all things.

●

SEPTEMBER 5

charles wright

from: A Journal of the Year of the Ox

—Ashes know what burns
               clouds savvy which way the wind blows . . .
Full moon like a bed of coals
As autumn revs up and cuts off:
Remembering winter nights like a doused light bulb
Leaning against my skin,
               object melting into the image
Under the quickly descending stars:
Once the impasse is solved, St. Augustine says, between matter and
    spirit,
Evil is merely the absence of good;
Which makes sense, if you understand what it truly means,
Full moon the color of sand now,
               and still unretractable . . .

In a bad way,
> I don't even know what I don't know,
Time like a one-eyed jack
> whose other face I can't see
Hustling me on O hustling me on,
Dark of the moon, far side of the sun, the back half of the sky.
Time is memory, he adds:
It's all in the mind's eye,
> where everything comes to one,
Conjecture, pure spirit, the evil the matter cannot present us—
As the sentence hides in the ink,
As dark hides in the light,
> as cancer hides in the smoke,
Time hides in our pockets, not stirring, not weighing much.

> *—5 September 1985*

SEPTEMBER 6

anonymous

White House Blues

Czolgosz, mean man,
He shot McKinley with his handkerchief on his hand,
In Buffalo.

Czolgosz, you done him wrong,
You shot McKinley when he was walking along,
In Buffalo, in Buffalo.

The pistol fires, then McKinley falls,
And the doctor says, "McKinley, can't find the ball."
In Buffalo, in Buffalo.

They sent for the doctor, the doctor come,
He come in a trot, and he come in a run,
To Buffalo, to Buffalo.

Forty-four boxes trimmed in lace,
Take him back to the baggage, boys, where we can't see his face,
In Buffalo, in Buffalo.

The engine whistled down the line,
Blowing every station, McKinley was a-dying,
In Buffalo, in Buffalo.

Seventeen coaches all trimmed in black
Took McKinley to the graveyard, but never brought him back,
To Buffalo, to Buffalo.

On September 6, 1901, Leon Czolgosz, a deranged anarchist, fatally shot President William McKinley while he was attending the Pan American Exposition in Buffalo, New York. McKinley died September 14th.

SEPTEMBER 7

edward dorn

On the Nature of Communication

September 7, 1966

As Dr. Verwoerd one day
sat at his appointed desk
in the parliament at Capetown
there came to him a green and black messenger.
(who did not, in fact, disagree with him)

and Dr. Verwoerd looked up
as the appropriately colored man
approached. He expected
a message. What he received
was a message. Nothing else.

That the message was delivered
to his thick neck
and his absolute breast
via a knife
that there was a part tied
to the innate evil of the man
is of no consequence
and as the condolences, irrelevant.

Thus, in the nature of communication,
Dr. Robert Kennedy is deeply shocked
and Dr. Wilson shocked
Dr. Portugal, that anonymous transvestite
is "with" the gentle people of
South Africa in this their moment
                    of grief
                    and wishes them well
in their mischief. A practical
and logical communication. Pope
Johnson also deplored etc.
Dr. Mennen Williams said something about "africa."

By its nature communication
ignores quality and opts for accuracy:
come on, tell us how many nigger's balls
tonight. Do not fold bend spindle or mutilate,
I needn't tell anyone
who has received a paycheck,
is each man's share in the plan.

james mcmichael

Each in a Place Apart

   When she ushers at an outdoor evening concert,
I meet her at the side gate. She can stay until ten.
On a bicycle to the eucalyptus grove, she brings her
This England book. She'd been there with the
parents of a friend one summer and wants to show me
London and the Cotswolds, Chester, Blenheim, Rye.
Standing on a felled tree, she pulls my ear to her shirt.
Every time for us is a rehearsal for September 8th
when we'll say good-bye. We know we'll write. We write
daily for a year. By thinking that on her way
south sometimes to see her grandmother I'd have
two hours with her in Union Station, I hold on.
My walk toward her from the car, her seeing me, her
face and how she'd feel against my chest. Of those

last minutes with her there would be a first, then others
after it, their series welling at my wrists and temples.
She'd let go of me, she'd turn to get her train and we'd have
lived it, we'd remember, it would have to be enough.
She writes that she is changing schools. Should she be
four hundred miles away or only sixty?

richard tillinghast

Today in the Café Trieste

> *Behind the red lacquered gates,*
> *wine is left to sour, meat to rot.*
> *Outside these gates*
> *lie the bones of the frozen and starved.*
> *The flourishing and the withered are just a foot apart.*
> *The thought of it is an open wound.*
> —Tu Fu, 8th Century

> *The Mountain Goddess, if she is still there,*
> *will see the world all changed.*
> —Mao Tse-tung, 1956

Today in the Café Trieste,
    in San Francisco,
I watch through high rippled windows
    flawed and old
the blue sky that reveals
        and resembles nothing.

A face in the mirror:
    someone else's for an instant
        as I order coffee.
A smile-line cuts the flesh on the left side
        like a scar
    in an otherwise balanced face,
as though everything I've smiled at in thirty-eight years,
        or accepted with irony,
pulled me toward one side of the universe.
My face returns my stare blankly.

326

I slip back into it.
The light slips off my lenses,
   the marine light of the hot afternoon,
      a little too bright for the wine
     I drank last night.

Mrs. Giotta says something in Italian:
La vita, life—
   or the world, *il mondo*,
      I think she is saying—
   is a solid, well-made glass.
This Italian lady sets a warm glass
        of something
         in front of you,
and you know the world is in order.
When order goes,
glass is the first thing to break.

Mindlessly I watch
   the North Italian daughter-in-law
      open the dishwashing machine
and roll out a tray
   on one-inch plastic wheels—
a tray of dishes like a story
      about the future of the world,
like Buenos Aires' walled-off gardens
      seen from a private plane.
In the upturned tops of green stemware—
   jade lakes, limpid
     half-moons
   of hot water, cooling,
redolent of jungle spring,
   clean steam rising in the café.

The daughter-in-law
   pumps the espresso machine
like a lady engineer
   in the cab of a steam locomotive
in Italy, after the Revolution.

I sit at my favorite table.

September 9, 1976,
   three years ago,
someone else's paper told me

Mao Tse-tung had died,
   ten minutes into that day.
I sat at this same corner table,
   looking at the newsprint photos,
      and watched the sky stream away—
   a wooden flagpole,
a Gothic rooftop wobbly in the old glass.

SEPTEMBER 10

 ramon guthrie

Death with Pants On

"Ace of aces." I saw him once in Harry's Bar
("Tell the taxi Sank Roo Doe Noo")
standing there with an untouched glass before him.
Georges Guynemer, the name had come to stand
beside Jeanne d'Arc's and Roland's. Apart those eyes
and the palm leaves on the ribbon of his Croix de Guerre
reaching to his belt, looked no more godlike
than any other slight tubercular boy of 22.
Not at all the lightning-hurling Zeus
that La Fresnaye's heroic portrait makes him.

Never too sharp a pilot, often shot down,
his Spad riddled, himself eight times wounded.
"But man, what eyes!" a fellow Cigogne told me.
"And nerve and—well, you've got to say, what luck!"
Two shots—tat-tat—two Fokkers down in flames.
Tat-tat-tat! Tat-tat-tat! Tat-tat-tat-tat!
Eleven bullets: a Rumpler and two more Fokkers.
That night I saw him, his score was 48.
He got five more before his string ran out.

Monday, September 10, sick, irascible,
he had three Spads conk out on him,
force-landed them and met the omen with a tantrum.
Tuesday even his mechanic begged him
to give his crippled luck a chance to heal.
Bright oblivion called him. His wing-man said,

"One moment he was there. The next the sky
was empty. Not a boche in sight. No flash!"
No trace of either his body or the Spad was found.
Fit apotheosis: the skies of France
his tomb and monument. Streets and schools
named for him, medals struck.

          I think of others
Chapin, Sayre, Comygies, Nick Carter
whom I last saw spinning down in flames
toward La Chaussée. Their first fight—
if you can call it that. Unmatched for unreality:
as we straggled out of clouds into a well
of open sky, the red-nosed hornets swooped.
Most of us
never found a chance to fire a shot.
There were others. I forget their names.

charlotte brontë

The Night-Wind

September 11, 1840

In summer's mellow midnight,
A cloudless moon shone through
Our open parlour window
And rosetrees wet with dew.

I sat in silent musing,
The soft wind waved my hair:
It told me Heaven was glorious,
And sleeping Earth was fair.

I needed not its breathing
To bring such thoughts to me
But still it whispered lowly,
"How dark the woods will be!

"The thick leaves in my murmur
Are rustling like a dream,
And all their myriad voices
Instinct with spirit seem."

I said, "Go, gentle singer,
Thy wooing voice is kind,
But do not think its music
Has power to reach my mind.

"Play with the scented flower,
The young tree's supple bough,
And leave my human feelings
In their own course to flow."

The wanderer would not heed me;
Its kiss grew warmer still—
"O come," it sighed so sweetly,
"I'll win thee 'gainst thy will.

"Have we not been from childhood friends?
Have I not loved thee long?
As long as thou hast loved the night
Whose silence wakes my song.

"And when thy heart is laid at rest
Beneath the church-yard stone
I shall have time enough to mourn
And thou to be alone."

michael dennis browne

Epithalamion/Wedding Dawn

for Nicholas & Elena

1

Happy the man who is thirsty.
And the moths, pilgrims to our screens.
The fisher stands waist-deep in the water,
waiting. Happy the man waiting.

Who is not alone? Who does not sleep
in the dark house of himself, without music?
The world, a collapsed fire, shows only its smoke,
and the smoke hides its hills,

hides, too, the places where we are sleeping,
the hand opened, the hand closed.
Fragments, the lovers lie. And the question,
saying:

Who is broken? No one is broken,
but the living are sleeping, like animals,
like the dead. Tree dreams
of the man he was, who walked

by the shore, who followed
the hill upward, who dragged his roots
through the universe, who lay down
to suffer there, and, loving the earth,

left it exhausted, returned to it renewed.
But the house is dark. The sky at such time
has no light. Even the lines in the hand
are a little desert without name, and silent.

2

Friends: in the hours before dawn, the day of your wedding.
What will I tell you then?
That solitude's thorn

breaks into bloom now? I think it is so.
I think that if we are scarred, light heals us now.
We can be heard, making our difficult music.
And for this the sun
drags itself up from the dark parts of the world,
again, again.
The windows take on the peculiar fire of the living.
The dog hoots like a wood-pigeon, he has *his* morning.

3

You must not be angry with this planet.
For we are in a company
whose music surpasses its pain.
For I tell you, I sat in the dark, also,
and the wedding light came onto my window,
and the hills were cleared for me,
and the field spread out in front of me, remarkable, like marble.
And I thought; this is their day,
how it breaks for them!
O sir, the angel flies, even with bruises
O lady, a bird can wash himself anywhere.
The dawn that came up the day of your wedding
took me in its hand like the creature that I am;
and I heard the dark that I came from
whispering "Be silent."
And the dawn said "Sing."
And I found the best words I could find around me,
and came to your wedding.

Nicholas Delbanco and Elena Greenhouse were married on September 12, 1970.

john clellon holmes

Out of a Fever

for Robert Lowell
(Sept. 13, 1977)

This is an age of elegy in our poetry.
He morning-aftered everyone from Ford to Berryman.
Now he's gone off in a cab (just as he used to do),
not to come back this time. Yet I can't feel the curses
of the young at death's fat yawn at seriousness,
just the illusion of the futility of our endeavors—
which is all that's left of youth in me.

An engineer of breath, a poet's fevers
burn on, year in, life out, until the
last expenditure's demanded—breath itself.

Maule's curse hung over him, and me—
exalte mothers, ne'er-do-wells for fathers,
Sunday roasts, linen stiff as board, awesome uncles,
dead leaves scuttling through a burying ground,
reviving stink of bilgy harbors after a carouse.
He got free with half his wits intact, and so did I.

His exemplary life caesuraed now—pacifist, poet,
teacher, inmate, drunk—a typical contemporary scribe.
Dogged by history, his attempts to leash it
were a True Believer's ethic in a beliefless age.
But what we'll miss next year will be his thorny line.

Cheating world, that woos a man's concern,
then kills him for his trouble with a grin—
But enough of that. This Holmes salutes that Lowell
on this day of his abrupt departure for Back Bay.

—1977

donald davie

Montcalm

It is reported of General Wolfe that as he drifted by night to the secret assault of the Heights of Abraham he quoted to his companions some famous stanzas of the elegy of Grey.

The French and the British commander were alike destined to die on the morrow, and thus to illustrate the melancholy truth of the poet's reflections. Montcalm was himself a poet, and appended pious verses in French and Latin to a cross erected on his field of victory at Ticonderoga. He had the sentiments and inclinations of a country gentleman.

He died before he could learn which of his children had predeceased him.

In Candiac by Nimes in Languedoc
He left a mill to grind his olives well
Who now must harvest laurels. Who had died
In Candiac? All Bougainville could tell
Was of a death. Mirète he thought had died
If it was Mirète. He never could decide
For whom the olives sighed in Languedoc.

To Candiac by Nimes in Languedoc
A murmur reaches from the perjured wave
That floats surprise and France's great reverse:
At dawn, too late, the cliffs will answer back.
"The paths of glory lead but to the grave"
—Marmoreal verses, plumes to tuft a hearse
and scutcheons black for squires of Candiac.

From Candiac by Nimes in Languedoc
Quoting Corneille—"though, Christian! not Montcalm
Nor his sagacity nor up-ended trees
Nor men nor deeds checked England, but God's arm"—
Coming from this and homelier pieties
In Candiac by Nimes in Languedoc
To earn the stucco tribute of a plaque,

Montcalm had met, if we should say his match,
We ought to mean his match in hardihood

Hardly in grace, James Wolfe, but most of all
His match in fate, his double. Did he catch
If not the low voice, still its tone, the mood?
The paths of glory led but to Quebec
From Candiac by Nimes in Languedoc.

Both earned their stucco. Marble was reserved
To honour the intrepid, the serene
And the successful Amherst. But it served,
Pompous and frigid as it was, the phrase
"A martial glory": common ground between
The public lives, the private, Kent, Quebec,
And Candiac by Nimes in Languedoc.

*The Battle of Quebec, in which both opposing Generals, Wolfe and Montcalm, lost
their lives, was fought on September 14, 1759.*

nathaniel tarn

For the Death of Anton Webern
Particularly

Sunday gardening, hoeing, trying to think of nothing but
hoeing—so that this at least can be an exercise in the true sense—
nevertheless I can think of little but the death of Anton Webern.
I just happened to read it. It just happened to be Webern.
One has ferreted out and written up at length how the Weberns
went out to dine some night with their daughter and their
(unbeknown to them) blackmarketeer of a son-in-law, shortly
after the American occupation. The G.I. agent provocateur went out
to block any escape. Just at that moment, in the black back yard,
the fragile Webern, out to puff a gift cigar, collided
with the decoy who shot him by mistake. Back home, not knowing
whom he'd killed, but withered by it, this kind man died of drink.

Sunday gardening, hoeing, I turn over the worms in their beds
and am shadowed by the blackbirds. And I have to ask again from what
body-stitching the worms are sundered and picked out writhing to die,
and from what soul-harrowing that Rome of blackbirds flutters down

to drill and gut the worms with javelin beaks, and in the fold of what
wedding of body and desire in Jerusalem I am conceived and born
to offer this show. I need to ask on what Sunday God first churned
his cauldron world in such a manner that we all deal death,
not knowing that we deal it, scarcely caring, yet dying of it too
from afar—in what stew God first mixed meat of worm,
feather and beak of bird and hand of man and what bubbles
send up each in turn to do the other in. And how, at last, the notes
composed by fragile Webern survive the boil and music in the bubbles.

Anton Webern was killed September 15, 1945.

 james merrill

16.IX.65

For Vassili and Mimi

Summer's last half moon waning high
Dims and curdles. Up before the bees
On our friend's birthday, we have left him
To wake in their floating maze.

Light downward strokes of yellow, green, and rust
Render the almond grove. Trunk after trunk
Tries to get right, in charcoal,
The donkey's artless contrapposto.

Sunrise. On the beach
Two turkey gentlemen, heads shaven blue
Above dry silk kimonos sashed with swords,
Treat us to a Kabuki interlude.

The tiny fish risen excitedly
Through absolute transparence
Lie in the boat, gasping and fanning themselves
As if the day were warmer than the sea.

Cut up for bait, our deadest ones
Reappear live, by magic, on the hook.
Never anything big or gaudy—
Line after spangled line of light, light verse.

A radio is playing "Mack the Knife."
The morning's catch fills one straw hat.
Years since I'd fished. Who knows when in this life
Another chance will come?

Between our toes unused to sandals
Each step home strikes its match.
And now, with evening's four and twenty candles
Lit among stars, waves, pines

To animate our friend's face, all our faces
About a round, sweet loaf,
Mavrili brays. We take him some,
Return with honey on our drunken feet.

alan ross

Off Brighton Pier

I saw him, a squat man with red hair
Grown into sideburns, fishing off Brighton pier:
Suddenly he bent, and in a lumpy bag
Rummaged for bait, letting his line dangle,
And I noticed the stiffness of his leg
That thrust out, like a tripod, at an angle.
Then I remembered: the sideburns, that gloss
Of slicked-down ginger on a skin like candy floss.
He was there, not having moved, as last,
On a windless night, leaning against the mast,
I saw him, rummaging a bag for numbers.
And the date was the 17th of September,
15 year back, and we were playing Tombola
During the last Dog, someone beginning to holler
"Here you are" for a full card, and I remember

He'd just called "Seven and six, she was worth it,"
When—without contacts or warning—we were hit.
Some got away with it, a few bought it.
And I recall now, when they carried him ashore,
Fishing gear lashed to his hammock, wishing
Him luck, and his faint smile, more
To himself than to me, when he saluted
From the stretcher, and, cadging a fag,
Cracked "I'm quids in, its only one leg,
They'll pension me off to go fishing."

SEPTEMBER 18

tod perry

For Nicholas, Born in September

You bring the only changes to this season.
Once more, Gomorrah has enjoyed its harvest;
old cards, discarded dominoes and chips
lie scattered on the patio; the beach
is quiet, half of its shells brought home to fade
like negatives. For miles the day is empty,
given to gulls that slide along the wind
and stab the shore. And I recall the way
so many autumns came. Bulbs on a cord
tottering upside down like icicles
above the wooden bandstand, a scarf of sand,
curling, begins to bury the cement.

We used to play there, in and out like moths
among the dancers, but more often owls,
perching along the edge of night, we'd screech
and try to disapprove of what we saw.
Our parents told us that before the war
the town was better, and certainly, with time,
things would improve; their dignity was silence,
and summers lean and lifeless as the winter
afternoons. Now you have proved the future
falls in slow progressions of the present.
The night the season ended, on Labor Day,
campfires roasted strings of unsold oysters

they'd given to us free. We'd watch sparks lift
across the fire, then finally disappear.
By morning the dancers were no longer there.

For two weeks after Labor Day, we'd spot
great herds of porpoises leap up the coast
in rain and ride out like September clouds.
Always, before, it was the saddest month,
the beach and water one monotonous sea
of careless stirrings and transparencies,
the cool breezes turning the white drifts gray.

Today, I saw a red oak tree—the one
they planted when the war was won—its leaves,
stubborn as winter, clawing in the wind
as if to tear it down. The tree in time
collapsed among the barren, upright elms,
but watching it drop here reminded me
how soon the days adjusted to the fall
and settled in to wait like seeds till June,
when porpoises return, salting the tides.

My first-born, the eighteenth of September
of my only season, you have risen
like a sapling among these barren trees.
Each day I watch you spread the deepest roots
in our common soil; I touch you with my hand,
veined and strong as a leaf. This time I feel
a wind I never knew blow through my bones.

john keats

To Autumn

Season of mists and mellow fruitfulness,
  Close bosom-friend of the maturing sun;
Conspiring with him how to load and bless
  With fruit the vines that round the thatch-eves run;
To bend with apples the moss'd cottage-trees,

And fill all fruit with ripeness to the core;
   To swell the gourd, and plump the hazel shells
With a sweet kernel; to set budding more,
And still more, later flowers for the bees,
Until they think warm days will never cease,
   For Summer has o'er-brimm'd their clammy cells.

Who hath not seen thee oft amid thy store?
   Sometimes whoever seeks abroad may find
Thee sitting careless on a granary floor,
   Thy hair soft-lifted by the winnowing wind;
Or on a half-reap'd furrow sound asleep,
   Drows'd with the fume of poppies, while thy hook
      Spares the next swath and all its twined flowers:
And sometimes like a gleaner thou dost keep
   Steady thy laden head across a brook;
   Or by a cyder-press, with patient look,
      Thou watchest the last oozings hours by hours.

Where are the songs of Spring? Ay, where are they?
   Think not of them, thou hast thy music too,—
While barred clouds bloom the soft-dying day,
   And touch the stubble-plains with rosy hue;
Then in a wailful choir the small gnats mourn
   Among the river sallows, borne aloft
      Or sinking as the light wind lives or dies;
And full-grown lambs loud bleat from hilly bourn;
   Hedge-crickets sing; and now with treble soft
   The red-breast whistles from a garden-croft;
      And gathering swallows twitter in the skies.

"How beautiful the season is now—How fine the air. A temperate sharpness about it. Really, without joking, chaste weather—Dian skies—I never lik'd stubble fields so much as now—Aye better than the chilly green of the spring. Somehow a stubble plain looks warm—in the same way that some pictures look warm—this struck me so much in my sunday's walk that I composed upon it." [Letter from Keats to J. R. Reynolds, Tuesday, September 21, 1819.]

charley george

Death of the Poet

september 18, 1830, sainte-beuve insulted his editor, pierre dubois. dubois slapped sainte-beuve and a duel was arranged for monday morning the 20th.

in a steady rain, sainte-beuve and his seconds took a carriage to the wooded suburb of romainville to meet dubois. stepping down from the carriage, sainte-beuve refused to hand over his silk umbrella. he did not mind getting killed, he told his seconds, but dreaded getting wet. at a distance of twenty paces, the umbrella'd sainte-beuve and exposed dubois fired at each other four times. neither being hit, they agreed to quit.

john ford

Perkin Warbeck's Wife Surrenders

from: The Chronicle History of Perkin Warbeck

Act V, scene i
[*Enter* KATHERINE *and* JANE *in riding-suits, with one* SERVANT.]

KATH   It is decreed; and we must yield to fate,
Whose angry justice, though it threaten ruin,
Contempt, and poverty, is all but trial
Of a weak woman's constancy in suffering.
Here in a stranger's and an enemy's land,
Forsaken and unfurnished of all hopes
But such as wait on misery, I range
To meet affliction wheresoe'er I tread.
My train and pomp of servants is reduced
To one kind gentlewoman and this groom.
Sweet Jane, now whither must we?

JANE   To your ships,
Dear lady, and turn home.

KATH   Home! I have none.
Fly thou to Scotland, thou hast friends will weep
For joy to bid thee welcome; but, O Jane,
My Jane, my friends are desperate of comfort,
As I must be of them; the common charity,
Good people's alms and prayers of the gentle,
Is the revenue must support my state.
As for my native country, since it once
Saw me a princess in the height of greatness
My birth allowed me, here I make a vow
Scotland shall never see me being fallen
Or lessened in my fortunes. Never, Jane,
Never to Scotland more will I return.
Could I be England's queen—a glory, Jane,
I never fawned on—yet the king who gave me
Hath sent me with my husband from his presence,
Delivered us suspected to his nation,
Rendered us spectacles to time and pity.
And is it fit I should return to such
As only listen after our descent
From happiness enjoyed to misery
Expected, though uncertain? Never, never!
Alas, why dost thou weep, and that poor creature
Wipe his wet cheeks too? let me feel alone
Extremities, who know to give them harbour;
Nor thou nor he has cause. You may live safely.

JANE   There is no safety whiles your dangers, madam,
Are every way apparent.

SERVANT   Pardon, lady;
I cannot choose but show my honest heart;
You were ever my good lady.

KATH   O dear souls,
Your shares in grief are too, too much!
[*Enter* DALYELL.]

DALYELL   I bring,
Fair princess, news of further sadness yet
Than your sweet youth hath been acquainted with.

KATH   Not more, my lord, than I can welcome; speak it;
The worst, the worst I look for.

DALYELL   All the Cornish
At Exeter were by the citizens
Repulsed, encountered by the earl of Devonshire

And other worthy gentlemen of the country.
Your husband marched to Taunton, and was there
Affronted by king Henry's chamberlain—
The king himself in person, with his army,
Advancing nearer to renew the fight
On all occasions. But the night before
The battles were to join, your husband privately,
Accompanied with some few horse, departed
From out the camp, and posted none knows whither.

KATH   Fled without battle given?

DALYELL   Fled, but followed
By Daubeney, all his parties left to taste
King Henry's mercy—for to that they yielded—
Victorious without bloodshed.

KATH   O, my sorrows!
If both our lives had proved the sacrifice
To Henry's tyranny, we had fallen like princes,
And robbed him of the glory of his pride.

DALYELL   Impute it not to faintness or to weakness
Of noble courage, lady, but foresight;
For by some secret friend he had intelligence
Of being bought and sold by his base followers.
Worst yet remains untold.

KATH   No, no, it cannot.

DALYELL   I fear you're betrayed. The earl of Oxford
Runs hot in your pursuit.

KATH   A' shall not need;
We'll run as hot in resolution gladly
To make the earl our jailor.

JANE   Madam, madam,
They come, they come!
[*Enter* OXFORD *with followers*]

*Katherine Gordon, wife of Perkin Warbeck, was captured by the Earl of Oxford on
September 21, 1497.*

edmund spenser

Sidney Wounded

from: Astrophel, A Pastorall Elegie

*Upon the Death of the Most Noble and Valorous Knight, Sir Philip
Sidney*

. . .

Such skill, matcht with such courage as he had,
Did prick him foorth with proud desire of praise
To seek abroad, of daunger nought ydrad,
His mistresse name, and his owne fame, to raise.
What needeth perill to be sought abroad,
Since, round about us, it doth make aboad!

It fortuned, as he that perilous game
In forreine soyle pursued far away;
Into a forest wide and waste he came,
Where store he heard to be of salvage pray.
So wide a forest and so waste as this,
Nor famous Ardeyn, nor fowle Arlo is.

There his welwoven toyles, and subtil traines,
He laid the brutish nation to enwrap:
So well he wrought with practice and with paines,
That he of them great troups did soone entrap.
Full happie man (misweening much) was hee,
So rich a spoile within his power to see.

Eftsoones, all heedlesse of his dearest hale,
Full greedily into the heard he thrust,
To slaughter them, and worke their finall bale,
Least that his toyle should of their troups be brust.
Wide wounds emongst them many one he made,
Now with his sharp borespear, now with his blade.

His care was all how he them all might kill,
That none might scape, (so partiall unto none:)
Ill mynd so much to mynd anothers ill,

As to become unmyndfull of his owne.
But pardon that unto the cruell skies,
That from himselfe to them withdrew his eise.

So as he rag'd emongst that beastly rout,
A cruell beast of most accursed brood
Upon him turnd, (despeyre makes cowards stout)
And, with fell tooth accustomed to blood,
Launched his thigh with so mischievous might,
That it both bone and muscles ryved quight.

So deadly was the dint and deep the wound,
And so huge streames of blood thereout did flow,
That he endured not the direfull stound,
But on the cold deare earth himselfe did throw;
The whiles the captive heard his nets did rend,
And having none to let, to wood did wend.

Ah! where were ye this while his shepheard peares,
To whom alive was nought so deare as hee:
And ye faire Mayds, the matches of his yeares,
Which in his grace did boast you most to bee?
Ah! where were ye, when he of you had need,
To stop his wound that wondrously did bleed?

Ah! wretched boy, the shape of dreryhead,
And sad ensample of mans suddein end:
Full litle faileth but thou shalt be dead,
Unpitied, unplaynd, of foe or frend!
Whilest none is nigh, thine eyelids up to close,
And kisse thy lips like faded leaves of rose.

. . .

On September 22, 1586, the Earl of Leicester unsuccessfully attempted to wrest the
city of Zutphen in the Netherlands from the Spanish. Sir Philip Sidney, Leicester's
thirty-two-year-old nephew, was fatally wounded in the skirmish (described by
Spenser in pastoral terms as a boar hunt) and died on October 17.

gerald w. barrax

First Carolina Rain

and
so
this is the way
it rains in carolina
23 sept 69
school started for them
in pittsburgh too
and they dont need this kind of rain
especially my second son
the grave serious one
needs dry weather
to carry his busted arm to school
(glad I tried to teach all three
ambi
     dexterity)
need it or not
i carry the rain to school with me
sometimes seeing in student's black faces
my own sons
wondering how it will be to face them
when they reach this age

geoffrey hill

September Song

born 19.6.32—deported 24.9.42

Undesirable you may have been, untouchable
you were not. Not forgotten
or passed over at the proper time.

As estimated, you died. Things marched,
sufficient, to that end.

Just so much Zyklon and leather, patented
terror, so many routine cries.

(I have made
an elegy for myself it
is true)

September fattens on vines. Roses
flake from the wall. The smoke
of harmless fires drifts to my eyes.

This is plenty. This is more than enough.

john greenleaf whittier

The Pipes at Lucknow

Pipes of the misty moorlands,
  Voice of the glens and hills;
The droning of the torrents,
  The treble of the rills!
Not the braes of bloom and heather,
  Nor the mountains dark with rain,
Nor maiden bower, nor border tower,
  Have heard your sweetest strain!

Dear to the Lowland reaper,
  And plaided mountaineer,—
To the cottage and the castle
  The Scottish pipes are dear;—
Sweet sounds the ancient pibroch
  O'er mountain, loch, and glade ;
But the sweetest of all music
  The pipes at Lucknow played.

Day by day the Indian tiger
  Louder yelled, and nearer crept;
Round and round the jungle-serpent
  Near and nearer circles swept.

"Pray for rescue, wives and mothers,—
  Pray to-day!" the soldier said ;
"To-morrow, death's between us
  And the wrong and shame we dread."

Oh, they listened, looked, and waited,
  Till their hope became despair;
And the sobs of low bewailing
  Filled the pauses of their prayer.
Then up spake a Scottish maiden,
  With her ear unto the ground:
"Dinna ye hear it?—dinna ye hear it?
  The pipes o' Havelock sound!"

Hushed the wounded man his groaning;
  Hushed the wife her little ones;
Alone they heard the drum-roll
  And the roar of Sepoy guns.
But to sounds of home and childhood
  The Highland ear was true;—
As her mother's cradle-crooning
  The mountain pipes she knew.

Like the march of soundless music
    Through the vision of the seer,
More of feeling than of hearing,
    Of the heart than of the ear,
She knew the droning pibroch,
        She knew the Campbell's call:
"Hark! hear ye no' MacGregor's,
    The grandest o' them all!"

Oh, they listened, dumb and breathless,
    And they caught the sound at last;
Faint and far beyond the Goomtee
    Rose and fell the piper's blast!
Then a burst of wild thanksgiving
    Mingled woman's voice and man's;
"God be praised!—the march of Havelock!
    The piping of the clans!"

Louder, nearer, fierce as vengeance,
    Sharp and shrill as swords at strife,
Came the wild MacGregor's clan-call,
    Stinging all the air to life.

But when the far-off dust cloud
    To plaided legions grew,
Full tenderly and blithesomely
    The pipes of rescue blew!

Round the silver domes of Lucknow,
    Moslem mosque and Pagan shrine,
Breathed the air to Britons dearest,
    The air of Auld Lang Syne.
O'er the cruel roll of war-drums
    Rose that sweet and homelike strain;
And the tartan clove the turban,
    As the Goomtee cleaves the plain

Dear to the corn-land reaper
    And plaided mountaineer,—
To the cottage and the castle
    The piper's song is dear.
Sweet sounds the Gaelic pibroch
    O'er mountain, glen, and glade;
But the sweetest of all music
    The Pipes at Lucknow played!

An incident of the Sepoy Mutiny. The Scotswoman who first heard the pipes was Jessie Brown. Reli
under the command of Colonel Campbell arrived on September 25, 1857.

SEPTEMBER 26

michael s. harper

Last Affair: Bessie's Blues Song

Disarticulated
arm torn out,
large veins cross
her shoulder intact,
her tourniquet
her blood in all-white big bands:

Can't you see
what love and heartache's done to me

I'm not the same as I used to be
this is my last affair

Mail truck or parked car
in the fast lane,
afloat at forty-three
on a Mississippi road,
Two-hundred-pound muscle on her ham bone,
'nother nigger dead 'fore noon:

Can't you see
what love and heartache's done to me
I'm not the same as I used to be
this is my last affair

Fifty-dollar record
cut the vein in her neck,
fool about her money
toll her black train wreck,
white press missed her fun'ral
in the same stacked deck:

Can't you see
what love and heartache's done to me
I'm not the same as I used to be
this is my last affair

Loved a little blackbird
heard she could sing,
Martha in her vineyard
pestle in her spring,
Bessie had a bad mouth
made my chimes ring:

Can't you see
what love and heartache's done to me
I'm not the same as I used to be
this is my last affair

Bessie Smith died of injuries suffered in a car accident on September 26, 1937.

dante gabriel rossetti

London to Folkestone

27 Sept. 1849

A constant keeping past of shaken trees,
And a bewildered glitter of loose road;
Banks of bright growth, with single blades atop
Against white sky; and wires—a constant chain—
That seem to draw the clouds along with them
(Things which one stoops against the light to see
Through the low window: shaking by at rest,
Or fierce like water as the swiftness grows);
And, seen through fences or a bridge far off,
Trees that in moving keep their intervals
Still one 'twixt bar and bar; and then at times
Long reaches of green level, where one cow,
Feeding among her fellows that feed on,
Lifts her slow neck, and gazes for the sound.

There are six of us: I that write away;
Hunt reads Dumas, hard-lipped, with heavy jowl
And brows hung low, and the long ends of hair
Standing out limp. A grazier at one end
(Thank luck not my end!) has blocked out the air,
And sits in heavy consciousness of guilt.
The poor young muff who's face to face with me,
Is pitiful in loose collar and black tie,
His latchet-button shaking as we go.
There are flowers by me, half upon my knees,
Owned by a dame who's fair in soul, no doubt:
The wind that beats among us carries off
Their scent, but still I have them for my eye.
Fields mown in ridges; and close garden-crops
Of the earth's increase; and a constant sky
Still with clear trees that let you see the wind;
And snatches of the engine-smoke, by fits
Tossed to the wind against the landscape, where
Rooks stooping heave their wings upon the day.
Brick walls we pass between, passed so at once
That for the suddenness I cannot know

Or what, or where begun, or where at end.
Sometimes a station in grey quiet; whence,
With a short gathered champing of pent sound,
We are let out upon the air again.
Now merely darkness; knees and arms and sides
Feel the least touch, and close about the face
A wind of noise that is along like God.
Pauses of water soon, at intervals,
That has the sky in it;—the reflexes
O' the trees move towards the bank as we go by,
Leaving the water's surface plain. I now
Lie back and close my eyes a space; for they
Smart from the open forwardness of thought
Fronting the wind.—

            —I did not scribble more,
Be certain, after this; but yawned, and read,
And nearly dozed a little, I believe;
Till, stretching up against the carriage-back,
I was roused altogether, and looked out
To where, upon the desolate verge of light,
Yearned, pale and vast, the iron-coloured sea.

c. p. cavafy

Theodotos

If you are one of the truly elect,
be careful how you attain your eminence.
However much you are acclaimed, however much
the cities praise the great things you have done
in Italy and Thessaly,
whatever honors
your admirers decree for you in Rome,
your elation, your triumph will not last,
nor will you feel yourself so superior—superior indeed—
when Theodotos brings you, in Alexandria,
on a blood-stained tray,
miserable Pompey's head.

And do not be too sure that in your life—
restricted, regulated, prosaic—
spectacular and horrible things like that do not happen.
Maybe this very moment Theodotos—
bodiless, invisible—
enters some neighbor's tidy house
carrying an equally repulsive head.

The rhetorician Theodotos of Chios persuaded the Egyptians to kill Pompey (September 28, 48 B.C.) when he landed in Egypt as a fugutive, after having been defeated by Julius Caesar at Pharsalus. There is no evidence that it was Theodotos who brought Caesar Pompey's head. [Note by translators]

Trans. Edmund Keeley and Philip Sherrard

SEPTEMBER 29

richard howard

September Twenty-Ninth

Decay is in the poplar,
    Darkness gathers
On even the simplest
    Leaf, and withers.

Never in this climate
    Of loss before
Could I have ascended
    To where you are

Standing—a place beyond
    Our foul weather
And all freezing. Yet I
    Have another

Comfort still to take, more
    Than keeping well
Or merely warm: ever
    Curious of all

Determinations, how
    Must I name this
Time and know this season?
    Like travellers

And other such strangers,
　　Calling places
They came to by titles
　　Of the countries

They had lost, can I do
　　Else in the wrong
Weather but look up and
　　Label it spring?

william shakespeare

Richard the Second Abdicates

from: King Richard the Second

Act IV, scene i
[*Enter* RICHARD (guarded) *with* BOLINGBROKE *and*
NORTHUMBERLAND.]

RICHARD	Give me the crown. Here, cousin, seize the crown.
	Here, cousin
	On this side my hand, and on that side thine.
	Now is this golden crown like a deep well
	That owes two buckets, filling one another,
	The emptier ever dancing in the air,
	The other down, unseen, and full of water.
	That bucket down and full of tears am I,
	Drinking my griefs, whilst you mount up on high.
BOLINGBROKE	I thought you had been willing to resign.
RICH.	My crown I am, but still my griefs are mine.
	You may my glories and my state depose,
	But not my griefs; still am I king of those.
BOL.	Part of your cares you give me with your crown.
RICH.	Your cares set up do not pluck my cares done.
	My care is loss of care, by old care down;
	Your care is gain of care, by new care won.
	The cares I give, I have, though given away,
	They 'tend the crown, yet still with me they stay.

BOL.	Are you contented to resign the crown?
RICH.	Ay, no; no, ay; for I must nothing be.
	Therefore no "no," for I resign to thee.
	Now, mark me how I will undo myself.
	I give this heavy weight from off my head,
	And this unwieldy sceptre from my hand,
	The pride of kingly sway from out my heart;
	With mine own tears I wash away my balm,
	With mine own hands I give away my crown,
	With mine own tongue deny my sacred state,
	With mine own breath release all duteous oaths;
	All pomp and majesty I do forswear;
	My manors, rents, revenues, I forgo;
	My acts, decrees, and statutes I deny.
	God pardon all oaths that are broke to me,
	God keep all vows unbroke are made to thee!
	Make me, that nothing have, with nothing griev'd,
	And thou with all pleas'd, that hast all achiev'd.
	Long may'st thou live in Richard's seat to sit,
	And soon lie Richard in an earthy pit.
	God save King Henry, unking'd Richard says,
	And send him many years of sunshine days!
	What more remains?
NORTH.	No more; but that you read
	These accusations, and these grievous crimes
	Committed by your person and your followers
	Against the state and profit of this land;
	That, by confessing them, the souls of men
	May deem that you are worthily depos'd.
RICH.	Must I do so? and must I ravel out
	My weav'd-up follies? Gentle Northumberland,
	If thy offences were upon record,
	Would it not shame thee, in so fair a troop,
	To read a lecture of them? If thou wouldst,
	There shouldst thou find one heinous article,
	Containing the deposing of a king,
	And cracking the strong warrant of an oath,
	Mark'd with a blot, damn'd in the book of heaven.
	Nay, all of you, that stand and look upon me
	Whilst that my wretchedness doth bait myself,
	Though some of you, with Pilate, wash your hands,
	Showing an outward pity—yet you Pilates
	Have here deliver'd me to my sour cross,
	And water cannot wash away your sin.

NORTH.	My lord, dispatch, read o'er these articles.
RICH.	Mine eyes are full of tears, I cannot see.
	And yet salt water blinds them not so much
	But they can see a sort of traitors here.
	Nay, if I turn mine eyes upon myself,
	I find myself a traitor with the rest.
	For I have given here my soul's consent
	T' undeck the pompous body of a king;
	Made glory base, and sovereignty a slave;
	Proud majesty a subject, state a peasant.
NORTH.	My lord—
RICH.	No lord of thine, thou haught insulting man;
	Nor no man's lord. I have no name, no title;
	No, not that name was given me at the font,
	But 'tis usurp'd. Alack the heavy day,
	That I have worn so many winters out,
	And know not now what name to call myself!
	O that I were a mockery king of snow,
	Standing before the sun of Bolingbroke,
	To melt myself away in water-drops!
	Good king, great king, and yet not greatly good,
	And if my word be sterling yet in England,
	Let it command a mirror hither straight,
	That it may show me what a face I have
	Since it is bankrupt of his majesty.
BOL.	Go some of you, and fetch a looking-glass.
	[*Exit an Attendant.*]
NORTH.	Read o'er this paper while the glass doth come.
RICH.	Fiend, thou torments me ere I come to hell.
BOL.	Urge it no more, my Lord Northumberland.
NORTH.	The commons will not then be satisfi'd.
RICH.	They shall be satisf'd. I'll read enough
	When I do see the very book indeed
	Where all my sins are writ, and that's myself.
	[*Enter one with a glass.*]
	Give me that glass, and therein will I read.
	No deeper wrinkles yet? hath sorrow struck
	So many blows upon this face of mine
	And made no deeper wounds? O flatt'ring glass,
	Like to my followers in prosperity,
	Thou dost beguile me. Was this face the face
	That every day under his household roof
	Did keep ten thousand men? Was this the face
	That like the sun did make beholders wink?

Is this the face which fac'd so many follies,
That was at last out-fac'd by Bolingbroke?
A brittle glory shineth in this face;
As brittle as the glory is the face,
[*Dashes the glass against the ground.*]
For there it is, crack'd in an hundred shivers.
Mark, silent king, the moral of this sport—
How soon my sorrow hath destroy'd my face.

BOL. The shadow of your sorrow hath destroy'd
The shadow of your face.

RICH. The shadow of my sorrow? ha! let's see—
'Tis very true, my grief lies all within,
And these external manners of lament
Are merely shadows to the unseen grief
That swells with silence in the tortur'd soul.
There lies the substance. And I thank thee, king,
For thy great bounty, that not only giv'st
Me cause to wail, but teachest me the way
How to lament the cause. I'll beg one boon,
And then be gone, and trouble you no more.
Shall I obtain it?

BOL.   Name it, fair cousin.

RICH. Fair cousin! I am greater than a king;
For when I was a king, my flatterers
Were then but subjects; being now a subject,
I have a king here to my flatterer.
Being so great, I have no need to beg.

BOL. Yet ask.

RICH. And shall I have?

BOL. You shall.

RICH. Then give me leave to go.

BOL. Whither?

RICH. Whither you will, so I were from your sights.

BOL. Go some of you, convey him to the Tower.

RICH. O, good! Convey! Conveyers are you all,
That rise thus nimbly by a true king's fall.
[*Exeunt* Richard *and Guard.*]

Richard II abdicated on September 30, 1399. See January 20.

October

stephen dobyns

No Map

How close the clouds press this October first
and the rain—a gray scarf across the sky.
In separate hospitals my father and a dear friend
lie waiting for their respective operations,
hours on a table as surgeons crack their chests.
They were so brave when I talked to them last
as they spoke of the good times we would share
in the future. To neither did I say how much
I loved them, nor express the extent of my fear.
Their bodies are delicate glass boxes
at which the world begins to fling its stones.
Is this the day their long cry will be released?
How can I live in this place without them?
But today is also my son's birthday.
He is eight and beginning his difficult march.
To him the sky is welcoming, the road straight.
Far from my house he will open his presents—
a book, a Swiss army knife, some music. Where
is his manual of instructions? Where is his map
showing the dark places and how to escape them?

rita dove

Parsley

1. The Cane Fields

There is a parrot imitating spring
in the palace, its feathers parsley green.
Out of the swamp the cane appears

to haunt us, and we cut it down. El General
searches for a word; he is all the world
there is. Like a parrot imitating spring,

we lie down screaming as rain punches
    through
and we come up green. We cannot speak
    an R—
out of the swamp, the cane appears

and then the mountain we call in whispers
    Katalina.
The children gnaw their teeth to
    arrowheads.
There is a parrot imitating spring.

El General has found his word: *perejil.*
Who says it, lives. He laughs, teeth shining
out of the swamp. The cane appears

in our dreams, lashed by wind and
    streaming.
And we lie down. For every drop of blood
there is a parrot imitating spring.
Out of the swamp the cane appears.

2. The Palace

The word the general's chosen is parsley.
It is fall, when thoughts turn
to love and death; the general thinks
of his mother, how she died in the fall

and he planted her walking cane at the
    grave
and it flowered, each spring stolidly
    forming
four-star blossoms. The general

pulls on his boots, he stomps to
her room in the palace, the one without
curtains, the one with a parrot
in a brass ring. As he paces he wonders
Who can I kill today. And for a moment
the little knot of screams
is still. The parrot, who has traveled

all the way from Australia in an ivory
cage, is, coy as a widow, practising
spring. Ever since the morning
his mother collapsed in the kitchen
while baking skull-shaped candies
for the Day of the Dead, the general
has hated sweets. He orders pastries
brought up for the bird; they arrive

dusted with sugar on a bed of lace.
The knot in his throat starts to twitch;
he sees his boots the first day in battle
splashed with mud and urine
as a soldier falls at his feet amazed—
how stupid he looked!—at the sound
of artillery. *I never thought it would sing*
the soldier said, and died. Now

the general sees the fields of sugar
cane, lashed by rain and streaming.
He sees his mother's smile, the teeth
gnawed to arrowheads. He hears
the Haitians sing without R's
as they swing the great machetes:
Katalina, they sing, *Katalina*

mi madle, mi amol en muelte. God knows
his mother was no stupid woman; she
could roll an R like a queen. Even
a parrot can roll an R! In the bare room
the bright feathers arch in a parody
of greenery, as the last pale crumbs
disappear under the blackened tongue.
    Someone

calls out his name in a voice
so like his mother's, a startled tear

splashes the tip of his right boot.
My mother, my love in death.
The general remembers the tiny green
   sprigs
men of his village wore in their capes
to honor the birth of a son. He will
order many, this time, to be killed

for a single, beautiful word.

On October 2, 1957, Rafael Trujillo (1891–1961), dictator of the Dominican Republic, ordered 20,00
blacks killed because they could not pronounce the letter "r" in perejil, the Spanish word for parsle
[Note by Dove].

OCTOBER 3

david wojahn

Dates, For Example

Branches nodding in the fog,
   the trees are bruised with
      afternoon light. I'm watching

Phil Alexander next door
   stoop to a purple dahlia blossom
      larger than a hat. He brings us cukes,

late plum tomatoes, oxeye
   daisies in jars, recipes
      in a wavering hand

for kale soup and chowder. The gardener
   for Dos Passos and O'Neill, his anecdotes
      commence with roses, the Japanese elm

in O'Neill's yard, the way
   Dos Passos cut his lawn and hair—
      "A big man with a cowlick, he was.

Had the first power mower on the Cape."
    From my book by a Turkish poet
        I read, "Dates, for example,

are very important to Hikmet.
    The date of the poem
        is part of the poem itself."

It's the third of October, 1983,
    and I'm listening
        to Lynda's typewriter hesitantly clatter

the stanzas of a poem I would like
    Nazim Hikmet, twenty years dead this month,
        to read with approval

her hunched-down shoulders, under
    the shimmering, supernoval waterlilies
        of Monet's Giverny adorning her wall.

I want him to read her lines
    from his prison cell in Istanbul,
        exclaiming like a child when a phrase

seems right, saying *"This*
    would sound almost as good
        in Turkish!" Saying, "Woman,

your hair is a steady
    pulsing lily made of light!"
        He will talk with her this way

for hours. The plummeting sun disperses
    its light on the hundred masts
        of sloops and freighters

in the port of Istanbul below
    his window. It's evening now:
        the bars of the window marry

the first steady darkness until
    they seem to waver and disappear.
        Nazim Hikmet removes his glasses,

cups his hand around
   the single candle he's been issued this week.
      And Phil Alexander, with garden shears,

is pounding the doorframe behind me:
   I brought you some rhubarb!
      I brought you some peppers!

OCTOBER 4

charles (tennyson) turner

On the Eclipse of the Moon of October 1865

One little noise of life remained—I heard
The train pause in the distance, then rush by,
Brawling and hushing, like some busy fly
That murmurs and then settles; nothing stirred
Beside. The shadow of our travelling earth
Hung on the silver moon, which mutely went
Through that grand process, without token sent,
Or any sign to call a gazer forth,
Had I not chanced to see; dumb was the vault
Of heaven, and dumb the fields—no zephyr swept
The forest walks, or through the coppice crept;
Nor other sound the stillness did assault,
Save that faint-brawling railway's move and halt;
So perfect was the silence Nature kept.

james reiss

The Breathers

(Jeffrey Andrew Reiss—October 5, 1969)

In Ohio, where these things happen,
we had been loving all winter.
By June you looked down and saw your belly
was soft as fresh bread.

In Florida, standing on the bathroom
scales, you were convinced—
and looked both ways for a full minute before crossing
Brickell Boulevard.

In Colorado you waited-out summer in a mountain
cabin, with Dr. Spock,
your stamps, and my poems in the faint
8000-foot air.

Listen, he had a perfect body,
right down to his testicles, which I counted.
The morning he dropped from your womb, all rosy
as an apple in season, breathing the thick
fall air of Ohio, we thought good things would happen.

Believe me, Dr. Salter and the nurses were right:
he was small but feisty—they said he was
feisty. That afternoon in his respirator
when he urinated it was something to be proud of.
Cyanotic by evening, he looked like a dark rose.

Late that night you hear . . .

Think of the only possible twentieth-century consolations:
Doris saying it might have been better this way;
think of brain damage, car crashes, dead soldiers.
Better seventeen hours than eighteen, twenty years
of half-life in Ohio where nothing happens.

Late that night you hear them
in the . . .

For, after all, we are young, traveling
at full speed into the bull's eye of the atom.
There's a Pepsi and hot dog stand in that bull's eye,
and babies of the future dancing around us.
Listen, the air is thick with our cries!

Late that night you hear them
in the nursery, the breathers.
Their tiny lungs go in and out like the air
bladder on an oxygen tank
or the rhythm of sex.
Asleep, your arms shoot towards that target
with a stretch that lifts you like a zombie,
wakes you to the deafening breathers.

And now you see them, crawling
rings around your bed, in blankets,
buntings, preemies in incubators circling
on casters, a few with cleft palates, heart trouble,
all feistily breathing, crawling
away from your rigidly outstretched arms—
breathing, robbing the air.

OCTOBER 6

thomas rice henn

_____

Burning of a House

(6 October 1970)

I
The grey west rain slakes ashes: turns carven oak to mire.
Journalists, casual visitors,
Come to wonder
At this fallen house: The broken roof-trees: gravel that
                                        smells of fire.

Rafters will stand for a while, like the dark ribs
Of the Galway Hooker sunk at the creek's mouth.
The urns on the balustrade have been stolen for souvenirs.
                        Once they had been
Heavy with geraniums, bright with lobelia.   And slowly
Bushes, rare climbing shrubs, the johnswort that edges the drive
Will sidle outwards, fighting, choking each other
In new raw life from the bone-dust of the house.
Pernettias cloak the sundial.
(But its bronze dial was stolen.)

Small birds roost secure in the rhododendron thickets
By the walk to the locked garden.
Only the jackdaws, companionable, compassionate,
Fly puzzled round a single crumbling stack
That gives no warmth for the nest.

II

We never know when we have done some act:
Walked that bracken edge, crisped with hail-stones,
Splashed through a rushy spring
Felt the soft gracious air on Lough Lomaùn,
Pushed through the saplings to the trout-pool's margin,
Walked by foot-touch—eyes far ahead—on the bog-lands
For the last time.

III

Here they have done more evil than fire or crowning bramble.
Torn gravel from ancient rivers:
Uprooted the bones of the Roman and of the mammoth
Hollowed the chalk downs whose springs gave life to the
                                     grass-lands.
Sealed for ever the small life beneath us:
Worm and questing ant and the groping grass roots:
They have sealed them under the tortured slabs of concrete
That quiver and tremble under the thudding pistons.

IV

Who am I that should blame
Greed   treachery   malice
Thievery in God's many names
Commandment to root out the heretic
As snouts of pig or badger tear a meadow:
Wrench out the iron palings, oak from mortice:

So we had once thought of destruction that hemmed us,
Yet planned that it would not fail.
But that was high ancestral arrogance
Of power and race and pride.
It is better that these cracked stones sink into history's footings
And that I remember actions of the last time.

OCTOBER 7

emery george

Bad Day at the Home Office

How the bridge fell; how our trucks collided.
Let the pros conduct the investigation.
Frankly, I've grown tired of all the gambling.
      First, it's the Hamburg

shipment: crashed October the 7th, just off
Greenland. Not one shred of the plane recovered.
Then that Cartwright order: the floodgates busted.
      One little bastard's

negligence in warning the crew of dam walls
fit to burst already when swollen river
waters slammed down out of the mountains, did us.
      Then the tornadoes,

cutting swaths: Kentucky and Indiana
closed to freight. I'm plumb on the point of asking,
Why the hell not take on that job for Squires?
      "Company Fires

Half Its Sales Force." Can't you just see the papers?
All our stiff insurance won't cover drinking,
migraine, eyes unchecked to the point of blindness.
      Dunder & Lawless . . .

Oh, they won't? Right. Then we'd prefer it. Roger.
They will not fork over a dime until this
once we've been through court and our claim is proven.
      Let's get a move on.

paul goodman

Don Larsen's Perfect Game

Everybody went to bat three times
except their pitcher (twice) and his pinch hitter,
but nobody got anything at all.
Don Larsen in the eighth and ninth looked pale
and afterwards he did not want to talk.
This is a fellow who will have bad dreams.
His catcher Berra jumped for joy and hugged him
like a bear, legs and arms, and all the Yankees
crowded around him thick to make him be
not lonely, and in fact in fact in fact
nothing went wrong. But that was yesterday.

Don Larsen of the Yankees pitched the only perfect game in the history of the World
Series against the Dodgers on October 8, 1956.

richard hugo

What Thou Lovest Well Remains American

You remember the name was Jensen. She seemed old
always alone inside, face pasted gray to the window,
and mail never came. Two blocks down, the Grubskis
went insane. George played rotten trombone
Easter when they flew the flag. Wild roses
remind you the roads were gravel and vacant lots
the rule. Poverty was real, wallet and spirit,
and each day slow as church. You remember threadbare
church groups on the corner, howling their faith
at stars, and the violent Holy Rollers
renting that barn for their annual violent sing
and the barn burned down when you came back from war.
Knowing the people you knew then are dead,
you try to believe these roads paved are improved,

the neighbors, moved in while you were away, good-looking,
their dogs well fed. You still have need
to remember lots empty and fern.
Lawns well trimmed remind you of the train
your wife took one day forever, some far empty town,
the odd name you never recall. The time: 6:23.
The day: October 9. The year remains a blur.
You blame this neighborhood for your failure.
In some vague way, the Grubskis degraded you
beyond repair. And you know you must play again
and again Mrs. Jensen pale at her window, must hear
the foul music over the good slide of traffic.
You loved them well and they remain, still with nothing
to do, no money and no will. Loved them, and the gray
that was their disease you carry for extra food
in case you're stranded in some odd empty town
and need hungry lovers for friends, and need feel
you are welcome in the secret club they have formed.

wendell berry

October 10

Now constantly there is the sound,
quieter than rain,
of the leaves falling.

Under their loosening bright
gold, the sycamore limbs
bleach whiter.

Now the only flowers
are beeweed and aster, spray
of their white and lavender
over the brown leaves.

The calling of a crow sounds
loud—a landmark—now
that the life of summer falls
silent, and the nights grow.

richard kenney

The Battle of Valcour Island

Although hindsight accords a degree of humored
panache to our performance that year, my heart
I own still lurches like a stallion fording
a rapid to remember my first battle, when Edward
shinned out to the tip of the bowsprit to free a fouled
jib, alone, and drew the fire that followed
from every more or less awestruck gunner aboard
the galley *Congress*. Balls and shells and shards
of every sort soughing around his deaf gallant
ears, and he chopping lines as nonchalant
as paring vegetables for his mother in a cooling rain
in England. His next birthday we drank *restraint
in action*, lest the natural span of adult
years lapse before one's ascent to the Admiralty—

It happened this way. We were on the lake at five
of the false dawn on 11 October, Sir Guy
Carleton aboard flotilla Captain Pringle's
ship the *Lady Maria*. Then the *Inflexible*,
the *Carleton*, the radeau *Thunderer* (the sow),
twenty gunboats, longboats, canoes, and bateaux,
following like farrow on a fresh north breeze,
and all for seven nutshells full of Yankees.
I sailed the *Carleton*'s cutter, feeling like an ass.
The boat still bore the stencil *HMS
Blonde*, my ship and Edward's ship, anchored
in the St. Lawrence, while we scurried
down this freshwater wilderness farther and farther
from a decent sea. I felt—lost there.

At four bells we blew by them like grape.
Tucked in the channel behind Valcour Island, sheep
in a pen, Pringle said (though led by a brilliant
goat, as he later learned): and the north wind sent
us gaily past like clowns. It took the *Inflexible*
two miles to come about. On a tactical pretext
several of Arnold's vessels feinted from Valcour
Sound, into the lake, and Lieutenant Dacres

instantly committed the *Carleton* to pursuit.
She sheered off like a razor, bow guns shooting
wide, and the rebels turned. Dacres dogged
them straight up the channel. Gunboats followed with lug-
sails and oars, but of five British ships, the *Carleton*
engaged the rebel battle line alone.

It went very badly. With the first exchange, Lieutenant
Dacres fell wounded, and Edward assumed command
of the ship. Not twenty years old, then, already twice
the man that Captain Pringle was, or was
capable of being (we've since toasted his vulgarity,
all birthdays, George, old age and flag
rank for every Jack-tar, *skoal*)—In ragged
fall crosswinds sneezing off those miserable Valcour
bluffs, the *Carleton* lost control, her slack
sails flapping like shot gulls. Slowly the black
schooner swung round, until she lay still before
the crescent enemy line: like a focused mirror
throwing gunlight on a single point, the surface
of the water buzzing like bees, and fire from the *Congress*.

The naval history will read *The* Carleton *fought*
like a British ship, or some such phlegmy
platitude to explain her vicious mauling, needless
to say; though long before the *Maria*'s recall
flag ran up it ceased to be a contest. The *Carleton*
was totally unresponsive by then, caught
bows into the breeze like a shivering compass needle,
helpless to come about, hulled, her flame-
lit decking raked by every shot from the galley
Congress, and at the same time powerless to lay
her own traversing guns. The command was saved by
one man, by the single most extraordinary
act of courage I had ever seen, high
on the bowsprit, the ship in his hands like a sword—

We rowed to him in longboats from the *Isis*
and the *Blonde;* Edward hurled a hawser,
and we towed the *Carleton* to safety. Soon it was night.
(Time for Pringle, the ninny, to dine—no doubt
he was helped to more than a gill of fine Madeira
to irrigate his spent, weary, dead
intelligence. Or as some later said, *courage*.

The British naval code is simple: *Engage*
the enemy. Engage: In 1766
a fleet admiral was shot for having neglected
to engage. The *Lady Maria* had hardly fired
a round—But the navy has had its inquiry;
that's done.) That night the plan was to blockade
the Americans in the sound, and sink them the next day.

We used only four ships! At night, half awake,
I still search my drowned memory for the clicks
of rowlocks, the breath of Benedict Arnold. . . . Lake
Champlain deep in fog that night; we'd
heard nothing. They went by like teal through marsh-reeds
and gently rocking masts, like thoughts
through a dreaming dog, whose feet paddle and eyelids
only quiver. What fools. The captain licked
his lips when he saw the sheepfold empty as the lake
below, and knew we all knew he was a horse's
ass beside his rebel adversary.
What came of that was Edward Pellew, Lieutenant
Dacres and I smelled no salt water all winter,
and kissed a number of ladies in Montreal.

OCTOBER 12

judith baumel

World Without End

If you believe the various records and registers,
on the very morning that the Genoese, in the commission
of King Ferdinand and Queen Isabella of Castile, set
foot on the island of Guanahani—San Salvador—Watling,
Piero della Francesca died at the Via Aggiunti,
in the town of his birth, Borgo Sansepolcro.
If you believe Vasari he was blind. The works
lead us to believe that this Euclidean scholar's
round-bellied women turned finally,
in the "Madonna of the Birth,"
into a sort of Riemannian proposition of beauty.
That enormous-bellied woman in Monterchi

may have been homage to Piero's own mother,
called Francesca or Romana, depending
on whom you believe. And she may have been
buried in the adjoining graveyard the year before
Piero drew the curtains open, held by his familiars,
his constant angels draped in red and green
with alternating, matching socks and wings.
They present one more enigma of Piero—
this utterly peculiar image, a single maternal face
of fear, peace, desperation, patience, exhaustion.
Beneath the bursting drapery of her blue dress,
a slit of white underdress covers a belly
expectant, low and round like the globe.
I believe the third Book of the Dead
of the Confraternity of San Benedetto,
which registers the end on 12 October 1492, and
I believe he left this world in peace at the very moment
that Columbus was confounded by the roundness of the earth.
And so believe that the master of perspective
closed his part of the Renaissance, a birth
in the Old World and a life that so loved
the even older East of Constantinople,
by ceding spirit to the new one, mother
of all manner of strange round fruit,
its baskets of tomatoes, corn kernels, potatoes,
and to what was being born there, a new form of innocence,
three dimensions of roundness where everything converges
without parallel lines. And where the son of my
future was, remains, and becomes a mystery of flesh.

william barnes

The Geäte A-Vallen to

n the zunsheen ov our zummers
  Wi the haytime now a-come,
low busy were we out a-vield
  Wi vew a-left at hwome,
Vhen waggons rumbled out ov yard
  Red wheeled, wi body blue,
nd back behind em loudly slammed
  The geäte a-vallen to.

rough day sheen ov how many years
  The geäte ha' now a-swung,
ehind the veet of vull-grown men
  And vootsteps of the young.
rough years o days it swung to us
  Behind each little shoe,
s we tripped lightly on avore
  The geäte a-vallen to.

n evenen time o starry night
  How mother zot at hwome
nd kept her bleäzen vire bright
  Till father should ha' come,

An' how she quickened up an' smiled,
  And stirred her vire anew,
To hear the trampen ho'ses' steps
  And geäte a-vallen to.

There's moon-sheen now in nights o fall
  When leaves be brown vrom green,
When to the slammen o the geäte
  Our Jenny's ears be keen,
When the wold dog do wag his tail,
  And Jeän could tell to who,
As he do come in drough the geäte,
  The geäte a-vallen to.

An' oft do come a saddened hour
  When there must goo away
One well-beloved to our heart's core,
  Vor long, perhaps for aye:
An' oh! it is a touchen thing
  The loven heart must rue,
To hear behind his last farewell
  The geäte a-vallen to.

tober 13, 1885. Barnes's daughter Lucy recalls him dictating his last poem: "It was a cold evening,
d he was sitting in his easy chair by the fire with his fur-lined cloak and red cap and his feet in a fur
t muff. The firelight fell warm on his face, and even dimly brought out the figures in the ancient tapes-
behind his bed."

lord herbert of cherbury

October 14, 1664

Enraging griefs, though you most divers be,
In your first causes you may yet agree
To take an equal share within my heart,
Since, if each grief strive for the greatest part,
You needs must vex yourselves as well as me.

For your own sakes and mine then make an end.
In vain you do about a Heart contend,
Which, though it seem in greatness to dilate,
Is but a tumor, which in this its state
The choicest remedies would but offend.

Then storm't at once. I neither feel constraint,
Scorning your worst, nor suffer any taint,
Dying by multitudes, though if you strive,
I fear my heart may thus be kept alive,
Until it under its own burden faint.

What is't not done? Why then my God, I find,
Would have me use you to reform my mind,
Since through his help I may from you extract
An essence pure, so spriteful and compact
As it will be from grosser parts refin'd.

Which being again converted by his grace
To godly sorrow, I may both efface
Those sins first caus'd you, and together have
Your pow'r to kill turn'd to a pow'r to save,
And bring my Soul to its desired place.

anonymous

Frankie and Albert

Frankie was a good girl
As everybody knows.
She paid a hundred dollar bill
For a suit of Albert's clothes,
Just because she loved him so.

Frankie went down to the bar-room;
She called for a bottle of beer;
She whispered to the bartender:
"Has Albert he been here?
He is my man and he won't come home."

"I am not a-going to tell you no story;
I am not a-going to tell you no lie;
He left here about an hour ago
With a girl called Alice Fry;
He is your man and he won't come home."

Frankie went to the house
As hard as she could run;
And under her apron
Concealed a smokeless gun;
"He is my man but he won't come home."

Frankie stepped out in the back yard;
She heard a bull-dog bark;
"That must be the man I love slipping out
in the dark.

If it is, I am a-going to lay him low;
He is my man, but he done me wrong."

Frankie went down to the river.
She looked from bank to bank:
"Do all you can for a gambling man,
But yet you will get no thanks;
For a gambling man won't treat you right."

Frankie reached down in her pocket,
And pulled that forty-four out,
And shot little Albert through that suit of
clothes
People been a-talking about;
"He's my man but he won't be long."

"Turn me over, Frankie,
Turn me over slow,
Turn me on my right side;
My heart will overflow;
I'm your man and I have done you wrong."

Frankie looked down on Broadway
As far as she could see—
Two little children just a-crying and
singing
"Nearer, My God, to Thee"—
Seems so sad little Albert is dead.

About 2:30 on Sunday morning, October 15, 1899, in St. Louis, Albert Britt staggered home drunk and was drawn by his mistress, Frankie Baker, into a violent argument about Alice Pryor, another woman he was seeing. When Albert attacked her with a knife, Frankie shot him in self-defense. The well-known "Frankie and Johnny" is a vaudeville version of this folk ballad.

langston hughes

October 16: The Raid

Perhaps
You will remember
John Brown.

John Brown
Who took his gun,
Took twenty-one companions
White and black,
Went to shoot your way to freedom
Where two rivers meet

And the hills of the
South
Look slow at one another—
And died
For your sake.

Now that you are
Many years free,
And the echo of the Civil War
Has passed away,
And Brown himself
Has long been tried at law,
Hanged by the neck,
And buried in the ground—
Since Harpers Ferry
Is alive with ghosts today,
Immortal raiders
Come again to town—

Perhaps
You will recall
John Brown.

See December 2.

laurence minot

The Battle of Neville's Cross

Sir dauid the bruse was at distance,
when edward the baliolfe rade with his lance;
the north end of ingland teched him to daunce,
when he was met on the more with mekill mischance.
Sir philip the valayse may him noght avance;
the flowres that faire war, er fallen in ffraunce.
    the floures er now fallen, that fers war and fell,
    A bare with his bataille has done tham to dwell.

Sir dauid the bruse said he suld fonde
to ride thurgh all ingland, wald he noght wonde;
at the west-minster hall suld his stedes stonde,
whils oure king edward war out of the londe.
    bot now has sir dauid missed of his merkes,
    and philip the valays, with all thaire grete clerkes.

Sir philip the valais, suth forto say,
Sent vnto sir dauid and faire gan him pray;
at ride thrugh ingland thaire fo-men to flay,
and said none es at home to let hym the way.
    none letes him the way to vende whore he will,
    bot with schipherd staues fand he his fill.

Fro philip the valais was sir dauid sent,
all ingland to win fro twede vnto trent.
he broght mani berebag with bow redy bent;
thai robbed and thai reued and held that thai hent.
it was in the waniand that thai furth went;
for couaitise of cataile tho schrewes war schent.
    Schent war tho schrewes, and ailed vnsele,
    for at the neuil cros nedes bud tham knele.

At the Erchbisschop of york now will I bigyn,
for he may with his right hand assoyl vs of syn.
both Dorem and Carlele thai wald neuer blin
the wirschip of ingland with wappen to win.
    Mekill wirschip thai wan, and wele haue thai waken,
    for sir dauid and bruse was in that tyme taken.

When sir dauid the bruse satt on his stede,
he said of all ingland haued he no drede;
bot hinde Iohn of Coupland, a wight man in wede,
talked to dauid and kend him his crede.
Thare was sir Dauid, so dughty in his dede,
the faire toure of londen haued he to mede.

Sone than was sir dauid broght vnto the toure,
and william the dowglas with men of honowre.
full swith redy seruis fand thai thare a schowre;
for first thai drank of the swete, and sethin of the sowre.

than sir dauid the bruse makes his mone,
the faire coroun of scotland haues he forgone:
he lurked furth into france, help had he none,
of sir philip the valais ne yit of sir Iohn.

The pride of sir Dauid bigon fast to slaken,
for he wakkind the were that held him-self waken.
for philyp the valaise had he brede baken,
and in the toure of londen his ines er taken.
    to be both in a place thaire forward thai nomen;
    bot philip fayled thare, and dauid es cumen.

Sir Dauid the bruse on this manere
said vnto sir philip, al thir sawes thus sere:
"Philip the valais, thou made me be here,
this es nought the forward we made are to-yere.
    ffals es thi forward, and euyll mot thou fare,
    for thou and sir Iohn thi son haues kast me in care."

the Scottes, with thaire falshede, thus went thai obout
for to win Ingland whils Edward was out.
for Cuthbert of dorem haued thai no dout;
tharfore at neuel cros law gan thai lout.
    thare louted thai law, and leued allane.
    thus was dauid the Bruse into the toure tane.

*David II of Scotland invaded England at the instigation of King Philip II of
France, who was trying to raise the siege of Calais. Although Edward III was pre-
occupied in France, his home garrisons were well prepared and defeated the Scots
at Neville Cross on October 17, 1346, capturing David and eliminating the threat
from Scotland.*

nicholas breton

from: Pasquil's Night-cap

. . .

And, that it might be done with more respect,
And Fortune's greater honour; they decree,
That at the time, when this should take effect,
Great store of *Kentishmen* in their degree;
    Knights, gentlemen and yeomen of the best,
    Of common people, should be ready drest,
    In all their braue accoutrements, to grace
    The forked piller to the fore-said place.
The 18. of October was proclaim'd
To be the day of this great celebration:
Against which time, ech long-taile before nam'd,
Made much prouision and great preparation:
    And vnto *Canterburie* tooke their way,
    There to be ready at th'appoynted day,
    To giue attendance in most sumptuous manner,
    On Fortune's piller, with all pompe and honour.
Now was the instant come to play this prize,
The day of good Saint *Luke*: which was of old,
The time when men were wont to sacrifice
At Fortune's temple, (as before was told)
    Chosen the rather, that their present might
    Better respected be in Fortune's sight:
    And that she might behold with what desire
    They were conform'd to pacifie her ire.
And now the long-tailes in their best array,
Preuenting the sun-rising by their haste,
Assembled were, before the dawning day
Had nights blacke curtains from the skie displac'd,
    The thundring drums did ratle through the towne,
    To summon euery gentleman and clowne:
    All which no sooner heard that lowd alarme,
    But like to bees together they did swarme.

. . .

*The "forked piller" was to be erected to placate Fortune, whose temple had been
destroyed by Wat Tyler and who, in despite, had caused all people in Kent to grow
long tails.*

anonymous

A Monk Poisons King John

from: The Troublesome Raigne of John, King of England

[*Enter* KING JOHN, *the* BASTARD (Phillip Falconbridge), *the* ABBOT, *and* THOMAS *the* MONKE.]

KING JOHN	Come on Lord Abbot, shall we sit together?
ABBOT	Pleaseth your Grace sit downe.
K. JOHN	Take your places sirs, no pomp in penury, all beggers and friends may come, where necessitie keepes the house, curtesie is bard the table, sit downe *Phillip*.
BASTARD	My Lord, I am loth to allude so much to the proverb honors change maners: a King is a King, though fortune do her worst, and we as dutifull in despight of her frowne, as if your highnesse were now in the highest type of dignitie.
K. JOHN	Come, no more ado, and you tell me much of dignitie, youle mar my appetite in a surfet of sorrow. What cheere Lord Abbot, me thinks you frowne like an host that knowes his guest hath no money to pay the reckning?
ABBOT	No my Liege, if I frowne at all, it is for I feare this cheere too homely to entertaine so mighty a guest as your Majesty.
BASTARD	I thinke rather my Lord Abbot you remember my last being heere, when I went in progresse for powtches—and the rancor of his heart breakes out in his countenance, to shew he hath not forgot me.
ABBOT	Not so my Lord, you, and the meanest follower of his majesty, are hartely welcome to me.
THOMAS	Wassell my Liege, and as a poore Monke may say, welcome to Swinsted.
K. JOHN	Begin Monke, and report hereafter thou wast taster to a King.
THOMAS	As much helth to your highnes, as to my own hart.
K. JOHN	I pledge thee kinde Monke.
THOMAS	The meriest draught that ever was dronk in *England*. Am I not too bold with your Highnesse.
K. JOHN	Not a whit, all friends and fellowes for a time.

THOMAS	If the inwards of a Toad be a compound of any proofe: why so it works. [*He dyes.*]
K. JOHN	Stay *Phillip* wheres the Monke?
BASTARD	He is dead my Lord.
K. JOHN	Then drink not *Phillip* for a world of wealth.
BASTARD	What cheers my Liege, your cullor gins to change.
K. JOHN	So doth my life, O *Phillip* I am poysond. The Monke, the Devill, the poyson gins to rage, It will depose my selfe a King from raigne.
BASTARD	This Abbot hath an interest in this act. At all adventures take thou that from me. There lye the Abbot, Abbey Lubber, Devill. March with the Monke unto the gates of hell. How fares my Lord?
K. JOHN	*Phillip* some drinke, oh for the frozen Alps, To tumble on and coole this inward heate, That rageth as the fornace sevenfold hote, To burne the holy three in *Babylon*, Power after power forsake their proper power, Only the hart impugnes with faint resist The fierce invade of him that conquers Kings, Help God, O payne, dye *John*, O plague Inflicted on thee for thy grievous sinnes. *Phillip* a chayre, and by and by a grave, My leggs disdaine the carriage of a King.
BASTARD	A good my Lege with patience conquer griefe, And beare this paine with kingly fortitude.
K. JOHN	Me thinks I see a cattalogue of sinne Wrote by a fiend in Marble characters, The least enough to loose my part in heaven. Me thinks the Devill whispers in mine eares And tels me tis in vayne to hope for grace, I must be damnd for *Arthurs* sodaine death, I see I see a thousand thousand men Come to accuse me for my wrong on earth, And there is none so mercifull a God That will forgive the number of my sinnes. How have I livd, but by anothers losse? What have I lovd but wrack of others weale? When have I vowd, and not infringd mine oath? Where have I done a deede deserving well? How, what, when, and where, have I bestowd a day That tended not to some notorious ill.

My life repleat with rage and tyranie,
Craves little pittie for so strange a death.
Or who will say that *John* disceasd too soone,
Who will not say he rather livd too long.
Dishonor did attaynt me in my life,
And shame attendeth *John* unto his death.
Why did I scape the fury of the French,
And dyde not by the temper of their swords?
Shamelesse my life, and shamefully it ends,
Scornd by my foes, disdained of my friends.

King John was poisoned the evening of October 19, 1216. See April 3 for his nephew Arthur's sudden death.

aeschylos

The Battle of Salamis

from: Persians

And when the light of the sun had perished
and night came on, the masters of the oar
and men at arms went down into the ships;
then line to line the longships passed the word,
and every one sailed in commanded line.
All that night long the captains of the ships
ordered the sea people at their stations.
The night went by, and still the Greek fleet
gave order for no secret sailing out.
But when the white horses of the daylight
took over the whole earth, clear to be seen,
the first noise was the Greeks shouting with joy,
like singing, like triumph, and then again
echoes rebounded from the island rocks.
The barbarians were afraid, our strategy
was lost, there was no Greek panic in
that solemn battle-song they chanted then,

but battle-hunger, courage of spirit;
the trumpet's note set everything ablaze.
Suddenly by command their foaming oars
beat, beat in the deep of the salt water,
and all at once they were clear to be seen.
First the right wing in perfect order leading,
then the whole fleet followed out after them,
and one great voice was shouting in our ears:
"Sons of the Greeks, go forward, and set free
your fathers' country and set free your sons,
your wives, the holy places of your gods,
the monuments of your own ancestors,
now is the one battle for everything."
Our Persian voices answered roaring out,
and there was no time left before the clash.
Ships smashed their bronze beaks into ships,
it was a Greek ship in the first assault
that cut away the whole towering stern
from a Phoenician, and another rammed
timber into another. Still at first
the great flood of the Persian shipping held,
but multitudes of ships crammed up together,
no help could come from one to the other,
they smashed one another with brazen beaks,
and the whole rowing fleet shattered itself.
So then the Greek fleet with a certain skill
ran inwards from a circle around us,
and the bottoms of ships were overturned,
there was no seawater in eyesight,
only wreckage and bodies of dead men,
and beaches and rocks all full of dead.
Whatever ships were left out of our fleet
rowed away in no order in panic.
The Greeks with broken oars and bits of wreck
smashed and shattered the men in the water
like tunny, like gaffed fish. One great scream
filled up all the sea's surface with lament,
until the eye of darkness took it all.

Trans. Peter Levi

The date traditionally given for the Battle of Salamis (the Greeks against the invading Persian army under Xerxes) is October 20, 480 B.C.

thomas hardy

The Battle of Trafalgar

from: The Dynasts

Part I, scene ii [*the quarter-deck of Nelson's flag ship, the "Victory."*]

NELSON

Bid still the firemen bring more bucketfuls,
And dash the water into each new hole
Our guns have gouged in the "Redoutable,"
Or we shall all be set ablaze together.

HARDY

Let me once more advise, entreat, my lord,
That you do not expose yourself so clearly.
Those fellows in the mizzen-top up there
Are peppering round you quite perceptibly.

NELSON

Now, Hardy, don't offend me. They can't aim;
They only set their own rent sails on fire.—
But if they could, I would not hide a button
To save ten lives like mine. I have no cause
To prize it, I assure 'ee.—Ah, look there,
One of the women hit,—and badly, too.
Poor wench! Let some one shift her quickly down.

HARDY

My lord, each humblest sojourner on the seas,
Dock-labourer, lame longshore-man, bowed bargee,
Sees it as policy to shield his life
For those dependent on him. Much more, then,
Should one upon whose priceless presence here
Such issues hang, so many strivers lean,
Use average circumspection at an hour
So critical for us all.

NELSON

                Ay, ay. Yes, yes;
I know your meaning, Hardy; and I know
That you disguise as frigid policy
What really is your honest love of me.
But, faith, I have had my day. My work's nigh done;
I serve all interest best by chancing it
Here with the commonest.—Ah, their heavy guns
Are silenced every one! Thank God for that.

HARDY

'Tis so. They only use their small arms now.
[*He goes to larboard to see what is progressing on that side between his ship and the "Santisima Trinidad."*]

OFFICER [*to a seaman*]
Swab down these stairs. The mess of blood about
Makes 'em so slippery that one's like to fall
In carrying the wounded men below.
[*While* Captain Hardy *is still a little way off,* Lord
Nelson *turns to walk aft, when a ball from one of the
muskets in the mizzen-top of the "Redoutable" enters his
left shoulder. He falls upon his face on the deck.* Hardy
looks round, and sees what has happened.]

HARDY [*hastily*]
Ah—what I feared, and strove to hide I feared! . . .
[*He goes towards* Nelson, *who in the meantime has been
lifted by* Sergeant-Major Secker *and two seamen.*]

NELSON Hardy, I think they've done for me at last!

HARDY I hope not!

NELSON Yes. My backbone is shot through.
I have not long to live.
[*The men proceed to carry him below.*]
Those tiller ropes
They've torn away, get instantly repaired!
[*At sight of him borne along wounded there is great
agitation among the crew.*]
Cover my face. There will no good be done
By drawing their attention off to me.
Bear me along, good fellows; I am but one
Among the many darkened here to-day!
[*He is carried on to the cockpit over the crowd of dead
and wounded.*]
[*To* Dr. Scott, the Chaplain]
Doctor, I'm gone. I am waste o' time to you.

HARDY [*remaining behind*]
Hills, go to Collingwood and let him know
That we've no Admiral here.
[*He passes on.*]

A LIEUTENANT Now quick and pick him off who did the deed-
That white-bloused man there in the mizzen-top.

POLLARD No sooner said than done. A pretty aim!
[*The Frenchman falls dead upon the poop.*]
[*The spectacle seems now to become enveloped in smoke,
and the point of view changes.*]

*Nelson's great victory over the French off Cape Trafalgar in Spain, and his death,
occurred on October 21, 1802.*

michael spence

Knowing What North Means: Letter to Hugo from Lopez Island

> *As a child, I believed life was a northern journey and at some unknown point in the north, all things end. The river found acceptance in the sea.*
> —Richard Hugo, 1923–1982, "The Real West Marginal Way"

Dear Dick: Surrounded by water, I begin to feel
What you said. Wind in the night blew down a huge fir—
It lies splintered on the beach. But even fallen
It has majesty. Ruined things always do. From a friend's shack
I see the house his folks have worked on ten years. Still
A shell. Will it ever hold people? Time to them flows endless
As water in the Strait of Juan de Fuca. Till we finish,
What is built? If we don't we build a different failure.
My friend's father accumulates everything—metal lathes,
Kegs of nails, chainsaws missing teeth, other houses
To store it all. Fourteen cars and trucks scattered from here
To Seattle; only one runs. The Depression stripped him: now
He can't bear to lose what's already gone. Port Townsend
Three years ago, I met you a single time, grinning
From the company of wine and writers. A blond girl wanted you
To sign her cork. She was nervous; I asked. *Sure*, you laughed,
And etched as though carving scrimshaw. Through her hangover
Next day, she smiled. No one knew: soon—like salmon flashing
As you caught them with lines of nylon, with lines of ink—
You'd come home for good. A year today since you died; the world
Circled the sun to get back to the same place. In my mind
The blond girl under a gray sky goes down to the Duwamish.
Like Longfellow Creek, the first you ever saw or fished,
It flows north. She turns the cork in her fingers, tracing
Your marks. Then she gives it to the river. Your signature
Dissolves, mixing with the current, heading for the Strait
And open water. Far to the north—at the unknown point
Where all things end—the sea accepts your name. Farewell. Mike.

October 22, 1983

dick davis

Richard Davis

> *. . . minding to have sent to Qazvin Alexander Kitchin, whom God*
> *took to his mercy the 23rd October last: and before him departed*
> *Richard Davis one of your mariners . . .*
> —Hakluyt, *Principal Voyages of the English Nation*

Our mariner's last landfall was this shore:
My namesake stood, four hundred years ago,
The empty Caspian at his back, and saw
A shelving view I intimately know—

Clean, silent air and noble poplar trees,
A marshy plain beyond which mountains rise,
The snow-line and the sky—all this he sees—
The colours fresh and calm before his eyes.

Fresh as your fading figure in my mind:
You look back to your little ship, then stare
As if the riches you had hoped to find
Were somehow present in the limpid air.

You walk towards the limits of my sight—
I see you stumble in the dusty light.

john moffitt

The Day Before the End

(October 24, 1962)

On this last day
The world is beautiful with doom:
Appropriately
A blue perfection rides the air
And all the houses shine

Distinct, electrical,
As if yet to enforce the old deceit
We so long nursed, that life was meaningful.

The wide city wears
An aspect of high holy days,
The streets are silent and the citizens few,
Each object, far or near,
Stands clean and right,
And men's faces take on
Solemnity and a quiet calm,
While the mind gathers to its last insight,
Seeing for the first time the weight
Of judgment in the thought
That I am who I am
And things are what they are.

Let us not, then, grudge fate its say
On this last day.

OCTOBER 25

william shakespeare

Agincourt

from: King Henry V

Act IV, scene iii.—The English Camp before Agincourt.

> [*Enter* KING HENRY *to* WESTMORELAND.]
> WESTMORELAND O that we now had here
> But one ten thousand of those men in England
> That do no work to-day!
> KING HENRY   What's he that wishes so?
> My cousin Westmoreland? No, my fair cousin:
> If we are mark'd to die, we are enow
> To do our country loss; and if to live,
> The fewer men, the greater share of honour.
> God's will! I pray thee, wish not one man more.
> By Jove, I am not covetous for gold,
> Nor care I who doth feed upon my cost;
> It earns me not if men my garments wear;

Such outward things dwell not in my desires:
But if it be a sin to covert honour,
I am the most offending soul alive.
No, faith, my coz, wish not a man from England:
God's peace! I would not lose so great an honour
As one man more, methinks, would share from me,
For the best hope I have. O do not wish one more!
Rather proclaim it, Westmoreland, through my host,
That he which hath no stomach to this fight,
Let him depart; his passport shall be made,
And crowns for convoy put into his purse:
We would not die in that man's company
That fears his fellowship to die with us.
This day is call'd the feast of Crispian:
He that outlives this day, and comes safe home,
Will stand a tip-toe when this day is nam'd,
And rouse him at the name of Crispian.
He that shall see this day, and live old age,
Will yearly on the vigil feast his neighbours,
And say, "To-morrow is Saint Crispian":
Then will he strip his sleeve and show his scars,
And say, "These wounds I had on Crispin's day."
Old men forget; yet all shall be forgot,
But he'll remember with advantages
What feats he did that day. Then shall our names,
Familiar in his mouth as household words,
Harry the king, Bedford and Exeter,
Warwick and Talbot, Salisbury and Gloucester,
Be in their flowing cups freshly remember'd.
This story shall the good man teach his son;
And Crispin Crispian shall ne'er go by,
From this day to the ending of the world,
But we in it shall be remembered;
We few, we happy few, we band of brothers
For he to-day that sheds his blood with me
Shall be my brother; be he ne'er so vile
This day shall gentle his condition:
And gentlemen in England now a-bed
Shall think themselves accurs'd they were not here,
And hold their manhoods cheap whiles any speak
That fought with us upon Saint Crispin's day.

*The weary English routed a numerically superior French force at Agincourt on
October 25, 1415.*

r. a. k. mason

Twenty-Sixth October

I strode with dry ironic gesture
   posing a high byronic posture
   towards your barred home, strutting the part
   of young man mocking broken heart

The sky was set for such a role:
   the great Cross glittered at the pole
   Orion and his wrath were red
   and the Milky Way white overhead
   all heaven a well-lit cyclorama
   for such a fine resounding drama . . .

I saw your house beneath the hill
   in the starlight gentle and still
   and a light struck the door denied

Then in one pulse the actor died

And through my heart wailed an old shrill
   wild keening that no art could kill
   an animal in lamentation
   for the dead of a long-dead nation:
   and in the macrocarpa trees
   I heard the sighing of the seas
   in some far ocean's centre moan
   for strong men dead with seed unsown

All my life leapt as one wild star
   breaks rank where its commandments are
   nor keeps the course of its appointment

The ulcer burst beneath the ointment

I turned: down a dull road I trudged
   hunched by a sky drawn close and smudged . . .
   for down a dreary road must travel
   an old man shuffling weary gravel

in night and pain timorous alone
with feet to whine at every stone

Give back the grease-paint and the mask
for shield against my unequal task:
give back the actor's godlike slickness
to smear over my mortal sickness.

dylan thomas

Poem in October

It was my thirtieth year to heaven
Woke to my hearing from harbour and neighbour wood
 And the mussel pooled and the heron
    Priested shore
   The morning beckon
With water praying and call of seagull and rook
And the knock of sailing boats on the net webbed wall
   Myself to set foot
    That second
 In the still sleeping town and set forth.

 My birthday began with the water-
Birds and the birds of the winged trees flying my name
 Above the farms and the white horses
    And I rose
   In rainy autumn
And walked abroad in a shower of all my days.
High tide and the heron dived when I took the road
   Over the border
    And the gates
 Of the town closed as the town awoke.

 A springful of larks in a rolling
Cloud and the roadside bushes brimming with whistling
 Blackbirds and the sun of October
    Summery
   On the hill's shoulder,

Here were fond climates and sweet singers suddenly
Come in the morning where I wandered and listened
    To the rain wringing
      Wind blow cold
In the wood faraway under me.

    Pale rain over the dwindling harbour
And over the sea wet church the size of a snail
    With its horns through mist and the castle
      Brown as owls
    But all the gardens
Of spring and summer were blooming in the tall tales
Beyond the border and under the lark full cloud.
    There could I marvel
      My birthday
Away but the weather turned around.

    It turned away from the blithe country
And down the other air and the blue altered sky
    Streamed again a wonder of summer
      With apples
    Pears and red currants
And I saw in the turning so clearly a child's
Forgotten mornings when he walked with his mother
    Through the parables
      Of sun light
And the legends of the green chapels

    And the twice told fields of infancy
That his tears burned my cheeks and his heart moved in mine.
    These were the woods the river and sea
      Where a boy
    In the listening
Summertime of the dead whispered the truth of his joy
To the trees and the stones and the fish in the tide.
    And the mystery
      Sang alive
Still in the water and singingbirds.

    And there could I marvel my birthday
Away but the weather turned around. And the true
    Joy of the long dead child sang burning
      In the sun.
    It was my thirtieth

Year to heaven stood there then in the summer noon
Though the town below lay leaved with October blood.
    O may my heart's truth
        Still be sung
On this high hill in a year's turning.

Dylan Thomas was born on October 27, 1914.

stephen scobie

McAlmon's Chinese Opera

I marched on Rome with Mussolini, arriving
the same day though by different routes.
His thugs were swarming in the streets,
force-feeding castor oil to those who failed
to sing the right words to a Fascist song
or raise their hands in the new salute.
Once watching a parade go by, I had
my hat knocked off my disrespectful head.

I've often wondered where they come from,
the wave of sadists, cretins, pimps,
who greet each new dictatorship, and crush
delightedly beneath their heels their own
identical twins of the previous reign.
History teaches them nothing—nor us, it seems,
applauding power when a gangster's hand
waves in the sky the imperial gesture,
his orator's voice ringing hollow as bells.

For a while as a tourist I followed
the guidebook round of ruined monuments
till polite pretence turned into farce:
too many ruins for the eye to hold,
Il Duce in the Colosseum watching
the games of death that raged
in the arena of my own sick heart.

*Mussolini's Blackshirts reached Rome on October 28, 1922. The speaker is the
American expatriate writer Robert McAlmon.*

robert lowell

Lady Ralegh's Lament

1618

Sir Walter, oh, oh, my own Sir Walter—
the sour Tower and the Virgin Queen's garden close
are deflowered and gone now . . .
Horrible the connoisseur tyrant's querulous strut;
an acorn dances in a girdle of green oak leaves
up the steps to the scaffold to the block,
square bastard of an oak. Clearly, clearly,
the Atlantic whitens to merge Sir Walter's head,
still dangling in its scarlet, tangled twine,
as if beseeching voyage. Voyage?
Down and down; the compass needle dead on terror.

Sir Walter Raleigh was beheaded on October 29, 1618.

edward hirsch

Devil's Night

He saw teenagers carrying flammable cans
of kerosene and boxes of wooden matches, torching
the discarded carcasses of Fords and Chevys,
spreading flames through abandoned buildings
and unused factories, lighting one-story houses
on narrow lots in small neighborhoods. He saw
old men standing on their front lawns in bathrobes,
holding shotguns and green garden hoses to stave off
the burning. A night of TV cameras and wailing
sirens, an hour of reckoning, moment of judgment.
He saw gas stations exploding like tinderboxes
and party stores being looted, and He understood
a new ritual of autumn, an annual reaping,

a fury that gathered night after night, until
it burst forth like a fever in late October.
He was one of the bystanders who waited
on the sidewalk, passing a thermos of steaming
coffee and a bottle of whiskey, watching fire-
fighters wading into a furnace of buildings.
He was there when the blaze finally calmed
and the radios quit bristling with static,
when the exhausted crowd dispersed and drifted
toward home. And He was one of the few
who were still awake to witness the sunrise,
to observe a smoky disc flaring over the river,
charring the rooftops, glistening in the ruins.
He closed his eyes and saw darkness visible.
Yellow flames brimmed over cinders and ashes.
A broken skyline smoldered in the distance.

*"Devil's Night" is set in Detroit, Michigan, on October 30th. A tradition of looting
and setting fires there has developed on the night before Halloween. [Note by
Hirsch]*

anthony hecht

Hallowe'en

    Tonight our streets are filled
With beardless pirates and their high-heeled wives
Who own no maps of treasure and have killed
Nobody with their aimless wooden knives;
They cry us charity for their cups of tin.
    Tonight their plea is styled
With signs of poison and the threat of crones,
While from behind a soap-scrawled windowpane,
A pumpkin with a candle for a brain
    Flashes its hacked-out grin
At Jolly Roger, ensign of the child
Who stalks the street, superfluous of bones.

    One time the children came
Souling with little songs for all the dead,

Soliciting in Mystery's full name
Apples and cakes and pies, for it was said
A hermit raised a trapdoor and was shown
    Where purgatory burned,
Whistled and hurt; he heard the demons yell
Against the monks of Cluny for their prayers
That lifted cripples up the spiraled stairs.
    And singing made it known:
To do grace to the dead, lest they returned,
Apples were prayers and giving was a spell.

    And singers have this right,
For hunger haunts the gut, but not for bread;
The troubled presence that returns this night,
When all the air is crowded with the dead,
Shivers for lack of body, and is claim
    To the community
Of the mad Prince disguised in seven ways,
The Riddling Knight who challenges our sleep,
The starving Goblin and the Hag who keep
    (To their perpetual blame)
Poor Tom o'Bedlam from his sanity,
And sent an English king into his craze.

    All of our enemies
Move through this night with polished, skinless jaws,
And kiss the daft ones into their disease,
Take from the poor, and are themselves the cause
That ghosts return upon us to be fed.
    Hearing the Death's Head cry,
"O hunger, hunger," shall I offer salt?
The pumpkin grins with idiotic mirth,
Laughs at the child whose bones were crossed at birth,
    Who moves among these dead,
Hungry for bread and salt, and ripe to die,
And likely to come, begging, from the vault.

p. j. kavanagh

November the First

A long farewell:
An All Souls' Day so bright I shift my seat
Out of the glare, and dying flies blacken the sill.

One window crawls,
The other taps with blown birds' beaks, torn leaves.
Today's a windy tunnel of farewells.

Farewell red-coated figure
Playing trains down lanes hairy with November.
We'll play the same again, next year, sometime, never.

A silly game,
My longing is, to keep you, when the sun
Never lights one blade of grass the same

Minute by minute.
Farewell's the only word wind ever says
And all we say is soundlessly lost in it.

Time blows
Clearest and clean round those who do not dream
Heavenly Waiting Rooms of renewed Hallos.

Farewell, red back.
I shall always dream so, mustily. Goodbye
Till then, red engine, on your single track.

william butler yeats

All Souls' Night

Midnight has come, and the great Christ Church Bell
And many a lesser bell sound through the room;
And it is All Souls' Night,
And two long glasses brimmed with muscatel
Bubble upon the table. A ghost may come;
For it is a ghost's right,
His element is so fine
Being sharpened by his death,
To drink from the wine-breath
While our gross palates drink from the whole wine,

I need some mind that, if the cannon sound
From every quarter of the world, can stay
Wound in mind's pondering
As mummies in the mummy-cloth are wound;
Because I have a marvellous thing to say,
A certain marvellous thing
None but the living mock,
Though not for sober ear;
It may be all that hear
Should laugh and weep an hour upon the clock.

. . .

But names are nothing. What matter who it be,
So that his elements have grown so fine
The fume of muscatel
Can give his sharpened palate ecstasy
No living man can drink from the whole wine.
I have mummy truths to tell
Whereat the living mock,
Though not for sober ear,
For maybe all that hear
Should laugh and weep an hour upon the clock.

Such thought—such thought have I that hold it tight
Till meditation master all its parts,
Nothing can stay my glance
Until that glance run in the world's despite

To where the damned have howled away their hearts,
And where the blessed dance;
Such thought, that in it bound
I need no other thing,
Wound in mind's wandering
As mummies in the mummy-cloth are wound.

NOVEMBER 3

roy fisher

3rd November 1976

Maybe twenty of us in the late afternoon
are still in discussion. We're talking
about the Arts Council of Great Britain
and its beliefs about itself. We're baffled.

We're in a hired pale clubroom
high over the County Cricket Ground
and we're a set of darkening heads,
turning and talking and hanging down;
beyond the plate glass, in another system, silent,
the green pitch rears up, all colour,
and differently processed. Across it in olive overalls
three performance artists persistently move
with rakes and rods. The cold sky steepens.
Twilight catches the flats rising out of the trees.

One of our number is abducted
into the picture. A sculptor innocent of bureaucracy
raises his fine head to speak out;
and the window and its world frame him.
He is made clear.

400

stephen sandy

The Heart's Desire of Americans

Squally Election Day, a few drops pebbling
The hood; we wanted a bite to eat but wanted
To vote, to get back to vote; although not voting
Counted, too. We turned in the drive of Concord
Prison, backtracked through drizzle and at the sign
For Walden Pond turned off, on impulse to pay
A visit; parked where a crowd in cars sat talking
In the rain or silently watching it spatter the pond.
Tuesday: they should have been at work. But clearly
They had the day off to vote; and here they were.
Walden, we guessed, had been a glacial kettle
Or the like; since the wooded banks were steep, no way
For the water to get in or out that we could see.
There was a concrete pier with ladders and a beach,
A women's bath house and a men's, and signs that said
"No Swimming." The rain on the wooden rails was beautiful.

Jim said, "I believe everything you say,"
Which made me feel good although I knew of course
There was more than a touch of irony in his voice
And the way he laughed I knew he doubted me
When I told him the last words of Thoreau, as who
Wouldn't. We split a granola bar and decided
To make up proverbs. "He who looks for dustballs
Under the bed is not looking" seemed the most
Likely, here. Goofer feathers, dust puppies, and
Angel fluff we acknowledged as acceptable
Variant wordings for this Concord saw.
We wanted to look, but the rain was not letting up
And still we could not go for coffee without
First changing the old, frayed windshield wipers
For new ones, which he had thoughtfully brought with him,
Some "fits all" kind, not simple to attach at all.

Slant capes of rain spilled down and fled, scoring
The dark waters till Walden simmered with light,
While more people arrived in sparkling cars.
Two women in running suits had remembered to bring
A flowered parasol and plain umbrella, which

They put up as they sauntered down the path
Of White Pine needles toward the shore. We decided
Not to waste our time, and be on our way. "Zen mind,
Weekenders' mind," Jim said, and so it seemed.
It was a beautiful time. Even the prison looked
Empty, and the girl at the ice cream counter smiled.
Later, the Deerfield River and its arrangement
Of ice-planed rocks streaming with rain and the late
Twilight gleaming beside Route Two urged us
To stop. And we pulled over. When you've seen
One perfect spot, you want to see them all.

*Election Day in 1980 was November 4. Stephen Sandy was returning from Boston
to Bennington, Vermont, to vote.*

NOVEMBER 5

 vernon scannell

Gunpowder Plot

For days these curious cardboard buds have lain
In brightly coloured boxes. Soon the night
Will come. We pray there'll be no sullen rain
To make these magic orchids flame less bright.

Now in the garden's darkness they begin
To flower; the frenzied whizz of Catherine-wheel
Puts forth its fiery petals and the thin
Rocket soars to burst upon the steel

Bulwark of a cloud. And then the guy,
Absurdly human phoenix, is again
Gulped by greedy flames: the harvest sky
Is flecked with threshed and glittering golden grain.

"Uncle! A cannon! Watch me as I light it!"
The women, helter-skelter, squealing high,
Retreat; the paper fuse is quickly lit,
A cat-like hiss and spit of fire, a sly

Falter, then the air is shocked with blast.
The cannon bangs, and in my nostils drifts
A bitter scent that brings the lurking past
Lurching to my side. The present shifts,

Allows a ten-year memory to walk
Unhindered now; and so I'm forced to hear
The banshee howl of mortar and the talk
Of men who died; am forced to taste my fear.

I listen for a moment to the guns,
The torn earth's grunts, recalling how I prayed.
The past retreats. I hear a corpse's sons:
"Who's scared of bangers?" "Uncle! John's afraid!"

richard corbett

In Quendam Anniversariorum Scriptorem

Ter circum Iliacos raptaverat Hectora muros

Even soe dead *Hector* thrice was triumph'd on
The Walls of *Troy*, thrice slaine when fate had done:
So did the barbarous *Greekes* before their Hoast
Torment his ashes, and profane his ghoast:
As *Henryes* vault, his *Peace*, his Sacred *Hearse*,
Are torne and batter'd by thine Anniverse.
Was't not enough *Nature* and *strength* were foes,
But thou must yearly *murther* him in Prose?
Or do'st thou thinke thy rauing phrase can make
A lowder Eccho then the Almanake?
Trust mee, November doth more ghastly looke
In Dade and Hoptons pennyworth, then thy booke:
And sadder record their sixt figure beares,
Then thy false-printed and ambitious teares.
For were it not for Christmas, which is nigh,
When spice, fruit, eaten, and digested pye,
Call for wast paper; noe man could make shift
How to imploy thy writings to his thrift.

Wherefore forbeare for pitty, or for shame,
And let some richer pen redeeme his fame
From rottennesse. Thou leaue him captive; since
Soe vile a Price ne're ransom'd such a Prince.

*When Prince Henry, elder son of James I, died on November 6, 1612, there was a
general outpouring of grief and heartfelt commemorative verses. Later the annual
tributes, especially by one Daniel Price, began to be thinly veiled criticisms of Prince
Charles, who was clearly the satyr to Prince Henry's Hyperion. Corbett says enough
is enough.*

NOVEMBER 7

prentiss moore

November 7

Today lovely low clouds with soft
grey underbellies, the grey almost
matching the blue of the sky.
Like Vermeer's *View of Delft*,
patches of sunlight moving slowly
across the city. There is such stillness
one notices time itself; some
would say "time stood still,"
like the women in Vermeer's painting
who stand near the water talking
though they are too far to hear.
There is less sunlight than
shade today; one sees it it seems
as in the painting
always on distant rooftops
and trees. A good day
for reading at a window
or beneath a tree, the light
shining at the edges of the clouds
and from the small open areas of sky.

allen curnow

An Excellent Memory

Brasch wrote 'these islands' and I
'two islands' counting one short,
and 'the islands' in our language
were remoter, palmier Polynesian chartings,
a there for a here.
              The cartographer
dots them in, the depth of his blue
denotes the depth of the entirely
surrounding water.
              The natives,
given time, with the help of an atlas,
come to recognize in the features of
the coastline a face
of their own, a puzzled mirror
for a puzzling globe.
              'Always in these
'islands', that was Charles Brasch
getting it right the very first time.

Pat Laking knew it by heart the whole sonnet
all the way down to 'distance
'looks our way' and it did,
over the martinis in Observatory Circle,
Washington D.C., demanding by way
of an answering look nothing more
than an excellent memory.
              That was
8 November 1974, just about
midnight, give or take a few minutes.

dannie abse

Elegy for Dylan Thomas

All down the valleys they are talking,
 and in the community of the smoke-laden town.
Tomorrow, through bird trailed skies, across labouring waves,
wrong-again Emily will come to the dandelion yard
 and, with rum tourists, inspect his grave.

Death was his voluntary marriage,
and his poor silence sold to that rich and famous bride.
 Beleaguered in that essential kiss he rode
the whiskey-meadows of her breath till, mortal, voiceless,
 he gave up his nailed ghost and he died.

No more to celebrate
his disinherited innocence or your half-buried heart
 drunk as a butterfly, or sober as black.
Now, one second from earth, not even for the sake
 of love can his true energy come back.

So cease your talking.
Too familiar you blaspheme his name and collected legends:
 some tears fall soundlessly and aren't the same
 as those that drop with obituary explosions.
 Suddenly, others who sing seem older and lame.

But far from the blind country of prose,
wherever his burst voice goes about you or through you,
 look up in surprise, in a hurt public house
 or in a rain-blown street, and see how
 no fat ghost but a quotation cries.

Stranger, he is laid to rest
not in the nightingale dark nor in the canary light.
 At the dear last, the yolk broke in his head,
 blood of his soul's egg in a splash of bright
 voices and now he is dead.

Thomas died at St. Vincent's Hospital in New York City on November 9, 1953.

elizabeth brewster

William Brewster Disembarking from the *Mayflower*

We sailed in September,
a hundred and two of us
crowded on one ship
after the *Speedwell* had been sent back,
unseaworthy vessel. We first had good weather.
There was some quarrelling: we were not all Saints,
and even Saints do not always agree.
All plain men we were, though;
None, thank, God, with pride of blood
or family tree; Sons of Adam:
James Chilton, tailor, of Canterbury;
Sam Eaton, of Bristol, ship's carpenter,
with his wife Sarah and a sucking child;
grave Richard Warren, a useful instrument;
Myles Standish, a good soldier;
the Billingtons of London, a most profane family
(doomed to be hanged, no doubt);
my own wife Mary,
my sons Love and Wrestling
(Jonathan left in Leyden
with Fear and Patience,
his young sisters).

The trip seemed long, the quarters narrow.
We tired of our diet of salt horse and hardtack.
The weather worsened. Many were seasick.
Stink of slop and vomit tainted the air,
and smell of unwashed bodies
crowded below deck.
The sailors (not Saints) swore at the sick.
But the hand of God struck one profane young man.
He died and was buried
in the swelling sea.
But Saints died too. Young William Butten,
Deacon Fuller's servant, died in November.

On the tenth of November,
after a long tossing,

the lookout at dawn cried "Land ahoy!"
And, not a little joyful, we crowded to the rails.
But we were nearly lost
in the treacherous water.
All night we lay at sea, and finally entered
this good harbour.

We have still much to fear:
mutiny, hunger, cold, hostile natives,
dissension among ourselves, a savage life
in a strange country.

We must not be homesick
for the flat fens of Lincolnshire
and its farmhouses dark with age,
nor for London streets, or Amsterdam,
no, nor for Leyden, that goodly city
where we lived twelve years.
For we are Pilgrims
who seek a City
beyond all earthly seas and bounds of space
where no waves break and God is Governor.

tom paulin

11/11/84

for David Williams

> *The public knows very well the distinction between wrestling and boxing; it knows that boxing is a Jansenist sport based on a demonstration of excellence.*
> —Roland Barthes

They're at it again
this wick decade
the Cartesian
and his female wrestler
who's just eaten
an omelette *baveuse*
off a porcelain plate.
She looks on him
as a peeled joker
kinda tulip poplar
that wants to poke
sème partout
between her wet lips.
He's no limbs but
this bodiless
light monster
you watch them flip
into a croupier's
dry feint—

M. Clemenceau
lending Woodrow Wilson
a steel cigarclipper
from the Quai d'Orsay.
Its toolsmooth light shone—
it shines still—
like the rails in the Metro.
Look they zip away
into a black hole
like a line by Mallarmé
or this cropped kid
they call him Dale
a warder's strapping
to a gurney.
Dale has nine minutes
on their deathwatch—
he shivers
delicate and brittle poor wee thing
as tinfoil.

ewart milne

Remembrance Day 1972

Lord, it's been a hell of a life
That's for those of us who somehow survived its strife
Nothing but wars crying after wars and bloody murders
World wars civil wars holy wars ritual wars and massacres
And always the peewit: plaintive over the guns' *sturmfest*
Wing-tumbling to con death away from his nest

Now we are again enjoined to remember
Those who died—especially in the Fourteen war
And *of the best among them* as Ezra Pound wrote
For an old bitch gone in the teeth
But how can we forget?

I remember a rainy moonless night Nineteen Fifteen
My cousin Gerald in Lieutenant's khaki uniform
Going off to war from Ashford near Rathnew
Deep in the Glens of Wicklow

I remember my aunt and my grown-up cousins cried
And brusquely pushed me to one side
Small, bullet-headed, and solemn jackeen
Watching that all-too-common family scene
I remember my mother sitting as if turned to stone
When the news came Gerald had been killed in the line
My elder brother an OTC cadet in uniform by Seventeen

The question is not whether we remember
But when a time out of war will let us ponder
And recall there was more to our yesterdays than war
Which if permitted we might without guilt uncover.

Remembrance Day in 1972 fell on November 12.

andrew marvell

Tom May's Death

As one put drunk into the Packet-boat,
Tom May was hurried hence and did not know't
But was amaz'd on the Elysian side,
And with an eye uncertain, gazing wide,
Could not determine in what place he was,
For whence in Stevens ally trees or grass?
Nor where the Pope's head, nor the Mitre lay,
Signs by which still he found and lost his way.
At last while doubtfully he all compares,
He saw near hand, as he imagin'd *Ares*.
Such did he seem for corpulence and port,
But 'twas a man much of another sort;
'Twas *Ben* that in the dusky Laurel shade
Amongst the chorus of old Poets laid,
Sounding of ancient Heroes, such as were
The Subject's Safety and the Rebel's fear.

. . .

Yet then with foot as stumbing as his tongue
Prest for his place among the Learned throng,
But *Ben*, who knew not neither foe nor friend,
Sworn Enemy to all that do pretend,
Rose more than ever he was seen severe,
Shook his gray locks, and his own Bayes did tear
At this intrusion. Then with Laurel wand,
The awful Sign of his supreme command.
At whose dread Whisk *Virgil* himself does quake,
And *Horace* patiently its stroke does take,
As he crowds in he whipt him o'er the pate
Like *Pembroke* at the Masque, and then did rate.
    Far from these blessed shades tread back agen
Most servile wit, and mercenary Pen.
Polydore, Lucan, Allan, Vandale, Goth,
Malignant poet and historian both.

. . .

When the sword glitters o'er the Judges head,
And fear has Coward Churchmen silenced,

Then is the poets time, 'tis then he draws,
And single fights forsaken Vertues cause.
He, when the wheel of Empire, whirleth back,
And though the World's disjointed Axel crack,
Sings still of ancient Rights and better Times,
Seeks wretched good, arraigns successful Crimes.
But thou base man first prostituted hast
Our spotless knowledge and the studies chast.
Apostatizing from our Arts and us,
To turn the Chronicler to *Spartacus.*
Yet wast thou taken hence with equal fate,
Before thou coudst great Charles his death relate.

. . .

Poor Poet thou, and grateful Senate they,
Who thy last Reckoning did so largely pay.
And with the publick gravity would come,
When thou hadst drunk thy last to lead thee home.
If that can be thy home where *Spencer* lyes
And reverend *Chaucer,* but their dust does rise
Against thee, and expels thee from their side.
As th' Eagles plumes from other birds divide.
Nor here thy shade must dwell, Return, Return,
Where Sulphrey *Phlegeton* does ever burn.
The *Cerebus* with all his Jawes shall gnash,
Megera thee with all her Serpents lash.
Thou rivited unto *Ixion*'s wheel
Shalt break, and the perpetual Vulture feel.
'Tis just what Torments Poets ere did feign,
Thou first Historically shouldst sustain.
    Thus by irrevocable Sentence cast,
    May only Master of these Revels past.
    And straight he vanisht in a Cloud of pitch,
    Such as unto the Sabboth bears the Witch.

Tom May, translator of Lucan's Pharsalia, *died in his cups on November 13, 1650. According to John Aubrey, he "came of his death after drinking with his chin tyed with his cap (being fat) suffocated." He had lived in Stevens Alley and had vainly tried to be selected poet laureate after Ben Jonson's death.*

peter klappert

Says What

Beauty and Poetry contain the same number
of letters, but Beauty requires all three
lines of a standard typewriter keyboard.
The typewriter, of course, has had great
impact on the form and content between which
there is no dichotomy in modern poetry.

> *"Let's talk about*
> *the poem as it stands on the page."*
> *Lou brought two small ones—*

A further distinction is Instinct. Instinct
refers to unlearned, patterned, goal-directed
behavior which is species-specific.
Freaks you would say.

> *two small ones which she wears high*
> *where no one can miss them.*
> *I should have been kind and noticed*
> *but*

. . .

Nov. 14, 1967

Dear Elsie,

    Can you put out the moon with a pea-shooter? I'm walk-
ing on nobody's eggs, I'm as moral as I can remember. What
if I were to call you William? What if I were to call you—
Lassie?

    But if Lassie like it, and I liked it . . .

Chink Chink says the Chaffinch
and a thousand chaffinches mob
the outline of an owl.

               Too bad
for the essential features of owlness.

robert phillips

The Unfalling

November fifteenth, and still no fall
of leaves. They cling tenaciously
to every branch and stem. Weeks ago
they turned color, now turncoat
and will not let go. Even last night's
Sturm und Drang left them unperturbed.

In the country the bushel baskets
are impatient, awaiting their legacies,
their windfalls. Wheelbarrows stand
unmoving. Each suburban garage and cellar
houses rakes and yard brooms which lean
upon one another, mourning next-of-kin.

The gutters at my roofline are amazed:
Each autumn they strangle on leaves—
yet last night's rain set them singing
clear and high, a castrati choir.
All the baseballs boys lost last summer
long to be blanketed down for winter.

Will the leaves never fall?
Will this be the fall that failed?

ben jonson

An Ode, or Song, by All the Muses. In Celebration of her Majesties Birth-day 1630

1. CLIO
Up publike joy, remember
This sixteenth of *November*,
 Some brave un-common way:
And though the Parish-steeple
Be silent, to the people
 Ring thou it Holy-day.

2. MELPOMENE
What, though the thriftie Tower
And Gunnes there, spare to poure
 Their noises forth in Thunder:
As fearfull to awake
This Citie, or to shake
 Their guarded gates asunder?

3. THALIA
Yet, let our Trumpets sound;
And cleave both ayre and ground,
 With beating of our Drum's:
Let every Lyre be strung,
Harpe, Lute, Theorbo sprung,
 With touch of daintie thum's!

4. EUTERPE
That when the Quire is full,
The Harmony may pull
 The Angels from their Spheares:
And each intelligence
May wish it selfe a sense;
 Whilst it the Dittie beares.

5. TERPSICHORE
Behold the royall *Mary*,
The Daughter of great *Harry*!
 And Sister to just *Lewis*!

Comes in the pompe, and glorie
Of all her Brothers storie,
    And of her Fathers prowesse!

6. ERATO
Shee showes so farre above
The fained Queene of Love,
    This sea-girt Isle upon:
As here no *Venus* were;
But, that shee raigning here,
    Had got the *Ceston* on!

7. CALLIOPE
See, see our active *King*
Hath taken twice the Ring
    Upon his pointed Lance:
Whilst all the ravish'd rout
Doe mingle in a shout,
    Hay! for the flowre of *France*!

8. URANIA
This day the Court doth measure
Her joy in state, and pleasure;
    And with a reverend feare,
The Revells, and the Play,
Summe up this crowned day,
    Her two and twenti'th yeare!

9. POLYHYMNIA
Sweet! happy *Mary*! All
The People her doe call!
    And this the wombe divine!
So fruitful, and so faire,
Hath brought the Land an Heire!
    And CHARLES a Caroline.

george peele

A Sonet—At the Tilt-Yard; Nov. 17, 1590

His Golden lockes Time hath to Siluer turn'd,
   O Time too swift, o Swiftnesse neuer ceasing!
His Youth gainst Time and Age hath euer spurn'd,
   But spurn'd in vain, Youth waineth by increasing.
Beauty, Strength, Youth, are flowers, but fading seen,
Dutie, Faith, Loue, are roots, and euer greene.

His Helmet now shall make a hiue for Bees,
   And Louers sonets turne to holy Psalmes:
A man at Armes must now serue on his knees,
   And feede on praiers, which are Age his almes.
But though from Court to Cottage he depart,
His Saint is sure of his vnspotted heart.

And when he saddest sits in homely Cell,
   Heele teach his swaines this Caroll for a Song,—
Bless'd be the heartes that wish my Soueraigne well,
   Curs'd be the soules that thinke her any wrong!
Goddess, allow this aged man his right,
To be your Beads-man now, that was your Knight.

*Sir Henry Lee had been Queen Elizabeth's champion for many years at the annual
celebration of her accession to the throne. In the version reported by William Segar
in* Honor Military, and Civill, *Sir Henry speaks in the first person.*

jorie graham

Breakdancing

[Teresa: Saint Teresa of Avila]

Staying alive the boy on the screen is doing it,
   the secret nobody knows like a rapture through his limbs,
the secret, *the robot-like succession of joint isolations*
   that simulate a body's reaction to
electric shock.
   This is how it tells itself: pops, ticks, waves and the

float. What
    is poverty for, Mr. Speed, Dr. Cadet, Dr. Rage,
Timex? Don't push me the limbs are whispering, don't push
    'cause I'm close to the edge the footwork is whispering
down onto the sidewalk that won't give in won't go some other
    where while the TV

hums and behind me their breathings, husband, daughter, too slow,
    go in to that other place and come back out
unstained, handfuls at a time, air, air—
    The flag of the greatest democracy on earth
waves in the wind with the sound turned off. The current

rubs through the stars and stripes
    like a muttering passing through a crowd and coming out an
anthem,
    string of words on its search
and destroy
    needing bodies, bodies. . . .
I'm listening to where she must not choke. I'm listening
    to where he must not be betrayed. I'm trying

to hear pity, the idiom. I'm trying to lean into those
    marshes and hear
what comes through clean,
    what comes through changed,
having needed us.
    Oh but you must not fail to eat and sleep Teresa murmurs to
her flock,

staying alive is the most costly gift you have to offer Him—all the
                            while watching,

    (whispering Lord, what will you have me
do?) for his corporal
    appearance
in the light of the sixteenth century, in the story that flutters
    blowzy over the body of the land
we must now somehow ram
    the radioactive waste

into. He
    showed himself to her in pieces.
First the fingertips, there in mid-air,

clotting, floating, held up by the invisible, neither rising
nor falling nor approaching nor lingering, then hands, then a

few days later feet, torso, then arms, each part alone, each part
    free of its argument, then days, then eyes,
then face entire, then days again, then *His*
    most sacred humanity in its risen form
was represented to me

completely. "Don't try
    to hold me in yourself (the air, hissing) but try to hold yourself
in me," Nov 18, 1570. I'm listening to where she must not choke,
    I'm listening to where he must not, must not. . . . Air,
holding a girl in a man's arms now,
    making them look like wind,
what if they can't be returned to you
    the *things* now reaching me—the three

exhalings, hum, blue light, the minutes, the massacres, the strict halflife
    of radioactive isotopes, the shallow
graves, the seventeen rememberable personal
    lies? What if they go only this far, grounding
in me, staying
    alive?
Here is the secret: the end is an animal.
    Here is the secret: the end is an animal growing by

accretion, image by image, vote by
    vote. *No more pain* hums the air,
as the form of things shall have fallen
    from thee, no more pain, just the here and the now, the jackpot, the
watching, minutes exploding like thousands of silver dollars all over your
    face your hands but tenderly, almost tenderly, turning mid-air, gleaming,
so slow, as if it could last,
    frame after frame of nowhere

turning into the living past.

richard crashaw

from: Epithalamium

1. Come virgin Tapers of pure waxe
        made in the Hive of Love, all white
    as snow, and yet as cold, where lackes
        Hymens holy heate and light;
            where blooming kisses
                their beds yet keepe
            and steepe their blisses
                in Rosy sleepe;
    where sister budds yet wanting brothers
    kisse their owne lipps in Lieu of others;
    help me to mourne a matchlesse maydenhead
        that now is dead:

2. A fine thin negative thing it was
        a nothing with a dainty name,
    which pruned her plumes in selfe loves glasse,
        made up of fancy and fond fame;
            within the shade
                of its owne winge
            it sate and played
                a selfe crownd King;
    A froward flower, whose peevish pride
    within it selfe, it selfe did hide,
    flying all fingers, and even thinking much
        of its owne touch:

3. This bird indeed the phænix was
        late chaced by loves revengefull arrowes,
    whose warres now left the wonted passe
        and spared the litle lives of sparrowes;
            to hunt this foole
                whose froward pride,
            Loves noble schoole,
                and Courts denyed,
    And froze the fruite of faire desire
    which flourisheth in mutuall fire,
    'gainst nature, who 'mong all the webbs she spunn
        nere wove A Nunne:

4. She of Cupids shafts afraid
    left her owne balme-breathing East,
  and in a westerne bosome made
    a softer, and a sweeter neast;
    there did she rest
      in the sweet shade,
    of a soft breast,
      whose beauties made
Thames oft stand still, and lend a glasse
while in her owne she saw heavens face,
and sent him full of her faire names report
    to Thetis Court:

5. And now poore Love was at a stand
    the Christall castle which she kept
was proofe against the proudest hand;
    there in safest hold she slept;
    his shafts expence
      left there noe smart,
    but bounding thence
      broached his owne heart;
At length a fort he did devise
built in noble Brampstons eyes
and ayming thence, this matchlesse maydenhead
    was soone found dead:

6. Yet Love in death did wayte upon her,
    granting leave she should expire
in her fumes, and have the honour
    t' exhale in flames of his owne fire;
    her funerall pyle
      the marriage bedd,
    in a sighed smile
      she vanished.
So rich a dresse of death nere famed
the Cradles where her kindred flamed;
so sweet her mother phænixes of th' East
    nere spiced their neast:

. . .

The epithalamium celebrates the marriage of Sir John Branston and Alice Abdy on November 19, 1635, in London.

julius lester

from: In the Time of Revolution

IV.

One needs a lyric poet in these
now nights (dawns)
at 27 because revolution
is not
banners unfurling on clear
afternoons,
nor songs
(We Shall Overcome our own
inadequacies Someday,
O Lord.
Have mercy upon us.
Have Mercy upon us.)
heard in the distance.
the heartbeat of
revolution is
women
(in China and Algeria maybe it was
    different)
knowing that
(yes)
it must be
but in their
woman
(women)
souls
needing to ask him
(who lives only in now)
"do you think she needs a sweater today?"
    "Do you
think she has a temperature?" "What's

good on t.v. tonight?"
the minutiae of the day
un-
ra-
vels
(in the same way each day because God
rewinds the yarn each night and puts the
    neatly
wound ball back in your sewing basket
    each dawn)
and to keep from being
choked in its threads
the woman
(blood in the veins of poets)
needs someone to hold out their
(him)
un-
winds
because
night is
heavy
and as she lies down
it is like a
tombstone and her
bed a
grave dug by him in his
dawn
dawn
dawning of
now.

atlanta, georgia, November 20, 1966

422

fiona pitt-kethley

The Party

On my tenth birthday I had a really
dirty party—whoopee cushions, the lot.
The respectable list of games my Ma'd
planned were all despised. When eating-time came,
we renamed everything, sickening ourselves—
turds on sticks, bum sandwiches—and we shook
up the jellies like bosoms. Afterwards—
Pin the Pants on the Headmistress,
Truth or Dare and Dirty Consequences.
During Forfeits, we had a girl stripped down
to her red Ladybird tights. My mother came
to the rescue—not that my friend was pleased—
there had been a prize of threepence riding
on her silence. (We've kept in touch since school.
Some years back, on a train to Pitlochry,
she had the Canadian Ice Hockey team
for three quid—she's always been a sports fan.)
One Judas girl of the twelve sat silent—
like Queen Victoria, not amused—and went
rather early. The rest, combed and bourgeoised,
left with their parents, saying as usual,
"Thank you for having me."

Fiona Pitt-Kethley turned ten on November 21, 1964.

a. d. hope

Moschus Moschiferus

A Song for St. Cecilia's Day

In the high jungle where Assam meets Tibet
The small Kastura, most archaic of deer,
Were driven in herds to cram the hunters' net
And slaughtered for the musk-pods which they bear;

But in those thickets of rhododendron and birch
The tiny creatures now grow hard to find.
Fewer and fewer survive each year. The search
Employs new means, more exquisite and refined:

The hunters now set out by two or three;
Each carries a bow and one a slender flute.
Deep in the forest the archers choose a tree
And climb; the piper squats against the root.

And there they wait until all trace of man
And rumour of his passage dies away.
They melt into the leaves and, while they scan
The glade below, their comrade starts to play.

Through those vast listening woods a tremulous skein
Of melody wavers, delicate and shrill:
Now dancing and now pensive, now a rain
Of pure, bright drops of sound and now the still,

Sad wailing of lament; from tune to tune
It winds and modulates without a pause;
The hunters hold their breath; the trance of noon
Grows tense; with its full power the music draws

A shadow from a juniper's darker shade;
Bright-eyed, with quivering muzzle and pricked ear,
The little musk-deer slips into the glade
Led by an ecstasy that conquers fear.

A wild enchantment lures him, step by step,
Into its net of crystalline sound, until
The leaves stir overhead, the bowstrings snap
And poisoned shafts bite sharp into the kill.

Then, as the victim shudders, leaps and falls,
The music soars to a delicious peak,
And on and on its silvery piping calls
Fresh spoil for the rewards the hunters seek.

But when the woods are emptied and the dusk
Draws in, the men climb down and count their prey,
Cut out the little glands that hold the musk
And leave the carcasses to rot away.

A hundred thousand or so are killed each year;
Cause and effect are very simply linked:
Rich scents demand the musk, and so the deer,
Its source, must soon, they say, become extinct.

Divine Cecilia, there is no more to say!
Of all who praised the power of music, few
Knew of these things. In honour of your day
Accept this song I too have made for you.

The Feast of St. Cecilia, patron saint of music, is celebrated on November 22.

anonymous

St. Clement's Day Song

Clementsing, clementsing, apples and pears,
One for Peter, two for Paul, three for Him that made us all!
Up with your stockings and down with your shoes,
If you haven't got apples, money will do.
Put your hand in your pocket and fetch out your keys,
Go down in the cellar and fetch what you please,
An apple, a pear, a plum or a cherry,
A bottle of wine to make us all merry.
The roads are so dirty, our boots are so thin,
Our pockets are empty and got nothing in.

"So a pot against the 23rd of November for the feast of St. Clement, from the ancient custom of going about that night to beg drink with which to make merry."
(Natural History of Staffordshire, *Robert Plot, Oxford, 1686.*)

dan stryk

Quake in Turkey

November 24, 1976

If the old grey-beard whose cramped black fist
shoved up between iced lips for days
could talk, he'd tell you

of the "deafening roar," of earth-dolls
piled down the buckled roads
of Muriyadye. He'd tell you

of his youngest, twins, pressed into the grainfield
mud, a pair of fossil-doves, where they had frisked
to image promised spring,

thrill of the deep Islam light
upon their summer chores, elders bowing east
for Mecca's grain; while everywhere

the pierce of muezzin's cry. . . . He'd tell you
how the tremors had still gnarled
two frigid days, survivors like stiff cattle

round the blaze. What left?
American supplies, the NATO tents, distant
telegrammed regret—It didn't matter.

They'd lost more forty years ago, frozen
for three days. Survivors once again
they will rebuild—and, summer come,

will harvest grain and bear their young
and, kneeling, bow to Mecca
for the sweet unleavened

bread, browning on the stones that covered sons.

osip mandelstam

We Shall Meet Again

We'll meet in Petersburg
as if we'd buried the sun there,
and for the first time we'll say
the blessèd senseless word.
In the black velvet of Soviet night,
in the velvet of universal emptiness,
women's eyes sing on, belovèd eyes, blessèd women,
immortal flowers bloom on.

The capital, arched like a wild cat;
a patrol on the bridge:
only angry motors rush by in the haze,
shouting like cuckoos.
I need no night pass,
I'm not afraid of sentries:
and I'll pray, in this Soviet night,
for the blessèd senseless word.

A faint rustle, half deliberate,
and a girl's startled "Oh!"—
and a huge heap of immortal roses
in Venus' arms.
We sit at a campfire, bored, warming
our hands, maybe centuries will pass,
maybe blessèd women's belovèd hands
will gather the thin ash.

There are rows of red velvet seats, somewhere,
luxuriant *chiffoniers* of theatre boxes;
officers' clock-work dolls; but
nothing for black souls, for low hypocrites . . .
Well, maybe blow out our candles
in the black velvet of universal emptiness;
blessèd women, steep shoulders sing on,
and you'll never notice the night-time sun.

25 November 1920
Trans. Burton Raffel and Alla Burago

427

g. s. fraser

Instead of an Elegy

Bullets blot out the Life-time smile,
Apollo of the picture-page,
Blunt-faced young lion
   Caught by vile
Death in an everlasting cage:

And, no more young men in the world,
The old men troop to honour him.
The drums beat glum,
   Slight snow is swirled
In dazzling sun, pale requiem.

And pale dark-veiled Persephone,
A golden child in either hand,
Stands by white pillars;
   Silently,
It seems she might forever stand.

In bright grey sun, processionals
Of pomp and honour, and of grief,
Crown that dead head
   With coronals.
Some stony hearts feel some relief:

But not your heart, America,
Beating so slow and sure and strong,
Stricken in his
   Triumphal car,
Guard Caesar's bitter laurels long

With soldiers' music, rites of war:
He had proved bravely when put on:
The soldiers shoot.
   Rage echoes far
Above the grave at Arlington.

This was written in the emotional days following the assassination of John F. Kennedy. The images
the poem derive from watching the televising of the funeral on Monday, November 26, 1963. [Note
Fraser].

robert bly

At a March Against the Vietnam War

Washington, November 27, 1965

Newspapers rise high in the air over Maryland.

We walk about, bundled in coats and sweaters in the late November sun.
Looking down, I see feet moving
Calmly, gaily,
Almost as if separated from their bodies.

But there is something moving in the dark somewhere
Just beyond
The edge of our eyes: a boat
Covered with machine guns
Moving along under trees.

It is black.
The hand reaches out
But cannot touch it. . . .
Is it that darkness among pine boughs
That the Puritans brushed
As they went out to kill turkeys.

At the edge of the jungle clearing
It explodes
On the ground.

We have carried around this cup of darkness.
We hesitate to anoint ourselves.
Now we pour it over our heads.

anonymous

A Song on the Famous Peal of 7308 Grandsire Cators

Rung by the Society of All Saints Ringers, in Worcester, on the 28th of November, 1774

Ye lovers of ringing now give your attention
Unto these few words which my song it will mention:
It is of Seven Thousand Three Hundred and Eight,
By the Youths of All Saints that was rung quite compleat:
In the year Seventy-four, now remark what I say,
In the month of November, the twenty-eighth day,
This peal was compleated, which was to the fame
Of the Youths of All Saints, who shall still bear the name.

RICHARD PAINE to the treble, I speak in his praise,
That I ne'er heard a bell better rang in my days;
For over the large bells he struck her quite clear,
And his compass at lead kept as true as a hair:
THOMAS HILL he the Second did steadily ring,
And in the Tittoms she sweetly did sing;
Though some seem to sneer at his prophetic dream,
Yet the Youths of All Saints they shall still bear the name.

JOSEPH STONE to the Third, he kept her stiff in hand,
And just at his own pleasure did her command;
He cut her in compass, and tuck'd her so tight,
Through the whole Seven Thousand Three Hundred and Eight:
THOMAS SPINNER the Fourth, for a solid hand's he,
And in ringing a length he rings quite steadily;
He marks his course bell, and sticks close to the same,
And the Youths of All Saints they shall still bear the name.

GEORGE ROE to the Fifth he did cheerfully stand,
And he struck her right well, both at back stroke and hand;
"There's beauty!" he cry'd, and so smooth did he pull,
And smiled when the large bells at home they did roll:
At the Sixth RICHARD HERBERT, he looked quite sharp,
And ne'er was observ'd in his course once to warp;
For to finish the peal, Sir, it was his whole aim,
And the Youths of All Saints they shall still bear the name.

WILLIAM KENDAL the Seventh, so smart a young lad,
Did call the peal true, and he made each heart glad;
The Changes he plac'd in the Tittoms so tight,
And he told out just Fifty Times Nine, Seven, Eight:
JOHN BRISTOW, the Eighth, rang so solid and clear,
That no fault was discern'd by the most curious ear;
All his thoughts at that time he to ringing did frame,
And the Youths of All Saints they shall still bear the name.

To the Ninth THOMAS BARKER stood sturdy and stout,
And with hearty good-will he did swing her about;
Right boldly and bravely he stuck to her tough,
And he ne'er once faulter'd, or said he had enough:
To the Tenor GEORGE WAINWRIGHT stood like heart of oak,
And to this famous peal gave the finishing stroke;
When the clapper came out, which just answer'd the dream!
And the Youths of All Saints they shall still bear the name.

Four Hours and a Half and Six Minutes they were,
The people with watches in hands did declare;
And said the performers were worthy of praise,
For they ne'er heard a peal better rang in their days:
So here's a good health to those that wish us well,
And those that do envy us they cannot excell;
Those that wish us well, boys, we wish them the same,
And the Youths of All Saints they shall still bear the name.

wallace stevens

Lettres d'un Soldat

> *29 novembre au matin, en cantonnement Telle fut la beauté d'hier.*
> *Te parlerai-je des soirées précédentes, alors que sur la route, la lune*
> *me dessinait la broderie des arbres, le pathétique des calvaires,*
> *l'attendrissement de ces maisons que l'on sait des ruines, mais que*
> *la nuit fait surgir comme une évocation de la paix.*
> —André Chevrillon

LUNAR PARAPHRASE

The moon is the mother of pathos and pity.

When, at the wearier end of November,
Her old light moves along the branches,
Feebly, slowly, depending upon them;
When the body of Jesus hangs in a pallor,
Humanly near, and the figure of Mary,
Touched on by hoar-frost, shrinks in a shelter
Made by the leaves, that have rotted and fallen;
When over the houses, a golden illusion
Brings back an earlier season of quiet
And quieting dreams in the sleepers in darkness—

The moon is the mother of pathos and pity.

alfrredo navarro salanga

An Apocryphal Account of the Birthing of Andres Bonifacio

To greet him, post-partum,
on the thirtieth November,
the midwife in attendance
fished out a thimble of truth
from deep within the folds,
the creases of her ancient mind.

To the mother who lay folded up
in a blanket of reed mats,
round and bound like a wet cigar,
the old woman cackled, her voice
dry and wrinkled like rice straws:

"He cries loudly, like thunder,
But his thunder is not the sky.
The boy's thunder is of the bowels
of the earth, a thunder of caverns."

To the father who stood swaying
in a corner, like the bamboo in April,
she whispered a friar's instruction;

"Search out a name for him
in the calendar of all saints,"

His index finger trembling
like a blade of cogon grass,
he traced the nervous progress
of numbers planted across the face
of the year. What was written on
the bottom of the last box
he screamed across the room:

"San Andres Apostol!"

The brother of Simon Peter,
the first called, but not chosen
to sit as Rock of the Church.
Protoclete to the Greeks
to whom he preached
the Revolution of Christ Jesus.
Adopted of Scotland
and of Russia also where
he never trod.

"Of him I read a warning!" she hissed.

As, slowly, she slithered out
to bury cord and placenta
in the land of his birth.

"Keep watch. The pigs
are gathering in the yard."

From the window's ear,
they could hear them grunt,
their snouts buried deep
in hallowed ground.

"They are digging,
digging for what rooted him
to his mother.
        I read
a warning!"

But the man and the woman
had ceased to listen to her.
Deep in his mother's arms,
Andres continued to cry,
his voice filling the room
with the thunder of caverns.

December

marion montgomery

Winter Song

Four jorees, and now three sparrows,
Fluff the quince by the front walk.
   (It is the First of December.)

The moon wastes pale into daylight;
Breath hangs air in a still wash.
   (It is the First of December.)

Inside, my love stirs our ashes—
Our children stir in the firelight.
   (It is the First of December.)

DECEMBER 2

john beecher

One More River to Cross

For John L. Salter, Jr.

"The passage of the Patowmac through the Blue Ridge"
wrote the author of the Declaration of Independence
"is one of the most stupendous scenes in nature"
In the midst of this stupendous scene
on the second day of December 1859
the sovereign state of Virginia
hanged old Osawatomie Brown
(strange confluence of rivers)
for holding certain truths to be self-evident
which had been first enunciated
by the greatest Virginian of them all
A bystander at the hanging
one Thomas J Jackson
was struck by the incongruity of Brown's
"white socks and slippers of predominating red"
beneath sober black garb more appropriate to the occasion

A frivolous touch that "predominating red"
or could it have been a portent
Thomas J soon-to-be-dubbed "Stonewall" Jackson?
"Across the river and into the trees" you babbled
only four years later
while your blood ebbed away
ironically shot by one of your own
But it is still the second of December 1859
and you glowing with the vigor of a man in his prime
are watching while the body of Brown swings slowly
to and fro
in a cold wind off the mountains
for exactly 37 minutes before it is cut down
In less than half so many months
Thomas J Jackson
this stupendous scene plus 24,000 contiguous square miles
will no longer be Virginia
Its blue-uniformed sons will be ranged against you
in the Army of the Potomac singing
"John Brown's body lies a-mouldering in the grave
but his soul goes marching on"

Now you my friend
so akin in spirit to the earlier John
I have been seeing your picture in the papers
your head anointed with mustard and ketchup
at the lunch-counter sit-in
hoodlums rubbing salt in the cuts where they slugged you
or the police flailing you with clubs
blood sopping your shirt
but pure downright peace on your face
making a new kind of history
Now the people Harper's Weekly called
"this good-humored good-for-nothing half monkey race"
when John Brown sought to lead them out of bondage
are leading us toward that America
Thomas Jefferson foresaw and Abraham Lincoln
who once again sprawls dying in his theater box
(Why must we always kill our best?)
The dastard in the bushes spots the crossed hairs
squeezes the trigger and Medgar Evers pitches
forward on his face while the assassin scuttles
into the night his beady rat's eyes seeking where to hide
his incriminating weapon with the telescopic sight

He heaves it into the tangled honeysuckle
and vanishes into the magnolia darkness
"God Sees the Truth But Waits"
The sickness is loosed now into the whole body politic
the infection spreading from South to North and West
"State's rights" "Freedom of Choice" "Liberty of the Individual"
Trojan horse phrases with armed enemies within
In the name of rights they would destroy all rights
put freedom to death on the pretext of saving it
Under the cover of Jeffersonian verbiage
these men move to destroy the Constitution
they feign to uphold
but their plots will miscarry
Who knows but that some unpainted shack in the Delta
may house one destined to lead us the next great step of the way
From the Osawatomie to the "Patowmac"
the Alabama Tombigbee Big Black Tallahatchie and Pearl
and down to the Mississippi levee in Plaquemines Parish
it's a long road
better than a hundred years in travelling
and now the Potomac again . . .

Summer, 1963

DECEMBER 3

 clara claiborne park

Advent

(H.S.F., newborn December 3, 1980)

The waters flood;
hugely the body
rules, as flesh, perfected, ready,
begins in water what it will complete in blood,

one darker than the other,
yet not less cleansing nor less innocent.
Hours pass, as months did, till our mother,
no jot left unperformed

436

of nature's common work,
prepared in nature's dark,
is hugely rent,
hugely heaves forth
this common birth
into the winter wild;

another child
to be wrapped safe and warmed,

the skull,
its perfect eggshell full,
hazed, haloed with the usual hair,
and there,
passing belief, the fragile wrists, the fingers
starring our dark, green branching shoots in snow.

What passed belief the pulse proves out as true.
Hannah's small hands make all things new.

DECEMBER 4

haki r. madhubuti

One Sided Shoot-out

*(for brothers fred hampton & mark clark, murdered 12/4/69 by
chicago police at 4:30 A.M. while they slept)*

only a few will really understand:
it won't be yr/mommas or yr/brothers & sisters or even
   me,
we all think that we do   but we don't.
it's not *new*   and
under all the rhetoric the seriousness is still not serious.
the national rap deliberately continues, "wipe them niggers out."
(no talk do it, no talk do it, no talk do it, notalk notalknotalk do it)

& we.
running circleround getting caught in our own cobwebs,

437

in the same old clothes, same old words, just new adjectives.
we will order new buttons & posters with: "remember
   fred" & "rite-on mark."
& yr/pictures will be beautiful & manly with the deep-
   look/the accusing look
to remind us
to remind us that suicide is not black.

the questions will be asked & the answers will be the new
   cliches.
but maybe,
just maybe we'll finally realize that "revolution" to the
   real-world
is international 24hours a day and that 4:30AM is like
   12:00 noon,
it's just darker.
but the evil can be seen if u look in the right direction.
were the street lights out?
did they darken their faces in combat?
did they remove their shoes to *creep* softer?
could u not see the whi-te of their eyes,
the whi-te of their deathfaces?
didn't yr/look-out man see them coming, coming, coming?
or did they turn into ghostdust and join the night's fog?

it was mean.
& we continue to call them "pigs" and "muthafuckas"
   forgetting what all
black children learn very early "sticks & stones may break
                         my bones but names can
                         never hurt me."

it was murder.
& we meet to hear the speeches/ the same, the duplicators.
they say that which is expected of them.
to be instructive or constructive is to be unpopular (like:
   the leaders only
sleep when there is a watchingeye)
but they say the right things at the right time, it's like a
   stageshow:
only the entertainers have changed.
we remember bobby hutton. the same, the duplicators.

the seeing eye should always see.
the night doesn't stop the stars
& our enemies scope the ways of blackness in three bad
   shifts a day.
in the AM their music becomes deadlier.
this is a game of dirt.

only blackpeople play it fair.

horace

Odes. Book Three, XVIII

Faunus, who loves the Nymphs and makes
Them scamper, leap my boundary stakes,
Lightly and benignly pass
Across the sunny fields of grass,
Leave behind your blessing on
My lambs and kids, and so be gone.
In return receive your due:
A goat shall die to honour you
At the year's end, the ancient shrine
Smoke with thick incense, and the wine,
Liberally poured, keep filling up
Venus' friend, the drinking-cup.
When the December Nones come round,
All the farm beasts on the green ground
Gambol, and with time to spare
The world enjoys the open air,
Countryman and unyoked ox
Together; in among the flocks
Unfeared the wolf strolls; from the copse
The leaf, to be your carpet, drops;
And in three-time the son of toil
Jigs on his enemy the soil.

Trans. James Michie

In the Roman calendar the Nones of December occurs on the fifth.

louise glück

12.6.71

You having turned from me
I dreamed we were
beside a pond between two mountains
It was night
The moon throbbed in its socket
Where the spruces thinned
three deer wakened & broke cover
and I heard my name
not spoken but cried out
so that I reached for you
except the sheet was ice
as they had come for me
who, one by one, were likewise
introduced to darkness

And the snow
which has not ceased since
began

gerard manley hopkins

from: The Wreck of the *Deutschland*

To the happy memory of five Franciscan Nuns exiled by the Fulk
Laws drowned between midnight and morning of Dec. 7th, 1875

from: PART THE SECOND

12

On Saturday sailed from Bremen,
American-outward-bound,
Take settler and seamen, tell men with women,
Two hundred souls in the round—
O Father, not under thy feathers nor ever as guessing

The goal was a shoal, of a fourth the doom to be drowned;
Yet did the dark side of the bay of thy blessing
Not vault them, the millions of rounds of thy mercy not reeve even them in?

13

Into the snows she sweeps
Hurling the haven behind,
The Deutschland, on Sunday; and so the sky keeps,
For the infinite air is unkind,
And the sea flint-flake, black-backed in the regular blow,
Sitting Eastnortheast, in cursed quarter, the wind;
Wiry and white-fiery and whirlwind-swivelled snow
Spins to the widow-making unchilding unfathering deeps.

14

She drove in the dark to leeward,
She struck—not a reef or a rock
But the combs of a smother of sand: night drew her
Dead to the Kentish Knock;
And she beat the bank down with her bows and the ride of her keel:
The breakers rolled on her beam with ruinous shock;
And canvas and compass, the whorl and the wheel
Idle for ever to waft her or wind her with, these she endured.

15

Hope had grown grey hairs,
Hope had mourning on,
Trenched with tears, carved with cares,
Hope was twelve hours gone;
And frightful a nightfall folded rueful a day
Nor rescue, only rocket and lightship, shone,
And lives at last were washing away:
To the shrouds they took,—they shook in the hurling and horrible airs.

16

One stirred from the rigging to save
The wild woman-kind below,
With a rope's end round the man, handy and brave—
He was pitched to his death at a blow,
For all his dreadnought breast and braids of thew:

They could tell him for hours, dandled the to and fro
Through the cobbled foam-fleece, what could he do
With the burl of the fountains of air, buck and the flood of the wave?

17

They fought with God's cold—
And they could not and fell to the deck
(Crushed them) or water (and drowned them) or rolled
With the sea-romp over the wreck.
Night roared, with the heart-break hearing a heart-broke rabble,
The woman's wailing, the crying of child without check—
Till a lioness arose breasting the babble,
A prophetess towered in the tumult, a virginal tongue told.

. . .

DECEMBER 8

rodney hall

Feast of the Immaculate Conception

ITALY—DECEMBER, 1961

Rosary lamplight spills
in loops around three hills,
threads of the twisted glowing beads
hang over us. Our world recedes,
the eye that once explored so much
now strains and fails.

Sounding, bitter bells
are battered hollow shells
that chant so aching semibreves
tower out above the heaved on
rope, the backs, the leather hands
where flash rebels.

Weaving its way below
the lamps there climbs a slow
procession, up among the houses,

442

those evening walls where snowlight drowses
and sundry churchbell chimes are hung
to die or grow.

And as for any feast
(birth or death of Christ;
Mary conceived, conceiving) metal
angels croon, their belfries rattle,
and each tongue strikes from lip
the temporal rust.

This lame procession hobbles
up the village cobbles
chanting somewhere in its throat
uncertain words that trail remotely
past these piles of crumbling kitchens
past these hovels.

Underneath the long
insistent ringing song
of heaven creeps a human sound
—clinging to stone, tile and ground—
a gasp, a whisper from where the wind
and storm belong.

Eight hundred feet confess
their complex humbleness.
Candles cupped in turned-up hands
are floating chains of lilies, garlands
bobbing about on the liquid
of night's caress.

Madonnas ride on poles
and spin their aureoles
and pirouette and pitch and lurch
with arching cloaks toward the church
fluttering while the fretful angel
squeaks and tolls.

Twelve tall candlesticks
surround the crucifix.
*And there was darkness over all
the Earth, a blackness fell and the veil
of the temple was rent:* Catholic
from Orthodox.

443

Perhaps these streets, forlorn
and hungry, are like their worn
inhabitants; they also shamble
skyward, ravaged to gild the Lamb,
perhaps to claim their Mary also
virgin born.

Resplendently arrayed
Bishop and Priest parade
amid the drabness, tread their wise
advance—two polished jewel eyes
picked from some fabulous Madonna
they betrayed?

Still the bells are scourged
as the last few faithful nudge
their way to the smoky warmth inside
where strident organ Preludes ride
on nerves and clamp the brain; and finger
scrawny handbags.

Angel voices ending,
ancient backs unbend
and ropes hang loose. A tutored ear
can draw from the freshening atmosphere
dancing climaxes that silence
comprehends.

This gnarled old street like a dimly
remembered catacomb
now steers the healthy winds at will
to hunt through secret crannies till
they've cleaned away the least echo,
the faintest fume.

The Feast of the Immaculate Conception of the Virgin Mary is celebrated on December 8th.

david young

Notes on the Poems

1   Was found in an orchard;
is three or four thousand years old;
was probably made with poor tools
by the light of an oil lamp throwing
shadows against the wall
that would frighten us now.

2   Would never have been possible without
that famous fog of December 9th
for out of that fog came Geraldine
wearing a dress of chipmunk furze
with a grackle perched on her wrist.

3   Whole families were involved here
and the death wish and the industrial
revolution. You say the third line
about the bathroom in the grocery
was troublesome; I ask,
should a poem make more sense than Omaha?

4   It is right, little poem about
wandering and misunderstanding
that you kept coming back, unwanted.
Small avalanche,
always missing your victims,
come here—
I open my arms.

5   Of course the opening stanza
is like a cheap decal
of roses and tulips
on the side of a laundry hamper.
But as the poem progresses
you see something crawling
from one of the flowers.
An insect? Bend closer.
It is a very small man, holding a flashlight.
He snaps it on and swings the beam toward you.
You are blinded.

geoffrey chaucer

from: The House of Fame

Of Decembre the tenthe day,
Whan hit was nyght, to slepe I lay
Ryght ther as I was wont to done,
And fil on slepe wonder sone,
As he that wery was forgo
On pilgrymage myles two
To the corseynt Leonard,
To make lythe of that was hard.
　　But as I slepte, me mette I was
Withyn a temple ymad of glas;
In which ther were moo ymages
Of gold, stondynge in sondry stages,
And moo ryche tabernacles,
And with perre moo pynacles,
And moo curiouse portreytures,
And queynte maner of figures
Of olde werk, then I saugh ever.
For certeynly, I nyste never
Wher that I was, but wel wyste I,
Hyt was of Venus redely,

The temple; for in portreyture,
I sawgh anoon-ryght hir figure
Naked fletynge in a see.
And also on hir hed, pardee,
Hir rose garlond whit and red,
And hir comb to kembe hyr hed,
Hir dowves, and daun Cupido,
Hir blynde sone, and Vulcano,
That in his face was ful broun.
　　But as I romed up and doun,
I fond that on a wall ther was
Thus writen on a table of bras:
"I wol now singen, yif I kan,
The armes, and also the man
That first cam, thurgh his destinee,
Fugityf of Troy contree,
In Itayle, with ful moche pyne
Unto the strondes of Lavyne."
And tho began the story anoon,
As I shal telle yow echon. . . .

albert goldbarth

Water Pie: Tonight, 12/11/72

Tonight the air's too dry, the vents
offsetting winter cold with the enthusiasm
of retrorockets, until we're dry-mouthed
at the blast and the rims of our nostrils
cake. And in defense we scatter water

filled pie tins through the house;
in sleep, the nose sniffs in a wedge
of water pie, as much as, or more

than, the dog laps at night. Tonight,
when I wake you, my lips burn to lick

your silhouette so that it gleams in moonlight
like halved citrus, want to stop to suck
a flower of blood to your chillest hill
this season, but then continue and touch
you with my expenditure

of this wet as uniformly as it was breathed in.
There's just enough left, a circle
in the aluminum pan, to catch the arid
moon as if it snuck to drink from a gleaming
trap at our bedside. I've no sense,

it seems, of decorum; tonight there are men
on the moon. Well, let them look
down at us if they'd like! We're all
busy, reaching as far as we can,
and perhaps this makes us brothers. I know

when I walk the dog this morning he'll piss
at every tree on the block, his way of claiming
territory with water he's taken in, no pee
in the world smelling just like his. It's
a home. And I sight the sun through his flags,

his warm waves of stink on the cold wind.

william shakespeare

_____

from: Twelfth Night

Act II, scene iii.

CLOWN	Beshrew me, the knight's in admirable fooling.
SIR ANDREW	Ay, he does it well enough, if he be disposed, and so do I too: he does it with a better grace but I do it more natural
SIR TOBY	*O' the twelfth day of December—*
MARIA	For the love o' God, peace.

DECEMBER 12

*The song Sir Toby was about to sing is generally believed to be an
anonymous ballad called "Upon the Scots being beaten at
Muscleborough Field," which follows:*

On the twelfth day of December,
In the fourth year of King Edwards reign
Two mighty Hosts (as I remember)
At Muscleborough did pitch on a Plain.
For a down, down, derry derry down, Hey down a.
Down, down, down a down derry.

All night our English men they lodged there,
So did the Scots both stout and stubborn,
But well-away was all their cheere,
For we have served them in their own turn.

       For a down, &c.

All night they carded for our English mens Coats,
(They fished before their Nets were spun)
A white for Six-pence, a red for two Groats;
Wisdome would have stayd till they had been won.

       For a down, &c.

On the twelfth day all in the morn,
They made a fere as if they would fight;
But many a proud Scot that day was down born,
And many a rank Coward was put to his flight.

       For a down, &c.

And the Lord Huntley, we hadden him there,
With him he brought ten thousand men:
But God be thanked, we gave him such a Banquet,
He carryed but few of them home agen.

       For a down, &c.

For when he heard our great Guns crack,
Then did his heart fall untill his hose,
He threw down his Weapons, he turned his back,
He ran so fast that he fell on his nose.

       For a down, &c.

We beat them back till Edenbrough,
(There's men alive can witnesse this)

But when we lookt our Englishmen through,
Two hundred good fellowes we did not misse.

                    For a down, &c.

Now God preserve Edward our King,
With his two Nuncles and Nobles all,
And send us Heaven at our ending:
For we have given Scots a lusty fall.
For a down, down, derry derry down, Hey,
Down a down down, down a down derry.

john donne

A Nocturnall Upon S. Lucies Day,

Being the Shortest Day

Tis the yeares midnight, and it is the dayes,
Lucies, who scarce seaven houres herself unmaskes,
    The Sunne is spent, and now his flasks
    Send forth light squibs, no constant rayes;
        The worlds whole sap is sunke:
The generall balme th' hydroptique earth hath drunk,
Whither, as to the beds-feet, life is shrunke,
Dead and enterr'd; yet all these seeme to laugh,
Compar'd with mee, who am their Epitaph.

Study me then, you who shall lovers bee
At the next world, that is, at the next Spring:
    For I am every dead thing,
    In whom love wrought new Alchimie.
        For his art did expresse
A quintessence even from nothingnesse,
From dull privations, and leane emptinesse:
He ruin'd mee, and I am re-begot
Of absence, darknesse, death; things which are not

All others, from all things, draw all that's good,
Life, soule, forme, spirit, whence they beeing have;

449

I, by loves limbecke, am the grave
Of all, that's nothing. Oft a flood
   Have wee two wept, and so
Drownd the whole world, us two; oft did we grow
To be two Chaosses, when we did show
Care to ought else; and often absences
Withdrew our soules, and made us carcasses.

But I am by her death, (which word wrongs her)
Of the first nothing, the Elixer grown;
   Were I a man, that I were one,
   I needs must know; I should preferre,
     If I were any beast,
Some ends, some means; Yea plants, yea stones detest,
And love; All, all some properties invest;
If I an ordinary nothing were,
As shadow, a light, and body must be here.

But I am None; nor will my Sunne renew.
You lovers, for whose sake, the lesser Sunne
   At this time to the Goat is runne
   To fetch new lust, and give it you,
     Enjoy your summer all;
Since shee enjoyes her long nights festivall,
Let mee prepare towards her, and let mee call
This houre her Vigill, and her Eve, since this
Both the yeares, and the dayes deep midnight is.

England did not adopt the Gregorian calendar until 1752 (see February 22). During Donne's lifetime the winter solstice according to the Julian calendar occurred on St. Lucy's Day, December 13.

george peele

from: Edward I

Act I, scene i

GLOCESTER   My gratious Lord, as erst I was assignde,
     Lieutenant to his Majestie,
     Here render I up the crowne left in charge with me,
     By your princely father king Henrie,
     Who on his death bed still did call for you,
     And dying, wild to you the Diadem.

LONGSHANKES   Thankes worthie Lordes,
     And seeing by doome of heavens it is decreed,
     And lawful line of our succession,
     Unworthy Edward is become your king,
     We take it as a blessing from on hie,
     And wil our Coronation be solemnized,
     Upon the fourteenth of December next.

Q. ELINOR   Upon the fourteenth of December next?
     Alas my Lord, the time is all too short
     And sudden, for so great solemnitie:
     A yeare were scarse enough to set aworke,
     Tailers, Imbroderes, and men of rare device,
     For preparation of so great estate.
     Trust me sweete Ned, hardlie shal I bethinke me,
     In twentie weekes what fashion robes to weare,
     I pray thee then deferre it till the spring,
     That we may have our garments point device.
     I meane to send for Tailers into Spaine,
     That shall confer of some fantastickt sutes,
     With those that be our conningst Englishmen,
     What? let me brave it now or never Ned.

LONG.   Madam content ye, would that were greatest care,
     You shall have garments to your harts desire,
     I never red but Englishmen exceld,
     For change of rare devises every way.

james scully

Lt. Cmdr. T. E. Sanderson

15 December 1963

None of the brass hatters had seen
the flight plan, nor what orders were,
but judged the thing to be routine.

Part shooting star, the Grumman Tracker
harrowing a suburb . . . It left
headlines. Looked-at hard, the picture

grows atoms, ungathering grains.
He'd come of nothing and made it
after a fashion. What remains

is what to make of him: not torn
out of a dream but living it,
who took-off on Sunday, airborne

in Hingham, Mass. . . . I lie awake
mulling over my mother's note;
embossed, its plumes cap-off the wake:

"just like President Kennedy's,
the American Flag on it
& closed." Not having died at ease

nor in a war, he lay in state,
the case being shut (no news leak
nor angel to uncover it)

and screwed up, sealed the way he went.
All that he was, he had become
by virture of self government.

The thing is, what to make of it,
of the nation's arms his nation
made of him. Perhaps bit by bit

it all falls together, but then
the thing is Tommy Sanderson
my cousin, fellow citizen,

a uniform of flesh and blood
shoved back into the marshes, down
the Commonwealth, in Hingham mud.

Better to give up, than acquit;
whatever it was he meant
a whole creation weighs on it.

robert duncan

Passages 36 (These Lines Composing Themselves in My Head as I Awoke Early this Morning, It Being Still Dark December 16, 1971)

Let it go. Let it go.
Grief's its proper mode.

But O, How deep it's got to reach,
 How high and wide
 it's got to grow,
Before it come to sufficient grief . . .

. . .

House made of the changing of the light;
House made of darkness
    in which the stars again
            appear to view; House
made of appearances, House you
daily bring to me   I remember.

Waking to see your slumbering eyes,
your smile arrived or about to arrive
about your lips, and from that other
    world
from me you sleep in you return,
    Fugitive Aubade I stay by,
How tender the green tip before the leaf
    grows. Soon all
will be a-flame with spring.

The cut-worm sleeps in his cold.
And in a million eggs, greed grows.
The blood in a billion hearts beats at the locks.
Thought thickens in the veins and swells.
Bright arteries run into the pressures of the dark.
The meat grows restive.

At Xibalba they open the doors again.
It is not the First Year or the Last.
The priests in flayd skins
rip from their cages hearts
to feed the mind of an incoming nightmare.

Who pours into these streams what wastes
   where I come to drink?
What Salmon in this stink grows wise?

   Let it go. Let it go.

     Grief's its proper mode.

The poem rehearses its lines even as I wake,
   the passage from sleep to day again.

     But O, How deep it's got to reach . . .

It was about the end of an old friendship,
   the admission of neglect rancoring,
mine of her, hers of what I am,
   and festering flesh was there.

It was very like that coming to know
   my mother was at war with what I was to be;
and in the Courts of Love I raged that year
   in every plea declared arrogant
      and in contempt of Love.

It do not   as the years go by   grow tolerant
   of what I cannot share and what
refuses me. There's that in me as fiercely beyond
   the remorse that eats me in its drive
as Evolution is   in
   working out the courses of what will last.

In Truth   'tis done.   At last.   I'll not
     repair.

hart crane

from: Cape Hatteras

. . .

Stars scribble on our eyes the frosty sagas,
The gleaming cantos of unvanquished space . . .
O sinewy silver biplane, nudging the wind's withers!
There, from Kill Devils Hill at Kitty Hawk
Two brothers in their twinship left the dune;
Warping the gale, the Wright windwrestlers veered
Capeward, then blading the wind's flank, banked and spun
What ciphers risen from prophetic script,
What marathons new-set between the stars!
The soul, by naphtha fledged into new reaches
Already knows the closer clasp of Mars,—
New latitudes, unknotting, soon give place
To what fierce schedules, rife of doom apace!

Behold the dragon's covey—amphibian, ubiquitous
To hedge the seaboard, wrap the headland, ride
The blue's cloud-templed districts unto ether . . .
While Iliads glimmer through eyes raised in pride
Hell's belt springs wider into heaven's plumed side.
O bright circumferences, heights employed to fly
War's fiery kennel masked in downy offings,—
This tournament of space, the threshed and chiselled height,
Is baited by marauding circles, bludgeon flail
Of rancorous grenades whose screaming petals carve us
Wounds that we wrap with theorems sharp as hail!

. . .

The first successful flight of the Wright Brothers airplane, described here, occurred on December 17, 1903.

allen ginsberg

Continuation of a Long Poem of These States

S. F. *Southward*

Stage-lit streets
       Downtown Frisco whizzing past, buildings
       ranked by freeway balconies
          Bright Johnnie Walker neon
            sign Christmastrees
And Christmas and its eves
       in the midst of the same deep wood
          as every sad Christmas before, surrounded
            by forests of stars—
Metal columns, smoke pouring cloudward,
          yellow-lamp horizon
            warplants move, tiny
          planes lie in Avionic fields—
Meanwhile Working Girls sort mail into the red slot
       Rivers of newsprint to soldiers' Vietnam
       Infantry Journal, Kanackee
       Social Register, Wichita Star
And Postoffice Christmas the same brown place
       mailhandlers' black fingers
       dusty mailbags filled
          1948 N.Y. Eighth Avenue was
     or when Peter drove the mailtruck 1955
          from Rincon Annex—
Bright lights' windshield flash,
       adrenalin shiver in shoulders
          Around the curve
       crawling a long truck
          3 bright green signals on forehead
       Jeweled Bayshore passing the Coast Range
          one architect's house light on hill crest
. . . .negro voices rejoice over radio
       Moonlit sticks of tea
Moss Landing Power Plant
       shooting its cannon smoke
          across the highway, Red taillight

speeding the white line and a mile away
Orion's muzzle
raised up
to the center of Heaven.

December 18, 1965

john webster

from: The Duchess of Malfi

Act II, scene iii

[BOSOLA, *with a lantern, and* ANTONIO *at night.*]

ANTONIO	You libel well, sir.
BOSOLA	No sir, copy it out,
	And I will set my hand to't.
ANT.	[*Aside*]

My nose bleeds:
One that were superstitious would count
This ominous;—when it merely comes by chance.
Two letters, that are wrought here for my name,
Are drown'd in blood!
Mere accident:—[*To him*] for you, sir, I'll take order:
I'th' morn you shall be safe:—[*Aside*] 'tis that must
    colour
Her lying-in:—[*To him*] sir, this door you pass not:
I do not hold it fit that you come near
The duchess' lodgings, till you have quit yourself.
[*Aside*] *The great are like the base—nay, they are the same—*
When they seek shameful ways, to avoid shame.   [*Exit.*]

BOS.   Antonio hereabout did drop a paper—
Some of your help, false friend—O, here it is:
What's here? a child's nativity calculated!
[*Reads*] *The duchess was delivered of a son, 'tween the*
hours twelve and one, in the night: Anno Dom. 1504,—
that's this year—*decimo nono Decembris,*—that's this night—
taken according to the meridian of Malfi—that's our
duchess: happy discovery!—*The lord of the first house,*

being combust in the ascendant, signifies short life: and Mars
being in a human sign, joined to the tail of the Dragon, in
the eighth house, doth threaten a violent death; caetera non
scrutantur.
Why now 'tis most apparent: this precise fellow
Is the duchess' bawd:—I have it to my wish;
This is a parcel of intelligency
Our courtiers were cas'd up for! It needs must follow
That I must be committed on pretence
Of poisoning her; which I'll endure, and laugh at:—
If one could find the father now! but that
Time will discover. Old Castruchio
I'th' morning posts to Rome; by him I'll send
A letter, that shall make her brothers' galls
O'erflow their livers—this was a thrifty way.
Though lust do mask in ne'er so strange disguise,
She's oft found witty, but is never wise.

DECEMBER 20

alicia ostriker

Elegy

December 20, 1965

What may I tell? The sharp death that does not leave
nor rich men nor high: it him took.
—Saxon Chronicle

i

In Doom Year, the day of his number,
My sole striding father was humbled.
His heart hurt a moment, he fell vacated,
And hit that sidewalk, if there is mercy, dead.

ii

These are my visions: knife vision driving
Alone towards you the given stiffclothed bittercold man
Around whom vertical overcoats gaze
Horrified, gluttonous, breathing—

And vision in the hospital basement
While the dirty balding coroner jokes,
You and I meet, who never meet again,
Although I establish unalterably glassed
Hard forehead's breadth from temple to temple,
Sleeping eyes, left tightened cheek bruised brown,
Ironic mouth that speechlessly bids me
Stay with you, be eternal.
And vision of the burning
While we prayed to the spider God
And screamed behind our eyelids,
The boxed brainpot, depository
Of school verse and love's future gesture
Takes fire, steams, the diffident tongue is eaten,
The racing leg collapses,
The tender life of testicles withers,
Now the marrowbones lose their juice,
Now the teeth and vertebrae drop
Glowing, incandescent among cinders,
At last the stubborn clotted heart is punished,
While we sleepwalk from the chapel to the car
Quiet now, quiet now
Quiet now he is burning no more.

iii

Must not the widow pass strange hours
Having lain beside one man forever,
Having his odors still in the house,
Having us love one another because we grieve?

iv

Curse this. All our life swear hatred
Of the abominable enemy, that
Is the condition of our breath, and yet
Now no rage rises, why, no anger,
No outburst, why, but we are anchored
To quietude, as if a stranger
From the deep night entered a room
Blinking shyly at our bright lights,
Who, before anyone spoke to him,
Returned alone into his snowy night
As in tales the wild bird goes, takes flight.

james wright

Eisenhower's Visit to Franco, 1959

> *. . . we die of cold, and not of darkness.*
> —Unamuno

The American hero must triumph over
The forces of darkness.
He has flown through the very light of heaven
And come down in the slow dusk
Of Spain.

Franco stands in a shining circle of police.
His arms open in welcome.
He promises all dark things
Will be hunted down.

State police yawn in the prisons.
Antonio Machado follows the moon
Down a road of white dust,
To a cave of silent children
Under the Pyrenees.
Wine darkens in stone jars in villages.
Wine sleeps in the mouths of old men, it is a dark red color.

Smiles glitter in Madrid.
Eisenhower has touched hands with Franco, embracing
In a glare of photographers.
Clean new bombers from America muffle their engines
And glide down now.
Their wings shine in the searchlights
Of bare fields,
In Spain.

Eisenhower's visit began on December 21, 1959.

william trowbridge

Bearing Gifts

December 22

In the post office lobby, his evening haunt
at freezing or below, he hunkers by the trash can
in the corner, eyes white against his charcoal
face, cap and coveralls fouled to a tarry
stiffness. The smell of mildew, shit, and rancor
greets us at the doors and clings like a family
grudge as we line up for the last truckload
going out of town. He stares us in,
one by one, to where we wait with our assortments
ready for the proper postage. Soon, we'll return
to the kids and ribbons, our carols of nutmeg, sage,
and bourbon. He knows us all by now, for years
has watched us make our rounds from home to office,
church to mall. If you pass too close, he spits.
And always that stare: secretive and disapproving,
like the squirrel's when he spots you looming near his pulpit.

Some blame liquor, some the war,
but maybe it wasn't anything big or clear:
maybe on a night like this, for no reason
you could put your finger on, he found himself
one grasp from letting go, and, looking back
at his freshly shoveled walks, the Douglas fir
twinkling in his picture window, that snowman,
he said, "What the hell. Why not," and opened
the hand, let his mind tumble down its own
steep bluff to a plain of curbs and doorways.

But that was him, not us. Outside,
the snow floats down, contained in cones of light;
I long to pick one up and shake it, watch
the flakes swirl about the shoppers and the passing
cars till they vanish in a thick white blaze
but then return, like April, good as new.

The line advances, indulged beneath the mug shots
on the wall. Feeling his stare, I shift my load
of books and Christmas ties, my grip secure.

peter blue cloud

Hawk Nailed to a Barn Door

December 23, 1973

Hawk nailed to a barn door,
and rain makes you small and dark, and my muddy boots
are ankle-deep in ground fog,
far away dog barks sharp as cracking rifles
disked earth the hayfield's primal mud
    your brother and sister rough-legged hawks
of quick-beating wings and spread, down-pointed tails
momentarily transfixed in air as if fighting
    an up-slanting gale from earth.
Hobbling with practiced dignity, Chauncy, my new dog neighbor
with casts on front legs, limps forward
    to good-morning me the day, hesitant.
Yes, I am trying to fashion a scene to forget the maggots
and the stink, your hollow eaten eyes and tight closed
talons in last grasping, nailed through wing muscles,
head down to side, crucified,
    curved beak slightly open to my own questions
who has lost another particle of faith.
    Your wings and claws dry now above the stove,
and the rising heat gently revolves them.
It is 4:30 a.m. and cold and dark and your feathers
will be passed on to sky lovers.
    I was choking slightly, deep down, as I removed
your wings, claws, and tail feathers, then one by one
I took a handful of breast down,
    so warm looking.
Buried you behind the barn with two pepperwood leaves
and a mumbled se-sa-ton-ti, o-nen,
    go-home, now
Sat down in anger for your senseless murder,
all set to write a bitter song,
    it is 5:00 a.m. now
and your feathers so close send me no messages of hate.
I look at your beautiful wings
    and sense your flight.

karl shapiro

The Jew at Christmas Eve

I see the thin bell-ringer standing at corners
Fine as a breath, in cloth of red,
With eyes afar and long arm of a reed
Weakly waving a religious bell,
Under the boom of caroling hours
I see the thin bell-ringer standing still,
Breasting the prosperous tide on the Christmas pave.

I see the thin bell-ringer repenting himself
From corner to corner, year to year,
Struggling to stand beneath the windy blaze
Of horns that carol out of walls.
He would attract a crying waif
Or garrulous old woman down-at-heels
Or a pair of lovers on the icy pave.

Whom do you summon, Santa of the spare?
Whom do you summon, arm of the reed?
Whom do you cheer with ringing and whom chide,
And who stops at the tripod at your side
And wishes you the time of year?
A few who feed the cauldron of the unfed,
The iron cauldron on the fireless pave.

I see the thin bell-ringer as a flame
Of scarlet, trying to throw the flame
With each sweep of the bell. The tide pours on
And wets the ringer in cloth of red
And parts around the ringer of flame
With eyes afar and long arm of a reed
Who shakes the fire on the snowy pave.

george herbert

Christmas-Day

All after pleasures as I rid one day,
   My horse and I, both tir'd, bodie and minde,
   With full crie of affections, quite astray;
I took up in the next inne I could finde.

There when I came, whom found I but my deare,
   My dearest Lord, expecting till the grief
   Of pleasures brought me to him, readie there
To be all passengers most sweet relief?

O Thou, whose glorious, yet contracted light,
   Wrapt in nights mantle, stole into a manger;
   Since my dark soul and brutish is thy right,
To Man of all beasts be not thou a stranger:

   Furnish & deck my soul, that thou mayst have
   A better lodging, then a rack, or grave.

The shepherds sing; and shall I silent be?
        My God, no hymne for thee?
My soul's a shepherd too; a flock it feeds
        Of thoughts, and words, and deeds.
The pasture is thy word: the streams, thy grace
        Enriching all the place.
Shepherd and flock shall sing, and all my powers
        Out-sing the day-light houres.
Then we will chide the sunne for letting night
        Take up his place and right:
We sing one common Lord; wherefore he should
        Himself the candle hold.
I will go searching, till I finde a sunne
        Shall stay, till we have done;
A willing shiner, that shall shine as gladly,
        As frost-nipt sunnes look sadly.
Then we will sing, and shine all our own day,
        And one another pay:
His beams shall cheer my breast, and both so twine,
Till ev'n his beams sing, and my musick shine.

joyce carol oates

An American Tradition

Returning gifts!

At the K-Mart in Marietta, Georgia,
the morning after Christmas morning,
there they wait, a small crowd,
waiting for the doors to open at ten.
Some carry bulky cardboard boxes: Mixmasters,
electric football games, chenille bedspreads.
Others grip paper bags into which gifts have been stuffed,
price tags still attached.

Excitement as ten o'clock nears!
By now the outer doors are opened;
they advance into the foyer, happily,
where vending machines offer
rubber lizards, 5-Minit Photos, and popcorn
kept fresh by yellow lights.
They wait.

But someone is not patient, someone is muttering—
no, it is a couple—
a woman in a fur-lined parka, her husband in his shirtsleeves—
You think you're so superior—You want to make me crawl—
Suddenly she is crying.
Suddenly she is elbowing her way back out, out
of the jammed-in pack, suddenly her face is contorted,
she is one of them, but a stranger.
What rage, what bitterness!—
this woman sensing a gift
she cannot return.

percy bysshe shelley

from: The Cenci

Act I, scene iii. A banquet in the Cenci Palace.
[*Enter* CENCI, LUCRETIA, BEATRICE, ORSINO, CAMILLO,
NOBLES.]

FIRST GUEST I never saw such blithe and open cheer
In any eye!

SECOND GUEST Some most desired event,
In which we all demand a common joy,
Has brought us hither; let us hear it, Count.

CENCI It is indeed a most desired event,
If, when a parent from a parent's heart
Lifts from this earth to the great father of all
A prayer, both when he lays him down to sleep,
And when he rises up from dreaming it;
One supplication, one desire, one hope,
That he would grant a wish for his two sons
Even all that he demands in their regard—
And suddenly beyond his dearest hope,
It is accomplished, he should then rejoice,
And call his friends and kinsmen to a feast,
And task their love to grace his merriment,
Then honour me thus far—for I am he.

BEATRICE [*To Lucretia.*] Great god! How horrible! Some dreadful
ill
Must have befallen my brothers.

LUCRETIA Fear not, Child.
He speaks too frankly.

BEATRICE Ah, my blood runs cold.
I fear that wicked laughter round his eye
Which wrinkles up the skin even to the hair.

CENCI Here are the letters brought from Salamanca;
Beatrice, read them to your mother. God!
I thank thee! In one night didst thou perform,
By ways inscrutable, the thing I sought.
My disobedient and rebellious sons
Are dead!—Why, dead!—What means this change of
cheer?
You hear me not, I tell you they are dead:

	And they will need no food or raiment more:
	The tapers that did light them the dark way
	Are their last cost. The Pope, I think, will not
	Expect I should maintain them in their coffins
	Rejoice with me—my heart is wondrous glad.
	[*Lucretia sinks, half fainting. Beatrice supports her.*]
BEATRICE	It is not true!—Dear lady, pray look up.
	Had it been true, there is a God in Heaven,
	He would not live to boast of such a boon.
	Unnatural man, thou knowest that it is false.
CENCI	Aye, as the word of God, whom here I call
	To witness that I speak the sober truth;—
	And whose most favouring Providence was shewn
	Even in the manner of their deaths. For Rocco
	Was kneeling at the mass, with sixteen others,
	When the Church fell and crushed him to a mummy,
	The rest escaped unhurt. Cristoforo
	Was stabbed in error by a jealous man,
	Whilst she he loved was sleeping with his rival;
	All in the selfsame hour of the same night;
	Which shews that Heaven has special care of me
	I beg those friends who love me, that they mark
	The day a feast upon their calendars.
	It was the twenty-seventh of December.
	Aye, read the letters if you doubt my oath.

DECEMBER 28

christopher smart

Hymn 35: The Holy Innocents

Love and pity are ally'd,
So are cruelty and pride;
But they never met till now,
As in Herod's hellish vow.

Ev'ry tyrant of his time
Stands abash'd at such a crime;
Not a monster since the flood
Was in equal guilt of blood.

Rachael, with a mother's grief,
Sees the ruffians and their chief,
Piercing heav'n and earth with cries,
For her children's rescue tries.

'Cherubs lend your aid in air;
Seraphim, ye shall not dare
Such a scene as this to see,
And not succour God and me.'

Woman, speed thee back to bliss—
At a greater price than this,
Ere the plan of Christ we build,
Prophecies must be fulfill'd.

Blessed be the Lord's escape,
When the gulf began to gape,
And the fiends from hell were sent,
Man's salvation to prevent.

By the hope which prophets give,
By the psalmist 'he shall live,'
Sav'd for a sufficient space
To perform his works of grace.

Though the heav'n and earth shall fail,
Yet his spirit shall prevail,
Till all nations have concurr'd
In the worship of the WORD.

The Slaughter of the Innocents, or Holy Innocents, is traditionally observed on December 28th.

alfred, lord tennyson

The Murder of Becket

from: Becket

Act V, scene iii
NORTH TRANSEPT OF CANTERBURY CATHEDRAL
[BECKET *enters, forced along by* JOHN OF SALISBURY *and*
GRIM, *a monk of Canterbury.*]

BECKET	No, I tell you!
	I cannot bear a hand upon my person;
	Why do you force me thus against my will?
GRIM	My lord, we force you from your enemies.
BECKET	As you would force a king from being crown'd.
JOHN	We must not force the crown of martyrdom.
	. . .

[*Noise of armed men in the cloisters. Monks who have
rushed to Becket's assistance carry him part way up stairs
to the choir.*]

BECKET	Shall I too pass to the choir,
	And die upon the patriarchal throne
	Of all my predecessors?
JOHN	No, to the crypt!
	Twenty steps down. Stumble not in the darkness,
	Lest they should seize thee.
GRIM	To the crypt? no—no,
JOHN	To the Chapel of Saint Blaise beneath the roof!
	That way or this! Save thyself either way.
BECKET	O, no, not either way, nor any way
	Save by that way which leads thro' night to light.
	Not twenty steps, but one.
	And fear not I should stumble in the darkness,
	Not tho'it be their hour; the power of darkness,
	But my hour too, the power of light in darkness.
	I am not in the darkness but the light,
	Seen by the Church in heaven, the Church on earth—
	The power of life in death to make her free!

[*Enter the four knights*, REGINALD FITZURSE,
RICHARD DE BRITO, WILLIAM DE TRACY *and* HUGH
DE MORVILLE.]

FITZURSE	Where is this treble traitor to the King?
DE TRACY	Where is the archbishop, Thomas Becket?
BECKET	Here.

No traitor to the King, but Priest of God,
Primate of England. [*Descending.*] I am he ye seek.
What would ye have of me?

FITZURSE   Your life.

Was not the great gate shut?
They are thronging in to vespers—half the town.
We shall be overwhelm'd. Seize him and carry him!
Come with us—nay—thou art our prisoner—come!
[*Lays hold of the archbishop's pall.*]

BECKET   Touch me not!

DE BRITO   How the good priest gods himself!
He is not yet ascended to the Father.

FITZURSE   I will not only touch, but drag thee hence.

BECKET   Thou art my man, thou art my vassal. Away!
[*Flings him off till he reels, almost to falling.*]

FITZURSE   Strike, strike. [*He strikes off the Archbishop's
mitre, wounding Becket in the forehead.*]

BECKET   [*As Grim wraps his arms about Becket.*] Spare this defense,
dear brother.

FITZURSE   Strike him, Tracy! Strike, I say!

GRIM   O God, O noble knights, O sacrilege!
Strike our archbishop in his own cathedral!
The Pope, the King, will curse you—the whole world
Abhor you; ye will die the death of dogs!
Nay, nay, good Tracy. [*Lifts his arm.*]

FITZURSE   Answer not, but strike.

DE TRACY   There is my answer then. [*His sword falls on Grim's
arm and glances from it, wounding Becket.*]

GRIM   Mine arm is sever'd
I can no more—fight out the good fight—die
Conqueror.

BECKET   [*Falling to his knees.*] At the right hand of Power—
Power and great glory—for thy Church, O Lord—
Into thy hands, O Lord—into thy hands! [*Sinks prone.*]

DE BRITO   This last to rid thee of a world of brawls! [*Kills him.*]
The traitor's dead and will arise no more.

FITZURSE	Nay, have we still'd him?
	What, the great archbishop?
	Does he breathe? No?
DE TRACY	No, Reginald, he is dead. [*Storm bursts.*]
DE MORVILLE	Will the earth gape and swallow us?
DE BRITO	The deed's done—
	Away!

Archbishop Thomas Becket was murdered on December 29, 1170. A tremendous thunderstorm broke over the Cathedral as the murderers were escaping.

chester the herald

Epitaph for Richard Duke of York

A remembrer à tous ceurs de noblesse
Que yey gist la fleur de gentillesse,
Le puissant duc d'York, Rychart ot nom,
Prince royal, preudomme de renom,
Saige, vaillant, vertueux en sa vie,
Qui bien ama loyaulté sans envie,
Droyt heritier, prouvé en mainte terre,
Des couronnez de France et d'Engleterre.
Ou parlement tenu à Vestmestre,
Bien fut congneu et trouvé vray heir estre.
Sy fut roygent et gouveneur de France,
Normandie il garda d'encombrance,
Sur Pontaysse la ryviere passa,
Le roy Francoyez et son doulfin chassa.
En Erllande mist tel gouvernement,
Tout le pais rygla paisiblement.
D'Engleterre fut long temps prottetur,
Le peuple ama, et fut leur deffendeur.
Noble lygne ot d'enfans, que Dieu garde.
Dont l'aysné fylz est nomé Edouarde,
Qui est vray roy, et son droit conquessta,
Par grant labeur qu'il en prinst l'aqueta,
Il est regnant solitaire ou jour d'uy,
Dieu et ses sainz sy le gardent d'enuy!

Ce noble duc à Wacquefylde mourut,
Doux paix traitant force sur luy courut,
L'an soixnte, le xxxᵉ de Decembre,
Cinquante ans ot d'age, comme on remembre,
En priant Dieu et la tresbelle dame
Qu'en Paradiz puist reposser son ame!
 Amen *Chester le II.*

TRANSLATION

Let it be remembered by all noble hearts
that here lies the flower of gentility,
the powerful duke of York, Richard was his name,
a royal prince, a gentleman of renown,
wise, valiant, virtuous in his life,
who loved well loyally without envy,
the right heir, proved in many a land,
of the crowns of France and England.
In the parliament held at Westminster
he was fully acknowledged and found to be the right heir.
And he was regent and governor of France,
Normandy he guarded from danger,
he passed the river at Pontoise,
and drove away the French king and his dauphin.
In Ireland he established such government,
that he ruled all the country peaceably.
Of England he was long protector,
he loved the people, and was their defender.
He had a noble lineage of children,
whom may God have in his keeping.
The eldest of whom is named Edward,
who is true king, and conquered his right,
he purchased it by great labour which he bestowed upon it,
he is reigning singly at the present day,
God and his saints preserve him from injury!
This noble duke died at Wakefield,
while treating of sweet peace, force rushed upon him,
the year sixty, the thirtieth of December,
he was fifty years of age, as people remember,
Praying God and the very fair lady
that his soul may repose in Paradise!
Amen.

 Trans. Anonymous

alfred, lord tennyson

The Passing of Arthur

from: Idylls of the King

* * *

And slowly answer'd Arthur from the barge:
"The old order changeth yielding place to new,
And God fulfils himself in many ways,
Lest one good custom should corrupt the world.
Comfort thyself; what comfort is in me?
I have lived my life, and that which I have done
May He within himself make pure! but thou,
If thou shouldst never see my face again,
Pray for my soul. More things are wrought by prayer
Than this world dreams of. Wherefore, let thy voice
Rise like a fountain for me night and day.
For what are men better than sheep or goats
That nourish a blind life within the brain,
If, knowing God, they lift not hands of prayer
Both for themselves and those who call them friend?
For so the whole round earth is every way
Bound by gold chains about the feet of God.
But now farewell. I am going a long way
With these thou seest—if indeed I go—
For all my mind is clouded with a doubt—
To the island-valley of Avilion;
Where falls not hail, or rain, or any snow,
Nor ever wind blows loudly; but it lies
Deep-meadow'd, happy, fair with orchard lawns
And bowery hollows crown'd with summer sea,
Where I will heal me of my grievous wound."

So said he, and the barge with oar and sail
Moved from the brink, like some full-breasted swan
That, fluting a wild carol ere her death,
Ruffles her pure cold plume, and takes the flood
With swarthy webs. Long stood Sir Bedivere
Revolving many memories, till the hull
Look'd one black dot against the verge of dawn,
And on the mere the wailing died away.

But when that moan had past for evermore,
The stillness of the dead world's winter dawn
Amazed him, and he groan'd, "The King is gone."
And therewithal came on him the weird rhyme,
"From the great deep to the great deep he goes."

Whereat he slowly turn'd and slowly clomb
The last hard footstep of that iron crag,
Thence mark'd the black hull moving yet, and cried:
"He passes to be king among the dead,
And after healing of his grievous wound
He comes again; but—if he come no more—
O me, be yon dark queens in yon black boat,
Who shriek'd and wail'd, the three whereat we gazed
On that high day, when, clothed with living light,
They stood before his throne in silence, friends
Of Arthur, who should help him at his need?"

Then from the dawn it seem'd there came, but faint
As from beyond the limit of the world,
Like the last echo born of a great cry,
Sounds, as if some fair city were one voice
Around a king returning from his wars.

Thereat once more he moved about, and clomb
Even to the highest he could climb, and saw,
Straining his eyes beneath an arch of hand,
Or thought he saw, the speck that bare the King,
Down that long water opening on the deep
Somewhere far off, pass on and on, and go
From less to less and vanish into light.
And the new sun rose bringing the new year.

Author Index

Title Index

First Line Index